Dwelling on the Green Line

Concealed within the walls of settlements along the Green-Line, the border between Israel and the occupied West-Bank, is a complex history of territoriality, privatisation and multifaceted class dynamics. Since the late 1970s, the state aimed to expand the heavily populated coastal area eastwards into the occupied Palestinian territories, granting favoured groups of individuals, developers and entrepreneurs the ability to influence the formation of built space as a means to continuously develop and settle national frontiers. As these settlements developed, they became a physical manifestation of the relationship between the political interest to control space and the ability to form it. Telling a socio-political and economic story from an architectural and urban history perspective, Gabriel Schwake demonstrates how this production of space can be seen not only a cultural phenomenon, but also as one that is deeply entangled with geopolitical agendas.

GABRIEL SCHWAKE is an architect, urban designer and researcher. He is a Lecturer at the Sheffield School of Architecture, at the University of Sheffield, and co-director of Studio Sabra. Gabriel's work focuses on the issues of identities, conflicts, and neoliberalism, as well as the influences of nation-building and privatisation on the process of spatial production.

Dwelling on the Green Line

Privatize and Rule in Israel/Palestine

GABRIEL SCHWAKE
University of Sheffield

CAMBRIDGE
UNIVERSITY PRESS

University Printing House, Cambridge CB2 8BS, United Kingdom

One Liberty Plaza, 20th Floor, New York, NY 10006, USA

477 Williamstown Road, Port Melbourne, VIC 3207, Australia

314–321, 3rd Floor, Plot 3, Splendor Forum, Jasola District Centre, New Delhi – 110025, India

103 Penang Road, #05–06/07, Visioncrest Commercial, Singapore 238467

Cambridge University Press is part of the University of Cambridge.

It furthers the University's mission by disseminating knowledge in the pursuit of education, learning, and research at the highest international levels of excellence.

www.cambridge.org
Information on this title: www.cambridge.org/9781316512890
DOI: 10.1017/9781009071246

© Gabriel Schwake 2022

This publication is in copyright. Subject to statutory exception and to the provisions of relevant collective licensing agreements, no reproduction of any part may take place without the written permission of Cambridge University Press.

First published 2022

A catalogue record for this publication is available from the British Library.

Library of Congress Cataloging-in-Publication Data
Names: Schwake, Gabriel, author.
Title: Dwelling on the green line : privatize and rule in Israel/Palestine / Gabriel Schwake, Delft University of Technology, The Netherlands.
Description: Cambridge, United Kingdom ; New York, NY : Cambridge University Press, 2022. | Includes bibliographical references and index.
Identifiers: LCCN 2021052941 (print) | LCCN 2021052942 (ebook) | ISBN 9781316512890 (hardback) | ISBN 9781009069397 (paperback) | ISBN 9781009071246 (ebook)
Subjects: LCSH: Land use – Political aspects – West Bank. | Land use – Political aspects – Israel. | Private roads – Israel. | Private roads – West Bank. | Israeli West Bank Barrier. | BISAC: POLITICAL SCIENCE / World / General
Classification: LCC HD850.Z7 S39 2022 (print) | LCC HD850.Z7 (ebook) | DDC 333.73/13095694–dc23/eng/20211129
LC record available at https://lccn.loc.gov/2021052941
LC ebook record available at https://lccn.loc.gov/2021052942

ISBN 978-1-316-51289-0 Hardback

Cambridge University Press has no responsibility for the persistence or accuracy of URLs for external or third-party internet websites referred to in this publication and does not guarantee that any content on such websites is, or will remain, accurate or appropriate.

It is possible to understand the Greeks without mentioning their economic relations; the Romans, on the other hand, can only be understood through these.

Oswald Spengler, The Decline of the West

Contents

List of Figures	page ix
Preface	xiii

1 Introduction	**1**
The Settlements along the Trans-Israel Highway	1
Book Focus	3
Political Historiography of (Israeli) Architecture and Urban Planning	5
Outline	16
2 Background: The Evolution of a National Project	**20**
Settle and Rule	20
An Evolving National Project	21
The Frontier: Rural Pioneers	26
The Internal Frontiers: From Pioneers and Proletariats to Shareholders	32
Privatizing and Privatization: The Trans-Israel Highway	43
The Evolving Domestication of the Eastern Frontier	50
The Privatizing Domestication of the Green Line	60
3 (Neo-)Ruralization and the Community Settlement: From a Pioneer Experience to an Individual Focus	**62**
Early Signs of Privatization	62
The Neo-Rural Experience	63
The Community Settlement	66
Standardization: Communal Spatial Privileges	70
Customization: Individual Spatial Privileges	84
Mass Commodification: Corporate Spatial Privileges	100
From a Neo-Rural Lifestyle to a Mass-Produced Suburbia	106
4 Gentrification and the Suburban Settlement: The New Israeli Bourgeoisie and the Green Line	**110**
Bourgeoisification for the Sake of Domestication	110
The Bourgeoisification of the Israeli Middle Class	111

vii

Settlement and Socioeconomic Classes	116
Political Capital and Spatial Privileges: The Private Associations	118
Political Capital and Development Monopolies: The Connected Developers	131
The Omnipotent Spatial Agent: The Military Settlement	144
Localized American Suburbs and State-Oriented Gentrification	155

5 Mass Suburbanization and the *Stars* Settlements: Supply-Side Territoriality   159
From Gentrification to Suburbanization	159
Peace Talks, Immigration, and a National Housing Crisis	160
Supply-Side Territoriality	163
From Private Associations to Private Corporations: The Low-Rise *Stars*	166
Slumurbia: El'ad	177
High-Rise Suburbia: Tzur Yitzhak	187
The State Creates a Market That Shapes the State	195

6 Financialization and Harish City: Merging Financial and Geopolitical Frontiers   198
Forming a Crisis	198
Financializing the Frontier	199
The Crisis and Emergency Measures	201
Kibbutz Harish and Moshav Katzir: Early Rural and Neo-Rural Attempts	204
Katzir-Harish: The Suburban Turn	209
Harish: The Next City of Israel	218
The Architecture of Exchange-Value	230

7 Conclusions   233
Ends and Means, Tools, and Products	233
The Privatized Settlement Mechanism	235
A Privatizing Settlement Mechanism	239
Post-Socialist Neoliberalism?	242
Architecture without Architects: The Neoliberal Vernacular	244

Bibliography	246
Index	273

Figures

1.1	The different development phases along the Trans-Israel Highway and the chosen case studies.	*page* 15
2.1	JNF fundraising poster to purchase land in the Jezreel Valley, 1925.	30
2.2	A kibbutz (left), a *moshav* (Nahalal) (middle), and a *Moshav Shitufi* (right).	32
2.3	"Planning or laissez-faire" – Sharon's plan for national decentralization and population dispersal from the coastal plain to the periphery and internal frontiers, 1951.	36
2.4	Models for new industrial towns illustrated by Arieh Sharon – Beer Sheva, Ashkelon, and Kiryat Shmona, 1951.	38
2.5	The evolution of Israeli housing typologies according to the different phases in the national settlement project.	42
2.6	*Upper row* – Alon Plan, 1968, the Double Column Plan, 1975, and Gush Emunim Plan, 1977. *Lower row* – the World Zionist Organization Plan ("Drobles" Plan), 1978, Hills' Axis Plan, 1978, and Baruch Kipnis, the "Stars Plan," 1992.	56
2.7	The development of the area along the Green Line.	59
2.8	Israeli tanks on the Green Line, 1996.	60
3.1	"Agency Houses" in Moshav Avivim, 1958.	64
3.2	Case studies along the Green Line and the West Bank Barrier, 2015.	71
3.3	The temporary site of Reihan, 1979.	74
3.4	Sal'it (left) and Reihan (right), 1979.	75
3.5	Infrastructure works and first houses in Sal'it, 1980.	77
3.6	Hinanit (left) and Shaked (right).	81
3.7	Houses in Hinanit, 1981.	82
3.8	Sal'it during the 1980s and early 1990s.	85

3.9	House of a new admitted family in Sal'it, 1986.	86
3.10	The new units in Reihan.	87
3.11	Initial and second phases of Nirit.	90
3.12	An example of a house in Nirit with a possible extension level.	92
3.13	Nirit's third (1991) and fourth (1996) stages.	93
3.14	Plan for Ya'arit, 1983.	97
3.15	Houses promoted by the Judea–Samaria Residential Neighbourhoods company, 1981.	98
3.16	Sa'it after 2008.	101
3.17	Standardization (left), customization (middle), mass commodification (right).	108
4.1	Suggested parcellation, setting, and distribution of housing types to increase "quality of life," 1982.	114
4.2	Case studies along the Green Line and the West Bank Barrier.	119
4.3	Kochav Yair zoning scheme, 1984.	124
4.4	Promotion drawings of housing models in Kochav Yair, 1984.	126
4.5	Houses in Kochav Yair, 1989 (left) and Tzvika Israel, 1986 (right).	127
4.6	Israeli Prime Minister Ehud Barak meeting Yasser Arafat at his private residence in Kochav Yair, 2000.	129
4.7	Alfei Menashe, Phases A and B, 1982.	134
4.8	Design regulations for Alfei Menashe, 1984.	136
4.9	Alfei Menashe, 1984.	136
4.10	Area of Alfei Menashe, 1986 (left), 1988 (middle), and 1992 (right).	138
4.11	Initial layout of Oranit (left) and amended layout of Oranit (right).	140
4.12	House models in Oranit, 1982.	142
4.13	Houses in Oranit, 1985.	142
4.14	Reut, 1986.	150
4.15	Houses in Reut, with the West Bank in the background, 1994.	152
4.16	Model for a house in Reut B, 1991.	152
5.1	Case studies along the Trans-Israel Highway and the West Bank Barrier.	160

List of Figures xi

5.2 Detailed lots of proposed sites: *upper row* (from left) Yad Hannah (Bat Heffer), Tzur Yigal, Matan, and Kfar Ruth (Lapid); *lower row* (from left) Holot Geulim (Tzoran), Khirbet Mazor (El'ad), and Budrus (not built). 169
5.3 Outline plans for the new sites: *upper row* (from left) Tzur Yigal, 1991, Matan, 1991, and Lapid, 1991; *lower row* Bat Heffer, 1991 and Tzoran, 1991. 172
5.4 A single-family house (left), a double-family house (middle), and a terraced house (right) in Tzur Yigal, 1991. 173
5.5 Allocation of the areas to developers, 1996: *upper row* (from left) Tzur Yigal, Matan (Yarhiv), and Lapid (Kfar Ruth); *lower row* (from left) Tzoran and Bat Heffer. 174
5.6 Houses in Bat Heffer, 2002. 176
5.7 El'ad masterplan, 1992. 182
5.8 Dwelling types in El'ad, 2007. 187
5.9 Illustration of the Tzur Nathan project, 1997. 190
5.10 Tzur Yitzhak, 2010. 192
6.1 Harish in 2015, located on the Green Line between the West Bank Separation Barrier and the Arab area of Wadi A'ara. 204
6.2 Temporary site of Harish, 1981. 208
6.3 Outline plan of Katzir, 1981 (left), 1985 (middle), 1994 (right). 210
6.4 Compounds of Harish, 1992. 213
6.5 First houses in Harish, 2000. 215
6.6 Compounds plan of HaParsa neighborhood, Harish, 2012. 223
6.7 *Upper row* – types of apartments (left), typical floorplan (middle), and a typical building (right); *lower row* – implementations of a typical building. 227
7.1 Screen shots of Rami Heuberger in *HaHamishia HaKamerit*. 234

Preface

For several years, I drove along the Trans-Israel Highway every other weekend while traveling to visit my parents in Nazareth. Leaving behind the modern Jewish Tel Aviv and returning to the Arab city where I grew up, I was glad that the new fast motorway enabled me to complete my biweekly trip in less than two hours. Yet when driving near the Palestinian city of Qalqilya, I always noticed the thick row of trees on my right side, which hides the eight-meter high concrete walls of the West Bank Separation Barrier, the military patrol road, and the guarding posts along it. This multifaceted scene emphasized to me the dissonance between the modern fast motorway, which I enjoyed using, and the violent act of territoriality which it was obviously part of.

Driving back to Tel Aviv, I put the highway and the Separation Barrier behind me, and I was ready to continue developing my architectural career. I was convinced that I would be spending the next years designing new affordable, livable, and people-oriented residential projects. However, I soon understood that I was basically designing the façades of buildings that were already dictated by the speculative interests of the different entrepreneurs that hired our services. Losing interest in the "architecture of 20 cm," as a colleague referred to the work we were doing, indicating the width of the exterior walls we were designing, I chose to move to urban planning. I was hoping that with the capacity to influence urban policy I would contribute to the development of better, more socially oriented and socially just residential environments. Working on a new neighborhood in southern Israel, I was asked by the client, the Ministry of Construction and Housing, to plan an outline scheme for 1,500 units that would blend with the natural landscape of the desert. During a work meeting, the project manager from the ministry mentioned that the plan we proposed was perhaps "nice," but far from being "marketable," and thus suggested replicating another outline from a neighboring town in order to appeal to a larger number of private developers.

Curious to understand how marketability became the main leading value behind the development of the local built environment, I decided to start a PhD focusing on this issue. Initially, I did not think that Israel's territorial aspirations were relevant to my study. However, during one of my recurrent trips along the Trans-Israel Highway, I noticed a new housing project that resembled the marketable layout I had been asked to implement. Remembering the trees near Qalqilya, I could not avoid linking the marketable new housing project to the state's territorial project. Consequently, I began to comprehend the area along the Trans-Israel Highway as the meeting point between the state's geopolitical interests in appropriating additional lands and the entrepreneurial considerations of growth. I understood that these seemingly contradictory interests are quite inseparable, coupled in a reciprocal relationship of national, individual, and corporate development. This book is the outcome of my doctoral research, which analyzed this relationship by focusing on the new settlements constructed along the Trans-Israel Highway, on both sides of the borderline with the occupied West Bank.

This book would not have been completed without the help of my family, friends, colleagues, supervisors, and many other Good Samaritans along the way. First, I would like to thank my supervisors, Professor Carola Hein and Dr Herman van Bergeijk, for their noncompromising standards, patience, and guidance. I would like to express my gratitude to all my colleagues and friends at TU Delft – Phoebus Panigyrakis, John Hanna, Maria Novas Ferradas (and her partner Martin), Armina Pilav, Mo Sedighi, Aleksandar Staničić, Amy Thomas, Elmira Jafari, Michiel Smits, Penglin Zhu, Fatma Tanis, Kaiyi Zhu, Rose Sarkhosh, Marc Schonderbeek, Grazia Tona, Nama'a Qudah, Stefan Hauser, Gül Aktürk, and those whose names I forgot to mention, for their feedback, cooperation, and, of course, friendship.

During my research, I received significant aid and support from various individuals who were willing to dedicate their time, knowledge, and documents. These include the many interviewees, residents, architects, planners, policymakers, and workers at all the archives I visited.

Moreover, I am more than thankful to all those who provided me with external feedback that enabled me to continue developing my research. These include Pieter Uyttenhove, Haim Yacobi, Philipp Oswalt, Marco Allegra, Ayala Ronel, Amnon Bar Or, and Wendy Pullan. A special thanks is dedicated to the Ernst Ludwig Ehrlich Foundation, for funding my doctoral research and making this project possible; without your material and spiritual support it would not have been possible. I would also like to thank Maria Ulatowski, my contact and supervisor at the foundation.

Last, and surely not least, I would like to thank my family – my parents Dalia and Norbert, my brothers Michael and Daniel, and especially my life partner and best friend, Rotem Shenitzer-Schwake, for her everlasting support, endless proofreading, and companionship, through good reviews and bad. Rotem, this book is dedicated to you.

1 Introduction

The Settlements along the Trans-Israel Highway

For a fee of 34 new Israeli shekels one can enjoy a private car ride along the entire 200 km of the Trans-Israel Highway and witness the ever-increasing construction boom that has turned the area from a frontier zone into a blooming real-estate market. Built in the early 2000s, the new, privately funded four-lane motorway presents the local driver with an uninterrupted journey at an average speed of 130 km per hour, bypassing the heavily crowded Tel Aviv metropolis all the way into the third millennium. Driving along the highway, one might forget that it runs parallel to the official border between the State of Israel and the Palestinian West Bank, the Green Line, which was successfully blurred by the extensive development of Israeli settlements on both of sides. Looking closely at the well-maintained landscape, the attentive driver might easily recognize shimmers of the West Bank Separation Barrier that was built east of the official border and surrounds the Palestinian cities of the Occupied Territories, despite efforts to hide it. The overt private highway and the covert state-constructed barrier constitute a mutually rewarding relationship, where the former contributes to the interests of the latter and vice versa.

This book attempts to understand the nature of this mutually rewarding relationship and how it shapes the local built environment. It has its feet in political economy, yet it is written from the perspective of architectural and urban planning history. Correspondingly, while architecture and planning are the subjects of this book, it uses political economic analyses as a perspective to understand how they are formed. Therefore, the book focuses on the production process, rather than the product, using the Israeli settlement mechanism as its object of research in order to understand the built environment it produced. This mechanism is part of a century-long process that began with the first waves of Zionist immigration to Palestine in the late 1800s, intensified during the British Mandate and continued to form official policy even after the establishment of the State of Israel in 1948. Consequently, it forms an integral part of the spiritual and physical Jewish national revival and constitutes a leading case study of a state-led geopolitical process of spatial development. With the global neoliberal turn during the 1970s and the liberalization of the local economy, the state began to privatize its settlement project, merging individualistic interests and speculations with geopolitical considerations.

This book claims that the increasing privatization of the settlement mechanism since the late 1970s is the result of a state-directed effort to facilitate its continuation by harnessing it to the logic of the market, leading to a coalition of national and private interests that dictate the formation of the local built environment in an evolving process of *privatize and rule*.[1] I focus on settlements constructed on both sides of the Green Line that are located between the Trans-Israel Highway built in 2002 and the West Bank Separation Barrier erected in 2006. The metamorphosis of this former frontier area was enabled by intense state-led development efforts following the occupation of the Palestinian territories in 1967 and the election of the first right-wing and economically liberal government a decade later. This process relied on the growing involvement of the private sector, marked by the first privatized national infrastructure project – the new cross-country motorway, also known as Highway 6.

Embracing the term *settlements along the Trans-Israel Highway*, which was used by the state more than a decade before the road's paving even began,[2] I emphasize the connection between the privatized highway and the territorial settlements around it. It therefore highlights the use of the seemingly neutral façade of private development to blur the Green Line and to facilitate Israel's eastward expansion into the West Bank. There is rarely any physical connection between the settlements and the highway, which is a national arterial road and thus consists of minimal intersections. Yet, it is these settlements that incorporated the area into Israel's main metropolitan region and enabled the highway's construction. Simultaneously, they also enabled

---

[1] Schwake, "Settle and Rule: The Evolution of the Israeli National Project."
[2] MCH Directorate of Rural Construction and New Settlements, "Plan for the Development of New Suburban Settlements along Highway 6," 6.

the erection of the West Bank Separation Barrier several kilometers east of the Green Line, de facto annexing parts of the Occupied Territories.

This book shows that the settlements along the Trans-Israel Highway are an outcome of evolving modes of privatized spatial production, which relied on a system of *spatial privileges* and have produced different housing typologies over the past four decades. These modes of production are based on the state granting favored groups of individuals, developers, and entrepreneurs the ability to influence the formation of built space as a means to continuously develop and settle national frontiers. The settlements along the Trans-Israel Highway therefore constitute a unique case study of the relationship between the political interest to control space and the ability to carry it out.

Analyzing these modes of production, the spatial privileges they relied on, and the housing typologies they produced, I examine how the state incorporated a variety of private groups into its territorial project, ensuring its continuation while transforming the local built environment. Thus, unlike the research perspective that sees privatization as a state-led effort to ensure the survival of capitalism, *privatize and rule* depicts a contrary scenario, functioning as an economic means to a geopolitical end. Accordingly, this book challenges the conception of the built environment as a cultural product, as it sheds light on the ability of political and economic agendas to dictate the production of space – drawing a continuous line from the strategic regional level, through urban planning and design, all the way to the architecture of the single dwelling unit.

Book Focus

As an outcome of a privatized geopolitical project, the settlements between the Trans-Israel Highway and the West Bank Separation Barrier are a servant of several masters. Accordingly, this book claims that as the state was interested in expanding its *power over* space, it granted select groups spatial privileges that included the *power to* inhabit, plan, and construct it. Therefore, the production of these settlements followed the different functions they were meant to serve. First, the national-territorial aspect of controlling space dictates the location and spread of new settling points and in strategic plans appears as dots or continuous ink stains. Second, the individual and speculative interests of the different private groups that the state has involved in its territorial project since the late 1970s dictate the manner in which each ink stain is materialized. The book also claims that with the changes in local economic, political, and cultural values, the nature of these select groups altered, and with it the spatial privileges they received, thus creating a series of evolving modes of spatial production that transformed the local architectural and urban products accordingly. I first identify the changing geopolitical, individual, and corporate considerations that form the basis of the evolving modes of production. Then, I analyze the spatial manifestation of each mode of production, thus identifying the architectural and urban components that define the privatized Israeli national project. I examine how the development of Israeli settlements on both sides of the Green Line has evolved since 1977, in line with transforming national economic and geopolitical agendas, and how these were manifested in the settlements' architectural and urban form.

This book focuses on the border area with the West Bank since 1977, as both the location and period signify the privatization and financialization of the Israeli economy and the expansion of the national settlement enterprise. This area was only sporadically settled by the state during the 1950s and 1960s, as it preferred to develop other national frontiers.[3] With the occupation of the West Bank in 1967 and the election of the first right-wing and pro-laissez-faire government in 1977, the geopolitical status of the area became a leading national interest, while its relative proximity to the Tel Aviv metropolis gave it the potential to satisfy personal desires and economic speculations.[4] Located on the fringes of the West Bank, it was ideological enough to become an area of national importance, yet not too ideological like the depths of the Occupied Territories, and thus appealed to almost all sectors of Israeli (Jewish) society.[5] Correspondingly, it turned into a platform for one of the most intense development processes, which, in less than twenty years, concluded in the construction of over thirty new localities. As an extension of the Tel Aviv metropolis, these new settlements attracted thousands of upper-middle-class families with strong affiliations to the secular and centre-left political sector, giving the territorial project a seemingly apolitical and neutral mask.

[3] Gazit and Soffer, *Between the Sharon and Samaria*; Schwake, "Normalizing War: Protective Spaces and National Resilience."
[4] Berger, *Autotopia: Suburban In-between Space in Israel*.
[5] Newman, "Settlement as Suburbanization: The Banality of Colonization."

Developed by a coalition of geopolitical, personal, and financial objectives, the settlements on both sides of the Green Line represent the privatization of the Israeli national geopolitical project. The construction of the adjacent cross-country highway in the early 2000s, the first privately built and operated road in Israel, further emphasizes the role of both privatization and geopolitics – creating a geographical unit of privatized national projects. Focusing on the manner in which the development mechanism was privatized and the different settlement typologies it produced, this book shows how the location, urban fabric, and architecture of the houses corresponds with national territorial aspirations, private interests, and profitability concerns.

To explain how the settlements along the Trans-Israel Highway took shape, I focus on four different development phases, each with its specific modes of production and unique settlement phenomenon. First is the neo-rural development of the late 1970s, which was based on young urban families seeking a pioneer-like experience in the national frontiers and the small-scale Community Settlements they established. Second is the gentrification of the Green Line and the new Suburban Settlements that housed the Israeli upper-middle-class during the 1980s, in its quest for detached private houses within commuting distance from Tel Aviv. Third is the mass suburbanization of the 1990s, which witnessed the increasing involvement of private developers, leading to reproduced and high-rise residential environments. Finally, the current financialization phase and its speculative projects promotes the construction of corporate-led settlements, suburban in terms of everyday life, yet urban in terms of scale.

Political Historiography of (Israeli) Architecture and Urban Planning

The built environment is the human-made space in which we conduct our everyday lives. This consists of the buildings, streets, infrastructure, and nonnatural landscapes that surround them. Being a cultural artifact, the built environment reflects the social context in which it was produced. Therefore, in a basic Marxist analysis, the built environment would be part of the *superstructure*, shaped by the *base* that consists of the means and relations of production.[6] Expanding this analysis,

---

[6] Marx, *Capital: A Critique of Political Economy*, Vol. 1, 12.

Adorno and Horkheimer, in their writings on the *Dialectic of Enlightenment*, coined the term *culture industry*, classifying culture as an integral part of the means of production and the base that produces the societal superstructure.[7] Correspondingly, Lefebvre, in his analyses of built space, claimed that it is not a mere reflection of the existing social order but rather an integral part it, ensuring its continuation while functioning as "a means of production" and also as "a means of control, and hence of domination."[8] While most Marxist and neo-Marxist theoreticians focused on economic classes, Gramsci introduced the concept of *hegemony*, the ruling social class, to explain additional ruling interests and values that go beyond the simple economic rationale, such as nationalism, conservatism, and orthodoxy. The influence of the ruling class, according to Gramsci, is rendered in the built environment, as it controls "everything which influences or is able to influence public opinion, directly or indirectly ... even architecture, and the layout and names of the streets."[9] However, whether the built environment is produced by the social order or whether it reproduces it, they both correlate one to the other and as the means and relations of production are constantly changing, the ruling hegemonic values change in harmony. Respectively, their spatial manifestations are supposed to transform as well. Thus, by studying the planning history of a given place – in the case of this book, Israel – we are able to understand the prominent political, economic, and cultural values that dictated the formation of the built environment and how they changed over the years.[10]

The existing scholarship on the politics of built space is vast and multifaceted. Nevertheless, it is possible to identify several leading approaches that characterize the main research perspectives, which analyze the way the power of the state is both reproduced and represented in the built environment. The representational perspective focuses on the manner architecture "symbolises," "expresses," "houses," or "displays" the power of the state.[11] Accordingly, the

---

[7] Adorno, *The Culture Industry: Selected Essays on Mass Culture*; Adorno and Horkheimer, *Dialectic of Enlightenment*.
[8] Lefebvre, *The Production of Space*, 26.
[9] Gramsci, *Selections from Cultural Writings*, 389.
[10] Hein, "The What, Why, and How of Planning History," 5–6.
[11] Molnar, *Building the State: Architecture, Politics, and State Formation in Post-War Central Europe*, 11.

focal point of this approach is primarily iconic governmental buildings or national compounds,[12] usually of totalitarian regimes such as Nazi Germany, the USSR, or Fascist Italy, whose aesthetics are supposed to idealize the state and thus legitimize and enforce its rule.[13] Besides the common attention to fascist aesthetics, other researchers also considered democratic regimes, like the metaphoric aspects of transparency in West Germany,[14] or the adoption of Bauhaus architects by the American establishment as part of its efforts to depict the USA as the protector of democracy and freedom.[15] Similarly, at the urban level, Lawrence Vale's analyses of capital cities focus on the manner in which they were used to emphasize the authority of the state and its dominant culture.[16] Alternatively, James Holston and James Scott analyze capitals as a state-led social engineering process, intended to enforce certain behavior and modes of everyday life that confirm the ruling sociopolitical order.[17] Here, the focus is more on the built environment's ability to *reproduce* the existing power relations and less on its *representational* capacities.

The emphasis on spatial practices, rather than representation, originates from social studies theories in the 1960s and 1970s and the "spatial turn."[18] Whether in Pierre Bourdieu's concept of *habitus* and the divisions and hierarchies that create a common ideological construct,[19] Anthony Giddens' analyses of privacy and rules as spatial domination structures,[20] Michel Foucault's study of space's disciplinary power,[21] they all focused on the dominance mechanism produced through built space as an attempt to subjugate the individual to the rule

[12] Sklair, "Iconic Architecture and Urban, National, and Global Identities."
[13] Sontag, "Fascinating Fascism"; Lane, *Architecture and Politics in Germany, 1918–1945*.
[14] Barnstone, *The Transparent State: Architecture and Politics in Postwar Germany*, 27–60.
[15] Betts, "The Bauhaus as Cold War Legend: West German Modernism Revisited."
[16] Vale, *Architecture, Power and National Identity*, 3–47; Vale, "The Temptations of Nationalism in Modern Capital Cities."
[17] Holston, *The Modernist City: An Anthropological Critique of Brasilia*, 74–84; Scott, *Seeing Like a State: How Certain Schemes to Improve the Human Condition Have Failed*, 117–30.
[18] Brown, *The Black Skyscraper: Architecture and the Perception of Race*, 204.
[19] Bourdieu, "The Berber House."
[20] Giddens, *Central Problems in Social Theory*.
[21] Foucault, *Discipline and Punish*.

of the state. The innovation and popularity of this social perspective led to a vast architectural and planning history research that is based on the theories of the scholars mentioned above, as well as on other similar approaches.[22]

At the same time, as stated by architectural and urban critic Kim Dovey, the spatial adaption of the social sciences perspective usually diminishes the role of individuals, considering them solely as *subjects*, rather than *agents*. He therefore suggests a pluralistic approach that considers them as both, with the ability to be *"empowered"* and *"disempowered"* by the built environment.[23] Drawing on the work of Jeffrey Isaac,[24] Dovey emphasizes the difference between *power over*, the ability to harness the capacities of others to one's interests, and *power to*, "[t]he 'capacity' to imagine, construct and inhabit a better built environment."[25] Applying this distinction to the development of Israeli settlements, we could easily claim that this was a process in which the state enhanced its *power over* space by providing its citizens with housing opportunities in frontier areas. Accordingly, this was a state-led social engineering project, which created a spiritual bond between the citizens and the state while securing its legitimacy and territorial rule; using built space to control citizens on the one hand, and using citizens to control space on the other.

Allegedly, the privatization of housing development is a process with the potential to turn the individual from a mere subject into an agent. By transferring the responsibility from the state to the individual, the latter is granted the *power to* inhabit, plan, and create the built environment. Lisa Findley highlights the role of architecture as a liberating tool for subjected people, confirming their participation in cultural production. She refers to Le Corbusier's contention that "taking possession of space is the first gesture of living things" and that "the

---

[22] Scott, *Seeing Like a State: How Certain Schemes to Improve the Human Condition Have Failed*; Holston, *The Modernist City: An Anthropological Critique of Brasilia*; Findley, *Building Change: Architecture, Politics and Cultural Agency*; Hirst, *Space and Power: Politics War and Architecture*; Stanek, "French Post-War Architecture and Its Critics," 113–25; Molnar, *Building the State: Architecture, Politics, and State Formation in Post-War Central Europe*; Barnstone, *The Transparent State: Architecture and Politics in Postwar Germany*.
[23] Dovey, *Framing Place. Mediating Power in Built Form*, 20.
[24] Isaac, "Beyond the Three Faces of Power."
[25] Dovey, *Framing Place. Mediating Power in Built Form*, 10.

occupation of space is the first proof of existence."[26] In this sense, the power to occupy space is seen as an essential component of individual liberty that turns one into a spatial agent.[27] Similarly, the neoliberal order, which shifts the focus from the state's role as *provider* to that of *enabler*, adopts the same discourse of individuals as agents. At the same time, as David Harvey shows, neoliberal economies that claim to reduce state involvement eventually conclude in major "special interventions," meant to encourage " '[a] good business or investment climate' for capitalistic endeavours."[28] Ultimately, this limits the individual's power to affect the formation of the built environment while harnessing their interests to those of the market.[29] Nevertheless, while Marxist geographical analyses usually depict geopolitics as means serving capitalist objectives,[30] complex ethno-territorial contexts, like Israel, usually present an opposing scenario.

Superficially, a privatized national settlement project seems an oxymoron, as individual interests usually contradict those of the state. In his analysis of architectural production, Charles Jencks depicts three separate systems, *private, public,* and *corporate,* all of which have their own motivation – *usage, budget,* and *profit,* respectively.[31] Nevertheless, Jencks does not mention the ideological or political incentives of the state. Most importantly, he ignores the fact that it is the state that enables the private and corporate systems to operate, and that their produced architecture is thus subject to the state's interests as well, especially in a case like Israel.

To analyze the evolving modes of production and the role private agents began to play in them, I use the term *spatial privileges*. The term is usually used to describe the advantages members of a hegemonic group enjoy within the built environment,[32] whether this is due to race,

---

[26] Le Corbusier, quoted in Findley, *Building Change: Architecture, Politics and Cultural Agency*, 5.
[27] Ibid. [28] Harvey, *A Brief History of Neoliberalism*, 70.
[29] Graeber, *Debt: The First 5000 Years*, 376.
[30] Brenner and Elden, "Henri Lefebvre on State, Space, Territory"; Brenner et al., "State Space in Question."
[31] Jencks, *The Language of Post-Modern Architecture*, 25.
[32] Logan, Zhang, and Chunyu, "Emergent Ghettos: Black Neighborhoods in New York and Chicago, 1880–1940"; Wilton, "Colouring Special Needs: Locating Whiteness in NIMBY Conflicts"; Leonard, "Landscaping Privilege: Being British in South Africa"; Dirsuweit and Wafer, "Suburban Road-Closures and the Ruinous Landscapes of Privilege in Johannesburg"; Neupane and Chesney, "Violence against Women on Public Transport in Nepal: Sexual

ethnicity, gender, or social class.[33] Thus, it is an integral part of Logan and Molotch's "place stratification model,"[34] which describes the ability of privileged groups to manipulate the production of space for their own socioeconomic benefit.[35] Re-explaining the model, Logan defines "spatial privilege" as the objective of hegemonic groups seeking segregation, eventually creating a "rigid hierarchy of places."[36] However, in this book, I use the term to describe the exclusive rights members of favorable groups receive from the state as a means to incorporate them into the national geopolitical project with the purpose of ensuring its continuation and constantly recreating the hierarchy of places. Returning to Dovey's analysis, these spatial privileges are an outcome of a quid pro quo relationship that is based on granting favored groups the *power to* plan, construct, and colonize space, as a means to enforce the state's *power over* it. Therefore, in the privatization of a geopolitical project, it is by enabling (select) groups and corporations to participate in the production of new settlements that the state is capable of domesticating its frontiers.[37]

Ethnically oriented, the State of Israel granted spatial privileges to specific socioeconomic groups that could ensure the geopolitical objectives of its territorial project and the evolving economic rationale behind it. Haim Yacobi and Erez Tzfadia refer to this process as "selective privatisation," as the Israeli Government granted substantial spatial rights to "selected elites" in order to promote the settlement of its

---

Harassment and the Spatial Expression of Male Privilege"; Van Slyck, "The Spatial Practices of Privilege."

[33] Other uses include pedagogy studies that explain the relations between pupils and teacher inside a classroom, and even in computer science, examining the user experience design; see Niu and Gang, "Enforcing User-Space Privilege Separation with Declarative Architectures"; Engle, Langer-Osuna, and McKinney de Royston, "Toward a Model of Influence in Persuasive Discussions: Negotiating Quality, Authority, Privilege, and Access within a Student-Led Argument."

[34] Logan and Molotch, *Urban Fortunes: A Political Economy of Place*; Alba and Logan, "Variations on Two Themes: Racial and Ethnic Patterns in the Attainment of Suburban Residence."

[35] Pais, South, and Crowder, "Metropolitan Heterogeneity and Minority Neighborhood Attainment: Spatial Assimilation or Place Stratification?," 261.

[36] Logan, Zhang, and Chunyu, "Emergent Ghettos: Black Neighborhoods in New York and Chicago, 1880–1940," 1058.

[37] Prescott, *Political Frontiers and Boundaries*, 36–55; Weizman, "Principles of Frontier Geography."

national frontiers and to expand its territorial control.[38] This *selective privatisation* is precisely a case of Harvey's *special interventions*, intended to produce a certain economic climate and, subsequently, create a unique coalition of private, corporate, and national interests, which changed along with transformations in the Israeli economy, politics, and culture.

The privatization of Israel is a long and meandering process that benefited different social groups in various ways. The global decline of the welfare-state approach, which began in the late 1960s and early 1970s, affected the Israeli economy as well, and the government promoted more liberal approaches instead. This ignited a process of privatization that intensified throughout the 1970s and 1980s, concluding in the comprehensive reorganization of state-led projects, including the development of new settlements and housing estates. The state continued to act as the initial planner and initiator of these projects as it still controlled more than 90 percent of available land; its construction and marketing, however, were conducted by private individuals, associations, corporations, and entrepreneurs,[39] consequently privatizing the Israeli project. Subsequently, the reciprocal relations between the state's *power over* and the private *power to* transformed, leading to new modes of production that relied on granting diverse spatial privileges to various select groups.

The fact that it was developed by a coalition of individual, corporate, and national interests makes the Israeli settlement project a unique case of privatization and thus an exceptional case study of the influence of political–economic interests on the production of the built environment. To understand the politicization of housing under a privatized economy, we will consider seemingly mundane, ordinary, and banal housing projects. These, unlike iconic public or commercial buildings that are usually the focal point in the research on politics, economy, and architecture, constitute the vast majority of the built environment while shaping the everyday lives of the individuals who live in them,[40] thus

---

[38] Yacobi and Tzfadia, "Neo-Settler Colonialism and the Re-Formation of Territory: Privatization and Nationalization in Israel," 6.

[39] Yiftachel and Avni, "'Privati-nation' – Privatization, Nationalization, Housing and Gaps."

[40] Lane, *Architecture and Politics in Germany, 1918–1945*; Findley, *Building Change: Architecture, Politics and Cultural Agency*; Molnar, *Building the State: Architecture, Politics, and State Formation in Post-War Central Europe*.

forming the ultimate research object in the study of the relationship between state, individual, and spatial production processes.

This book considers the role of the built environment in the national geopolitical project while focusing on its production, instead of its architectural and urban products. Similar to Rafi Segal and Eyal Weizman's *A Civilian Occupation*, it discusses how architecture and planning became part of the national territorial agenda. At the same time, focusing on production, I aim to avoid possible oversimplifications. For example, Segal and Weizman cite a 1984 report by the Ministry of Construction and Housing, which recommended orienting the living rooms in settlements toward an open view. Relying on Paul Virilio, they explain that this was intended to create a "network of observations," which would control the local Palestinian population.[41] In *Hollow Land*, Weizman repeats this analysis again, mentioning the Hebrew term "*Mitzpe*" (lookout) that is used to refer to a new settling point.[42] Nevertheless, as the same guidelines had already been published in 1982 by the Jewish Agency's (JA) Settlement Division, in a document with clear instructions on how to increase "quality of life" in mountainous sites,[43] the desire to provide each household with an open panorama constitutes a more reasonable explanation than Weizman's panoptic analysis. Thus, the Hebrew translation of *Hollow Land* was mockingly criticized in the right-wing national-religious *Makor Rishon* newspaper. Concentrating specifically on this issue, the review claimed that the book was based on unsupported political statements, and that "in the twisted world of the extreme left, every settler is a spy."[44] Schnabel, the reporter who wrote the review, was not horrified by the territorial role attached to settlements, which he clearly supports and believes in, but rather by the claim that the architecture of the houses relied on militaristic principles.

To understand the geopolitical role of the built environment this book considers it as the product of the *settlement mechanism*. Compatibly, the JA's plan for the West Bank spoke of "settlement tools,"[45] which are the different incentives used to attract people to

---

[41] Segal and Eyal, "The Mountain," 85–86.
[42] Weizman, *Hollow Land*, 130–32.
[43] Naim, "Lot Sizes in Toshavot and Community Settlements with Mountainous Topography," 1–4.
[44] Schnabel, "In the Twisted World of the Extreme Left, Every Settler Is a Spy."
[45] Settlement Division, "The 100,000 Plan," 15.

the Occupied Territories; these include grants, subsidies, real-estate speculations, and social seclusion. Built space was not, therefore, a *settlement tool* meant to attract settlers or to function as a reconnaissance device, but rather an outcome of the various policies that were intended to stimulate the development of new settlements. This book thus discusses the *settlement mechanism,* which is the coalition between the state, the various agents it used, and the spatial privileges they were granted. To understand how the settlement mechanism works, I concentrate on the gradual changes it went through, examining the evolving *modes of production* it relied on and analyzing how these transformed the local built environment. With the focus on production, rather than the product, this book deliberately ignores the role of architects and planners as the masterminds of the production of built space, referring to them as mere executors of the settlement mechanism. Furthermore, comparing case studies on both sides of the Green Line, I show that the new modes of production were enacted both in the pre-1967 borders and in the Occupied Territories, thus highlighting the efficiency of privatized territoriality and its ability to blur the former border.

Most of the current literature focuses on ideological and political aspects, while relatively neglecting the economic standpoint. At the same time, scholars who focus on the privatization of Israel usually do not deal with its spatial urban and architectural morphology. Accordingly, the focal points are frequently politically contested case studies like the West Bank, as in the varied works of Weizman, Segal, Newman, Cahaner, Allegra, and many others;[46] or ethnically divided cities, former Palestinian neighborhoods, and peripheral towns inside Israel, such as the studies of Pullan, Yiftachel, Nitzan-Shiftan, Yacobi, Tzfadia, and Jabaraeen.[47] While they all discuss the political agenda in detail, the link with political-economics is quite preliminary, including

---

[46] Weizman, *Hollow Land*; Segal and Eyal, *A Civilian Occupation: The Politics of Israeli Architecture*; Newman, "Settlement as Suburbanization: The Banality of Colonization"; Cahaner, "Between Ghetto Politics and Geopolitics: Ultraorthodox Settlements in the West Bank,"; Allegra, "The Politics of Suburbia: Israel's Settlement Policy and the Production of Space in the Metropolitan Area of Jerusalem."

[47] Pullan, "Frontier Urbanism: The Periphery at the Centre of Contested Cities"; Yiftachel, *Ethnocracy*; Nitzan-Shiftan, *Seizing Jerusalem: The Architectures of Unilateral Unification*; Yacobi, "Architecture, Orientalism and Identity: The Politics of the Israeli-Built Environment"; Tzfadia, "Public Housing as Control:

several papers such as Yacobi and Tzfadia's "Neo-Settler Colonialism," Gutwein's concept of "alternative welfare state," and Yiftachel and Avni's short introduction in "Privati-nation."

Moreover, the existing literature usually studies the regional and urban levels, creating a research gap at the architectural level that would draw a continuous line from the national to the individual scale. Efrat's groundbreaking work *The Israeli Project* and Allweil's brilliant *Homeland* are in fact written from an architectural and regional perspective.[48] Yet, they mainly focus on the nation-building process, discussing its representational and social engineering roles, and thus do not address territorial, individual, and corporate interests post-1977. Researchers that have dealt with the architecture of settlements over the past four decades analyze it as an attempt to normalize occupation through banal and aesthetic spatial practices.[49] This book, however, takes a contrary position, claiming that architecture is the product of privatization and normalization, rather than their producer. It focuses on settlements on both sides of the Green Line, a comparison that is usually avoided, showing that despite the differing legal status, these settlements relied on the same modes of production and thus consisted of the same architectural and urban characteristics.

The case studies examined in this book represent the increasing privatization of the settlement mechanism and its evolving modes of production (Figure 1.1). Sal'it, the Reihan Bloc, Nirit, and Ya'arit demonstrate the early privatization measures of the late 1970s, which were based on granting small homogeneous groups the right to form an exclusive Community Settlement. Kochav Yair, Alfei Menashe, Oranit, and Reut, represent the mid-1980s, when privileged groups of well-connected private associations and private developers were granted the right to develop and/or populate a new Suburban Settlement. Bat Heffer, Tzoran, Tzur Yigal, Matan, Lapid, El'ad, and Tzur Yitzhak represent the mass suburbanization of the 1990s and the shift to private

   Spatial Policy of Settling Immigrants in Israeli Development Towns"; Jabareen and Dbiat, *Architecture and Orientalism in the Country*.
[48] Efrat, *The Israeli Project: Building and Architecture 1948–1973*; Allweil, *Homeland: Zionism as Housing Regime, 1860–2011*.
[49] Handel, Rand, and Allegra, "Wine-Washing: Colonization, Normalization, and the Geopolitics of Terroir in the West Bank's Settlements"; Newman, "Settlement as Suburbanization: The Banality of Colonization"; Allegra, "'Outside Jerusalem – Yet So Near': Ma'ale Adumim, Jerusalem, and the Suburbanization of Israel's Settlement Policy."

Political Historiography 15

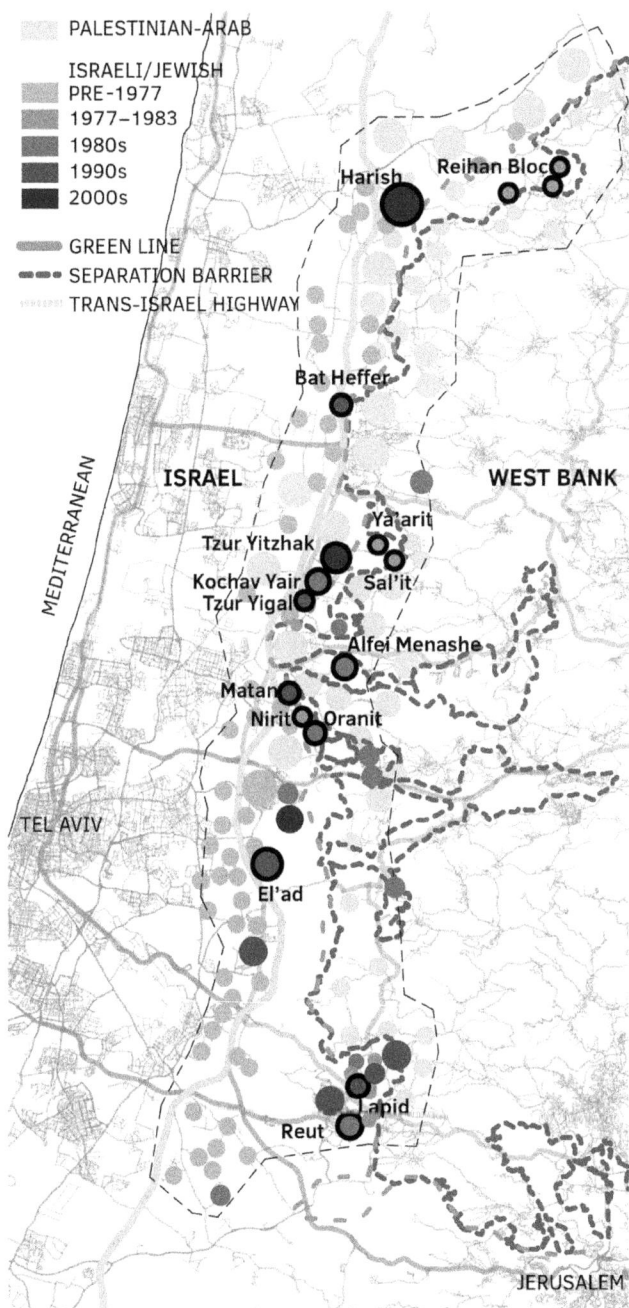

Figure 1.1 The different development phases along the Trans-Israel Highway and the chosen case studies (highlighted in black) (illustration by the author)

corporations, while Harish, the last case study, illustrates the current finance-led development that is based on the power to speculate as the main feature in the settlement mechanism.

To understand the development mechanism behind the production of these case studies, we will rely on different types of primary and secondary resources. These include meeting protocols, correspondences, ministerial reports, aerial photos, maps, national strategic plans, urban outline schemes, architectural drawings, photographs, and historical news articles. These sources also include relevant statistical information on the population and the development process and combine interviews with key figures and documentation of the settlements' current situation. To analyze the mutual geopolitical, individual, and corporate interests, I first examine each case study at the strategic level – analyzing its location along the Green Line, and its size and affinity to other existing Jewish and Arab towns, while considering the state's incentive to increase its power over this specific space. Then, identifying the relevant spatial agents, their interests and desires in correspondence with the spatial privileges they were granted, we will analyze each new mode of production and the way it matched the state's geopolitical agenda.

Subsequently, to understand the spatial manifestation of each mode of production, we will analyze each case study from its urban outline to the layout of the single dwelling unit – starting from the street system, its arrangement and hierarchy, moving to the zoning and distribution of public and private functions, as well as the sites' gross and net density. We will then examine the residential buildings' sizes, height, volume, and envelope, as well as the composition and distribution of dwelling units, their inner layout and relationship with the buildings' envelope, explaining how architectural and urban products are an outcome of the settlement mechanism.

Outline

This chapter has introduced the main features of the book. Following on from this, Chapter 2 provides the historical and theoretical context to the development of the settlements along the Trans-Israel Highway. It starts by identifying the geopolitical role of settlements in Israel/ Palestine and how they relied on evolving modes of territoriality. Relying on key theories on the welfare nation-state and the global turn toward neoliberalism and the market economy, the chapter presents the Israeli version of the phenomenon and how it led to a new mode of territoriality that was based on privatized modes of spatial production. Illustrating the entangled relations between nationalism, territoriality, and privatization this chapter clarifies the complexity of the subject and explains its unique profile. Presenting a general view of the development mechanism of the settlements along the Trans-Israel Highway, on both sides of the Green Line, the chapter prepares the reader for those that follow, explaining what makes the area a privately developed national project.

Each of the following chapters focuses on a singular frontier domestication mechanism and the new modes of privatized spatial production it relied on. Accordingly, each chapter examines different select groups that enjoy particular spatial privileges, or *powers to* produce built space, as a means to secure and expand power over it, thus generating specific settlement phenomena that correspond with the enacted mode of spatial production.

Chapter 3 focuses on the neo-ruralization of the frontier, which constituted the first privatized mode of spatial production and formed a new phase in the domestication of the Green Line. Accordingly, it deals with the Community Settlements – small-scale nonagricultural villages that consist of a limited number of families and a relatively homogeneous character. These were first used by the Israeli Government and its various planning agencies during the 1970s in order to attract city dwellers to frontier areas by offering them a pioneer-like experience, granting them the power to form their own secluded ex-urban communities while strengthening the state's power over areas of national interest. This chapter examines six different settlements that were initiated during 1977–81 on both sides of the Green Line and constitute the first example of early privatization. These include Sal'it, Reihan, Shaked, Hinanit, Nirit, and Ya'arit. Analyzing the development of these six case studies, and how they changed over the years, the chapter shows how the neo-rural experience and the concept of community became the leading force behind the national territorial project in the early 1980s, forming a new mode of spatial production. In examining the shift toward the individual during the 1990s and the growing emphasis on corporate interests in the early 2000s, the chapter illustrates how this mode of production continued to evolve, relying on new spatial privileges and producing new housing typologies.

Chapter 4 deals with the gentrification of the Green Line, a state-led effort to attract upper-middle-class families to settle the area. Accordingly, it focuses on the Suburban Settlement – a spatial phenomenon of the early 1980s that offered the option of spacious houses in a homogeneous commuter community that suited the desires of the newly forming bourgeois class. Focusing on this new settlement mechanism, this chapter illustrates how the power to develop space became a privilege given to upper-middle-class families and contractors the state wanted to attract to the area, thus gentrifying the former frontier and eventually enabling its further domestication. The chapter considers the first Suburban Settlements established along the Green Line, Kochav Yair, Alfei Menashe, Oranit, and Reut. Analyzing the new mode of spatial production and examining the (sub)urban and architectural typologies it produced, the chapter illustrates how changes in the settlement development mechanism led to alterations in housing practices and transformed the local built environment. Moreover, it shows how the emerging upper-middle-class was able to promote its own segregated suburban communities, and how the state used the suburban aspirations of this class to incorporate the former frontier into the main metropolitan area.

Chapter 5 considers the mass suburbanization of the 1990s, which formed a new mode of production that relied on the unprecedented involvement of the private sector. Unlike earlier examples, where the construction of new settlements was a collaboration between national institutions, settling movements, and small-scale private initiatives, by the early 1990s the state moved the process forward into the hands of large-scale private developers. This resulted in the mega suburbs of the 1990s – mass-produced residential environments consisting of tract housing developments and repetitive architectural typologies. The chapter focuses on the 'Stars' settlements – seven new sites initiated by the state in the early 1990s that demonstrate the completion of the transition into a privatized national project. Analyzing the architectural and urban characteristics of these new settlements, as well as their development mechanism, location, and intended target population, the chapter provides additional insight into the changing relationship between the private *power to* and the state's *power over* space.

Chapter 6 focuses on the financialization of the Green Line, which derived from increasing attempts to develop frontier settlements by creating a real-estate market and relying on the speculative interests of entrepreneurs and investors. This chapter considers the case of

Harish, a project that different governments unsuccessfully tried to develop over the last forty years. Its peripheral location and proximity to the West Bank and other Arab towns, on the one hand, and the lack of interest in rural settlement, on the other, repeatedly prevented the site's development. By 2010, the widespread demand for new dwelling units, the construction of the Trans-Israel Highway and the newly built West Bank Separation Barrier all contributed to turning Harish into an attractive piece of real estate, enabling the Israeli Government to designate it as a city with a target population of 60,000. While focusing on the case of Harish, the chapter analyzes the new financialized mode of production and illustrates how the power to invest, speculate, and develop real estate became the main tool in the national geopolitical campaign. By analyzing the urban layout and housing units in Harish, the chapter explains how this future city corresponds with the new mode of production and forms the pinnacle in the privatization of the national settlement project, embodying the manner in which architecture turned into a mere product of economic speculation.

Chapter 7 discusses the book's main findings. It draws a continuous line between the different modes of production and settlement phenomena presented in the previous chapters and explains how they constitute a gradual process of privatization. It summarizes the various national and private interests in the development of the area along the Trans-Israel Highway and explains how this influence was manifested in the local built environment and everyday civilian life. Reviewing the case studies presented in the book, the chapter concludes with insights that explain the relations between nationalism and neoliberalism, considering how the local materialization of this coalition presents a unique example with global significance that goes beyond the context discussed here.

2 Background
The Evolution of a National Project

Settle and Rule

To understand the privatization of the Israeli settlement mechanism, we must first grasp the physical and spiritual role of the local built environment and how it has evolved over the past century. While the initial essence of Zionist settlement in Palestine during the late nineteenth century was equivocal and consisted of multiple interpretations, it rapidly turned into a territorial project in which land control played a leading part. Endeavoring to create a territorial sequence of Jewish settlements, while simultaneously dismantling the Arab one, several leading Zionist organizations (and later the State of Israel) asked to fortify and expand their presence, securing their power over space. Therefore, focusing on the act of settlement as a governance apparatus, I claim that this territorial strategy could be understood as a *settle and rule* policy, adopting and adapting the phrase "*divide et impera,*" translated from Latin as *divide and rule*.[1] This strategy began to form at the turn of the twentieth century and it continues to dictate the development of the local built environment into the third millennium. However, as the hegemonic cultural, economic, and political values of Zionism and the State of Israel transformed over the last century, so did the spatial implementation of this strategy.

In this chapter, we will see how the concept of ruling by settling remained the core strategy of the national territorial project, although its materialization transformed with changing modes and the relations of production. We will first focus on the national geopolitical role of the local territory and built space, which began in the pre-statehood days and continued with the establishment of the State of Israel in 1948. Then we will identify three different modes of territoriality,

---

[1] The phrase is sometimes translated as "divide and conquer."

each with its particular state-led effort to attract people to settle the national frontiers according to the leading societal values of their time. We will first discuss the *cultivate and rule* mode of territoriality, which was led by several Zionist movements in the pre-statehood years and included an emphasis on frontier rural settlements. Continuing the discussion of the early statehood decades, we will then move to the *industrialize and rule* mode of territoriality and its focus on peripheral development towns. Third, focusing on the liberalization of the local economy during the 1970s, we will analyze the *privatize and rule* mode of territoriality, which was based on granting spatial privileges to select private groups. Accordingly, this chapter shows how the state endorsed new modes of spatial production that first harnessed the growing desire for better living standards to the national territorial agenda, while later turning investments and real-estate speculation into the main driving force behind the development of new settlements.

Zooming in on the Green Line, we will explore the privatization of the Israeli settlement mechanism. Using the Trans-Israel Highway as a paradigm of the local implementation of the global neoliberal turn, we will discuss the selective nature of Israeli privatization, explaining what makes it a unique case of a national-oriented market economy. In presenting an overview on the development of settlements on both sides of the Green Line, this chapter provides an insight into the evolving alliance between individual and corporate interests and the state's geopolitical project, preparing the ground for the remainder of the book.

An Evolving National Project

It is not our historic claims that will determine the borders of the land, but rather our posts. Our role now is to seize and settle.

Moshe Shertok[2]

Before analyzing the Israeli settlement project, we must first focus on the terms *territory* and *territoriality*. As Elden shows, *territory* is usually used to refer to a bounded space, or to the product of *territoriality*, which is the human behavior intended to achieve a bounded space.[3]

---

[2] The quote is from 1937; Sharet, *Political Diary B*, 175 (Shertok changed his name to Sharet).
[3] Elden, "Thinking Territory Historically," 757.

This corresponds with Agnew's concept of the "territorial trap," which refers to the essential connection between territory and sovereignty,[4] and Max Weber's definition of the modern state as a "human community that (successfully) claims the monopoly of the legitimate use of physical force within a given territory."[5]

As a territorial project, the Israeli settlement campaign focused on bounding space as a means to promote sovereignty. However, as Elden and Brenner have explained, the geopolitical and geoeconomic aspects of territoriality are inseparable, and building on Lefebvre's analyses of the "statification of space,"[6] they explain territory as the "site, medium and outcome of statecraft."[7] Territoriality, which is the constant production of space by the modern state, is thus an essential part of the capitalist mode of production as it facilitates continuous accumulation through unceasing economic growth. Therefore, territorial borders function both as the means and the ends of continuous endeavors to "shape the geographies of political-economic activities."[8] Territoriality and spatial production are thus entangled and complementary processes.

The fusion of geopolitics and geoeconomics is a highly noticeable historical phenomenon. Accordingly, Spengler's quote, which is cited as an epigraph at the beginning of this book, highlights the economic rationale of Rome's historical territorial drive. Colonial campaigns were based on the use of economic power to reinforce political dominance; and early forms of capitalist colonialism, like mercantilism, could be defined as the "subordination of the economic to the political."[9] Nineteenth-century European imperialism, a direct outcome of industrial capitalism, mixed means and ends, and, in the words of Hannah Arendt, functioned as a "process of never-ending accumulation of power necessary for the protection of never-ending accumulation of capital."[10] Subsequently, as explained by Lefebvre, the modern nation-state formed a new phase in the capitalist mode of production, with its constant focus on allocating surplus value. This "state mode of

---

[4] Agnew, "The Territorial Trap: The Geographical Assumptions of International Relations Theory," 56; Sassen, *Territory, Authority, Rights*.
[5] Weber 1946, quoted in Brenner et al., "State Space in Question," 1–2.
[6] Brenner and Elden, "Henri Lefebvre on State, Space, Territory," 359–63.
[7] Ibid., 365.   [8] Brenner et al., "State Space in Question," 8–9.
[9] Agnew, "The Territorial Trap: The Geographical Assumptions of International Relations Theory," 74.
[10] Arendt, *The Origins of Totalitarianism*, 186.

An Evolving National Project 23

production," he claimed, provided capitalism with the necessary spatial and societal support.[11] Correspondingly, as Elden and Brenner have shown, the "production of the nation by the State, dominating a territory," played a key role in continuously "facilitating the survival of capitalism."[12] *Privatize and Rule* defines a different scenario, based on the implementation of new modes of production intended to continuously facilitate the survival of Israeli territoriality during neoliberalism.

Prior to analyzing the privatization of the Israeli territorial project, we must first understand its roots, seen in the development of the first Zionist settlements in Palestine at the turn of the twentieth century. Despite the inability to speak of "a" unified Zionist doctrine, the leading Practical Zionism approach supported a variety of activities focusing on immigration, land acquisition, and settlements, in order to actively promote the establishment of a homeland for the Jewish nation in Palestine.[13] What began as a sporadic and relatively insignificant presence, soon turned into a large settlement enterprise, fueled by the growing demand for Jewish independence and additional waves of immigration. During the British Mandate (1921–48), as the dispute with the local Arab-Palestinian population continued to grow, it became clear that the future of the area would conclude in a territorial division. This meant that the designated Jewish homeland would be established on the areas owned and settled by Jews in Palestine, and that the Arab State would be created in areas owned and settled by Arabs. Therefore, land acquisition turned into a zero-sum game of *power over* space. Consequently, the Zionist Federation, the Jewish National Fund,[14] the Jewish Agency,[15] the Palestine Land

---

[11] Lefebvre, "Space and the State," 240.
[12] Brenner and Elden, "Henri Lefebvre on State, Space, Territory," 359–63.
[13] Kimmerling, *Zionism and Territory: The Socio-Territorial Dimensions of Zionist Politics*.
[14] *Jewish National Fund* (JNF, קק״ל, קרן קיימת לישראל, KKL, *Keren Kayemet Le'Israel*): a nonprofit organization founded in 1901, during the Ottoman rule over Palestine, with the aim of raising donations and purchasing, developing, and preparing lands for Jewish settlement in the area. The JNF took a leading part in afforestation efforts and the creation of national parks.
[15] *Jewish Agency for Israel* (JA, הסוכנות היהודית, *HaSochnut HaYehudit*): an international nonprofit Zionist organization, founded in 1929 as the executive arm of the World Zionist Organization (WZO, originally the Jewish Agency for Palestine). The JA was comprised of the representatives and administrative

Development Company,[16] and other Zionist organizations made an intense effort to purchase additional lands and to establish new settlements across all parts of Palestine. Accordingly, the words of Moshe Shertok, secretary of the Jewish Agency in Palestine during those years, quoted at the beginning of this section, demonstrate how the *settle and rule* approach turned into the official national policy.

This mission continued to evolve after the formation of the State of Israel in 1948 as the built environment maintained its geopolitical role. The new government aimed to strengthen and secure its control of former Arab territories and the new border areas while decentralizing the local Jewish population that was heavily concentrated in the Tel Aviv metropolitan area (*Gush Dan*).[17] Taking responsibility over the settlement mechanism while acting jointly with the pre-state organizations, the state wanted to settle millions of Jewish immigrants across its new borders;[18] consequently, planning, funding, and constructing a series of new industrial towns aimed to offer housing, subsistence, and occupational opportunities, while creating a unified national identity and promoting its territorial control.[19]

The Israeli territorial project is of an ethnocentric nature, aiming to ensure the sovereignty of a specific group.[20] Even in its definition, the term *Leom* that is used as the Hebrew equivalent of *nation* could also be translated into *ethnicity*. In the pre-statehood days, it was clear that

institution of the Jewish population in Palestine, in charge of education, immigration, governance, and security, laying the ground for the future Israeli Government. After the establishment of the State of Israel, the JA concentrated on promoting Jewish immigration (Aliya), education (for Jews outside Israel), economic development, and settlement. The status of the JA (as well as that of the WZO), was formalized by the Israeli parliament in 1952. The Settlement Department (not division) of the JA played a significant role in the development of rural settlements in Israel.

[16] Israel Land Development Company (הכשרת היישוב; *Hachsharat HaYeshuv*): formed by the British Zionist Federation in London in 1909 under the name of Palestine Land Development Company to act as an executive arm of the WZO in aiding the development of Jewish rural (and later also urban) settlements in Palestine. It went public during the 1950s, focusing on construction, development, hotels, and commercial buildings. In 1988 the Zionist institutions decided to sell the company and it was privatized.
[17] Efrat and Dash, *The Israel Physical Master Plan*.
[18] Efrat, *The Israeli Project: Building and Architecture 1948–1973*; Efrat, *The Object of Zionism: The Architecture of Israel*.
[19] Carmon, "Housing Policy in Israel: Review, Evaluation and Lessons."
[20] Yiftachel, *Ethnocracy*, 11–50.

the use of the word *Leom* referred exclusively to the Jewish nation; for example, the Jewish National Fund, which was in charge of acquiring *Admot Leom* (lands for the nation) for the sake of a *Bayit Leomi* (national home). Nonetheless, even after the establishment of the State of Israel, with a 20 percent Arab-Palestinian population, the term is seldom used to refer to an Israeli nation.[21] Evidence of this is the Israeli civil registration, which, from the variety of possible classifications for the term *Leom*, does not include *Israeli*; the majority of Israeli citizens are registered either as members of the Jewish *Leom* or the Arab one.[22] Despite several petitions and appeals, the state's official position remains that there is no such thing as an Israeli *Leom*; a position that was defended by the Israeli High Court of Justice.[23] Respectively, the terms national considerations, national lands, national priorities, and nation-state refer mainly to ethno-national Jewish. This would become official in 2018 with the "Nation-State Bill" that defined Israel as the nation-state of the Jewish people.[24] In this sense, the national settlement mechanism of the State of Israel continued the former pre-state ethno-national Jewish efforts,[25] turning the terms Israeli settlements and Jewish settlements into synonyms.

The Israeli territorial project has intensified since the 1970s. The endeavors to settle the recently occupied West Bank, Sinai Peninsula, and Golan Heights, which were seized during the 1967 War, as well as the attempts to fortify Jewish presence in other peripheral areas, were an outcome of a state-directed effort to enact its sovereignty.[26] Although the right-wing religious settlements in the heart of the West Bank were considered controversial in the eyes of large parts of the

---

[21] Sand, *The Invention of the Jewish People*.
[22] Occasionally, *Leom* is used to denote nationality, as the civil registration does include an East and West German *Leom*. A better possible explanation of the term *Leom* is the difference between the Arabic term for nation, *Qaumiya*, which refers to the general Arab nation, and *Wataniya*, which refers to a specific Arab nation such as Syrian, Lebanese, Iraqi, etc. See: Sheikh, "Pan-Arabism: A Tool of Ruling Elites or a Politically-Relevant Ideology?"
[23] Israel High Court of Justice, Ruling 8573/08 – Uzi Arnon against the Ministry of Interior.
[24] Knesset of Israel, Israel as the Nation State of the Jewish People.
[25] Yiftachel, *Ethnocracy*; Tzfadia, "Abusing Multiculturalism: The Politics of Recognition and Land Allocation in Israel."
[26] Benvenisti, *The West Bank Data Project: A Survey of Israel's Policies*; Portugali, "Jewish Settlement in the Occupied Territories: Israel's Settlement Structure and the Palestinians"; Segal and Eyal, "The Mountain."

Israeli public, those inside the pre-1967 borders, as well as those slightly over the former border, became an integral part of the national consensus. Furthermore, while the efforts in the West Bank were intended to fortify the Israeli occupation and prevent the formation of an independent Palestinian entity by expanding the state's territory, those in Galilee, the Negev, and west of the Green Line focused on strengthening the state's control inside the pre-1967 borders. Although these endeavors were allegedly different, they used the same basic tactics of establishing new settlements as a tool to secure territorial dominance by bounding additional space. Accordingly, the same planning discourse was used, "*Hesech*" – "scarcity of Jewish settlement," "*Havira*" – "Interconnections between Jewish settlements," and "*Hayetz*" – "Separation between Arab areas," to define the "national priority" of a certain area.[27]

The *settle and rule* strategy still forms an official development policy even today, more than seventy years after the establishment of the State of Israel.[28] Even when the state aimed to officially tie the national development process to the needs of the liberalizing local economy and to implement a more market-oriented approach during the 1980s and 1990s, it did not desert national geopolitical aspirations.[29] Territoriality was not forsaken, yet its implementation and method of realization adjusted to the new market-led development perspective. Therefore, the state applied a new mode of territoriality, which continued to focus on bounding space as a means to promote sovereignty while relying on changing modes of privatized spatial production.

The Frontier: Rural Pioneers

The logic behind the Israeli territorial endeavors to bound space is based on the concept of frontier domestication. Frontiers, unlike borders, are zones of varying widths that are either between two neighboring states, unpopulated areas within a state, or areas that have not yet been incorporated into an adjacent political entity.[30] Frontiers are usually sparsely settled areas or populated by indigenous peoples who

[27] Benvenisti, *The West Bank Data Project: A Survey of Israel's Policies*, 29.
[28] Yiftachel and Kader, "Landed Power: The Making of the Israeli Land Regime."
[29] Shachar, "Reshaping the Map of Israel: A New National Planning Doctrine."
[30] Prescott, *Political Frontiers and Boundaries*, 36–40; Ron, *Frontiers and Ghettos: State Violence in Serbia and Israel*, 1–13.

the settling society considers as part of the natural landscape that needs to be tamed.[31] The act of settling frontier areas dates to premodern times, yet in the era of nation-building it became an instrument of the modern state to enforce its sovereignty.[32] Weizman describes frontier settlements as an archipelago of enclaves and exclaves that are isolated from the geographical context that surrounds them. They constitute an extraterritorial geographic system of settling points and connecting lines, where law and order is temporarily exempted, until the frontier is domesticated and larger populations are able to migrate and inhabit it.[33] Frontier settlement, Weizman claims, is a chaotic and lawless situation which is directed by the remote entity it serves, functioning as a means to expand its control and enforce its law,[34] applying its *power over* space.[35] Through the act of settlement, the modern state has imposed both its empirical and its juridical sovereignty over its frontiers,[36] eventually replacing them with borders,[37] while fulfilling the modern western trinity of "state-people-territory."[38]

The manner in which the domestication of the frontier and statification of territory are practiced corresponds with contemporary modes of production. While premodern examples usually consisted of civilianized military strongholds, modern examples are often an integral part of the nation-state's attempts to create a national identity and a unified economy.[39] Therefore, the frontier answered the material need of settler societies for land and resources, as well as their spiritual aspiration to create a new culture.[40] Perhaps the most immediate example is the American westward expansion, which is usually linked with groups of pioneers, outlaws, and vigilantes;[41] yet, despite its association with the values of individualism and personal freedom, it was heavily dependent on the growth interests of the capitalist urban

---

[31] Mbembe, "Necropolitics"; Weizman, "Principles of Frontier Geography."
[32] Prescott, *Political Frontiers and Boundaries*, 30–40.
[33] Weizman, "Principles of Frontier Geography."
[34] Pullan, "Frontier Urbanism: The Periphery at the Centre of Contested Cities."
[35] Dovey, *Framing Place. Mediating Power in Built Form*, 10.
[36] Ron, *Frontiers and Ghettos: State Violence in Serbia and Israel*.
[37] Prescott, *Political Frontiers and Boundaries*.
[38] Arendt, *The Origins of Totalitarianism*, 282.
[39] Turner, *The Frontier in American History*.
[40] Yiftachel, "Nation-Building or Ethnic Fragmentation? Frontier Settlement and Collective Identities in Israel."
[41] Turner, *The Frontier in American History*.

establishment that funded it.[42] The "Wild West" was thus a coordinated state of chaos, directed by the urban centers, intended to lead to the domestication of the frontier and to the statification of territory.[43]

Kibush HaShmama, conquering the wilderness, or frontiers, was a leading narrative in the Practical and Labor Zionist approaches that led to the establishment of the State of Israel.[44] In that sense, the well-known concept of "a land without a people to a people without a land," portrayed Palestine as an empty, undeveloped, and unsettled area waiting for redemption.[45] Similar to the American westward expansion, settling the frontier was not only a means to appropriate lands but also to form a territorial-based national identity.[46] A shared identity, as Hobsbawm claimed, was a crucial feature in the formation of the modern nation-state, which significantly relied on a union between geographic and ethno-national entities.[47] Thus, it was by the act of settling the "land without people" that the "people without land" would become a nation. Consequently, settlements, housing, and dwelling units were a leading national mission. The method by which these were developed, however, transformed significantly over the years. While the *settle and rule* approach was maintained, the manner in which it was implemented adapted to changes in the local economy and culture. Eventually, what began as a pioneering act of conquering the frontier, turned into an elaborate and complex real-estate venture.

In the pre-statehood years, the main frontier settlement efforts were carried out by the various Labor Zionism movements and relied on a rural mode of territoriality. These movements, headed by the Zionist–Socialist *Mapai* party, the ruling hegemony of the Jewish population during the British Mandate, promoted the establishment of small-scale rural settlements right across Palestine. Agriculture and rural

[42] Hirst, *Space and Power: Politics, War and Architecture*.
[43] Weizman, "Principles of Frontier Geography"; Pullan, "Frontier Urbanism: The Periphery at the Centre of Contested Cities."
[44] Kemp, "The Frontier Idiom on Borders and Territorial Politics in Post-1967 Israel."
[45] Said, *The Question of Palestine*, 9.
[46] Yiftachel, "Nation-Building or Ethnic Fragmentation? Frontier Settlement and Collective Identities in Israel," 150.
[47] Hobsbawm, *Nations and Nationalism since 1780*; Hobsbawm, "Identity Politics and the Left"; MacIver, *The Modern State*.

settlements were thus used in order to expand the borders of the future Jewish state; or, as stated in the famous quote by Zionist leader Joseph Trumpeldor "Wherever the Jewish plough cultivates its last furrow, that is where the border will run."[48] This led to the communal agricultural settlements of the *moshavim* and *kibbutzim*, which expanded the areas populated by Jews while also acting as a disciplinary mechanism, meant to reconnect the Jewish nation to its historic fatherland through its active cultivation. The pioneer agricultural rural experience was thus both end and means: all focused to promote the physical and spiritual Jewish national revival.[49]

These actions, called *land redemption* (*Geulat Adama*), meaning redeeming of the Land of Israel to its *rightful* owners, included the construction of settlements intended to eventually secure the redeemed land. They were mostly carried out by the Palestine Office of the World Zionist Organization (*Hamisrad Haeritzyisraeli*),[50] which coordinated the land purchasing procedures funded by various contributors and the Jewish National Fund; the construction activities were executed by a variety of settling groups. These groups were usually part of what was known as The Labor Settlement (*Hahityashvut Haovedet*), an umbrella term that refers to the different national movements that promoted a mixture of Zionist and socialist values and advocated for pioneer rural settlements.[51]

The pioneer experience was an integral part of the land redemption efforts (Figure 2.1). The new settlements were supposed to enlarge the area populated by Jews, while promoting the formation of a healthy and idealistic society. *Conquering the labor* (*kibush haavoda*) and

---

[48] Gordis, Avishay, and Levi, *Israel's National Security and West Bank Settlements*, 6.
[49] Troen, "Frontier Myths and Their Applications in America and Israel: A Transnational Perspective."
[50] World Zionist Organization (WZO, ההסתדרות הציונית העולמית, *HaHistadrut HaTzionit HaOlamit*): an umbrella organization established in 1897 to coordinate the activities of all Zionist movements in terms of land acquisition, settlement, immigration, education, and absorption. In 1929, the Jewish Agency took over the practical actions of the WZO, which remained as a policymaking and administrative body. After 1948, its role focused on Jewish immigration, development of Jewish settlements, and education of Jewish communities outside of Israel.
[51] Kimmerling, *Zionism and Territory: The Socio-Territorial Dimensions of Zionist Politics*; Douer, *Our Sickle Is Our Sword*.

Figure 2.1 JNF fundraising poster to purchase land in the Jezreel Valley, 1925 (Central Zionist Archive). Tonal differences represent areas "redeemed" and those to be "redeemed."

conquering the wilderness (*kibush hashmama*) were thus complementary terms, as the physical cultivation of the land would eventually complete the rebirth of the Jewish nation in its historic homeland.[52] The *Halutz*, the pioneer, was perceived as an adventurous, firm, and ideological character involved in conquering the wilderness through cultivation and establishing new rural settlements. The image of the Halutz turned into the ideal prototype of Labor and Practical Zionism; a contra to the anti-Semitic image of Jews as a nation of wandering and deformed moneylenders and merchants.[53] Settling the frontier was thus an act of *Hagshama*, fulfillment, where one fulfills one's individual calling as part of the greater national mission.[54]

---

[52] Kemp, "The Frontier Idiom on Borders and Territorial Politics in Post-1967 Israel," 80.
[53] Troen, "Frontier Myths and Their Applications in America and Israel: A Transnational Perspective"; Neuman, *Land and Desire in Early Zionism*; Almog, *The Sabre – A Profile*.
[54] Kemp, "The Frontier Idiom on Borders and Territorial Politics in Post-1967 Israel," 81.

The centrality of rural settlements is highlighted by the lack of proportion between their extensive influence and significantly small size. In fact, the majority of Jews living in Mandatory Palestine resided in the main cities, and rural settlers constituted barely 10 percent of the Jewish sector. Moreover, while Labor Zionism endorsed socialist values, private initiative was a key component in the development of the main metropolises of Jerusalem, Tel Aviv, and Haifa.[55] Still, in terms of territorial efficiency, it was the rural sector that expanded Jewish bound space in Palestine, and the image of the *Halutz* and the pioneer lifestyle became the role model for rural and urban Zionists alike.[56]

The pioneer rural settlements in these years followed their settling group's level of communality and agricultural considerations. The kibbutzim, being a communal agrarian settlement, consisted of a hierarchal layout that emphasized its collective nature while limiting the role of the individual. Correspondingly, they were made out of a shared public core that contained the dining hall and all other public functions, surrounded by a ring of communal dwelling units. On the edge of the kibbutz, one could find the shared industrial and farming functions. The less communal *moshavim*, consisted of a more balanced correlation between the collective and private spheres. Accordingly, they were based on a public core, surrounded, in this case, by single-family detached houses and their private farmlands. Nahalal, designed by the architect Richard Kaufman, is an archetype of a moshav, presenting an almost perfect arrangement of a collective entity made out of private units. The *moshav shitufi* was a hybrid prototype, somewhere between the communal kibbutz and the more individualistic *moshav*. It consisted of a system of private households with communal ownership of the means of production. The layout of a *moshav shitufi* thus limited the private sphere to the individual family house, while highlighting the shared public areas for farming, labor, and education (Figure 2.2).[57]

Whether as a kibbutz or a *moshav*, the various rural settlements were the leading territorial tool in the pre-statehood years. Although they differed in their layout and architecture, all these settlements had

---

[55] Marom, *City of Concept: Planning Tel Aviv*.
[56] Gutwein, "Pioneer Bourgeoisie."
[57] Sharon, *Physical Planning in Israel*; Chyutin and Chyutin, *Architecture and Utopia: Kibbutz and Moshav*.

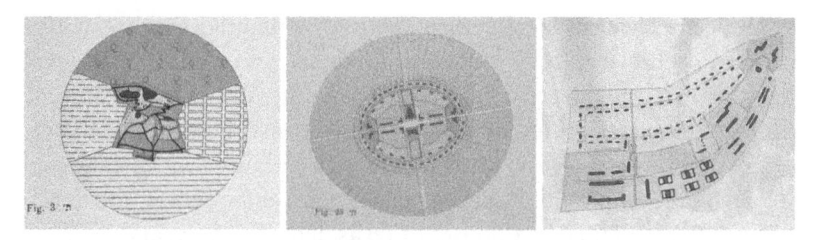

Figure 2.2 A kibbutz (left), a *moshav* (Nahalal) (middle), and a *Moshav Shitufi* (right). Illustrated by Arieh Sharon, 1951 (Arieh Sharon Archives)

a principal joint concept – the alliance between agriculture and land redemption. Through rural labor, the settlers were able to physically reclaim the land and secure its control while fulfilling their pioneer aspirations. This combination forms the essence of the *cultivate and rule* mode of territoriality.

The Internal Frontiers: From Pioneers and Proletariats to Shareholders

The 1948 Arab–Israeli War significantly altered the local demographic and territorial balance. In November 1947, the United Nations (UN) assembly agreed the Partition Plan of Mandatory Palestine, which followed the ethnic land ownership and designated most of the Jewish-owned land as part of the future Jewish state, and the Arab-owned land as part of the future Arab state. The partition plan ignited a series of skirmishes between local Arab and Jewish militias, which, with the end of the British Mandate and the declaration of the establishment of the State of Israel in May 1948, escalated into full-scale war between the young Jewish state and its Arab neighbors. In 1949, when the war ended, the Jewish state was larger than that proposed under the UN Partition Plan, and included several Arab areas as well as around 600 depopulated Arab villages and towns that were vacated by their 700,000 inhabitants, who fled or were deported to neighboring states.

The ethnocentricity of the nation-building process was highly apparent in the management of state-owned lands. On the eve of the 1948 War, less than 13.5 percent of the future area of the State of Israel was under Jewish ownership. After mass confiscations, more than 90 percent of the area became state-owned, of which the state sold some 15 percent to the JNF which incorporated them into its pool of *Admot Leom*. In 1960, the state established the Israel Land Administration, a body in charge of managing all state-owned lands in Israel, including those belonging to the JNF. The treaty between the JNF and the Israeli Government granted the former half of the seats on the executive council of the Israel Land Administration, while stating its obligation to "support the JNF in fulfilling its goal to redeem the wastelands,"[58] thus officially turning state-owned lands into an ethno-national resource.

To ensure that the newly bounded space promoted the sovereignty of the desired ethnic group, the official Israeli policy was to prevent Palestinian refugees from returning to their homes.[59] To preserve this situation, the construction of new settlements on formerly Arab lands, which were now state-owned, began immediately after the war.[60] These areas, which were either unsettled by Jews or predominantly populated by Arabs, became the state's internal frontiers, where the government continued the mechanism of *settle and rule*. Settling was now not only an act of physical control, but also of consciousness and narrative, as the Israeli Government aimed to cleanse the area of its Arab heritage through the construction of new localities.[61]

Unlike the pre-state years, the scale and scope of the post-1948 settlement efforts were significantly larger. The new Israeli Government had at its disposal a state to form and spread its ideology to the increasing influx of Jewish immigrants who doubled the local population over several years. Therefore, the former settling practices, which were sporadic and quite tactical, were replaced by a government-controlled strategy that harnessed the development of the state's industry and infrastructure. Thus, the Israeli nation-building process, like

---

[58] Abreek-Zubeidat and Ben-Arie, "To Be at Home: Spaces of Citizenship in the Community Settlements of the Galilee," 209; Government of Israel, *Treaty between the Government of Israel and the JNF*, 2.

[59] Morris, *The Birth of The Palestinian Refugee Problem Revisited*.

[60] Benvenisti, *Sacred Landscape*; Khalidi, *All That Remains: The Palestinian Villages Occupied and Depopulated by Israel in 1948*; Abu Kishk, "Arab Land and Israeli Policy," 121–30.

[61] Yiftachel, *Ethnocracy*; Yacobi, "Architecture, Orientalism and Identity: The Politics of the Israeli-Built Environment"; Jabareen and Dbiat, *Architecture and Orientalism in the Country*; Rotbard, *White City, Black City: Architecture and War in Tel Aviv and Jaffa*; Schwake, "Post-Traumatic Urbanism: Repressing Manshiya and Wadi Salib."

the pre-state efforts, had both spiritual and physical aspects as well, with the newly developed settlements providing shelter and housing opportunities but also promoting socialization and territorial control.[62]

The new mode of territoriality matched the concerns of the young state and its quasi-socialist *Mapai* government.[63] These included the transformation of an amalgam of Jewish immigrant communities into one unified society, providing them with proper housing, establishing a national industry, and securing the state's new borders. The new strategic plan for the young state called for a hierarchal system of development towns, and focused on industry and infrastructure that were meant to disperse the local population, secure the borders, and strengthen the state's control over its territory. While the earlier pioneer experience provided an educational role model, now, as a state, the Israeli establishment was able to use its various apparatuses in order to create a bond with its citizens and to form a nation.[64] In this sense, Israel's actions resembled the Fordist–Keynesian welfare state model,[65] which provided the individual with a range of social services in exchange for her labor and civil obedience, tying her personal interests to that of the state and its industry.[66] Housing, as Peter Marcuse claims in his critique of the postwar welfare system, was a seemingly benevolent act that tightened the dependence of the individual on the state, and actually helped the latter in controlling the former,[67] thus forming an integral part of the state's disciplinary institutions.[68] Corresponding with Marcuse's claims, the modernistic Israeli industrial towns of the early statehood years were a governance tool, intended to construct

---

[62] Yiftachel and Kader, "Landed Power: The Making of the Israeli Land Regime"; Allweil, *Homeland: Zionism as Housing Regime, 1860–2011*, 1–28.

[63] I prefer to refer to Israeli socialism as quasi-socialism, or semi-Keynesian, as the state welfare system was highly selective, especially with respect to the local Arab population, which, although state citizens, was under martial law until 1966.

[64] Allweil, *Homeland: Zionism as Housing Regime, 1860–2011*, 6–7.

[65] Filc, *Hegemony and Populism in Israel*.

[66] Adorno, *The Culture Industry: Selected Essays on Mass Culture*; Lefebvre, *Writings on Cities*; Marcuse, *One-Dimensional Man*.

[67] Marcuse, "Housing Policy and the Myth of the Benevolent State."

[68] Foucault, *Discipline and Punish*.

and shape a new form of collective belonging.[69] Appropriately, they granted the new Jewish immigrants the ability to inhabit certain places, while aiding the state's efforts to bound additional space – in other words, a territorial mode of *industrialize and rule*.

The young state's strategic plan, created by Arieh Sharon,[70] continued the prewar geopolitical aspirations and corresponded with the new mode of territoriality. Based on Walter Christaller's Central Places Theory from the 1930s,[71] Sharon suggested dispersing the Israeli population from the heavily populated coastal plain into a hierarchal system of new industrial towns that extended into the country's periphery (Figure 2.3). This national decentralization of the (Jewish) population was, according to Sharon, "imperative for national and defence standpoints,"[72] preserving the result of the 1948 War by urban development. Therefore, if Michel Foucault was able to claim that "[p]olitics is the continuation of war by other means,"[73] inverting the famous quote of Prussian General Carl von Clausewitz, in Israel the war was continued by the state's territorial policy and its focus on securing geographical dominance.

Sharon's plan was based on a coalition between the state's industrial needs and its political interests. In the Introduction to the 1951 masterplan he stated: "The physical planning of a country must be based on economic, social, and defence considerations."[74] According to Sharon, the new industrial towns would secure the country's geographical frontiers, while enabling the development of the state's industry, which would be much more productive due to the low operation

---

[69] Holston, *The Modernist City: An Anthropological Critique of Brasilia*; Yacobi, *Constructing a Sense of Place: Architecture and the Zionist Discourse*.
[70] Arieh Sharon (1900–84), was an Israeli architect. After studying at the Bauhaus, Sharon returned to Palestine where he became a leading architect, earning several commissions for the Histadrut – the main Zionist workers' union in pre-state Palestine and, later, in the state of Israel – and gaining the admiration of its leader, David Ben Gurion. After creating the Physical Plan for Israel in 1950, he continued his private practice, leading several major projects in Israel and Africa. He should not be confused with military general and politician Ariel Sharon (1928–2014).
[71] Efrat and Dash, *The Israel Physical Master Plan*; Trezib, *Die Theorie der zentralen Orte in Israel und Deutschland: Zur Rezeption Walter Christallers im Kontext von Sharonplan und "Generalplan Ost."*
[72] Sharon, *Physical Planning in Israel*, 5.
[73] Foucault, *Society Must Be Defended*, 15.
[74] Sharon, *Physical Planning in Israel*, 9.

Figure 2.3 "Planning or laissez-faire" – Sharon's plan for national decentralization and population dispersal from the coastal plain to the periphery and internal frontiers, 1951 (Sharon Archive)

costs on the periphery. Therefore, on the one hand, the new state-owned lands, seized in the 1948 War, functioned as a platform for the development of a dispersed urban system that would provide Jewish immigrants with proper habitation, education, and employment and "expedite their integration into one organic and productive unit,"[75] as appropriate to the nation-building process. On the other hand, the same state-owned lands also functioned as an objective, safeguarded by the new system of industrial towns that ensured the state's control over formerly Arab space.

At the strategic level, Sharon proposed twenty-four planning regions, which would decentralize the local Jewish population and enhance the state's territorial control while developing a balanced industry and proper housing opportunities. Each of the regions included a medium-sized industrial town, which was supposed to function as its hub and civil center. In the centralized Israeli economy of the 1950s and 1960s, the state was not only in charge of the planning process, but acted also as the initiator, financer, and constructer of the new towns. Accordingly, the massive state-led construction of new industrial towns on the Israeli periphery became known as the *Israeli Project*.[76] The towns' spatial characteristics followed the state's ideology, promoting homogeneous and uniform residential environments that emphasized the role of the individual as an integral part of the collective national organism. Subsequently, they had a top-down hierarchal plan that relied on single-use zoning and a series of reproduced residential estates. The use of separate residential and industrial areas not only correlated with the state's desire for homogeneity, but also with its aspiration to simultaneously appropriate and ignore the remains of depopulated Palestinian towns, settling the areas surrounding their remnants while leaving them to decay (Figure 2.4). This territorial mode was seen even in Tel Aviv, which began as a city of private initiative, yet expanded significantly after the war and witnessed expansive waves of state-controlled residential development,[77] turning private construction into a marginal phenomenon.

As part of a large state-led project, the construction of new residential neighborhoods and development towns was controlled by governmental ministries. During the 1950s, it was the Planning Directorate in

[75] Ibid., 4. [76] Efrat, *The Object of Zionism: The Architecture of Israel*.
[77] Marom, *City of Concept: Planning Tel Aviv*.

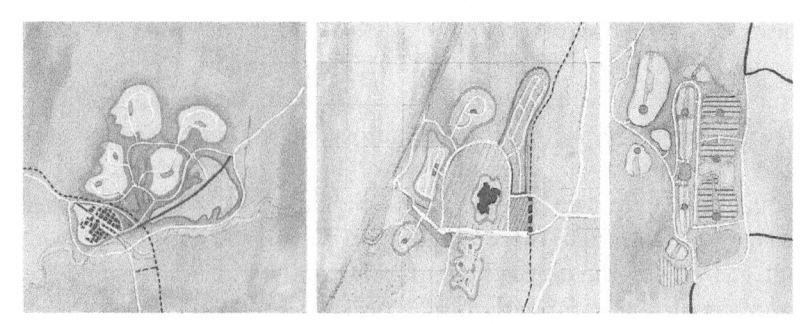

Figure 2.4 Models for new industrial towns illustrated by Arieh Sharon – Beer Sheva, Ashkelon, and Kiryat Shmona, 1951 (Arieh Sharon Archives). Note the remains of depopulated Palestinian settlements in black.

the Ministry of Labor and Construction and the Housing Directorate that guided the development of new residential environments.[78] With the growing need to coordinate and concentrate the national development of dwelling units, the Israeli Government established the Ministry of Housing in 1961.[79] Although the new ministry did not have additional responsibilities compared to the former directorate, its establishment highlights the key role dwelling units played in the young state.

Mass produced and forcibly populated,[80] mostly by underprivileged *Mizrahi* immigrants,[81] the new industrial development towns were a futile attempt to industrialize the periphery, turning into a synonym for urban failure, discrimination, and neglect.[82] In this sense, participation in the national territorial project was based on a lack of spatial privileges – settling nonhegemonic Jewish groups in anonymous, alienating, and reproduced housing estates on the state's periphery. With the economically liberalizing society of the early 1970s and the shifting focus on self-expression and self-fulfillment, the *industrialize and rule* mode of territoriality, promoted throughout the 1950s and 1960s, was replaced by a new mode, which focused on living standards and private

[78] Shadar, *The Foundations of Public Housing*, 14–15.   [79] Ibid., 76.
[80] Cohen, "Problems of Development Towns and Urban Housing Quarters," 117–25; El-hanani, "Feelings of Ethnic Discrimination in Two Development Towns."
[81] Jews originated from Arab or Islamic countries.
[82] Efrat, "New Development Towns of Israel (1948–93)"; Shenhav, *The Arab Jews: A Postcolonial Reading of Nationalism, Religion, and Ethnicity*.

initiative. This initially began as an attempt to prevent negative immigration from development towns by providing better dwelling opportunities locally, and later developed as a model for new settlements.[83]

Alongside the focus on industrial towns, the agricultural effort continued to develop. In the early 1950s, the state initiated a series of kibbutzim and *moshavim* along its new internal frontiers, mainly adjacent to the newly established borders with Lebanon, Egypt, and Jordan. The military *Nahal* corps, established under the direct orders of prime minster Ben Gurion, played a key role in these efforts,[84] taking an active role in the construction of around 150 new settlements in less than 30 years. This was carried out in concentrated operations resembling the pre-state Tower and Stockade settlements and consisted of a preliminary *Gari'in* (core group),[85] made up of Nahal soldiers, which was in charge of the first preparation stages. After a given period, they were handed over to a civilian settling group, in what came to be known as a civilizing or naturalization ceremony. Turning fully civilian, the new settlement would develop according to the new group's ideology: a kibbutz in the case of a socialist group, and a fully private *moshav* in more liberal cases. The rural Nahal settlements were accompanied by similar initiatives, promoted by other national agencies, such as the JNF, the Ministry of Agriculture and the World Zionist Organisation.[86]

In the late 1960s, the Israeli economy entered a process of liberalization and privatization, which accelerated in 1977 with the election of the first liberal-oriented right-wing government. With the gradual privatization of key national enterprises,[87] the national mission of developing and settling was privatized as well. Consequently, alongside the existing national considerations of ideology, identity, security, and sovereignty, the production of

---

[83] Berger, *Autotopia: Suburban In-between Space in Israel*; Hatuka et al., *Neighborhood-State*.
[84] Douer, *Our Sickle Is Our Sword*.
[85] Gar'in (גרעין; plural, Gari'inim): Hebrew for kernel. Used to refer to the initial core of a settling group, which would carry out the first phases of foundations. A Gari'in could be civilian, belonging to one of the settling movements, or military, as part of the Nahal corps.
[86] Abreek-Zubeidat and Ben-Arie, "To Be at Home: Spaces of Citizenship in the Community Settlements of the Galilee."
[87] Hason, *Three Decades of Privatisation*; Filc, *Hegemony and Populism in Israel*.

new settlements was now also influenced by economic and personal concerns. Accordingly, the Ministry of Housing became the Ministry of Construction and Housing in 1978,[88] emphasizing the shift from state-led construction to state-sponsored private development[89] and demonstrating the departure from the old Labor and Socialist Zionist ideology.[90]

Simultaneously, the national settlement campaign intensified with the occupation of several new territories during the 1967 War, receiving an additional boost following the 1977 political changeover. Initially, the post-1967 settlements continued former modes of territoriality, consisting of communal kibbutzim in the Occupied Territories,[91] or urban examples like Yamit in the Sinai Peninsula and Katzrin in the Golan Heights, which were heavily based on the development town model, despite some early signs of privatization.[92] Nevertheless, with the economic measures enacted by the new pro-laissez faire government, the national territorial mission began transforming; while in the early statehood days the pioneer spirit was the main driving force behind frontier settlements, in liberalizing Israel this act was no longer a mere ideological deed, but one that was also based on individual and economic interests.[93] Consequently, the national focus on creating a unified society gave way to the individual chase for "quality of life" in formerly urban and suburban contexts.[94] New settlements, offering larger houses in small communities within commuting distance from the main city centers, became the main logic behind the national geopolitical project.[95] This new territorial mode

---

[88] Schwake, "The Americanisation of Israeli Housing Practices."
[89] Shadar, *The Foundations of Public Housing*, 164.
[90] Kimmerling, *The End of Ashkenazi Hegemony*.
[91] Benvenisti, *The West Bank Data Project: A Survey of Israel's Policies*.
[92] The Subcommittee on Immigration and Naturalization of the Committee on the Judiciary, United States Senate Ninety-Fifth Congress, "The Colonization of the West Bank Territories by Israel."
[93] Allegra, "The Politics of Suburbia: Israel's Settlement Policy and the Production of Space in the Metropolitan Area of Jerusalem"; Newman, "Settlement as Suburbanization: The Banality of Colonization"; Gutwein, "The Settlements and the Relationship between Privatization and the Occupation."
[94] Billig, "The Jewish Settlements in Judea and Samaria (1967–2008): Historical Overview."
[95] Allegra, "The Politics of Suburbia: Israel's Settlement Policy and the Production of Space in the Metropolitan Area of Jerusalem," 497–510; Allegra, "'Outside Jerusalem – Yet So Near': Ma'ale Adumim, Jerusalem, and the Suburbanization of Israel's Settlement Policy."

of *privatize and rule*, where the national *Hagshama* (fulfillment) was tied to *Hagshama Atzmit* (self-fulfillment) relied on privatized modes of spatial production that were based on the state granting members of favored groups the privilege to consume space.

The decline of the Israeli welfare state was parallel to the decline globally, followed by the rise of postmodernism, neoliberalism, and the market economy.[96] With the new metropolitan-based local decentralization efforts of the 1980s and 1990s, which changed the former national distribution strategy,[97] the state began to attach the national development process to the rationale of the market, thus increasing the involvement of private capital in the settlement mechanism while enhancing the commodification of the residential environments.[98] The only way individuals were able to participate in this process was by investing from their private funds, literally buying a "piece of capitalism" while being complicit in the "financialisation of the everyday life."[99]

The *privatize and rule* mode of territoriality was not static at all, and continued to evolve over the years, relying on new modes of spatial production. What began with attracting families by promising them better living standards, later included a growing reliance on large-scale private corporations. Therefore, as the state began granting private developers the spatial privilege to produce space, the settlement mechanism transformed into a real-estate project. Subjected to the financial logic of the market, a house in a new settlement turned into an investment, its development was based on speculation, and its owner became a shareholder in the national territorial mission of *settle and rule*. Therefore, in each phase, the state used a different mode of territoriality in order to force its interests on individuals; whether by *forcing* them to move to the periphery, *seducing* them by the suburban lifestyle, or by incorporating the territorial project into existing social structure, as an integral part of the market economy.[100]

This book focuses on the *privatize and rule* mode of territoriality and analyzes the evolving modes of spatial production it relied on,

---

[96] Harvey, *The Condition of Postmodernity*; Harvey, *A Brief History of Neoliberalism*.
[97] Shachar, "Reshaping the Map of Israel: A New National Planning Doctrine."
[98] Harvey, *A Brief History of Neoliberalism*.
[99] Graeber, *Debt: The First 5000 Years*, 367.
[100] Dovey, *Framing Place. Mediating Power in Built Form*, 3.

Cultivate and rule

Industrialize and rule

Privatize and rule

| Neo-ruralization | Gentrification | Mass suburbanization | Financialization |
| Chapter 3 | Chapter 4 | Chapter 5 | Chapter 6 |

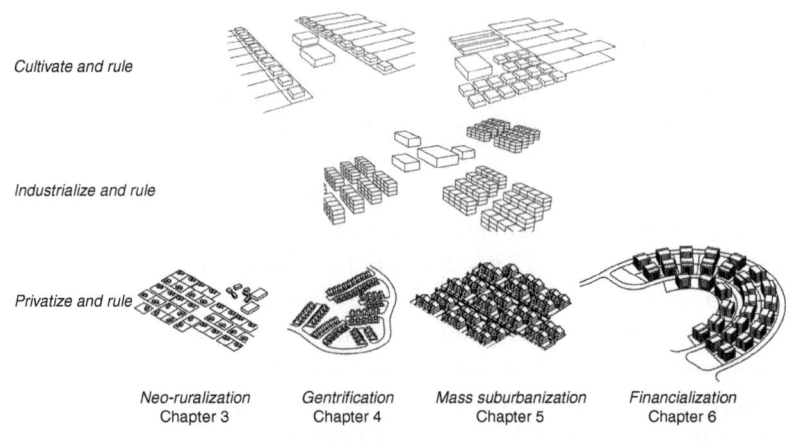

Figure 2.5 The evolution of Israeli housing typologies according to the different phases in the national settlement project (illustration by the author)

beginning with the neo-ruralization of the Green Line during the late 1970s, then moving to its gentrification in the mid-1980s and mass suburbanization during the 1990s, eventually ending with its current financialization (Figure 2.5).

The geopolitical role of the built environment received official status with the approval of the controversial Nation-State Law by the Israeli parliament in 2018. Among the law's eleven clauses, which have constitutional status and define Israel as the nation-state of the Jewish people, a paragraph is devoted to the issue of Jewish settlement, stating that: "The state views the development of Jewish settlement as a national value and will act to encourage and promote its establishment and consolidation."[101] In mentioning Jewish settlement as a national interest, this law shows that the strategy of *settle and rule* has not ceased, and that it still constitutes a leading ideological principle. During the different periods, from the pre-statehood efforts, through the nation-building decades and the current neoliberal era, the *settle and rule* ideology evolved and changed, adapting to societal, political, and economic transitions. Focusing on the settlements along the Green Line, which witnessed the growing involvement of private capital, this book illustrates how the gradual

---

[101] Knesset of Israel, Israel as the Nation State of the Jewish People.

privatization of the settlement mechanism developed over the years, relying on new modes of production and transforming the local built environment.

Privatizing and Privatization: The Trans-Israel Highway

Privatization is a process in which the state transfers its properties, responsibilities, and control into private hands. The term is often associated with the sale of government companies or public services to private corporations. These include the control of natural resources, the development of civil infrastructure and national industry, or even basic welfare services such as education, security, or health. Privatization is basically the liquidation of the postwar Fordist–Keynesian state that controlled development of the economy, securing employment and providing basic welfare services. The logic behind privatization is that a profit-driven private entity would be able to provide the same services as the state, yet better and more efficiently, and, most importantly, without "spending public money."[102] With the challenges of the 1970s, which were characterized by a global monetary recession and widespread national debts, privatization turned into the common economic approach of the industrialized western world, perceived as a means to recover and salvage failing financial systems.[103] This was the key logic behind the new global neoliberal agenda, which was to return to the main concepts of the liberal, prewar economic rationale.

The privatization of Israel followed a similar path, yet it had its own unique characteristics. David Harvey describes neoliberalism as an attempt by the old economic elites to retain their former financial powers by reducing the control of the state. In fact, in industrialized western countries, where economic inequality had decreased significantly during the 1950s and 1960s, it began increasing once again during the 1970s.[104] In Israel, which was a young quasi-socialist country, with an economic system heavily controlled by the state, it is quite hard to speak of an old economic elite trying to retain its power. Private initiative did exist, yet it was irrelevant in comparison to the centralized

---

[102] Graeber, *Debt: The First 5000 Years*; Harvey, *The Condition of Postmodernity*.
[103] Harvey, *A Brief History of Neoliberalism*.   [104] Ibid., 15–19.

state-controlled market. Moreover, as a country with a specific dominant group and based on an ethnic-oriented nationalism, Israel was a semi- or quasi-welfare state, with an Arab population that was under military rule until 1966 and an underprivileged *Mizrahi* sector, that received very different conditions compared to the privileged *Mapai* affiliated Ashkenazi hegemony.[105] Therefore, the neoliberalization of this quasi-welfare state had its own unique trajectory.

The early privatization measures of the 1960s stimulated the formation of a local middle class. This group consisted of liberalizing members of the Labor Zionism hegemony and other urban white-collar families; there is evidence for this in the foundation of the Israeli Liberal Party in 1961.[106] These would later join forces with marginalized right-wing Revisionist Zionists and large segments of the *Mizrahi* sector,[107] creating the Likud party and eventually overthrowing the socialist *Mapai* regime in 1977. Promoting a liberal economic agenda was thus both an antiestablishment act, a protest against discriminating *Mapai* protectionism, and an attempt to support the interests of the emerging middle class.[108] At the same time, as the state-controlled market and industry was of an ethno-national nature, its privatization followed a similar path.

The year 1977 was crucial in the privatization of Israel. Under the new government of Menachem Begin,[109] the process, already underway, significantly intensified as further and more crucial steps were made to

[105] Ashkenazi (אשכנזי): a term that refers to Jews of western or European origin. Kimmerling, *The End of Ashkenazi Hegemony*, 21–29; Shenhav, *The Arab Jews: A Postcolonial Reading of Nationalism, Religion, and Ethnicity*, 136–84.
[106] Gutwein, "The Class Logic of the 'Long Revolution,' 1973–1977."
[107] Revisionist Zionism (ציונות רוויזיוניסטית): a right-wing ideology within Zionism, founded by Zeev Jabotinsky as an ideological counter to socialist Labor Zionism. Revisionist Zionism advocated for a Jewish sovereign state in the greater area of Eretz Israel, which includes both banks of the Jordan, and the rejection of territorial compromises. The political party of Revisionist Zionism was *HaTzhoar* (*HaTzionim HaRevizionistim* [הרוויזיוניסטים הציונים]), while the *Irgun* was its paramilitary force and *Beitar* its youth movement. After 1948, the *Herut* Party became the representative of Revisionist Zionism, followed later by the Likud.
[108] Filc, *Hegemony and Populism in Israel*.
[109] Begin, Menachem (מנחם בגין; 1913–92): Israeli politician and head of state. Before the establishment of the State of Israel, he was the leader of the paramilitary *Irgun Zevai Leumi* (*Irgun*). He was founder of the *Herut* Party, main opponent of the Labor governments from 1948–77, and Israeli Prime Minister (1977–83).

finally free the market from Ben Gurion's "Bolshevism."[110] Subsequently, the Israeli economy experienced acute inflation in the early 1980s, which led to a stock crash and the bankruptcy of the labor union and later the Kibbutzim Movement (the two main *Mapai* institutions). The varied consequences of that time included the loss of union power, further privatization, and a devaluation of the expedience and profitability of agriculture.[111] According to Gutwein, the hegemony of the socialist Ashkenazi sector fully cooperated with the post-1977 privatization measures in order to retain power by turning its privileges into financial capital.[112] Gutwein highlights the role of the 1985 Economic Stabilization Plan.[113] The fact that the plan was promoted and approved by the national coalition headed by Prime Minister Shimon Peres of the Labor Party and concluded in significant cuts in governmental expenditures and the privatization of many state-owned businesses, provides clear proof of this collaboration. Thus, if 1977 accelerated the process of privatization, 1985 became a point of no return when the neoliberal agenda became the obvious way "things are done."[114]

The transformation from state-controlled and ethnic-based socialism into a market-oriented economy retained the existing social structures. In most cases, the transfer of governmental and public-owned companies into private hands involved a limited number of emerging businessmen. Through their political contacts these well-connected entrepreneurs were able to receive extremely favorable conditions that allowed them to purchase public companies way below their real value. This eventually transformed the state market concentration into a privately owned one, where, in a short period of time, a limited number of new tycoons were able to take over the local market.[115] Moreover, with its ethnocentricity, the privatization of the Israeli economy was accompanied by the creation

---

[110] Segev, *Elvis in Jerusalem: Post-Zionism and the Americanization of Israel*, 49.
[111] Hason, *Three Decades of Privatisation*.
[112] Gutwein, "The Class Logic of the 'Long revolution,' 1973–1977."
[113] 1985 Economic Stabilization Plan (תכנית הייצוב הכלכלית; *Tochnit Hayitzov Hakalkalit*): An economic plan that consisted of several steps that aimed to reduce the public deficit. The plan, which included a significant reduction in public spending and a sharp decrease in subsidies, symbolizes the official transition in Israel from a quasi-social democratic economy toward a liberal one.
[114] Rabinowitz and Vardi, *Driving Forces: Trans-Israel Highway and the privatization of Civil Infrastructures in Israel*, 15.
[115] Ibid.

of a series of *ethno-classes*, thus retaining ethnic segregation by widening socioeconomic gaps. Yiftachel and Avni refer to this process as *privati-nation*, as it consists of selective privatization, meant to economically empower a specific ethnic group and thus enhance its social dominance.[116] Correspondingly, Yacobi and Tzfadia highlighted the same "selective privatisation" as a means to attract privileged groups to frontier areas by promising them exclusive spatial rights, thus promoting the state's control while creating their own ethnically secluded communities.[117] Consequently, the forces of the market that are supposedly color-blind turned into a tool used to prevent social and ethnic integration, promoting spatial privileges as a means to ensure geopolitical and demographic dominance.

The Trans-Israel Highway is perhaps one of the best examples of the local privatization mechanism. Zionist settlement has historically relied on the construction of infrastructure as part of the aforementioned acts of land redemption. The construction of roads, bridges, power stations, and the efforts to drain the swamps[118] were an integral part of the Zionist concepts of "conquering the land" and the national renaissance ideology "to build and be built."[119] *Solel Boneh*, the public works company of the *Histadrut*, the Jewish trade union, was a leading actor in these efforts and continued developing infrastructure and other construction projects after the establishment of the State of Israel. Consistently, during the 1950s, the young Israeli Government commissioned *Solel Boneh* to start work on the National Water Carrier, an unprecedented national infrastructure project intended to efficiently manage and distribute the country's water and transfer precipitation from the rainy north to the arid south. Inaugurated in 1964, the National Water Carrier became a symbol of Israel's industrialization and its success in taming the local landscape and conquering the wilderness.[120] Not surprisingly, one of the first attacks carried out by

---

[116] Yiftachel and Avni, "'Privati-nation' – Privatization, Nationalization, Housing and Gaps," 225.
[117] Yacobi and Tzfadia, "Neo-Settler Colonialism and the Re-Formation of Territory: Privatization and Nationalization in Israel," 2.
[118] Shapira, *Land and Power: The Zionist Resort to Force, 1881–1948*; Sofian, *Healing the Land and the Nation: Malaria and the Zionist Project in Palestine, 1920–1947*.
[119] Zakim, *To Build and Be Built*, 1–22.
[120] Schattner and Biger, "The Real 'Fathers' of the 'National Water Carrier' of Israel."

Fatah,[121] the Palestinian National Liberation Movement, in 1965, targeted the National Water Carrier;[122] this action, despite its failure, marked the movement's official anniversary. The scope and ambitions of the Trans-Israel Highway, which began operating in 2002, made it the twenty-first-century version of the National Water Carrier. Designed to enable the flow of private cars – instead of aiding endeavors to make the desert bloom – and being the first national infrastructure project in the history of the State of Israel to be developed and operated by private means, the Trans-Israel Highway constitutes the ultimate symbol of neoliberal Zionism.

The idea of constructing such a highway, which would constitute an eastern parallel to the coastal routes, emerged in the late 1960s.[123] A minimized version of the road even appeared in the 1976 National Outline Plan, yet concrete planning did not begin before the late 1980s. With the construction boom that followed the immigration waves of the early 1990s, the Public Works Department (PWD – *Maatz*) resurrected the idea and turned it into a 300 km road connecting Beer Sheva in the south and Yokneam in the North. In 1991 *Netivei Israel*, the National Transport Infrastructure Company Ltd, conducted a feasibility study that showed an urgent need to construct the road, which led to the establishment of the Trans-Israel Road Ltd, a governmental company intended to promote and manage the construction of the new highway.[124] The company conducted several additional analyses, which pointed to the feasibility and economic potential of such a road. Although the studies ignored other possibilities, like developing the national train system, and used selective data to support the car-oriented approach,[125] the Israeli Government and all the relevant offices supported the construction of the new road. This decision was backed by the main political parties, and while the hawkish right-wing factors saw it as helping to strengthen the Jewish

---

[121] Fatah (فتح: حركة تحرير فلسطين; *Harakat Tahrir Falastin*): a nationalist Palestinian movement, political party, and paramilitary group established in 1959. It constituted the largest faction of the Palestinian Liberation Organization, as both were led by Yasser Arafat. Fatah and its subgroups led the armed struggle against Israel, which defined it as a terrorist organization, in 1986.
[122] Davar, "Attempts to Sabotage Water Carrier Foiled."
[123] Efrat, "Israel's Planned New 'Crossing Highway'."
[124] Trans-Israel Ltd, "Transisrael."
[125] Garb, "Constructing the Trans-Israel Highway's Inevitability."

settlement along the Green Line, the more dovish factors pictured it as a utopian road of peace, which would one day connect Egypt and Lebanon via Israel.[126]

The decision to privatize the road was encouraged by Trans-Israel Road Ltd and other governmental agencies. Eventually, Yitzhak Rabin's Labor government promoted the proposal to fund the construction process through extrabudgetary sources, with a private corporation funding, paving, and operating the freeway as a toll road during a thirty-year franchise (a BOT format – Built, Operate, Transfer). This decision was undisputed on almost all sides of the political spectrum and shortly after approving the road's construction in 1994, the Israeli parliament approved the toll road option as well.[127] The rationale behind the decision was that an experienced private corporation would have better managerial skills and planning competencies that would lead to quicker, more efficient, and professional execution. Privatization of the process was also justified by a profit-minded risk management approach, which anticipated low toll prices resulting from the private franchisee's incentives to attract as many drivers as possible.[128] However, as Rabinowitz and Vardi note, the governmental guarantees given to the private franchisees promised significant subsidies in case of low usage, which prevented major losses, as well as insignificant dividends in case of overusage, ensuring major profits. Rabinowitz and Vardi have also shown that the government repeatedly supported raising the toll prices further, leading to rates that were significantly higher than in comparable examples elsewhere.[129] Thus, the profit was privatized, but the risk remained public.

The franchisee of the Trans-Israel Highway is a private congregate called *Derech Eretz* that enjoyed significant support from the state. It started when Canadian Highways International Corporation (CHIC) was interested in competing in the national tender for the highway. Looking for a local partner, they first turned to Bank Leumi, which at that time was nationalized along with all other banks following the local 1980s crisis, and it directed CHIC to Africa–Israel Ltd,

---

[126] Azrayahu, "Rabin's Road: The Politics of Toponymic Commemoration of Yitzhak Rabin in Israel."
[127] Garb, "Constructing the Trans-Israel Highway's Inevitability."
[128] Trans-Israel Ltd, "Transisrael."
[129] Rabinowitz and Vardi, *Driving Forces: Trans-Israel Highway and the Privatization of Civil Infrastructures in Israel.*

a construction and holding company owned by Bank Leumi. Africa–Israel had almost no knowledge and experience in infrastructure, yet it was interested in the project due to its recent acquisition of the sub-companies Packer Steel and Alon energy. Africa–Israel saw the economic potential in the construction materials that Packer Steel would provide for the project and the filling stations that Alon would build along it. Moreover, as a real-estate company, the development of the area created new potential investments for Africa–Israel. For CHIC, the partnership with inexperienced Africa–Israel promised the needed contacts and connections with the local authorities.

In 1996, as part of the privatization efforts, the state sold its shares in Bank Leumi to Lev Leviev, an Israeli–Uzbek businessman and diamond trader, who would also become the owner of Africa–Israel. In 1998, the French *Société Générale*, the third partner in *Derech Eretz*, sold its shares to the Israeli *Shikun U'Binui* Ltd. *Shikun U'Binui* was a construction company owned by the *Histadrut*, the decades-old central workers' union, which also owned the aforementioned *Solel Boneh*, in charge of building the National Water Carrier. In 1995, as part of its economic recovery measures, the *Histadrut* sold its share in *Shikun U'Binui* to Israeli American businessman Ted Arison, granting him almost full control of the company. Arison had already purchased the previously nationalized *Bank Hapoalim*, one of the main banks in Israel, in 1997. This was the bank that gave Derech Eretz the credit to build the highway that same year; a deal which was done only after a clear governmental guarantee that would lower the risks taken by the franchisees yet again.[130] The soap opera behind Highway 6 thus reveals a national infrastructure project, constructed by privatized construction companies owned by the same conglomerates as the banks that funded the process, yet all backed by the government and public funds. With the state's support, the private conglomerate was also able to minimize opposition to the project by harnessing the interests of Jewish landowners, fragmenting any Arab objections, and conducting an elaborated "green-washing" campaign – eventually, actively enhancing the existing ethno-economic stratification.[131]

This entangled story of the Trans-Israel Highway turns it into a typical example of post-socialist and ethno-nationalist Israeli neo-liberalism. The governmental company Netivei Israel was headed by

[130] Ibid.   [131] Ibid.

Moshe Levi, a highly decorated and well-respected general and former Israel Defense Forces (IDF) Chief of Staff. He was regarded as an honest, trustworthy, and genuine officer, whose height and *Mizrahi* origin added to his public persona. His appointment as head of the Israeli military was an attempt to cleanse it from the controversies of the Lebanon War of 1982. Selecting Levi as CEO of Netivei Israel gave the project the aura of an undisputed national and patriotic mission – an aura that continued to function as Netivei Israel promoted the interests of the private franchisees building the highway. Levi's transformation from promising young officer to Chief of Staff, and then into a patriotic mask for a privatized project, illustrates the Israeli version of neoliberalism.

The Evolving Domestication of the Eastern Frontier

The border area between the Israeli coastal plain and the occupied West Bank has undergone major transformations during the past eight decades. Before the 1948 War, the area had limited Jewish presence and consisted mainly of Arab Palestinian towns and villages and their farmlands. After the war, the area was depopulated of its Arab Palestinian inhabitants and the 1949 Armistice Agreements shaped the new international border, creating a divide between the new State of Israel and the kingdom of Jordan. This border, which came to be known as the Green Line,[132] followed the topographical features of the area, leaving the Samarian hills on the Jordanian side and their western plains on the Israeli side. Consequently, the Israeli coastal plain and the Tel Aviv metropolitan area and its eastern fringes was a mere 15 km wide, and, being the only connector between Israel's northern area and its center, it thus became known as the country's *narrow waist*.[133] During the 1950s, with the intention of strengthening its control over this internal frontier, Israel promoted the construction of more than twenty new rural settlements in the area, built on the sites of former Palestinian villages and along the new border.[134]

Despite the state's plans to enhance its control over this area, it preferred to develop other internal frontiers instead. A scheme drafted

---

[132] The name derives from the color of the ink that was used to draw the line on the map.
[133] Gazit and Soffer, *Between the Sharon and Samaria*.
[134] Tal, *The Frontier Fortresses Plan*.

by the Ministry of Defense, called the Frontier Fortresses Plan, was only partially executed, producing an insignificant number of new settlements. While the plan demonstrates the state's perception of the area as a neglected, vacant, breached, and dangerous zone, which needed to be fortified and protected, its lack of fulfillment points to the state's preference to settle other internal frontiers, such as Galilee and the Negev.[135] The strategic perspective of the young state was to focus on a wide national-scale decentralization effort, and it thus chose to locate the newly built development towns far from the heavily populated coastal plain.[136] Therefore, this part of the Green Line was not frontier-like enough to receive the necessary attention, functioning more as a peripheral border zone.

The occupation of the West Bank in 1967 changed the status of the Green Line, enhancing its national importance. The fact that Israel ruled over both sides of the former border, even though the West Bank was not officially annexed, turned the area into a transition zone from the Israeli coastal plain to the occupied West Bank. With the new status of the area as a *Seam Zone (Kav HaTefer)*, which simultaneously detaches and connects Israel and the Occupied Territories, the Green Line turned into a frontier to be domesticated. Nevertheless, in the early years following the 1967 War, the state lacked a clear agenda for the development of the area. The first plan for the future of the Occupied Territories, prepared by Defense Minister Yigal Alon, suggested either returning the areas adjacent to the Green Line to Jordanian custody or including them in a future Palestinian autonomous rule;[137] Israel would annex the Judean Desert, the Jordan Valley, and areas around Jerusalem. While never formally endorsed, this plan formed the basis of Israel's unofficial settlement policy during the 1970s, which focused mainly on the areas Alon had suggested annexing. Therefore, in the 1970s, the Labor Government initially tried to limit the actions of the religious right-wing movement, *Gush Emunim*, which wanted to construct Jewish settlements right across the West Bank.[138] Even the far-reaching Double Column Plan (*HaShidra HaKfula*) of 1975, which called for

---

[135] Gazit and Soffer, *Between the Sharon and Samaria*; Tal, *The Frontier Fortresses Plan*.
[136] Efrat, "Geographical Distribution of the Soviet-Jewish New Immigrants in Israel"; Efrat, *The Object of Zionism: The Architecture of Israel*.
[137] Tessler, *A History of the Israeli-Palestinian Conflict*.
[138] Gush Emunim, "Proposal for Settlement in Judea and Samaria."

the development of an eastern counterpart to the Israeli coastal plain, all along the borders with Jordan and the eastern part of the occupied Sinai peninsula, left out the majority of the West Bank.[139] This approach changed in 1977 with the rise of the first right-wing Likud regime and Ariel Sharon's term as Minister of Agriculture.[140]

Despite the different perspective that followed the 1977 political changeover, the area remained relatively undeveloped. The national-religious settlers like members of *Gush Emunim*, preferred to settle the core of the West Bank, especially areas with some affiliation to the biblical texts. Accordingly, their plan consisted of small-scale settlements on the Samarian hills, while the joint vision of the World Zionist Organization's Settlement Division and the Israeli Government, in 1978, focused on creating groups of settlement blocs inside the Occupied Territories. Beyond a few new settlement points, the Seam Zone was relatively untouched, and the majority of the new sites developed between 1977 and 1981 had already been authorized by the former Labor Government prior to the 1977 elections.[141] Nonetheless, both plans introduced a new mode of spatial development to the area, and with it a new settlement typology – the Community Settlement, which would instigate the eventual metamorphosis of the Green Line.

The Community Settlements lacked almost all means of production – industrial, commercial, as well as agricultural. Nevertheless, as their objective was not to create a commuter-based community but rather one connected to the local natural landscape, they were quasi- or neo-rural settlements, and much more counter urban than simply suburban. As such, they were part of an early privatized mode of production and relied on small-scale previously organized groups, which were usually affiliated with a certain settlement movement or a political party. Their mode of production was based on the state granting these select groups the spatial privilege of exclusively settling a site and establishing their own homogeneous community away from the urban centers, as a means to increase state presence and control.[142] Mimicking the pre-statehood mode of territoriality and adopting a frontier-like discourse

---

[139] Wachman, "The Double Column Plan."
[140] Weizman, "Principles of Frontier Geography"; Yiftachel, "From Sharon to Sharon: Spatial Planning and Separation Regime in Israel/Palestine."
[141] Douer, *Our Sickle Is Our Sword*.
[142] Yiftachel, "Bedouin-Arabs and the Israeli Settler State."

and lifestyle,[143] these new sites first consisted of a pioneer-like phase of temporary houses that eventually turned into a permanent settlement.

During the early 1980s, the state began to promote a more suburban perspective. This occurred in light of the changes in the national economy and culture, which included additional privatization measures and an increasing demand for suburban environments.[144] Accordingly, the 1981 Settlements Division's plan continued to insist on settling the entire West Bank, yet it began to incorporate terms such as "areas of high demand," "commuting," "private initiative," "living standards," and "middle-class families."[145] The main assumption of the Settlement Division was that the heart of the West Bank would attract a more ideologically motivated population, while the area close to the Tel Aviv metropolis and the coastal plain – the Green Line – would attract middle-class and upper-middle-class families looking for better, affordable living standards.[146]

Simultaneously, both the Ministry of Agriculture and the Ministry of Construction and Housing began to encourage private-led construction in the area, relying on a new mode of spatial production.[147] The official policy was that "west Samaria [the area close to the Green Line] would become a part of Gush Dan," while directing the "Pioneer population" to settle other parts of the West Bank.[148] The new private mode of production provoked a public dispute between the Ministry of Housing and the Ministry of Agriculture;[149] this did not question the legitimacy of privatized settlements, but rather revolved around

---

[143] Rotbard, "Wall and Tower"; Kemp, "The Frontier Idiom on Borders and Territorial Politics in Post-1967 Israel," 79.

[144] Gutwein, "The Class Logic of the 'long revolution,' 1973–1977"; Allegra, "The Politics of Suburbia: Israel's Settlement Policy and the Production of Space in the Metropolitan Area of Jerusalem," 497–510.

[145] Settlement Division, "The 100,000 Plan," 8–20.   [146] Ibid.

[147] Weismann, "Private Settlements in Samaria."

[148] Ministry of Agriculture, "Renewal of Settlement Momentum in Judea and Samaria," 2.

[149] Levi, David (דוד לוי; 1937): an Israeli politician, who acted as a member of parliament between 1969 and 2006 on behalf of several parties that included Gahal, Likud, Gesher, and Israel Ahat. Levi acted as Minister of Aliyah and Integration (1977–81), Minister of Housing and Construction (1979–90), and Minister of Foreign Affairs (1990–2; 1996–8; 1999–2000). Dekel, Michael (מיכאל דקל; 1920–94): an Israeli politician and member of parliament (1977–88) on behalf of the Likud party. He served as deputy minister of agriculture (1981–84), where he coordinated the development of Jewish settlements in the West Bank and Galilee.

responsibility and credit concerning their development.[150] Both Ministries emphasized their role in promoting private settlement, with the CEO of the Ministry of Construction and Housing, Asher Wiener, claiming his office was a "pioneer in bringing private developers to build from their own money," while the Ministry of Agriculture stated that the latter was not using the "[market] demand forces" as needed.[151] The dispute needed the direct intervention of Prime Minister Menachem Begin; eventually, besides the allocation of sites, the establishment of new settlements became a mission of the Ministry of Housing, leading to a more organized and controlled suburbanization process that began to rely on larger and more experienced contractors and developers.

With this new mode of production, the state promoted the gentrification of the area through the construction of new Suburban Settlements during the 1980s. Unlike the earlier neo-rural examples, these new settlements relied on residential environments that were based on spacious houses and a well-maintained landscape, and, most importantly, an easy commute to the Tel Aviv metropolitan area. Not surprisingly, the new settling families far from resembled the allegedly more ideological religious settlers of *Gush Emunim*; they consisted mainly of city dwellers looking for improved living standards. The new population was characterized as upper-middle class, more secular and politically left-central leaning, and usually not part of the right-wing religious bloc.[152] These new Suburban Settlements began to form the sought after territorial sequence between the coastal plain and the West Bank, while attracting large segments of Israeli society; only the recession of the mid-1980s stopped this process from being even more widespread.[153]

The 1980s' gentrification of the Green Line enabled its mass suburbanization during the 1990s. These years witnessed two crucial events, the first being waves of Jewish immigration from the former Soviet

[150] Barel, "CEO of MH Warns Apartment Buyers in the West Bank," 1; Maoz, "MA and MH Agree on Cooperation in Construction in JS," 1.
[151] Wiener, *Letter to Michael Dekel*, 1; Settlement Division, "Population Dispersal Policy and Development of Judea and Samaria," 2.
[152] Portugali, "Jewish Settlement in the Occupied Territories: Israel's Settlement Structure and the Palestinians"; Benvenisti, *Report: Demographic, Economic, Legal, Social, and Political Developments in the West Bank*; ICBS, "Socio-Economic Index Value 2013, Cluster of Locality."
[153] Razin, "Urban Economic Development in a Period of Local Initiative: Competition among Towns in Israel's Southern Coastal Plain."

Union, increasing the Israeli population by 20 percent in less than ten years, and the second being the Israeli–Palestinian peace talks.[154] To meet increased demands for new dwelling units while simultaneously improving its territorial claims in any future negotiations, the Israeli Government promoted the construction of additional Suburban Settlements along the Green Line. The objective of the new governmental scheme, known as the Stars Plan, was to offer middle-class families affordable suburban housing in the recently gentrified frontier. This would lead them to evacuate their apartments in the Gush Dan area for the use of the coming immigrants while enhancing the state's control over the Green Line,[155] completing the suburban turn and finalizing the domestication of the former border. Approved in 1991, the Stars Plan relied on the similar unexecuted 1978 "Hills' Axis" plan, prepared by Baruch Kipnis for the Ministry of Construction and Housing, and even mentioned it in its subtitle.[156] However, while the 1978 plan spoke of creating an alternative urban system that would run parallel to the existing coastal plain, the new plan extended the coastal plain eastward, toward the Green Line (see Figure 2.6).

The suburbanization of the Green Line was part of the new national planning initiative. If, during the first statehood decades, the planning strategy was oriented toward national decentralization of the population and means of production, the approach of the 1990s began to favor a concentrated local decentralization. Both National Outline Plan 31 (1993) and National Outline Plan 35 (2005) proposed a metropolitan-based approach, which tied the national planning strategy to the rationale of the market. At the same time, the territorial agenda was not entirely forsaken, and both plans addressed the importance of settling frontier areas.[157] Therefore, as the government wanted to merge *areas of high demand* with *areas of national interest*, internal frontiers with economic potential became the main focus of national

---

[154] Efrat, "Geographical Distribution of the Soviet-Jewish New Immigrants in Israel"; Tolz, "Jewish Emigration from the Former USSR since 1970."
[155] Nahoum Dunsky Planners, "Development of the Hills' Axis: The Seven Stars Plan."
[156] Kipnis, "Potential of Developing Urban Housings along the Hills Axis."
[157] Shachar, "Reshaping the Map of Israel: A New National Planning Doctrine," 209; Yacobi and Tzfadia, "Neo-Settler Colonialism and the Re-Formation of Territory: Privatization and Nationalization in Israel," 17–19.

56   2 Background

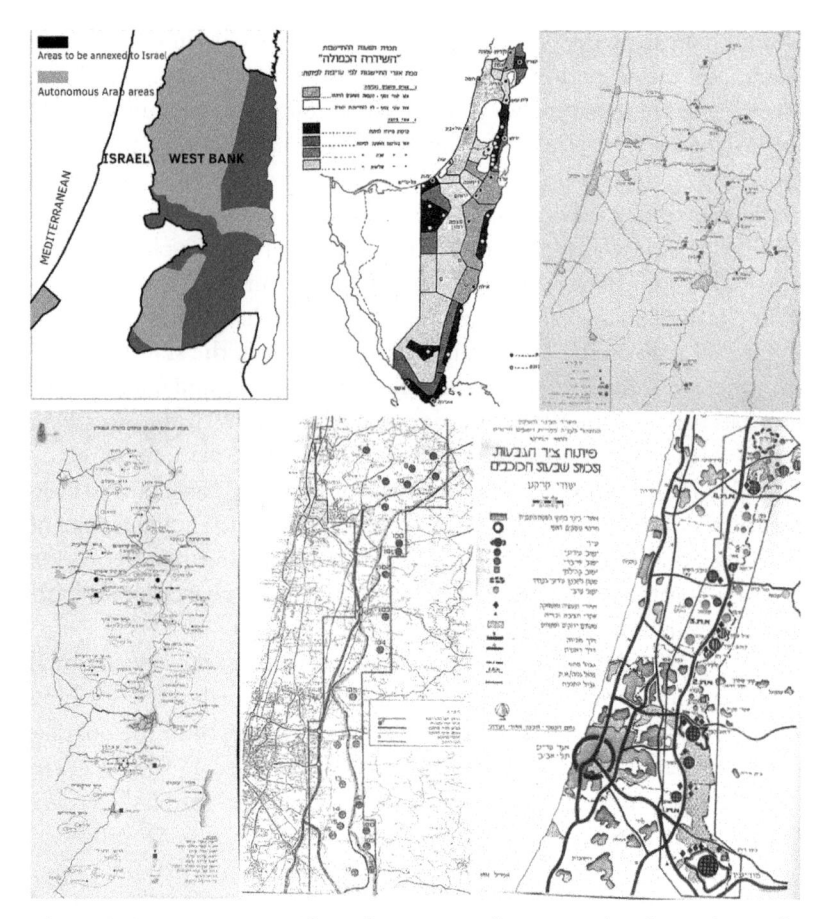

Figure 2.6 *Upper row* – Alon Plan, 1968 (illustration by the author); the Double Column Plan, 1975, (Avraham Wachman – MCH), note the areas designated for intense Jewish settlement in black; and Gush Emunim Plan, 1977. *Lower row* – the World Zionist Organization Plan ("Drobles" Plan), 1978 (WZO); Hills' Axis Plan, 1978; and Baruch Kipnis, the "Stars Plan," 1992 (Dunsky Planners – MCH)

development efforts.[158] Consequently, the Green Line was blurred, and what was once considered the country's eastern frontier turned into an integral part of the Tel Aviv metropolis.

[158] Charney, "A 'Supertanker' against Bureaucracy in the Wake of a Housing Crisis: Neoliberalizing Planning in Netanyahu's Israel," 1243.

The development of the area ceased by the early 2000s but regenerated less than ten years later. After the construction boom that followed mass immigration from the former Soviet Union, the Israeli building industry entered a recession, caused by an overflow of supply. Subsequently, the construction of new settlements and new dwelling units significantly decreased and the state decided to freeze some of the planned projects along the Green Line, fearing their economic failure. The violent incidents of the Second Intifada, which began in 2000, decreased interest in the area and the proximity of the Green Line settlements to the ongoing attacks, clashes, and raids in the West Bank turned them into a frontier zone once again.[159] Concurrently, the Ministry of Defense began to carry out the construction of the West Bank Separation Barrier. This land obstacle, which consists of six-meter concrete walls, barbed wires, patrol roads, guarding posts, and an elaborate surveillance system, did not follow the Green Line, leaving as many Jewish settlements as possible on the "Israeli side," thus expanding the metropolitan area of Gush Dan further into the West Bank. The completion, during the same years, of the first segments of the privately developed Trans-Israel Highway adjacent to the Separation Barrier retained the status of the area as a safe, well-connected region, far enough away from the coastal plain (the Tel Aviv metropolis) to be regarded by the government as fulfilling ideological and national interests, yet still close to it, thus attracting commuters.

The West Bank Separation Barrier and the Trans-Israel Highway laid the necessary infrastructure and created the desired economic feasibility, yet it was the post-2008 housing crisis that enabled the Israeli Government to make use of this potential. With increasing demand for housing, the government sought to enlarge the overall supply of dwelling units by stimulating a national construction boom. Nonetheless, as it was not able to do so in the areas of demand inside the main metropolises, it tried to expand into the internal frontiers by tendering state-owned lands to private developers.[160] The state hoped that the profitable land prices would lead private entrepreneurs to produce the needed units at affordable prices, which would eventually attract large numbers of Israeli families. Financializing the territorial

---

[159] Levi-Barzilai, "A House with an Attached Tank," 16.
[160] Charney, "A 'Supertanker' against Bureaucracy in the Wake of a Housing Crisis: Neoliberalizing Planning in Netanyahu's Israel," 1223–25.

mode of production meant that formerly unbuilt or small-scale settlements turned into large-scale housing schemes, and the former frontier turned into a real-estate project.

Over the past forty years, the state has promoted the construction of over thirty new settlements on both sides of the Green Line. What was once a frontier area, which the state sought to domesticate through sporadic *moshavim* and kibbutzim during the 1950s and 1960s, witnessed gradual modes of privatized production that led to the formation of new settlement typologies. First were the small rural, or neo-rural, Community Settlements of the late 1970s and early 1980s, which gave way to the first Suburban Settlements of the mid-1980s. These were followed by the intense development of the 1990s and its mass-produced suburbs, which eventually led to the high-rise construction boom of the early 2000s (Figure 2.7).

The private development of both the Trans-Israel Highway and the current large-scale housing projects along it have created a seemingly market-oriented area. However, as David Graeber claimed: "Whenever someone starts talking about the 'free market,' it's a good idea to look around for the man with the gun. He's never far away."[161] In the case of the settlements of the Trans-Israel Highway, the "man with the gun" is located on the adjacent Separation Barrier, proving Graeber's claims that it is *states* that create *markets*, and not the other way around (Figure 2.8). This market was created by the gradual involvement of private capital, yet in a selective manner, as the state sought to enhance its territorial project by directing the free market to the use of specific groups.[162] Thus, privatization was not simply an instrument utilized to fulfill the national settlement agenda, but actually an integral part of it, as the seemingly color-blind liberal economic discourse was used to promote the construction of ethnically homogeneous gated suburban communities.

The free-market façade the state gave to the area eased its merger into the wider national consensus. In 2014, Minister Naftali Bennet, from the religious right-wing *HaBayit HaYehudi* Party, addressed the Israeli Institute for National Security Studies (INSS). In his thirteen-minute

---

[161] Graeber, The Utopia of Rules, 120.
[162] Yacobi and Tzfadia, "Neo-Settler Colonialism and the Re-Formation of Territory: Privatization and Nationalization in Israel"; Yiftachel and Avni, "'Privati-nation' – Privatization, Nationalization, Housing and Gaps."

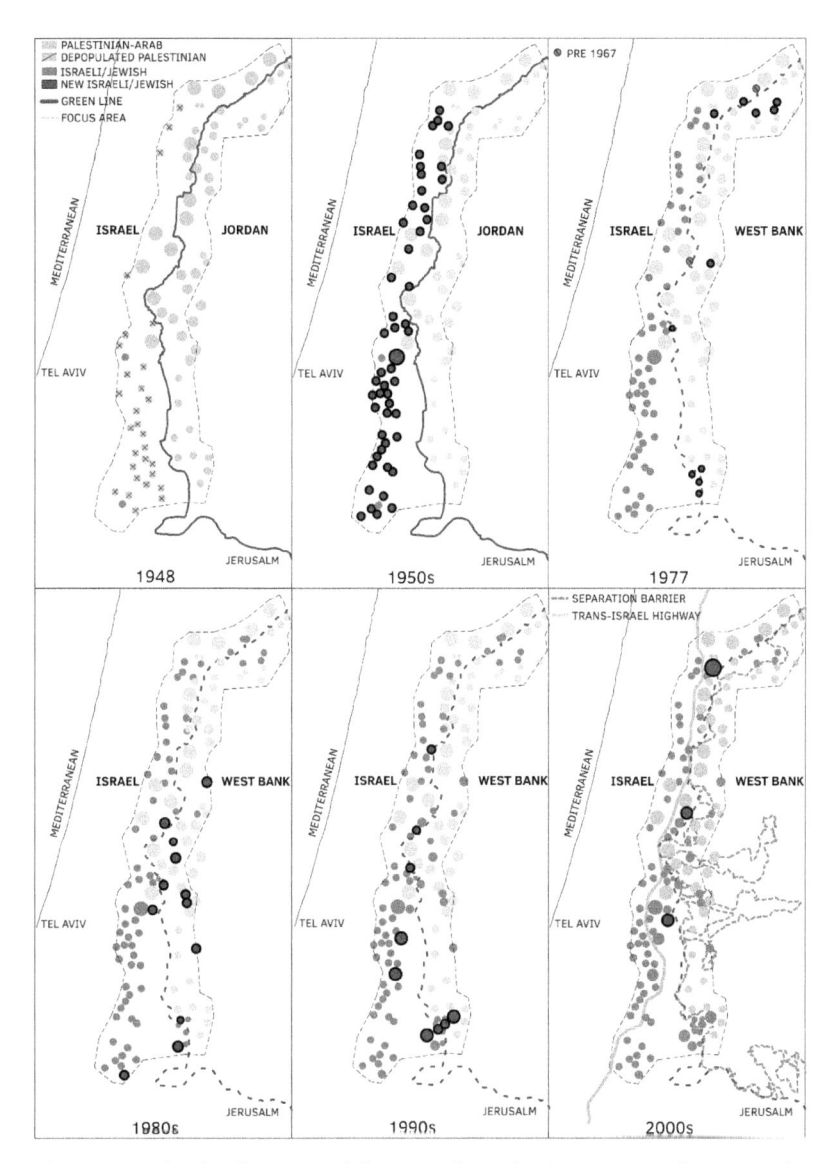

The Evolving Domestication of the Eastern Frontier 59

Figure 2.7 The development of the area along the Green Line (illustration by the author)

speech, Bennet cited the threats of the establishment of a Palestinian state on "Highway 6" and of having "hundreds of thousands of Palestinian refugees protesting" on its fences, and asked "[do] you think they would

Figure 2.8 Israeli tanks on the Green Line, 1996. In the background are houses in the settlement of Bat Heffer (Moshe Milner – GPO)

stop there?"[163] In the following years, Bennet would repeatedly use the highway as a cause in preventing the formation of a Palestinian state, using intimidatory expressions such as "ISIS sovereignty on Highway 6," "millions of Palestinians on Highway 6," or a "Palestine on Highway 6."[164] A young and charismatic politician, Bennet is known for his ability to appeal to a wide Israeli consensus, as seen in his appointment as Prime Minister and head of the national coalition government in 2021. His references to the highway thus indicate its wide perception as an integral part of the country, illustrating that for Israelis the Green Line does not exist, and that although de jure it is still the official border of the State of Israel, de facto, the privately developed Trans-Israel Highway and the settlements around it had moved this border eastward.

The Privatizing Domestication of the Green Line

As we have seen in this chapter, the Israeli built environment retained its geopolitical role over the past century by relying on different modes of territoriality that corresponded with the relevant socioeconomic order.

[163] Bennet, *Speech at the INSS*.   [164] Bennet, Facebook Profile.

From the early agricultural settlements in the pre-statehood days to current corporate development, the concept of ruling by settling has remained a leading national value, a political agenda, and a governance strategy that ensured the state's power over space. Contrary to the popular conception of privatization, based on decreasing state control, this version of privatization was meant to increase state control by introducing a new mode of territoriality – *privatize and rule*. In this sense, privatization of the settlement mechanism was a state coordinated effort that continuously harnessed the national territorial agenda to the constantly changing economic climate and cultural values by endorsing evolving modes of production, thus persistently ensuring the survival of the national geopolitical project by tying it to the changing rationale of the market.

The special circumstances of the area along the Green Line make it a unique case study of the privatizing settlement mechanism. As the national interest to develop the area grew only in the 1970s, it did not witness a substantial state-led development like other internal frontiers. Consequently, its increasing national importance and economic potential, together with the relatively undeveloped environment, turned the eastern frontier into a clean slate, ready to be developed by the various settlers, contractors, speculators, and entrepreneurs. Therefore, missing out on the first phases of *cultivate and rule* and *industrialize and rule*, the Green Line witnessed mainly the post-1977 *privatize and rule* mode of territoriality and its corresponding modes of production.

Using the settlements along the Green Line as a case study, the following chapters analyze and clarify how the settlement mechanism has transformed since 1977. Each chapter focuses on a particular stage in the privatizing settlement mechanism, first analyzing the evolving and entangled geopolitical, individual, and economic interests. Accordingly, each chapter analyzes a different mode of production in the settlement mechanism and the spatial privileges it was based on, examining the differing reciprocal relationships of granting settling groups, or spatial agents, the power to colonize, inhabit, plan, develop, or market space, as a means to increase the state's power over it. Examining the settlement typologies, each chapter then considers how architecture and urban forms are a product of the modes of production that generated them, and an outcome of the evolving territorial, individual, and corporate coalition – from the strategic level of locating new sites on both sides of the border, through the settlement's (sub)urban layout, all the way to the architecture of the single dwelling unit.

3 | (Neo-)Ruralization and the Community Settlement

From a Pioneer Experience to an Individual Focus

Early Signs of Privatization

The privatization of the Israeli geopolitical project was not a sudden occurrence, but rather a long and gradual process such that one could identify its origins in the Community Settlements of the late 1970s.[1] While the former frontier domestication efforts of Labor Zionism focused on communal agricultural or industrial development, these aspects were no longer evident in privatizing Israel. Thus, the Community Settlements were based on the desire of homogeneous groups to create their own small-scale localities away from the city and the larger societal context.[2] They were an outcome of an early mode of privatized production, which relied on granting select groups spatial privileges that consisted of the power to exclusively colonize the frontier by establishing their own ex-urban communities while securing and enhancing the state's power over space. As an early example of the privatized settlement mechanism, the development of the Community Settlements was a fusion of individualistic desires and pre-privatization residues. Consequently, they were inspired by former rural examples, using a pioneer-like framework and the spatial syntax of communal agricultural settlements.[3] Lacking any means of production, the Community Settlements were a neo-rural phenomenon, using agricultural concepts and pioneer discourse as a mere façade, rather than an essential component of the group's everyday life.

Focusing on the cases of Sal'it, the Reihan Bloc, Nirit, and Ya'arit, this chapter discusses the evolution of the Community Settlements.

---

[1] Schwake, "The Community Settlement: A Neo-Rural Territorial Tool."
[2] Yiftachel, "From Sharon to Sharon: Spatial Planning and Separation Regime in Israel/Palestine."
[3] Kemp, "The Frontier Idiom on Borders and Territorial Politics in Post-1967 Israel," 79.

Exploring these case studies, it sheds light on the gradually privatizing modes of production the Community Settlements relied on, starting with standardization, then shifting to customization and ending with mass commodification. Studying the transforming mode of production and its evolving materialization over the years, this chapter explains how the Community Settlements at first continued the previous rural focus on communal aspects, yet later began shifting toward individual characteristics and, eventually, toward corporate interests. By analyzing the changes in the spatial privileges each mode of production was based on, we will come to understand the changing role of architecture and planning, starting from a territorial and societal function and concluding as an artifact of the privatizing settlement mechanism.

The Neo-Rural Experience

There are individual men and women, and there are families . . . . There is no such thing as society.

Margaret Thatcher[4]

Rurality, in the Israeli context, was an integral part of the nation-building process. Despite their relatively small part in the local Jewish population, the early agricultural settlements of the kibbutzim and *moshavim* of the pre-state years formed the ideological backbone of the leading Labor Zionist ideology. These rural settlements were not only a territorial tool of land redemption, but also an educational one, intended to lead to the formation of a new and healthy nation connected to its historic land, and thus to its past. With the changes in Israeli society, economy, and culture, the old pioneer ideology gave way to a pioneer experience, which embraced the pioneer discourse and the act of frontier settlement as a lifestyle.[5] Consequently, the rural communal layouts, as this chapter shows, formed the (sub)urban muse for this new mode of territoriality. Synchronously, the *Agency House* (*Beit Sochnut*) (Figure 3.1), a simple white cube unit covered by a pitched roof, which the Jewish Agency supplied to moshavim and kibbutzim during the 1950s and represented a suitable dwelling for an

---

[4] Thatcher, "Margaret Thatcher's Interview in *Women's Own*."
[5] Kemp, "The Frontier Idiom on Borders and Territorial Politics in Post-1967 Israel."

Figure 3.1 "Agency Houses" in Moshav Avivim, 1958 (Central Zionist Archive)

ideological and modest pioneer, formed the architectural inspiration for the neo-rural experience.

Neo-rurality is a postindustrial phenomenon that involves the immigration of middle-class and upper-middle-class city dwellers to rural areas. Fueled by different incentives, such as the despair of urban centers or the renaissance of the countryside, it took various manifestations, although it usually included the transformation of the rural built environment in order to adapt to the lifestyle sought by the newly arriving ex-urban settlers.[6] The rural, therefore, became an experience consumed by the migrating urban upper-middle-class, as part of the postindustrial course of *"Rurbanisation."*[7] This global phenomenon, which emerged during the 1960s and 1970s, was characterized by a transformation in patterns of population distribution that included an increase in rural

---

[6] Chevalier, "Neo-Rural Phenomena"; Smith and Phillips, "Socio-Cultural Representations of Greentrified Pennine Rurality"; Halliday and Coombes, "In Search of Counterurbanisation: Some Evidence from Devon on the Relationship between Patterns of Migration and Motivation."

[7] Chevalier, "Neo-Rural Phenomena," 176. Hines, "In Pursuit of Experience: The Postindustrial Gentrification of the Rural American West," 285–303.

settlements at the expense of urban ones. Categorized by several scholars as *rural gentrification*, it is much more complex than a simple replacement of local low-income communities by new higher-income ones.[8] Neo-rurality refers also to the new ways of life city dwellers moving to rural areas were seeking to adopt or develop; whether they were working-class families looking to escape the hardship of urban centers, or others seeking to pursue a peasant-like or artisan-like lifestyle.[9]

Neo-rurality is not mere suburbanization. People who move away from urban centers are usually interested in improving their current living standards while searching for a more tranquil way of life. In *suburbia* the emphasis is on being away from the city's disadvantages while still being close enough to all of its advantages. In counterurban examples of neo-rurality, the emphasis is on remoteness from the entire urban system,[10] with the distance from the city enhancing the rural idyll. Therefore, although it is sometimes hard to draw a line between these phenomena, counterurbanization and suburbanization are not synonyms, but rather two different manifestations of rural gentrification and neo-rurality. As an expression of postindustrialism, which focuses on the production and consumption of experiences, neo-rurality offers a seemingly new "authentic" experience,[11] based on a pleasant way of living in affinity with nature that is further enhanced by a "sense of community" and social empowerment.[12]

The search for a sense of community was not unique to the neo-rural phenomenon but rather part of the wider neoliberal turn. The decline of the welfare state and the rise of the neoliberal order during the 1970s not only challenged the economic system, but also the concept of society.[13] With the diminishing of the welfare state, the tie between individuals and society was weakened, forcing them to seek alternative or compensatory

---

[8] Guimond and Simard, "Gentrification and Neo-Rural Populations in the Québec Countryside: Representations of Various Actors"; Rose, "Rethinking Gentrification: Beyond the Uneven Development of Marxist Urban Theory."
[9] Halliday and Coombes, "In Search of Counterurbanisation: Some Evidence from Devon on the Relationship between Patterns of Migration and Motivation."
[10] Ibid.
[11] MacCannell, *The Tourist: A New Theory of the Leisure Class*; Liechty, *Suitably Modern Making Middle-Class Culture in a New Consumer Society*.
[12] Hines, "In Pursuit of Experience: The Postindustrial Gentrification of the Rural American West," 296.
[13] Harvey, *A Brief History of Neoliberalism*, 23; Bauman, *Community Seeking Safety in an Insecure World*.

systems, often found in smaller, more homogeneous groups or communities that offered a sense of security and belonging.[14] Marxist historian Eric Hobsbawm claimed that this led to a greater focus on smaller, fragmented *Gemeinschafts* (communities), in contrary to a single unified *Gesellschaft* (society), as seen in separatism, identity politics, sectarianism, and neo-nationalism;[15] thus, it is not surprising that former British Prime Minister Margaret Thatcher, one of the leading figures of neo-liberalism, undermined the concept of society.[16] The neo-rural experience could therefore be understood as an attempt by the postindustrial individual to escape the unauthentic context of the urban *Gesellschaft*, in search of a small-scale and authentic rural *Gemeinschaft*. The Israeli Community Settlements, with their emphases on landscape and community life, therefore constitute a new territorial mode of production, in which the Israeli administration turned the neo-rural experience into a new method of frontier domestication. Moreover, the Community Settlements illustrate how neo-rurality might eventually become suburban, as it forms a mere extension of the urban context it initially opposed.

The Community Settlement

The Community Settlement model was an integral part of the West Bank project.[17] It was first mentioned in a report of the Movement for New Urban Settlement in 1975, which represented six West Bank Jewish localities planning to develop a new settlement framework that differed from the traditional *moshav* or kibbutz. The report proposed to focus the settlement's inner structure on community life while promoting a more flexible economic framework than in the cooperative rural settlements.[18] Unity in this new framework was not in respect of labor or production, but rather in the societal aspect of creating a homogeneous group interested in living together. Consequently, one of the main features of the Community Settlements was their relatively

---

[14] Filc, *Hegemony and Populism in Israel*.
[15] Tönnies, *Community and Civil Society*; Hobsbawm, *Nations and Nationalism since 1780*; Hobsbawm, *Globalisation, Democracy and Terrorism*.
[16] Gutwein, "The Settlements and the Relationship between Privatization and the Occupation."
[17] Newman, "Gush Emunim and Settlement-Type in the West Bank."
[18] Appelbaum and Newman, *Between Village and Suburb: New Forms of Settlement in Israel*.

small size, 250–500 families, and the central role of the admission committee, which made sure that the settling core would have common characteristics, thus promoting a "closed society" that would function better than "larger" and "open" ones.[19] Essentially a *gemeinschaft*-oriented framework, this new model expressed the desires of middle-class families for "quality of life" in "gated localities," protected from the wider society.[20] The Ministry of Agriculture, the Jewish Agency, and the World Zionist Organization endorsed this report, embracing the Community Settlements and their exclusionary criteria as a means to attract families to areas of national interest.[21]

Lacking farming uses, yet mimicking previous agricultural models, the Community Settlements were a neo-rural territorial phenomenon. This new prototype reused several concepts from agricultural settlements, such as reliance on an association and the division into households sharing a communal system, thus reproducing the experience of a rural lifestyle without having to physically engage in agricultural work. Not by chance, the development of Community Settlements was carried out by the same institutions that were in charge of the former cooperative rural settlements, such as the Jewish National Fund (JNF), the Jewish Agency (JA), and the Ministry of Agriculture, while being planned and initiated by the Jewish Agency's rural settlement unit. The newly established Settlement Division, which was separated from the Settlement Department and focused on the Occupied Territories,[22] continued the former apparatus and encouraged small-scale groups, often with a common ideological background, to form an

---

[19] Movement for New Urban Settlements, "The Community Settlement," 2; Gush Emunim, "Proposal for Settlement in Judea and Samaria."
[20] Yiftachel, "Bedouin-Arabs and the Israeli Settler State," 27; Allegra, "The Politics of Suburbia: Israel's Settlement Policy and the Production of Space in the Metropolitan Area of Jerusalem," 497–510.
[21] Settlement Division, "Community Settlements."
[22] *Settlement Department* (המחלקה להתיישבות, *HaMahlaka LeHityashvut*): the executive arm of the JA, in charge of establishing agricultural settlements in the State of Israel, and previously in Palestine during the British Mandate. Its activities later dissolved into other departments of the JA. *Settlement Division* (החטיבה להתיישבות, *HaHativa LeHityashvut*): an independent unit of the World Zionist Organization and the executive arm of the State of Israel in terms of new settlements in the West Bank and the Golan Heights (previously also in the Sinai Peninsula) and, since 2004, Galilee and the Negev. Founded in 1967, the Settlement Division first operated as part of the Settlement Department, under the same management (though with different funding sources).

initial settling core for a future settlement.[23] In promoting these homogeneous communities, planning officials sought to attract families that were seeking to move out of the city and into small-scale ex-urban communities.[24] Thus, the Community Settlement model became an integral part of the state's new vision for the West Bank, forming one of the main features of the Drobles Plan (1979),[25] and the more elaborate 100,000 Plan (1981).[26]

The pursuit of better "quality of life" was a fundamental feature in the development of Community Settlements, yet the interpretation of the term was equivocal. Whether targeting religious and ideological families, or more secular and politically neutral ones, all territorial plans highlighted the potential of the better living standards that the new small-scale settlements could provide. In the late 1970s, "quality of life" and "living standards" revolved around the ability to live in small homogeneous communities, surrounded by a natural landscape. The Gush Emunim Plan thus called for the creation of "closed societies" as promoters of "vivid communal life" where "the individual's participation is willingly and consciously" sought.[27] The Drobles Plan stated: "In order to create a wide spread of settlements that would consist of high living standards, it is suggested that the settlements in Judea and Samaria would be constructed as Community Settlements."[28] In the 100,000 Plan, Community Settlements were mentioned once again as a way to create "special social qualities," that would attract potential settlers.[29] Nevertheless, as the later plans began tying the development of the Green Line to the private market, the emphasis shifted toward a growing focus on the affordability of spacious, large detached houses, in comparison to the expensive and small apartments of the dense coastal plain.[30] Thus, by the mid-1980s, the Community Settlements were no longer minimalistic and isolated

---

[23] Benvenisti, *The West Bank Data Project: A Survey of Israel's Policies*, 49–58.
[24] Rosen and Razin, "Enclosed Residential Neighborhoods in Israel: From Landscapes of Heritage and Frontier Enclaves to New Gated Communities."
[25] Drobles, "Master plan for Settlement Development in Judea and Samaria, 1979–1983," 2.
[26] Settlement Division, "The 100,000 Plan."
[27] Gush Emunim, "Proposal for Settlement in Judea and Samaria," A3.
[28] Drobles, "Master plan for Settlement Development in Judea and Samaria, 1979–1983," 2.
[29] Settlement Division, "The 100,000 Plan," 13–14.   [30] Ibid.

residential environments but rather a platform that provided luxurious and attractive living standards.

The various settlement agencies applied the Community Settlement model both inside and outside of the West Bank. The Settlement Department, in charge of promoting settlement in areas inside official Israeli territory, began using this new model in the late 1970s to attract families to its areas of responsibility.[31] This would usually start with an open call for settlers through public media, and families interested in joining one of the new settlements would sign up and then attend a tour of the area. After passing a selection process, which would ensure the family's suitability for the project and the future community, they would be included in the first settlement phase that consisted of temporary houses and limited infrastructure. Once the permanent houses had been constructed, new families would be accepted only after passing an admissions committee, which was made up of representatives of the JA, the regional council, and the settlement's members, ensuring the homogeneity of the community.

The spatial privileges enacted in the early Community Settlements were based on the ability of small-scale and uniform groups to exclusively use a certain site and to create their own segregated ex-urban compounds. The settlements' admission committees excluded vast portions of wider Israeli society, guaranteeing the desired social seclusion.[32] The better "quality of life" the Community Settlements had to offer was thus manifested in small gated communities, isolated from cities and connected with nature. Later, as this chapter will show, the "quality of life" would consist of spacious detached single-family houses, which were significantly more luxurious than the urban dwellings middle-class families usually inhabited, shifting the focus from the community to the individual. Subsequently, in the 1980s, the pursuit of "quality of life," whether due to the Community Settlements' pseudo-rural character or better living standards, became the most effective promotion strategy to settle the state's internal frontiers.

---

[31] Abreek-Zubeidat and Ben-Arie, "To Be at Home: Spaces of Citizenship in the Community Settlements of the Galilee"; Yiftachel, "The Internal Frontier: Territorial Control and Ethnic Relations in Israel," 493; Shafir, "From Overt to Veiled Segregation: Israel's Palestinian Arab Citizens in the Galilee," 1.

[32] Shafir, "From Overt to Veiled Segregation: Israel's Palestinian Arab Citizens in the Galilee," 20–22.

The Community Settlements combined individual fulfillment (*Hagshama Atzmit*) with national fulfillment (*Hagshama Leomit*). With the growing emphasis on better living standards, the Settlement Division, Settlement Department, the various planning administrations, and the settling families still portrayed the Community Settlement as a pioneering act that was an integral part of the national territorial mission. The Community Settlements were thus a neo-rural phenomenon that merged "quality of life" and a pioneer-like lifestyle, an ideal postindustrial neo-rural experience. This could not be better described than in a recent commercial for the new neighborhood of Haspin in Galilee:

> Welcome to Haspin – a religious community located in the heart of nature and Jewish history. Residents of the community enjoy a wide range of services such as a library ... a grocery store, swimming pool, dental clinic, youth hostel and many Torah institutions .... Haspin combines an excellent way of fulfilling the values of settlement with quality of life and community.[33]

The settlements discussed in this chapter, Sal'it, Reihan, Hinanit, Shaked, Nirit, and Ya'arit, demonstrate the manner in which the Community Settlement model started as a counterurban pioneer-like phenomenon that was eventually incorporated into the national suburban turn and ever-growing corporate involvement (Figure 3.2). It thus shows how the focus was initially on homogenous intimate communities, which gradually gave way to "individual men and women" and their commodities.

Standardization: Communal Spatial Privileges

The initial mode of production in the neo-ruralization of the Green Line began as an extension of former agricultural modes of territoriality. The appeal of the first settlements was not just due to the high living standards they offered to future inhabitants, but also the ability of select groups to establish their own isolated communities away from the larger societal context. The focus was on the *gemeinschaft* and it was the community as a whole that received the spatial privilege to exclusively settle a certain site, while the power to develop and form space was retained by the state. Accordingly, the early mode of production relied on communal seclusion

---

[33] Homee, *Website for Rural Living*.

Standardization: Communal Spatial Privileges 71

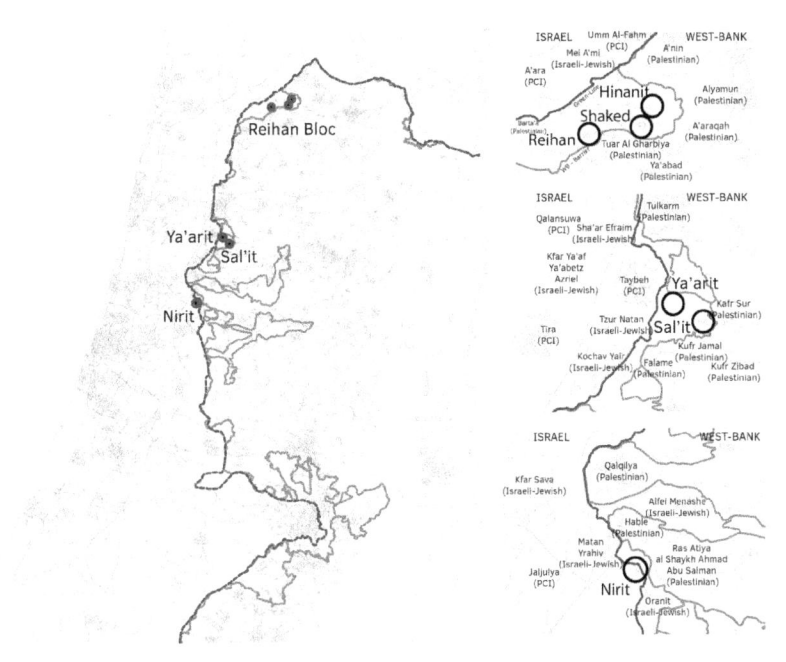

Figure 3.2 Case studies along the Green Line and the West Bank Barrier, 2015 (illustration by the author) Note: PCI – Palestinian Citizens of Israel.

and standardization, and promoted the formation of a segregated settlement that fitted the new distinctive desires, on the one hand, and uniform and simplistic residential environments that matched the settlers' pioneer-like aspirations, on the other. The first sites were Nirit and Reihan, established in 1979, followed by Hinanit and Shaked a couple of years later.

Territorially oriented and located inside the West Bank, the new sites were drawn by the Settlement Division of the World Zionist Organization. Just a few kilometers east of the rural settlements of Tzur Nathan (1966) and Kibbutz Eyal (1950), Sal'it (Hebrew for "rocky") formed an extension of the pre-1967 efforts to strengthen Jewish presence in the area, which in the early 1980s consisted of a few thousand, in comparison to almost 30,000 Palestinians living on both sides of the Green Line, and was thus first named Tzur Nathan B.[34]

[34] Davar, "The Three Settlements," 2.

Placed between the Palestinian villages of Kufr Sur, Kufr Jamal, and Falame in its east and the Arab town of Taybeh,[35] inside of Israel, in the west, Sal'it formed a territorial wedge in the area, extending Israeli control eastward while preventing any possible Arab cross-border connections. The Reihan Bloc followed similar considerations, and was located south of the predominantly Arab region of Wadi A'ara, inside the State of Israel and north of the Palestinian region of Jenin, which altogether included some 60,000 Palestinians and around 1,000 Israeli Jews at that time.[36]

Located on the fringes of the West Bank, slightly over the Green Line, the new settlements were ideological, yet not "too" ideological. Sal'it and Reihan, for example, had already been authorized by the Labor establishment in 1977, before the formation of the right-wing Likud government later that year. The decision was even declared as "administrative" and "not political" by the interministerial Settlement Committee,[37] and received the support of Ra'anan Weitz,[38] head of the JA's Settlement Department, who advocated for settling sites inside the official borders of Israel, rather than in the Occupied Territories. According to Weitz, the new sites were compatible with the unofficial Alon Plan of 1967, which limited Israeli territorial expansions to the border area of the Green Line, greater Jerusalem and the Jordan Valley.[39]

As a residue of the pre-privatization days, the sites of Sal'it and Reihan first took the form of a temporary military *Nahal* settlement. This custom of a military *Nahal* settlement was quite common in developing frontier areas, and usually consisted of a preliminary military outpost settled by a small group of soldiers that safeguarded the area and prepared it for its future as a civilian settlement. They were housed either by former *Nahal* soldiers, or by members of another political settling movement.[40] With the military taking the lead, the territorial importance of the sites derived from their strategical

---

[35] Taybeh housed Palestinian citizens of Israel.
[36] JA and WZO, "Nahal Eron Project," 16.
[37] Waxman, "Green Light for Three Settlements over the Green-Line," 3.
[38] Weitz, Ra'anan (רענן וייץ; 1919–98): a key figure in the Settlement Department since 1948, and its director from 1963–84. Although he was in charge of settlement development, he ideologically opposed the West Bank enterprise and advocated for other areas.
[39] Ibid.
[40] Douer, *Our Sickle Is Our Sword*, 233; Davar, "The Three Settlements," 2.

importance as a defensive shield for the coastal plain. In his speech to the soldiers of the Sal'it outpost, Moshe Nehorai, head of the *Nahal* division in the Ministry of Defence, stated that in "every peace arrangement" the lights of Sal'it "on top of the mountain" will "expand the breath of Israel," increasing the safety of all "mothers and children in their sleep, [and the] workers in the fields and factories in the lowlands."[41] Similar words were also sounded at the ceremony in Reihan, where the settling soldiers who belonged to the left-leaning *HaShomer HaTzair* movement,[42] mentioned the strategical importance of the site, intending to appease their general anti–West Bank approach.[43]

As temporary outposts, Sal'it and Reihan followed the typical lines of a military settlement. They both consisted of five prefabricated buildings that were used as barracks and as a communal kitchen and dining area. Arranged in a U-shaped form and positioned at the highest topographical point, the units created a defendable inner courtyard suitable for a military base, which the soldiers used for informal and formal activities (Figure 3.3). As these were sites of future rural activity, the soldiers maintained a daily routine that consisted of guarding duties and agricultural work in nearby settlements.[44]

Continuing in rural course, the settlement's permanent phase was planned by the Settlement Department's rural unit.[45] It was officially the Settlement Division that was responsible for new sites in the West Bank, but as it was still in its initial stages it relied on the experience and knowledge of the Settlement Department and the JA. In fact, the division between these organizations was of a bureaucratic manner, meant to prevent an affiliation between the JA and the Occupied Territories, which could hinder its budget that relied on donations by Jews living abroad who were not always keen on supporting the West Bank project. The Settlement Division was thus basically a cover that enabled the planners and administrators of the Settlement Department to operate freely in the West Bank. Dealing with some aspects of the pre-privatized

---

[41] Douer, *Our Sickle Is Our Sword*, 233.
[42] *Shomer HaTzair, ha* (השומר הצעיר): a Socialist-Zionist youth movement established in 1919, literally "the young guardian." It is also the name of Marxist-Zionist Party active in Mandatory Palestine, which later became part of the Israeli *Mapam* (*Mifleget HaPoalim HaMeuhedet*; the united workers' party).
[43] Walter, "Nahal Reihan Outpost Goes on Site," 4.
[44] Douer, *Our Sickle Is Our Sword*, 233.
[45] Settlement Department, "Outline Plan for Sal'it."

Figure 3.3 The temporary site of Reihan, 1979 (Chanania Herman – GPO)

mode of production, the JA controlled the entire planning process, and the future settlers had almost no power to influence the proceedings, thus leading the planners to focus on the site's restrictions while using existing settlement practices.[46]

With the rural unit taking the lead, its planners continued using settlement patterns they were familiar with. They gave both sites the form of a *Moshav Ovdim*: a rural settlement made up of private family households with a cooperative system of purchasing supplies and marketing produced goods. Accordingly, they turned the former military posts on the hilltop into the new settlements' focal point, while forming a spatial arrangement of private houses sharing a communal open space. This *compound model* resembled a common rural *moshav*, and promoted a clear hierarchy that emphasized the reliance of the individuals on the community they were part of (Figure 3.4). In view of the rural focus, planners initially intended to designate areas for agricultural use; however, as we will see later in the chapter, this was never fully realized.

Until this point, proceedings were conducted according to the common practice of rural settlement, yet the first signs of privatization

---

[46] Settlement Department, "Outline Plan for Reihan."

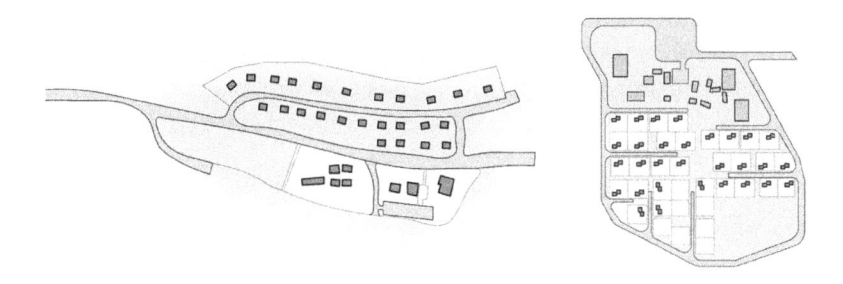

Standardization: Communal Spatial Privileges 75

Figure 3.4 Sal'it (left) and Reihan (right), 1979 (illustration by the author)

started to appear in the efforts to find a proper settling group. The selective privatization enacted in this phase relied on the ability to become a member of a prearranged settling group, which would receive the spatial privilege of exclusively populating one of the sites. The site of Sal'it was assigned to the right-wing *Herut-Beitar* settling movement and, as it was unable to find a suitable group in time,[47] Matityahu Drobles,[48] head of the Settlement Division and the former head of *Herut-Beitar*, approached the *B'nai Brith* organization,[49] which had already organized a settling group and was looking for a suitable location. As members of a politically neutral movement, this group was not focused on strengthening Jewish presence in the West Bank per se, and was simply interested in leaving the city and adopting a new rural way of living. Unsure as to whether there would be another possible site in the near future, Drobles' offer was too attractive to refuse and the *B'nai Brith* members agreed to join the West Bank project as well as the *Herut-Beitar* movement.[50] The same selective measures were enacted

[47] *Mishkei Herut Beitar* (משקי חירות בית״ר): a Zionist settlement movement affiliated with Revisionist Zionism, the *Beitar* movement, and the *Herut* Party (later Likud).
[48] Drobles, Matityahu (מתיתיהו דרובלס; 1931–2018): an Israeli politician and parliament member (1972–7) for *Gahal* and the Likud. From 1978–92 he acted as the head of its Settlement Division. He composed the "Master Plan for Settlement Development in Judea and Samaria 1979–1983," which became known as the Drobles plan, and supervised the 100,000 plan.
[49] *B'nai Brith* (בני ברית): a Jewish social organization founded in New York in 1843. Today, it has about half a million members in 60 countries and is one of the largest Jewish organizations worldwide.
[50] Gilboa, Interview in Salit.

in Reihan, which the Ministry of Agriculture assigned to the *HaOved HaTzioni* movement.[51] The movement did not have a prearranged group, and thus began enlisting young families and married couples, originating mainly from cities in the Israeli coastal plain,[52] who were seeking a change to a more rural lifestyle by moving into the geographical periphery.[53]

With the seemingly light ideological affiliation, the settlers of both sites were far from the typical right-wing religious settlers. Located slightly over the Green Line, both groups were much closer to the center of the Israeli political spectrum, and clearly nonreligious. This was echoed in the contrasting statements made by settlers from Reihan in the early phases. These included hawkish declarations such as "establishing a Jewish settlement in the core of the Arab one was close to our heart"[54] and "[those opposing us] don't understand the strategical necessity of Reihan,"[55] as well as more dovish comments like "we are from HaOved HatZioni, the liberals, we are not Gush Emunim, we are not settlers ... we are in the consensus ... agreed upon by all parties" and "We are for settling in Judea and Samaria, but not in the sole of the Arabs ... we have good relations with the Arabs."[56]

The transition from the temporary outpost to the permanent settlement lasted almost two years, emphasizing the lack of sincere defense justifications. The Settlement Division was ready to populate the sites quite quickly, yet budgetary considerations caused several delays.[57] With the long transition period, the military, who initially highlighted the importance of controlling the sites, was not interested in maintaining its presence and declared that it would leave the outposts by the end of 1979. The Settlement Division, afraid of losing its foothold, pressurized the groups to replace the soldiers and to inhabit their barracks

---

[51] *Oved HaTzioni, ha* (העובד הציוני; The Zionist Worker): a settlement movement established in 1936, affiliated with the nonsocialist line of Zionism (yet nonrevisionist), later the liberal Israeli Progressive Party and the General Zionists.
[52] Davar, "Rozolio: Setbacks in Settlement in Undisputed Areas," 2; Pripaz, "Nahal Reihan: Moshav Shitufi," 4.
[53] Cohen, Interview in Reihan.
[54] Levav, "In Reihan Are Worried from Controversy over Other Settlement with the Same Name," 20.
[55] Harif, "Prof Zamir: Haven't Yet Finished My Examination Regarding Reihan and Dotan," 1.
[56] Levav, "JNF to Establish 3 More Points in the Triangle Area," 4.
[57] Tzuriel, "Samaria Is Open for Settlement," 17.

Standardization: Communal Spatial Privileges   77

temporarily while planning and construction were still underway.[58] Despite this being a temporary arrangement, the "naturalisation" of Sal'it was marked by a ceremonial occasion attended by Minister of Agriculture Ariel Sharon, in which *Nahal* soldiers handed the flag of the settlement over to the settling families, symbolizing the transition from a military occupation to a civilian one, and from defense concerns to geopolitical considerations.

After several months of living in the former barracks, the Ministry of Construction and Housing began to supply the first permanent houses, which clearly matched the neo-rural profile of the settlements. They were standardized prefabricated concrete units assembled on site, resembling other mass-produced dwellings built by Ashdar Ltd for the Ministry of Construction and Housing, which became known as *Ashkubit* – a portmanteau of *Ashdar* and *Cube*.[59] The houses consisted of two 36 m² cubes, one dedicated to the "night-uses" of bedrooms and bathroom, and one to the "day-uses" of the living room and kitchen. Simplistic and quite spartan, the state-supplied units were covered by a sloping asbestos roof that granted the houses the desired appearance of an idyllic countryside home, while disguising the prefabricated concrete cubes (Figure 3.5).

Figure 3.5 Infrastructure works and first houses in Sal'it, 1980 (Smadar Gilboa)

[58] Gilboa, Interview in Salit.   [59] Ashtrom, "Milestones."

The arrangement of the units on site corresponded with the communal lifestyle of the settlers. As the cubes did not completely overlap, they gave each of the units an L-shaped form, with a minimal private entrance area that continued the communal approach. In Reihan, with a public core consisting of pedestrian paths and lacking any significant fences or barriers, the private front yards formed an extension of the open public space, connecting each household to the greater community. In Sal'it, the units were placed parallel to each other, creating a shared entrance area between every two houses, thus enhancing the communal aspect once more. At the same time, because there was an external staircase at the front of each house to bridge the height difference between the dwelling unit and ground level, the internal part of the unit was cut off from its surroundings, ensuring the privacy of the nuclear family.

Despite the apparent standardization, the settlers of Sal'it did have some ability to influence the design of their houses. According to the first settlers, owing to the group's connections to the Settlement Division, they were able to convince the Ministry of Construction and Housing to improve the common model and to turn it into a split-level unit,[60] which merged with the site's topography and oriented the living room area toward the open view. However, as the units were made with three load-bearing walls, the opening toward the panorama was quite limited and consisted of a narrow window. Still, this minor difference is indicative of future plans and shows how the same developments were carried out differently, according to the spatial privileges of each settling group.

While the initial ability to influence the design of the housing units was quite limited, once the families moved into their new homes they were able to start changing them and transforming the unified form and quite minimalistic conditions. Consisting of two bedrooms, the original houses fitted the needs of young families in their first years.[61] Yet, as these families began growing, the 72 m² units were no longer big enough, and the modifications that followed were mainly intended to provide the expanding household with more space. The modifications in Reihan were comparably limited and consisted of minimal additions, while in Sal'it the split-level model enabled the easier construction of

[60] Gilboa, Interview in Salit.
[61] Samaria Local Construction Committee, "Permit 8/908/0 (Sal'it)."

a second floor and an extension to the lower cube, which, as it no longer depended on the existing load-bearing walls, could be opened toward the landscape, providing the house with an open panorama fitting for a family living in the countryside.[62] Eventually, the changes that were made turned the units from small, spartan, prefabricated elements into multi-level houses, which several families expanded further, even adding a basement.

The significant signs of privatization began appearing with the undeveloped means of production, which turned both rural *moshavim* into Community Settlements. Although the Ministry of Agriculture helped to develop some agricultural industries on both sites, these were insufficient, and, as they were not officially categorized as rural settlements, the ministry was unable to provide them with additional means of production. Fearing a lack of development, the Sal'it council sent a complaint letter to the JA in 1984, protesting their treatment as "any other Community Settlement," that is, referring to Community Settlement as a derogatory term.[63] As the local means of production were not provided, Sal'it and Reihan began to lose their already limited rural characters, and the majority of families soon left their new agricultural professions.[64] Consequently, both sites continued to be remote, small and still counterurban, while remaining nonagricultural and neo-rural. While this halted the development of Sal'it, Reihan witnessed a severe communal crisis that caused sharp divisions inside the group and concluded in the departure of several families and changes in its leadership.[65] With the fragmentation of the initial settling group, Reihan suffered from continuous changes in its composition and an acute lack of new families interested in joining the community. Consequently, several of the sixteen houses were repeatedly vacant, left uninhabited for long periods, and several families declined sale offers, even at significantly low prices.[66]

The neighboring settlements of Hinanit and Shaked constituted a further step toward individuality and neo-rurality. Both sites were part of ongoing state efforts to expand its power over the area through the construction of additional Jewish settlements. Hinanit (Hebrew for Daisy flower) was formed from a *Herut-Beitar* group which consisted of Jewish

---

[62] Samaria Local Construction Committee, "Permit 852/84 [Sal'it]."
[63] Ilan, "Letter to the Jewish Agency regarding payment for house redemption," 1.
[64] Gilboa, Interview in Salit.   [65] Ibid.   [66] Cohen, Interview in Reihan.

immigrants from the Caucasus that came to Israel in the 1970s, giving it the name "*Caucasian Gar'in.*"[67] Shaked (Hebrew for Almonds) started out as a private initiative of upper-/middle-class families with connections to the Herut party that were interested in forming a settlement of their own. With their political connections, they were endorsed by Ariel Sharon's assistant for rural settlement, who personally assigned the site to the group and promoted the necessary development works.[68] Unlike Reihan, both Hinanit and Shaked were originally declared as Community Settlements, forming a clear neo-rural example.[69]

Superficially, the layouts of both settlements continued the communal rural orientation we saw in the cases Sal'it and Reihan, yet a closer look suggests a different picture. While both spatial settings included an array of houses sharing a public space, they present a further step toward an individualized mode of production. In Hinanit, the layout was very similar to that in Reihan;[70] however, the basic lot was much larger, around one dunam,[71] almost double the size of those in neighboring settlements.[72] This was mainly due to the unique profile of Hinanit's settlers that consisted of older, larger, and more conservatives families that were interested in maintaining small-scale agriculture and livestock in their private plots, and later expanding their units in order to meet the demands of their substantially sizable households.[73] Moreover, unlike Reihan, where the settling group made up more than half of the settlement's initial layout, in Hinanit this was much more limited, so that it was the future settlers who developed the majority of the settlement. This was further emphasized in Shaked, where the initial group settled around 10 percent of the planned layout, thus, relying on individuals' power to produce space to complete the settlement's development (Figure 3.6).

---

[67] Caucasian: originating from the Caucasus – not the term used to describe a white person in the USA; JA and WZO, "A Plan for the Development of Jewish Settlements in the Ara Hills – Reihan."
[68] Maariv, "Samaria: Uri Bar on Road," 19.
[69] JA and WZO, "A Plan for the Development of Jewish Settlements in the Ara Hills – Reihan."
[70] Settlement Department, "Hinanit Local Outline Plan."
[71] Ottoman Turkish (دونم; Turkish: dönüm): an ottoman measurement unit that is equivalent to 1,000 m^2.
[72] JA and WZO, "A Plan for the Development of Jewish Settlements in the Ara Hills – Reihan."
[73] Ibid.

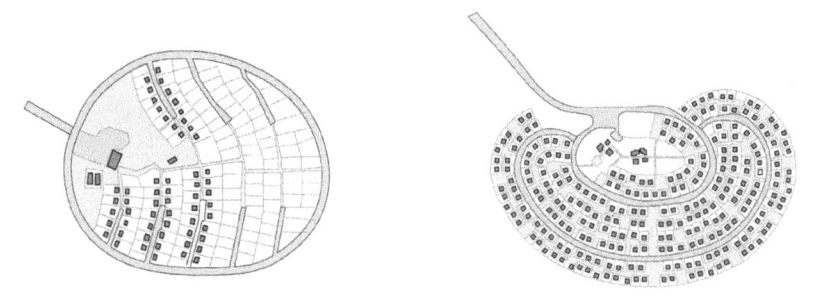

Standardization: Communal Spatial Privileges 81

Figure 3.6 Hinanit (left) and Shaked (right) (illustration by the author)

The spartan and minimalistic houses provided in Shaked and Hinanit also demonstrate the shifting responsibility from the state to the individual. Unlike earlier examples, Hinanit and Shaked did not include a preliminary *Nahal* outpost and the Ministry of Construction and Housing supplied the units before the arrival of the *Gar'in*.[74] Allegedly, these houses corresponded with the pioneer-like character of the early 1980s, as they were simple and minimalistic units. This minimalism continued even further into the units' design, which did not consist of prefabricated walls but rather of two precast cubes assembled on site, reducing construction time and the need for manpower. The simplified character of this model was augmented by the lack of the popular ornamental pitched roof; the houses retained the flat roof of the prefabricated cubes (Figure 3.7). On the one hand, this might indicate that the conditions were harsher than in previous case studies; on the other hand, using these simple cubes meant that the houses in Hinanit and Shaked formed an initial unit that the settling families could alter and adapt more freely. Thus, from the beginning, the Settlement Division promoted self-expression and individual initiative, passing the power to produce space to the settlers, who immediately began modifying their houses, starting with the addition of a tilted roof and continuing with further expansion and alterations.[75]

During the 1980s, it seemed that shifting the production of space from the state to the individual did not assist in developing the Reihan Bloc. As frontier localities, yet not exactly rural, these settlements lacked both the agricultural means of production needed for an

[74] Levav, "First Members of the Caucasian Gari'n Arrive in Reihan B," 4.
[75] Samaria Local Construction Committee, "Permit 1503/85 (Hinanit)."

Figure 3.7 Houses in Hinanit, 1981 (Amos Levav – Ma'ariv newspaper)

independent ex-urban context, and the proximity to central areas necessary for a suburban environment. Although the Settlement Division initially intended to develop local employment opportunities, most settlers worked either in other localities in the West Bank or in nearby Afula, a town that lacked appropriate employment opportunities.[76] Thus, the Reihan Bloc provided the neo-rural experience of living outside the city, yet it did not provide adequate commuting options or sufficient occupational opportunities, resulting in stagnation and lack of development. Moreover, as it was a long way from the heart of the West Bank, the area of Reihan was relatively ignored by the mainstay of the settlement enterprise, the religious Zionist sector. Consequently, even the relatively successful Shaked, with its upper-middle-class profile and individualistic layout was able to attract only around eighty families by 1989, while Hinanit had twenty-one and Reihan around ten.[77]

---

[76] JA and WZO, "Nahal Eron Project," 23–25.
[77] JA and WZO, "A Plan for the Development of Jewish Settlements in the Ara Hills – Reihan," 18–20.

Sal'it witnessed the same challenges as the Reihan Bloc, yet with its less peripheral location it enjoyed a smoother development process. Due to the absence of agricultural uses, Sal'it was basically an empty shell, mimicking former settlement methods while lacking its main component – means of production. At the same time, its location, on the fringes of the coastal area and a couple of kilometres into the West Bank, ensured the necessary distance that would provide the desired disconnection from the city, while staying in proximity to it. Placed on a hilltop, Sal'it enjoyed uninterrupted panoramic views, which strengthened its physical and spiritual affinity to rurality and nature. It continued to attract families interested in a rural-like lifestyle; however, this was done in a significantly slow manner. Each new family would be admitted only following a trial period of one year residing in the former barracks, and after passing the settlements' admission committee that decided whether the family fitted with the community's desired character. The slow admission process was aggravated by the frontier location of Sal'it at that time, which still meant a significantly long car journey from main urban centres and even a duty to guard the settlement during the night. Sal'it, in the 1980s, was therefore still an ex-urban frontier settlement with a small community, limited accessibility, and quite spartan conditions which included interrupted water and electricity supplies.[78] Accordingly, the main changes in the spatial characteristics of Sal'it were primarily the parcellation of the settlement into private households, dispensing with the initial communal layout. However, as we will see, Sal'it continued to transform during the 1980s and 1990s, attracting more commuters while the focus moved further from the community toward the individual.

Shifting the spatial privileges to the individual was a gradual process intended to reignite the stagnating neo-rural phase. Consequently, the settlements started to lose their communal aspects while slowly adopting a more suburban character. This, as we will see in the next section, led to new architectural typologies and (sub)urban models, which were an outcome of the transformations in the mode of production, a shift from standardization to customization, while relying on the power to develop space as the main settlement tool.

---

[78] Aigen, *35 Years for Sal'it*.

Customization: Individual Spatial Privileges

The increasing focus on the individual brought a new mode of production that altered the societal composition of the Community Settlements and their spatial characteristics. Consequently, the *gemeinschaft* orientation and the initial humble designs began to give way to more individualistic settings and custom-made spacious houses. Thus, while the spatial privileges had been granted to the community, they were now granted to the individual. At the same time, as they were selectively privatized, individuals' ability to receive these privileges depended on their affiliation to a specific collective.

In the gradual expansion of Sal'it, newly arriving families began to gradually expand the initial site, fragmentizing the original *compound model*. By the end of the 1980s, the development of regional infrastructure and the rise in demand for the area exposed Sal'it to a larger group of potential members.[79] The admission process was not revoked, yet the settlement was now also open to families interested in improving their living standards while staying within the greater metropolitan area. Accordingly, Sal'it began to shift from a frontier settlement to an exclusive community of commuters,[80] while taking the form of a *star model*, a housing-based layout based on a public centre and a diverging system of cul-de-sac streets surrounded by private parcels (Figure 3.8). This change was strengthened by the emergence of surrounding fences and walls, pavements, and even a swimming pool,[81] thus replacing the former spartan pioneer characteristics with a growing emphasis on private family life and attractive living standards.

With its slow expansion, the spatial privilege of being able to construct a private house in the midst of nature became the main settling tool in Sal'it, leading to more individualistic models than the first units. The new houses were no longer provided by the Ministry of Construction and Housing, nor built as part of a joint process; rather, this was now an individual process carried out by each family at its own pace and according to its needs, demands, and tastes.[82] As homes for members that did not belong to the original group, the newly built houses were more family focused than community oriented. While the earlier arrangement consisted of shared entrance areas, the new houses

---

[79] Benvenisti, *The West Bank Data Project: A Survey of Israel's Policies*, 49–58.
[80] Sal'it Council, *40 Years for Sal'it*.   [81] Ibid.
[82] Shomron Regional Council, "Building Permits Archive."

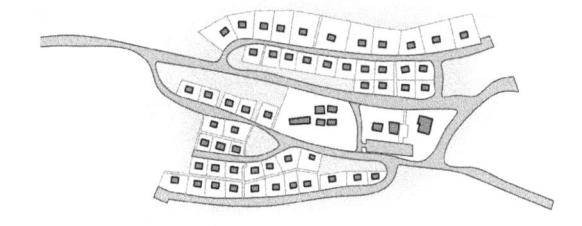

Customization: Individual Spatial Privileges   85

Figure 3.8 Sal'it during the 1980s and early 1990s (illustration by the author)

were fully detached, separated from their surroundings through natural or artificial height difference, and enhanced by a closed-off façade and the placement of the family living room area at the rear. Unlike the early prefabricated state-supplied units, the new houses were much larger and more spacious. However, using simple building materials, such as concrete blocks, white plastered walls and common terrazzo tiles, the new houses were modest cubes with minimal openings covered by a double-slope roof, and, despite their size, they were far from being extravagant.[83] Affordably built and simply designed, they were an enlarged version of the common Israeli countryside house (Figure 3.9).

The improvement of nearby infrastructure during the 1990s enhanced the development of a commuter community. Consequently, the connection to the coastal plain was tightened and more families arrived due to the site's location, landscape, and the ability to build a substantially large detached house rather than the desire to adopt a new lifestyle or reinforce Jewish presence in the area.[84] Sal'it, therefore, turned into an attractive Community Settlement and the *moshav* character remained as a residue from its early years, expressed in the

[83] Samaria Local Construction Committee, "Permit 8/1 (Sal'it)"; Samaria Local Construction Committee, "Permit 8/77 (Sal'it)."
[84] Berger, *Autotopia: Suburban In-between Space in Israel*, 50–54.

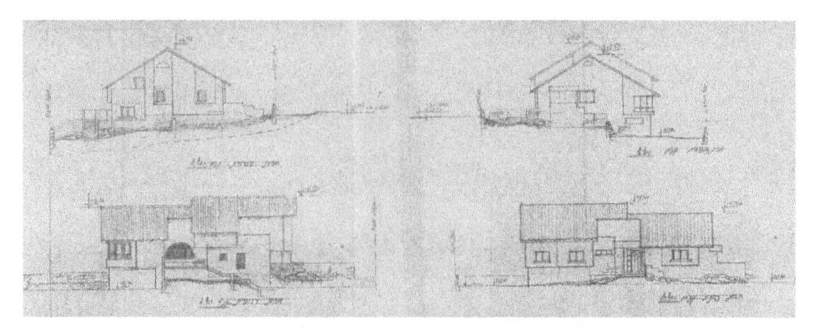

Figure 3.9 House of a new admitted family in Sal'it, 1986 (Braslavi Architects)

official classification of the settlement, its public core, and the Agricultural Council, which includes only the veteran families and has minimal symbolic responsibilities. However, these excesses still grant Sal'it a neo-rural chic that forms a basic element in its appeal.[85] Later, as the final section of this chapter shows, this neo-rural character would form a leading role in corporate-led suburban development, which became the main settlement tool in the early 2000s.

Similar individual-oriented attempts were carried out in the Reihan Bloc during the same period, when the Settlement Division tried to regenerate development by transforming the communal rural villages into individualistic Community Settlements. These efforts were not meant to enlarge the overall area of the settlements, but rather to fill the underpopulated existing fabrics through the construction of new housing units.[86] Subsequently, the Settlement Division commissioned the Samaria Central Development Company and the right-wing-affiliated Amana Ltd to construct dozens of new houses,[87] which, unlike the first spartan prefabricated units, were more spacious and family oriented. The Amana houses were detached from the public sphere by height differences and surrounding fences. This detachment was enhanced through the orientation of the bedrooms toward the neighboring environment, creating a closed main façade, while orienting the

[85] Gilboa, Interview in Salit.
[86] Samaria Local Construction Committee, "Permit 12–38/99–01 (Reihan)," 12.
[87] *Amana* (אמנה): a settlement movement established in 1976 by Gush Emunim. Samaria Central Development Company (פ״החל :השומרון לפיתוח המרכזית החברה; *HaHevra HaMerkazit LePituah HaShomron, Halap*): a private company owned by various communities in the Samaria Regional Council, which does not receive government assistance.

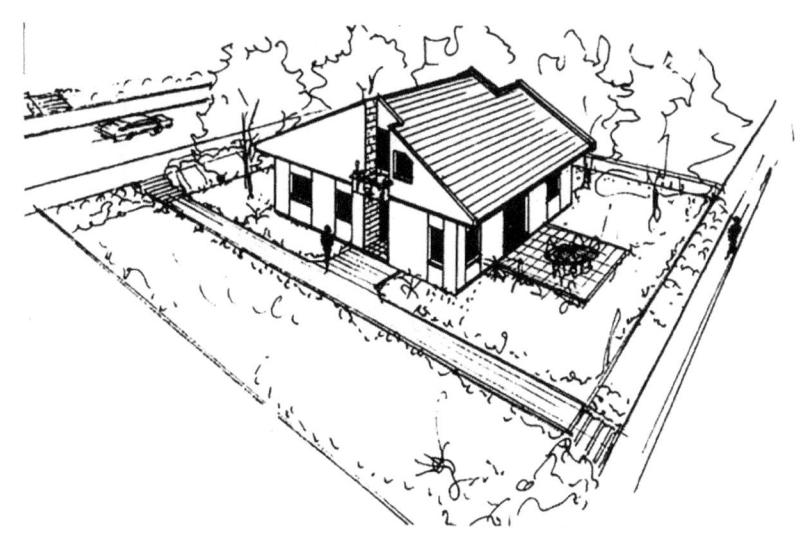

Customization: Individual Spatial Privileges   87

Figure 3.10 The new units in Reihan, Samaria Central Development Company (WZO)

joint living room and kitchen area rearward, emphasizing the role of the private backyard rather than the front lawn, as seen in former examples (Figure 3.10). The emphasis on detachment was manifested also in the self-built units, which slowly began to appear in the Reihan Bloc, as they consisted of the same spatial characteristics as the Amana houses.[88] This individualistic approach was highly visible in the amendment plan promoted by the Settlement Division for Shaked, which further fragmentized its layout by turning open communal areas into roads.

While the focus on the individual transformed Sal'it and the Reihan Bloc, this was an integral part of the development in Nirit, the southernmost site of the case studies presented here, lying adjacent to the Green Line, yet western to it, making it the only example inside official Israeli borders. Furthermore, promoted by the *Moshavim Movement* and the Agricultural Centre,[89] it began as an initiative of the rural

---

[88] Shomron Regional Council, "Building Permits Archive."
[89] *Moshavim Movement* (תנועת המושבים; *Tnuat HaMoshavim*): Established in 1933, it is the largest settlement movement in Israel, representing 254 *moshavim*. It represents the *moshavim* in all matters relating to land ownership, agricultural and rural policy, and economic development in rural areas. *Agricultural Centre* (המרכז החקלאי; *HaMirkaz HaHaklai*): a settlement movement established in the pre-statehood years as a joint framework of the Labor Settlement and the

sector. In *moshavim* constructed on state-owned lands, only a single child in each family has the right to inherit the parents' household and continue cultivating and inhabiting it. As small settlements surrounded by farmlands, *moshavim* usually lack substantial expansion options, causing members of the younger generation to search for alternative housing. Consequently, the 1970s and 1980s witnessed a growing demand for new settlements for future generations of the rural sector. Nirit thus started as an attempt to provide young couples from the *moshavim* of the area with a *moshav*-like community, though with no agricultural functions. It was therefore first defined as a "landless village" and later as a Community Settlement.[90] While the rural affiliation might implicate a more communal approach, it actually granted the families in Nirit the support of well-established settlement movements which the members were able to transform into spatial privileges, eventually promoting their individualistic interests.

Despite being located to the west of the Green Line and on official Israeli territory, the site of Nirit had clear territorial aspirations and it was part of the Settlement Department's efforts to develop a counterpart to the Settlement Division's work inside the West Bank. With the area consisting of some 20,000 Palestinians living on both sides of the Green Line, and fewer than 2,000 Israeli Jews, Nirit was a first step in the attempts to balance these demographic differences.[91] The site was mentioned in the department's plan in 1978, under the name of Mitzpe Zchor, due to the nearby ruins of a former Palestinian village of the same name. Outside the Occupied Territories, the Nirit site became an attractive option for members of the Agriculture Centre and the *Moshavim Movement*, who were relatively less supportive of the West Bank settlement project.[92] At the same time, while it was close to the West Bank, Nirit was a frontier settlement and thus received the

---

agricultural education workers. It is made up of representatives of the Agricultural Labourers' Union (established in 1919), which later formed a central part of the *Histadrut* (established in 1920). With the organizational change in the *Histadrut* in 1994, the Agricultural Centre disengaged from it, though it still represents the interests of farmers and rural settlements vis-à-vis government institutions. In 2001, the Agricultural Centre, together with representatives of other agricultural organizations and settlements, formed a joint body named the Israel Farmers Union.

[90] Davar, "First Experiment in Eastern Sharoin," 7.
[91] ICBS, "Localities in Israel"; PCBS, "Localities in the Palestinian Authority."
[92] Davar, "First Experiment in Eastern Sharoin"; Dor, Development of Nirit.

support of the JA, the Israel Land Administration, and the Ministry of Construction and Housing.

Rurally affiliated, the planning process was handled by the Settlement Department's rural unit and it followed the common trajectory of a *moshav*.[93] This included a first temporary outpost phase that consisted of a small number of families, a *Gar'in*, that would hold and safeguard the site while the preparation works and the search for new members were underway. Fifteen families, organized by the Agricultural Centre, settled the site in 1981. As the site was located on state-owned lands, inside the official Israeli borders, the temporary outpost phase was unnecessary, yet it gave the entire process the required pioneer-like aspect. Correspondingly, plans for the temporary phase were *gemeinschaft*-oriented resembling the typical *compound model*, and consisted of minimalistic dwelling units sharing a communal open space. Meanwhile, the *Moshavim Movement* launched a call for families interested in joining the future settlement. First, the search was in the *moshavim* of the Sharon area, but, due to low responses, it expanded to *moshavim* in other places and eventually even outside the *Moshavim Movement*.[94] In 1985, eighty-five families were admitted to the settling group, from which more than half were from cities and towns and seeking a more rural lifestyle. Still, each joining family had to go through a selection process handled by the Agricultural Centre, to make sure they fitted the rural profile.[95]

In keeping with the changing shift to the individual, the initial compound was merely a preliminary and temporary stepping-stone toward a better-organized development. In Nirit, the first units were shacks made out of tin walls and an asbestos roof supplied by the JA, giving them their common name, *Asbestonim*, as opposed to the concrete *Ashkubit*. These units were clearly designed for the temporary phase and were intended to be replaced during the settlement's transition to its permanent stage. Matching the *compound model*, the planners oriented the entrance of all the units toward the settlement's centre, forming a continuation of it. Nevertheless, the plan for the permanent phase did not use the initial site as the center of the future settlement, thus indicating that this step was merely a residue of former rural examples, which perhaps enabled the

---

[93] Settlement Department, "Mitzpe Yarhiv."
[94] Glick, "Nirit: Labour Pain," 21.   [95] Dor, Development of Nirit.

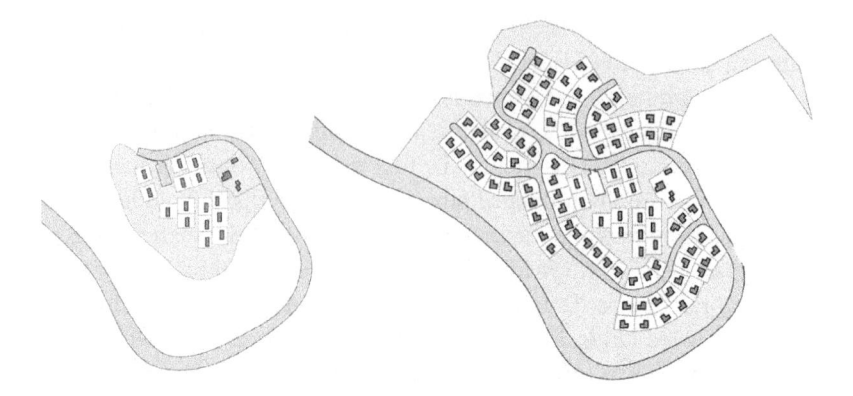

Figure 3.11 Initial and second phases of Nirit (illustration by the author)

Settlement Department to begin the necessary infrastructural works although it did not constitute the core of the future community.

With the decreasing communal focus, Nirit's proposed layout was much more family oriented. Matching the initial rural character, the planners of the rural unit attempted to designate an area for small industrial and agricultural uses; however, they eventually had to revoke this intention and focus on housing, mainly due to lack of lands and the need to preserve forests in the area.[96] Maintaining some spatial concepts of a *moshav*, Nirit had a clear public core, which included the settlement's public functions and an area for civic buildings in front of them. At the same time, the circular *moshav*-like layout began to take the form of a suburban-like *star-shaped model* of winding cul-de-sac streets, spreading out of the public area at the entrance to the settlement (Figure 3.11). This suburban character would continue to grow with the development of the settlement over the years.

Although the increasing focus on the individual decreased the communal aspect, the latter was not entirely forsaken as the community enabled collective bargaining that enhanced the spatial privileges of each of the members. While most members of Nirit lived outside the settlement, it functioned as a community in exile, with an active council that, together with the Agricultural Centre, managed the construction process. Both bodies were also in charge of monitoring and negotiating the payments made by all the families, leading to a subsidized fee for the

---

[96] Israel Planning Administration, "Meeting Regarding Nirit Outline Plan," 1–2.

cost of the parcel paid to the Israel Land Administration, infrastructure development costs made to the Ministry of Construction and Housing, and installments for the construction of each dwelling unit.[97] To foster a sense of community, the Agricultural Centre and Nirit council organized meetings and trips, and even an on-site guarding duty, where one of the couples was responsible for guarding the site every night (even though most couples did not yet reside in the settlement).[98]

Using their collective power, the members endorsed a distinctive construction method, a hybrid of customization and standardization. Despite being interested in implementing a Build Your Own House method, both members and the Agricultural Centre were aware of the economic implications of such a process, which the young couples moving to Nirit would not have been able to sustain. The Agricultural Centre therefore contacted two architects, with experience in designing private family houses in the area,[99] and asked them to propose several housing models, producing a pool of possible variants. Each model had a full and a partial option, according to the families' needs and abilities, as well as the possibility to add a basement, at additional cost. Each family was then able to choose one of the six models, while the parcels were assigned through a raffle.[100]

Although they were a product of a collective effort, and despite the uniform architectural design, the housing models in Nirit were significantly family oriented. With the ability to reach almost 250 m², the houses were spacious and highly individualistic as seen in the separation from the nearby surroundings, enforced artificial height differences, and the orientation of the living room area toward the backyard. The use of a split-level model, which created additional height differences while arranging the different inner functions according to height, continued these separations into the interior architecture while enabling an expansion of another level, whether in the first construction phase or later (Figure 3.12). At the same time, individualism did not mean complete self-expression and, despite their size and spatial features, the design of the houses was homogeneous and quite simplistic, consisting of cubic volumes with small windows, made out of inexpensive construction materials, and thus forming affordable large versions of the ideal rural house. The entire process experienced several setbacks and administrative

[97] Dor, Development of Nirit. [98] Nirit Council, "Guard Duty in Nirit."
[99] Sofer, Nirit: Sofer Architects. [100] Dor, Development of Nirit.

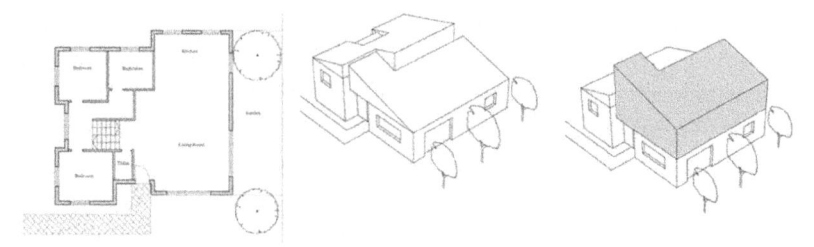

Figure 3.12 An example of a house in Nirit with a possible extension level (illustration by the author)

issues, causing the Agricultural Centre and the Nirit council to devolve their organizational responsibilities to the member families and grant them the power to manage the construction of their own houses, thus dismantling the communal aspects the settlement originally relied on.

With the completion of the first permanent houses, Nirit fulfilled its pioneer-like phase and was on course to a much more individualistic and, later, corporate development. By 1990, the construction of an additional forty-two houses was underway; these were built using the same method as the earlier eighty-five units, utilizing the same models and the same construction concept. However, they were slightly detached from the first complex, built in a separated compound that consisted of two cul-de-sac streets. Moreover, the attractive lease conditions the Israel Land Administration granted the first settling families were no longer available, and this affected the socioeconomic composition of the newly admitted members and attracted more upper-class urban families. In the mid-1990s, the regional council of Drom HaSharon, rather than the Agricultural Centre, initiated another residential neighborhood. Using the services of a private firm, the planned layout was of a single winding access road surrounding the settlement, designed to produce as many private parcels as possible (Figure 3.13). While the first two phases utilized the same housing models, the third phase was built using the Build Your Own House method, contributing to the suburban image of self-expression.[101] At the same time, almost half of the units were built by a single developer that constructed the houses and sold them to the newly admitted members;[102] implying the corporate turn the area was anticipating.

[101] Drom HaSharon Local Council Construction Committee, "Permit 416/87 (Nirit)."
[102] Drom HaSharon Local Council Construction Committee, "Permit 98288 (Nirit)."

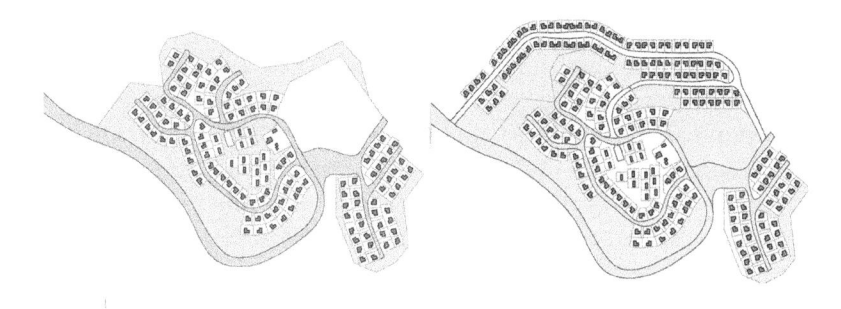

Customization: Individual Spatial Privileges 93

Figure 3.13 Nirit's third (1991) and fourth (1996) stages (illustration by the author)

Despite the individualistic turn, the members of Nirit aspired to maintain their rural affiliation. With its rural-based layout and background, Nirit turned into a Community Settlement with the aura of a pioneer settlement. Considered as a frontier settlement in the 1980s, Nirit, had all the necessary attributes to become an attractive Community Settlement, offering affordable land and spacious houses, just at the fringes of the main metropolitan region. Most importantly, it was in a politically undisputed location, therefore preventing any ideological constraints to its development. Nevertheless, Nirit was not yet fully suburban, as it still suffered from the lack of a good connection to the cities of the coastal plain, disrupted electricity supply, and inadequate development of local facilities.[103] Even as this changed during the 1990s, the rural-like image was still important and, besides the civilian council, the original families are still represented in the pseudo-cooperative Agricultural Council, which retains a symbolic role and is still responsible for managing the water system and the swimming pool.[104] The rural affiliation also had a spiritual function, intended to prevent Nirit from becoming a simple Community Settlement. Still, this rural affiliation, as we will see, was also consumed by corporate development, and used to promote future real-estate projects.

While the individual turn shifted the focus toward the individual family, it was also gradually steered toward the private parcel, as we will see in Ya'arit. Unlike the other case studies discussed in this chapter, Ya'arit was a private-led West Bank Community Settlement

[103] Dor, Development of Nirit.   [104] Ibid.

that, ultimately, was never realized. Nevertheless, as it was initiated by a private entrepreneur and intended to be marketed to private individuals interested in purchasing a home in the West Bank, it incorporated almost all the characteristics of the entwined political and economic agenda of the 1980s. The intent to manage, fund, and execute such a project by private means points to the rising demand for spacious, detached houses in Israel during these years, while highlighting the shift from the seemingly ideological pioneer settlement to a real-estate-oriented one, fueled by the considerations of supply and demand.

The developers of Ya'arit, Judea–Samaria Residential Neighbourhoods Ltd, demonstrated the growing involvement of private capital, which concentrated on purchasing privately owned lands and then using political connections to receive substantial spatial privileges that included the power to plan, develop, and market a future settlement. Using a semiclandestine modus operandi, the company would start by contacting Palestinian touts, or profiteers, that would act as middlemen between the company and the landowners. Then, they would start to involve the relevant bodies like the Ministry of Agriculture, the Ministry of Housing and Construction, and the regional planning committees, in order to start planning and executing the settlement's construction. Deputy Minister of Agriculture Michael Dekel called Judea–Samaria Residential Neighbourhoods Ltd "ground-breaking in regard to private initiative,"[105] mixing ideological objectives with economic speculations.

The new operative approach was to opt for a client oriented and economically efficient process.[106] Using an assembly line method, the process would be accompanied by a *setup team*, in charge of the bureaucratic aspect of contacts and discussions with the relevant authorities and agencies, as well as an *execution team*, responsible for the construction of the settlement's infrastructure, enabling the eventual development of each private parcel.[107] Infrastructure works were to be funded directly by the families purchasing lots in the settlement, and this, according to the company, would lead to significantly decreased development costs, in comparison to those charged by the

[105] Maariv, "Ideology and Money," 45.
[106] Judea–Samaria Residential Neighbourhoods, "Residential Neighbourhoods in Judea and Samaria."
[107] Ibid.

Ministry of Construction and Housing.[108] The individual houses, customized according to each family's wishes, were intended to be built according to a *cost-plus* method, in which the company offered the services of a project manager who divided the entire procedure into smaller, manageable tasks that were passed to smaller contractors. According to the company, this would allow better control of the project and significantly reduce construction costs, thus "[e]nabling a larger number of families to move to Judea and Samaria."[109] By applying this work method, the company thought it could persuade the various governmental agencies with an interest in cutting public spending, as well as individuals seeking the luxuries of a private house at an affordable price.

The focus on the individual was highly apparent in the marketing used by the entrepreneurs, which targeted families as part of a clientele, rather than ideologically affiliated groups. The main target group was upper-middle-class professionals, usually owning an apartment in the coastal area, and looking for an affordable, private, detached house in a smaller community. According to the company's analysis, people in this group were not willing to change their place of work and aspired to live no further than a 20 km journey from their workplace.[110] Young couples were the next group targeted, who, with sufficient government aid, would be able to purchase a house in the West Bank, rather than an apartment in the city. The third target group was Jews living abroad who would like a second house in Israel, yet who might hesitate to settle in the depths of the West Bank and might therefore be interested in a settlement of a lighter mode, on its fringes. The company acknowledged that these three groups were not usually the target of the existing public policy of encouraging West Bank settlement; attracting them to the Green Line area would thus incorporate them into the national geopolitical project.[111]

In Ya'arit, rising living standards was a central and crucial aspect. In a brochure handed out to potential clients, the discourse repeatedly revolved around the political aspect of living in the West Bank, but

---

[108] Kotler, "The Construction Frenzy in Judea and Samaria – at Skyrocketing Prices," 17.
[109] Judea–Samaria Residential Neighbourhoods, "Residential Neighbourhoods in Judea and Samaria," 5.
[110] Ibid., 2. [111] Ibid.

also – and more emphatically – around the new "quality of life" families in the West Bank could achieve for a relatively low price:

> The massive settling of Judea and Samaria is a national objective of the first order .... The "Judea–Samaria Residential Neighbourhoods" Company is a private corporation which has taken [upon itself] to establish, by independent means, residential neighbourhoods in Judea and Samaria .... The ways and means employed by the company in establishing the settlements are such as to enable a broad cross-section of the population to build their homes in Judea and Samaria, at a cost not exceeding that of an average flat in central Israel.[112]

The brochure, written in both Hebrew and English, highlighted the value of community life in West Bank settlements. Based on the Community Settlement method, the newly developed sites would consist of a small number of families, ensuring the intimate and amiable neighborhoods most potential buyers were seeking. At the same time, the brochure warned of planning settlements that are too small, which would later have problems in attracting private investors willing to invest in local commercial centers and shops.[113]

Ya'arit followed the exact lines of the work method of the Judea–Samaria Residential Neighbourhoods company. The site was allegedly purchased from Arab landowners living in Taybeh and, with their connections, the private entrepreneurs were able to receive the initial approval of the Ministry of Agriculture, and other relevant authorities like the Israel Defense Forces, to start planning and marketing the settlement, selling almost half of the planned parcels between 1981 and 1982.[114] Subsequently, in June 1984, the Ministerial Settlement Committee authorized the establishment of Ya'arit, and gave its approval to the ongoing construction works.

The layout of Ya'arit corresponded with the private initiative behind it and the ever-growing focus on the individual. It was planned by a private architect from Tel Aviv, rather than by the Settlement Division's internal team, which usually carried out the planning in the case of settlements in the early 1980s. Consisting of a public core containing a school, a civic and commercial centre, a synagogue, and a series of winding cul-de-sac streets, the layout resembled other

---

[112] Ibid., 3. [113] Ibid.
[114] Jerusalem District Court, Arnon et al. against the District Judea–Samaria Residential Neighbourhoods Ltd.

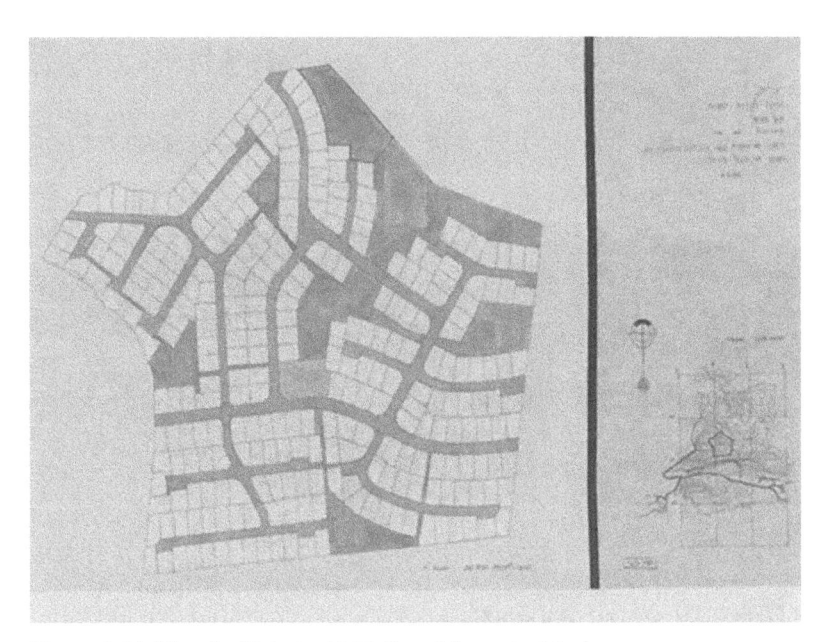

Customization: Individual Spatial Privileges 97

Figure 3.14 Plan for Ya'arit, 1983 (Israel State Archive)

Community Settlements. Nevertheless, while efficiently and resourcefully using the site, the proposed layout was an effective way to parcel the area of the settlement and generate the maximum amount of independent, marketable private plots (Figure 3.14). There was thus a shift from the common *star model* into a suburban tract development system, which simultaneously fragments and homogenizes space as a means to turn it into a commodity while transferring attention from the private house to the private parcel where the house is built. Accordingly, the cul-de-sac streets followed the site's topographical lines, allowing immediate, vehicle access to each of the private lots as well as the independent development of each parcel. The private houses were planned along the ridgeline, while the open green spaces were placed in the less assessable sloping areas. The split-level houses ensured integration with the site's topography, while increasing the orientation toward the panoramic view.

The houses in Ya'arit, like the ones promoted by the company, focused on high and luxurious living standards, with an emphasis on individuality and singularity of design (Figure 3.15). Spacious and planned with an emphasis on design and detail, the houses promoted

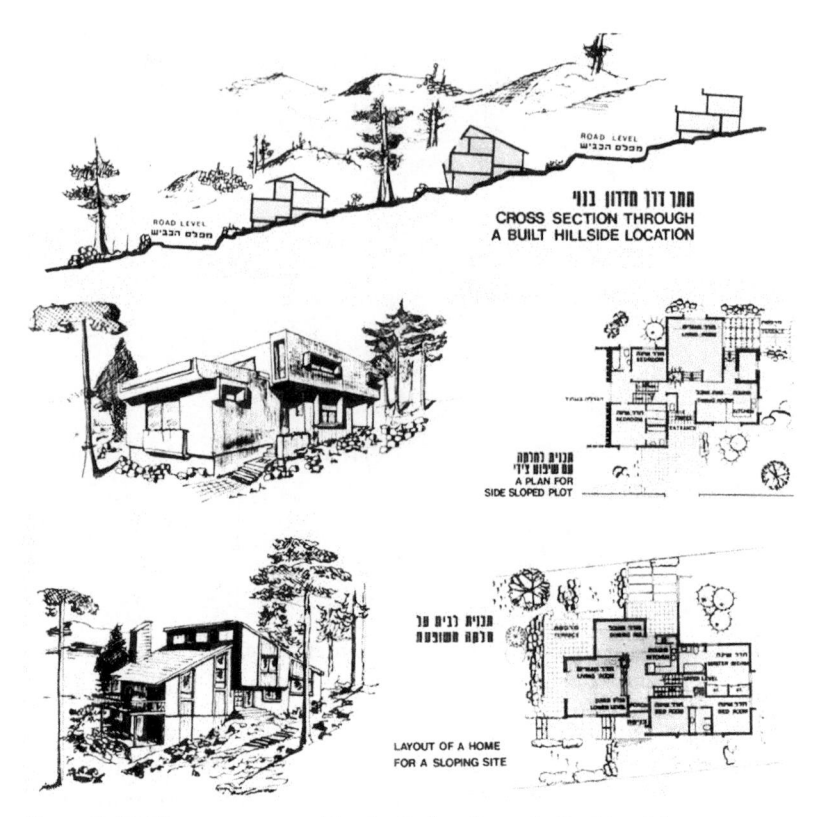

Figure 3.15 Houses promoted by the Judea–Samaria Residential Neighbourhoods company, 1981 (Israel State Archive)

in the marketing brochure were depicted as villas in the midst of nature, merging with the local topography and landscape and far from the simplistic, ideal, former rural houses.[115] So, urban middle-class families interested in upgrading their living conditions were targeted, rather than those in search of a pioneer experience; this corresponded with the new settlement approach in the 100,000 Plan earlier in 1981.[116]

The favorable status of the private developers enabled them to receive the necessary political and bureaucratic support to launch the process, yet not to complete it. Initially, the Ministerial Settlement Committee approved the construction of Ya'arit on condition that the Judea–Samaria Residential Neighbourhoods company owned the

[115] Ibid.   [116] Settlement Division, "The 100.000 Plan," 14.

entire site of the future settlement. The company, however, was able to prove only shared and partial ownership, which was not sufficient to get the necessary approval to continue the project. Deputy state attorney Plia Albeck,[117] famous for her prosettlement line, affirmed that as long as full ownership had not been proven, it would be illegal to start construction, and that the state would not be able to defend this action in a court of law.[118] By that time, the plan for Ya'arit had been approved by the regional committee, and the project received the approval of the Israel Land Administration. Moreover, the Judea–Samaria Residential Neighbourhoods company had already managed to sell almost 250 lots and had begun the first stages of infrastructure planning and execution.[119] However, by 1986, as the company and the other owners of the land parcels were unable to agree on the terms of a deal,[120] the Ya'arit project was canceled and the decision of the Ministerial Settlement Committee was revoked.

Ya'arit represented a new mode of production that relied on the ability of private entrepreneurs to develop new settlements as its main tool. Ya'arit was the outcome of a pairing between politics and real-estate investment, and thus had both characteristics. Its geographical location in the West Bank was highly ideologically motivated, yet its relative proximity to the coastal area made it an ideal commuter settlement. Thus, unlike other Community Settlements which began as a counterurban phenomenon, Ya'arit was already suburban from its inception. The enacted tract housing development model followed the economic and individual interests that lay behind it, as it divided the site into a reasonable number of private parcels available for sale while promoting a more individualistic setting. The layout of Ya'arit was therefore less intended to create a community and focused more on turning the site into a commodity. Furthermore, Ya'arit was based on a highly dichotomic everyday life – work in the city, and family time at home. Community here, unlike in earlier examples, was merely the combination of private households in one settlement, and a promotion

[117] Albeck, Plia (פליאה אלבק; 1937–2005): a former Israeli jurist who dealt with the legal status of the settlements and the area on which they were established. She was in charge of a huge land survey of the West Bank that declared unclaimed and unregistered lands as "state-owned," thus legitimizing their use for settlement purposes.
[118] Albeck, "The Site of Ya'arit," 1.
[119] Judea–Samaria Residential Neighbourhoods Company, "Ya'arit."
[120] Albeck, "The Site of Ya'arit," 1.

technique designed to attract buyers. This focus on the individual, as the next part shows, continued to evolve with the corporate turn, which shifted the mode of production from customization to a property-oriented mass commodification.

Mass Commodification: Corporate Spatial Privileges

During the early 2000s, the private initiative took the lead, moving to a new mode of production where it was mainly the corporate sector that enjoyed the spatial privilege of developing space. Private initiative, as we have seen, began to modify the settlement mechanism during the 1980s. However, the economic conditions and the state of the market did not yet enable a real-estate-oriented development. Therefore, even corporate-led development, like that in Ya'arit, was based on the individual ability to construct one's own private house. The long commute from the main metropolises and the proximity to Palestinian localities prevented the area from becoming a site worthy of corporate development. This was eventually resolved with the construction of the West Bank Barrier, a land obstacle that was intended to block Palestinians' access to Israel. The barrier, constructed in segments from 2002, did not follow the Green Line and in many areas ran eastern to it, de facto annexing parts of the West Bank to Israel. Consequently, the settlements studied here were cut off from their neighboring Arab environment and incorporated into the Jewish-Israeli geographical sequence.[121] This, together with wide national investment in infrastructure, laid the foundations for the mass development of the area; yet, it was the post-2008 housing crisis that created the demand. Suddenly, former remote and undesired places like the Reihan Bloc became reasonably priced potential investments; this eventually enabled the expansion of the stagnating periphery.[122]

Ex-urban, communal and selective until the early 2000s, Sal'it remained within its original boundaries, despite its steady growth. While the settlement continuously attracted a stream of young families that were interested in moving to a rural-like environment during the 1980s and 1990s, this was still quite limited. The lack of available

---

[121] Cohen, "Israel's West Bank Barrier: An Impediment to Peace?"
[122] Charney, "A 'Supertanker' against Bureaucracy in the Wake of a Housing Crisis: Neoliberalizing Planning in Netanyahu's Israel."

vacant and unbuilt lots, the selection procedure that lasted for more than a year, and the fact that the settlement was still quite remote and too close to the West Bank all served to restrict the number of families that were willing and able to move to Sal'it.[123]

With massive national investment in the area during the 1990s, the Ministry of Construction and Housing and the Settlement Division began promoting a new and more suburban vision for Sal'it. By the turn of the millennium, the Settlement Division issued an extension neighborhood for Sal'it, doubling its existing size. The first part was merely a westward extrusion of the existing layout and an additional part that included five more cul-de-sac streets located on the southern side of the settlement (Figure 3.16). Although authorized in 1999, construction was very limited in the early years, and consisted merely of sporadic built houses.[124] With the decline in violent incidents during the Second Intifada and increasing investment and property values, this part of the extension witnessed a construction boom in the post-crisis era. The Build Your Own House units, which initially were enlarged variations of the previous rural mode, gave way to more prestigious and luxurious houses. Consisting of white cubic volumes and built from

Figure 3.16 Sa'it after 2008 (illustration by the author)

---

[123] Sal'it Council, *40 Years for Sal'it*.
[124] Moshe Ravid Architects and Planners, "Sal'it: Urban Outline Plan 112/1/2."

expensive, high-end construction materials with details like metal beams, large windows, marble, wooden panels, and architectural concrete, they were seemingly minimalistic, yet practically exclusive. Lacking the common pitched red roof, which had previously decorated all rural settlements, and designed in simple lines, the new houses in Sal'it were neomodern, suiting the revival of the international style in Israel during the early 2000s,[125] that characterizes the secular upper-middle-class.[126]

While the Build Your Own House construction stimulated self-expression, the suburban turn and the growing reliance on private corporations promoted a more corporate-led development. Consequently, the second wave of construction in the southern section at Sal'it was carried out by a single private entrepreneur. Correspondingly, the new houses followed the lines of retail construction, consisting of repetitive models reproduced in the different parcels. Design-wise, they resembled the architectural features of the neighboring Build Your Own House units and were mainly white cubes with a closed façade toward the street and wide windows toward the backyard and open view.[127] The pinnacle of the corporate turn was the third expansion neighborhood, which was no longer an extension of the existing fabric of Sal'it, but rather a new compound outside of it. It was a pure tract housing development focused on generating an optimal number of private parcels. Although it was authorized in 2003, construction began only in 2017, due to the Second Intifada and the lack of real-estate potential. With the rise in property values, the Israel Land Administration granted a single entrepreneur the spatial privilege to exclusively develop the entire neighborhood. Consequently, this compound too consisted of repetitive cubic models that characterized all the new houses.

These suburbanization patterns were not exclusive to Sal'it, and the Reihan Bloc followed similar lines. By the late 1990s the Settlement Division promoted new expansion neighborhoods for all three settlements, prepared by private offices that replaced the division's internal team, as adequate to the privatization of planning. With the growing emphasis on the private family lot, all the new plans were based on a nonhierarchical system of streets and cul-de-sac lanes that parceled

---

[125] Nitzan-Shiftan, "Whitened Houses."
[126] Rotbard, *White City, Black City: Architecture and War in Tel Aviv and Jaffa*, 8–9.
[127] Samaria Local Construction Committee, "Permit 8–7/1/1 (Sal'it)"; Samaria Local Construction Committee, "Permit 8/84 (Sal'it)."

the site, creating independent marketable tracts.[128] Initially, the intentions were for a Build Your Own House mode of development, reproducing models of the Samaria Development Company.[129] The plans received official approval around the year 2000, yet they were barely developed until 2010, mainly due to the Second Intifada and lack of profitability.[130]

The increasing interest in rapidly developing the area shifted the power to construct the dwelling units from the individual to the private developer. Consequently, though initially the aim was to create Build Your Own House neighborhoods, this eventually gave way to a limited number of private construction companies. These entrepreneurs would lease the lots from the state and the Israel Land Administration in order to construct the houses in a concentrated effort, and then market them to families interested in moving to the settlements. This ensured the development of the new neighborhoods in a unified manner that would spread over a contracted and controlled period of time. Most importantly, it would reduce construction costs, enabling cheaper development and increased profitability, while absorbing the risk taken by individual families. Using this method, the likelihood of not developing the neighborhoods decreased significantly. The Build Your Own House model was not entirely forsaken but became a privilege for future generations.[131]

Built by a limited number of entrepreneurs, the houses in all the settlements discussed here followed similar lines. Made as two main cubic volumes – one consisting of the entrance and living room area and the second consisting of the bedrooms, these new houses were highly introverted dwelling units, designed to separate the family area from the surrounding environment. Enclosed by fences, vegetation, and a parking area, while using height differences, each house formed an isolated entity, focused on the private sphere of the nuclear family. Unlike earlier examples, which almost always included a tilted red-tiled roof, the new houses had a flat roof, strengthening and augmenting their cubic character.

While the expansion neighborhoods promoted the development of the Community Settlements, in some cases they hindered the former neo-rural affiliation. Besides the already mentioned expansions in Nirit, works on a new neighborhood began in 2004. Problems began

---

[128] Gonen Architects and Planners, "Shaked: Urban Outline Plan 102/3."
[129] Samaria Local Construction Committee, "Permit 15–231/99 (Shaked)."
[130] Samaria Local Construction Committee, "Permit 1008 (Shaked)."
[131] Cohen, Interview in Reihan.

because the site of the new project was east of the Green Line and outside official Israeli territory. Formally, the new neighborhood was not part of Nirit, but rather an extension to the settlement of Alfei Menashe, more than three kilometres away and separated from it by an Arab village and the West Bank Barrier. Promoting an *extension* of an existing settlement, rather than declaring a new one, enables the Israeli regime to continue settling the Occupied Territories while avoiding international pressure, in the pretense of natural growth. This was exactly the case in respect of the new neighborhood attached to Nirit. Afraid of being affiliated with a real-estate project in the West Bank, the residents of Nirit objected to the new neighborhood and their appeals reached the Israeli High Court of Justice. However, the court rejected their claims and authorized the construction of the new neighborhood of Nof HaSharon in 2005.[132]

As a private-led real-estate project, the layout of the new neighborhood was a tract housing arrangement that parcelled the site into a series of private lots. Consisting of a single access street, the new neighborhood was connected to Nirit and relied on it for basic municipal services. Therefore, although de jure Nof HaSharon was part of Alfei Menashe, in practice it was a part of Nirit. Moreover, while the residents of Nirit feared that the affiliation with a private real-estate project in the Occupied Territories would hinder the profile of their seemingly nonideological settlement, the developer of Nof HaSharon used the proximity to Nirit and its rural background to appeal to potential buyers, turning neo-rurality into an integral part of the promotion campaign.[133]

The extension neighborhoods followed a similar marketing method that matched their corporate mode of production. In the promotion of almost all new projects in Reihan, Hinanit, Shaked, and Sali't the focus was on four main aspects: a high "quality of life" depending on a relatively large detached private house surrounded by nature; a vibrant and intimate community; proximity to the main highways and cities in the coastal area; and a relatively affordable price. For example, in the promotion of the new

---

[132] Tzabari, "Nirit: From a Community Settlement in the Sharon Region to a Semi-Settlement"; Rotem, "Nirit Regrets: They Do Not Want a Neighborhood of Alfei Menashe."
[133] Glick, "Nadlan – Nof HaSharon."

Mass Commodification: Corporate Spatial Privileges 105

neighborhood in Shaked, the developing company, Ariel Yazamut. Proclaims:

[Shaked is a] Community Settlement in which about 250 high-quality families live in a rich communal life. Shaked is located about ... ten minutes from Route 6 and 7 minutes from Katzir-Harish. The attractive location gives quick access to the cities of central Israel, the Sharon and Haifa. The settlement overlooks the magnificent view of the Jezreel Valley to the north and the Mediterranean Sea to the west. In Shaked you will find a varied educational system for all ages, as well as activities after the school day that include classes, events and various activities. The community offers a wide range of services, such as a large grocery store, swimming pool, synagogues, club, library, animal corner and more.[134]

The new neighborhoods in the adjacent Hinanit, called "Villa in Nature," were also advertised using the same method, with the promotion brochure declaring that:

Hinanit is a rural secular community, located on one of the most spectacular mountains in the area above the settlement of Katzir, characterized by a unique tranquillity .... The settlement is located at a height of ca. 400 m above sea level. On the slope, its northern branches connect to Nahal Zabadun .... The Villa in Nature project combines modern concepts of advanced architectural design, a practical home plan that creates a comfortable living experience and large and pleasant living spaces ... a 5-Room Villa .... The size of the villa is about 120 square meters and the total land area is 500 square meters. The variety of financing tracks available to you will enable you to personally tailor your mortgage. You can purchase a house in the Villa in Nature project in an easy and convenient way for you. ... We will be happy to offer you the best and most convenient way to purchase your villa and fulfill your dreams. Hinanit is a Community Settlement with more than 100 high quality families and impressive construction momentum. In addition to a rich and diverse community life, there are community services that make the quality of life in the community especially high.[135]

Also interesting is the extension of Reihan, where the developer is a subsidiary company of Amana – Batei Amana – which, due to its political affiliation to the former *Gush Emunim* movement, is apparently a more ideological and less profit-driven company. Yet, it uses

---

[134] Ariel Yazamut, "Project Information."
[135] Laniv Engineering, "Villa in Nature," 2.

similar marketing techniques, and the discourse emphasizes the same points as the other examples, stating:

Reihan is only 7 minutes from Highway 6 and 25 minutes from Hadera and Afula and overlooks a spectacular view of the Samaria hills on the one hand and the reserve of the Reihan forest on the other. You are welcome to come and join us.[136]

In Sal'it, the developer of the new expansion neighborhood, Ampa Israel, emphasizes similar idealistic aspects, declaring:

In the heart of the country, next to Highway 6, lies the expansion of the Sal'it settlement, which overlooks an open panoramic view in all directions. The expansion of the settlement, which includes 40 charming homes in Stage A, which is fully occupied, and another 80 houses in Stage B, which is currently being populated, consists of quality families who have chosen to join the quality community.[137]

The shift that began by turning from a community-minded mode of production to an individual-focused one, continued toward property-oriented projects with the area's corporate turn. Accordingly, almost all extension neighborhoods followed the same outline and development method. They all formed a new detached compound that adjacent to the existing settlement and not an enlargement of the initial fabric. Unlike the former layout of the settlements that had a clear hierarchy based on the various public and private functions and relations between the community and the different households, the extension neighborhoods emphasized the private parcel. As private developers received the power to form space, they applied a uniform housing typology used in almost all settlements, appealing to a large number of families, or possible customers, while promoting an image of better "quality of life." Consequently, all Community Settlements had a relatively homogeneous and unified character, while the transition from a counterurban project to a territorial suburban real-estate enterprise was complete.

From a Neo-Rural Lifestyle to a Mass-Produced Suburbia

The settlements described in this chapter illustrate the transitions in the enacted mode of production, shifting from rural to neo-rural and

[136] Reihan Council, "Reihan." [137] Ampa Israel, "Ampa Israel Website."

then to suburban, as well as from state-led to private-led development. They started as an outcome of selective standardization, then moved to customization, and ended as a product of mass commodification. Initiated by the state and one of its affiliated organizations such as the JA or the World Zionist Organization while generating nonagricultural secluded, gated communities, the first stages of the case studies discussed here demonstrate the early privatization of the settlement mechanism. At the same time, while not yet completely privatized, the first steps were still carried out by the state, as it planned, funded, and developed the sites and even supplied the first dwelling units, as seen in Sal'it and the Reihan Bloc. Accordingly, the spartan housing units, ill-developed infrastructure, limited access, and lack of security highlighted the pioneer-like aspects of the settlements as moving to them was quite a challenging experience and thus inherently counterurban.

Returning to the equation of the state's *power over* space in return for the individual *power to* colonize it, which the privatized modes of production rely on, we see that in the early Community Settlements the individual spatial privileges derived from affiliation to the settling group. Therefore, the settlement tool enacted by the state was promoting the development of secluded and isolated communities. In later phases, with the suburbanization of the ex-urban neo-rural settlements, individuals' power to design and build their own private houses on lands provided by the state became the main settling tool. These increased spatial privileges shifted the focus from the community to the individual, encouraging additional families to join. Successively, the sharp rise in property values around the years 2008–10 enlarged the profitability of real estate in the former frontier settlements, and larger agents entered the scene. The state thus granted private developers the power to plan, develop, and market space, completing the shift from the individual to the corporate.

With increasing privatization, the spatial privileges behind the privatized mode of production consisted of the power to produce space as the main settlement tool, rather than the power to consume it, altering the layout of the Community Settlements. The first state-led and funded plans were meant to create a community-based settlement and were shaped according to the compound model that consisted of small and simple private households sharing a common open space, as in former examples of rural settlement. With the growing privatization and suburbanization, and as the state passed the settlement mechanism to the individual, the compound model gave way to the star model, which had a hierarchal setting with a center and branching cul-de-sac streets, thus leading to a more family-centered and private-house-focused community. Later, as private developers began to take the lead, Community Settlements started to utilize nonhierarchical and efficiently marketed parcelled layouts.

The transition from standardization to customization and then mass commodification was reflected not only in the layout of the settlements but also in their common houses. Accordingly, the early minimalistic state-provided units gave way to larger and grander houses, built according to the designs and wishes of the families moving into them; these were eventually followed by homogeneous models, mass-produced by corporate-led development (Figure 3.17).

The interior layout of the houses also reflected the changes in the development mechanism. In the earlier houses, the more public areas, consisting of the kitchen and living room, were oriented toward the open public space outside, functioning as a continuation of it. Later, the living room area was oriented toward the open view or toward the backyard, enhancing the feeling of a better standard of living and importance of the inner family circle. In the corporate-led development, the public sphere is even further renounced, set apart by a private parking spot and a small access area, emphasizing private car use while limiting pedestrian accessibility and any possible visual connections.

Initially emerging as an alternative to the city, the suburbanization of the Community Settlements turned them into a mere extension of it. Everyday life in all the case studies examined in this chapter consists of the same daily commute to work, school, and leisure activities. The pursuit of a better "quality of life" was the main driving force behind

Figure 3.17 Standardization (left), customization (middle), mass commodification (right) (illustration by the author)

the development of all the settlements discussed, and while the interpretation of "quality of life" changed over the years, it continued to mean the desire for a private house, small or large, in a rural-like location close to nature. This was emphasized in the names chosen for the settlements, as they all had a strong affiliation to the local flora and fauna, as in Shaked (almond), Reihan (basil), Hinanit (daisy flower), Ya'arit (forest), Sali't (rocky), and Nirit (false fennel). The logos of the settlements express this as well, as most consist of a house with a sloping roof and a tree.

The emphasis on personal living standards, instead of national ideology or self-fulfillment, was compatible with local cultural and societal changes. The transition from communal life to more introverted and individualistic housing paralleled key changes in the local political system and economy, as Israel began to shift from the old quasi-socialist *Mapai* regime to a more laissez-faire logic during the 1980s. The early pioneer Labor Zionism of the kibbutz and the *moshav* that focused on redeeming the land of Israel by cultivating it, thus gave way to a new Real Estate Zionism, which intended to redeem the land of Israel by commodifying it. The focus therefore shifted from society to the community, and then from the community to "individual men and women" and their properties.

The neo-ruralization of the Green Line was the first step in its privatized domestication, which later enabled its suburbanization and eventually its financialization. The next chapter focuses on the Suburban Settlements of the 1980s and illustrates the gentrification of the Green Line, which promoted the area's suburban turn and accelerated its inclusion into the Tel Aviv metropolis and the national consensus.

4 | *Gentrification and the Suburban Settlement*

The New Israeli Bourgeoisie and the Green Line

Bourgeoisification for the Sake of Domestication

The Suburban Settlements of the 1980s formed a new step in the privatizing domestication mechanism of the Green Line.[1] They were an integral part of the economic and cultural changes that Israel underwent during those years, which included the formation of a local upper-middle class and significant modifications in its popular culture. Therefore, unlike earlier examples of city dwellers moving to the periphery in order to adopt a neo-rural and counterurban lifestyle, the exodus of the 1980s was mostly suburban. Fueled by the desire for better living standards, manifested in a spacious private house in a small community away from the city yet a short commute from it, these new settlements were mainly an extension of the main metropolises rather than an alternative to them. Consequently, in contrast to former national decentralization efforts, which insisted on an equal dispersal of the population along the country's entire area, the focus in the 1980s shifted toward local decentralization, dispersing the population more equally inside the existing metropolises,[2] subsequently transforming the frontier area of the Green Line into suburbia. As a first step in the suburban turn, the Israeli planning administrations endeavored to attract the newly forming bourgeois upper-middle class to the area by using new modes of spatial production that were based on unprecedented spatial privileges that consisted of the power to plan, develop, and inhabit the frontier. Eventually, this enabled the area's domestication and further suburbanization, enhancing the state's power over it.

---

[1] Schwake, "The Bourgeoisification of the Green-Line: The New Israeli Middle-Class and the Suburban Settlement."
[2] Shachar, "Reshaping the Map of Israel: A New National Planning Doctrine."

This chapter argues that the Suburban Settlements were an outcome of a new phase in the national geopolitical project, which derived from the spatial privileges granted to the bourgeois middle class as a means to incorporate it in the evolving efforts to domesticate the Green Line. It focuses on the settlements of Kochav Yair, Alfei Menashe, Oranit, and Reut – the first Suburban Settlements in the area that demonstrate the new phase of privatization and the different modes of production it utilized. In studying their development, the chapter first explains the emergence of the local hegemonic middle class and how it was incorporated into the national geopolitical agenda. Analyzing the different modes of production involved in these case studies, the chapter illustrates how the new bourgeois middle class was able to influence the production of the local built environment, and how the power to produce space turned into the leading settlement tool. Accordingly, it analyzes how the bourgeois desire for social and cultural distinction was manifested in the settlements' (sub)urban and architectural form. Focusing on case studies on both sides of the Green Line, the chapter explains how this new phenomenon derived from the ability of the secular, politically central-left, upper-middle class to both produce and consume space. It demonstrates how the Suburban Settlements of the early 1980s were a state-directed gentrification effort, intended to domesticate the Green Line by turning it into the dormitory of the new Israeli bourgeoisie, thus using bourgeoisification for the sake of domestication.

The Bourgeoisification of the Israeli Middle Class

The Suburban Settlement phenomenon was an integral part of the *bourgeoisification* of Israel, a societal transformation that included a transition toward a more individualistic and consumerist culture.[3] These changes were not only manifested in the accumulation of wealth, but also in alterations in the patterns of consumption and living standards, as part of a long societal process that began during the 1960s.[4] Before the establishment of the state, and in the first proceeding decades after its establishment, the local hegemony was made up of the veteran

---

[3] Gutwein, "The Class Logic of the 'long revolution', 1973–1977"; Segev, *Elvis in Jerusalem: Post-Zionism and the Americanization of Israel*; Ram, *The Globalization of Israel*.
[4] Ram, *The Globalization of Israel*; Filc, *Hegemony and Populism in Israel*.

Jewish-socialist Ashkenazi sector,[5] which was linked to the ruling *Mapai* party and consisted of the proletarian agricultural–industrial classes.[6] The local nonsocialist white-collar class included professional academics, traditional middle-class merchants, landowners, and craftsmen who did not share the same concerns about a centralized state-led economy.[7] The socialist establishment regarded the emergence of a strong bourgeois class as threat that, according to Bareli and Cohen, caused it to minimize its members' involvement in decision-making and sociopolitical leadership,[8] thus actively diminishing its prestige.

With the economic growth of the 1960s, the middle class was expanded by an evolving group of public officials and executives, technocrats, military officers, and members of the private sector. Correspondingly, Ben Porat claims that it was during these years that the Israeli bourgeoisie became a leading social group.[9] According to Gutwein, the influence of this emerging class continued the *Mapai*-led apparatus and some of its pioneering cultural values, while it adopted bourgeois-like socioeconomic patterns, in what he refers to as "pioneer bourgeoisie."[10] The new bourgeois hegemony consisted of the emerging white-collar classes that, Gutwein notes, later aligned with the economic liberal, right-wing Herut party that represented the anti-socialist Zionist sector and large segments of underprivileged Mizrahi Jews; this enabled the 1977 political changeover that brought an end to the decades-long *Mapai* rule.[11]

The bourgeoisification of Israel corresponded with the national suburban turn. Gonen and Cohen highlight the growing focus on private family life during the 1970s, as an essential element in the new isolated private houses on the outskirts of cities.[12] Although such neighborhoods existed in the early statehood years, their scope was still limited, and the majority of white-collar, middle-class families inhabited urban

---

[5] Jews originating from European countries.
[6] Kimmerling, *The End of Ashkenazi Hegemony*.
[7] Rozin, *A Home for All Jews: Citizenship, Rights, and National Identity in the New Israeli*.
[8] Bareli and Cohen, *The Academic Middle-Class Rebellion: Socio-Political Conflict over Wage-Gaps in Israel*; Heilbronner, "The Israeli Victorians."
[9] Ben-Porat, *Where Are Those Bourgeois?*
[10] Gutwein, "Pioneer Bourgeoisie," 685.
[11] Gutwein, "The Class Logic of the 'Long Revolution', 1973–1977."
[12] Gonen and Cohen, "Multi-Faceted Screw-Up of Neighborhoods in Jerusalem."

quarters such as Rechavia in Jerusalem, Hadar in Haifa, or the Old North and Ramat Aviv in Tel Aviv. With the suburban turn of the 1970s and 1980s, the production of housing became entirely low-rise oriented, composing up to 80 percent of the yearly built dwelling units.[13] This suburban turn served the existing secular Ashkenazi middle and upper-middle class, as well as other socially upward groups such as the new *Mizrahi* middle class.[14] Consequently, while in the neo-rural phases "quality of life" was dependent on a small-scale community, surrounded by nature and away from the city, in suburbia this shifted toward the autonomy and detachment of the nuclear family. As shown in a 1982 document by the Settlement Division, and later by the Ministry of Construction and Housing, "quality of life" was basically a mathematical equation of optimally dividing a particular area while providing each family with a large private parcel, an enhanced perception of privacy, and maximized panoramic views.[15] Both documents advocated setting the residential parcels perpendicular to the street, using the topographic conditions to increase the seclusion of the private family while enlarging the achieved sight (Figure 4.1). These guidelines would become the standard parameters for frontier suburban development in the West Bank, Galilee, and the Negev alike.[16]

While seemingly similar, the bourgeois suburbanization patterns differed from other groups with similar socioeconomic backgrounds and focused on social and cultural distinctions. This need for distinction, as Bourdieu explains, is essential to the bourgeoisie as it enables its members to elevate their social status by distinguishing themselves from other parts of society through an emphasis on cultural capital, achieved through education, the arts, manners, specific consumer patterns, and taste.[17] Correspondingly, distinction is an integral part of Logan and Molotch's

---

[13] Ministry of Environmental Protection, *Residential Building Patterns in Israel*, 8.
[14] Cohen and Leon, "The New Mizrahi Middle Class: Ethnic Mobility and Class Integration in Israel."
[15] Naim, "Lot Sizes in Toshavot and Community Settlements with Mountainous Topography," 1–4; Segal and Eyal, "The Mountain," 85–86; Weizman, *Hollow Land*, 130–32.
[16] Naim, "Lot Sizes in Toshavot and Community Settlements with Mountainous Topography," 1–4; Segal and Eyal, "The Mountain," 85–86; Weizman, *Hollow Land*, 130–32.
[17] Bourdieu, *Distinctions*; Hines, "In Pursuit of Experience: The Postindustrial Gentrification of the Rural American West."

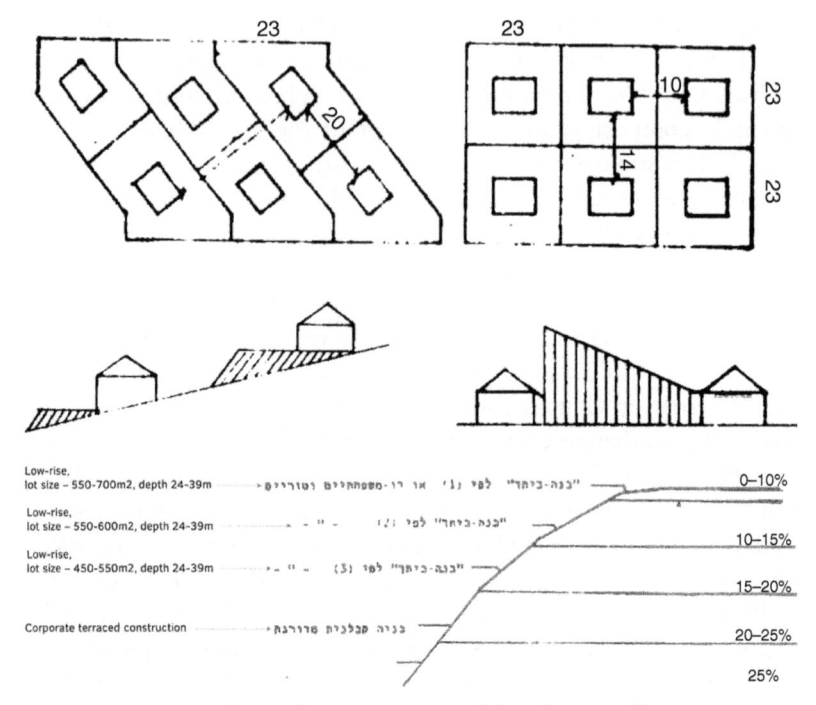

114   4 *Gentrification and the Suburban Settlement*

Figure 4.1 Suggested parcellation, setting, and distribution of housing types to increase "quality of life," 1982 (Settlement Division – WZO) "annotations added by the author"

"place stratification model,"[18] based on the desire, and ability, of hegemonic groups to preserve their social, physical, and cultural separation from other "groups they view as undesirable."[19] This was highly apparent in American suburbanization, which created racially and socially separated communities that went beyond economic classifications;[20] in Israel, this matched the national demographic-based geopolitical agenda.

The desire for distinction was first of all a matter of detachment and segregation, enabled by the capability of the bourgeoisie to influence spatial production. As noted by Yiftachel, this was expressed in the

---

[18] Logan and Molotch, *Urban Fortunes: A Political Economy of Place*; Alba and Logan, "Variations on Two Themes: Racial and Ethnic Patterns in the Attainment of Suburban Residence."
[19] Pais, South, and Crowder, "Metropolitan Heterogeneity and Minority Neighborhood Attainment: Spatial Assimilation or Place Stratification?," 261.
[20] Logan and Alba, "Minority Proximity to Whites in Suburbs: An Individual-Level Analysis of Segregation."

ability of "influential groups" to move to "suburban localities, 'protected' from the proximity of 'undesirables'."[21] Among these influential groups, Yiftachel includes the private developers who targeted "upwardly mobile groups who seek 'quality of life'" and thus profited from the construction of gated communities.[22] Yacobi and Tzfadia highlight the selective nature of Israeli privatization that consisted of granting social elites favorable conditions as a means to attract them to frontier areas.[23] Nevertheless, while Yacobi and Tzfadia emphasize property rights rather than planning rights as the main feature of these spatial privileges,[24] this chapter shows that in the early 1980s the bourgeois social elite still had a significant ability to impact the production of space. Therefore, applying the distinction between *power over* and *power to*, the state, in this case, granted the bourgeois upper-middle class and well-connected developers the power to organize, plan, and inhabit Suburban Settlements, as a means to expand its power over space.

The desire for distinction was not only expressed in the settlements' physical segregation, but also in their differing architectural and (sub) urban features. Accordingly, the bourgeois suburban environments were characterized by simplistic "good houses,"[25] in comparison to the nouveau riche and flamboyant Build Your Own House neighborhoods that housed many of the emerging *Mizrahi* middle class of the peripheral development towns and the rural frontier.[26]

The suburban turn did not only serve the new consumer patterns of the bourgeoisie, but also its economic aspirations. The significance of the different forms of capital, whether economic, social, or cultural corresponds with the leading hegemonic values of the relevant period.[27] In the early statehood years, one's social capital was of significant value, as the affiliation with the ruling *Mapai* party or the hegemonic Labor movement granted one substantial privileges regarding employment, housing, education, and other welfare services.[28] Therefore, as Bareli and Cohen note, the bourgeois middle class was first interested in gaining cultural capital and entering the existing

---

[21] Yiftachel, "Bedouin-Arabs and the Israeli Settler State," 36. [22] Ibid.
[23] Yacobi and Tzfadia, "Neo-Settler Colonialism and the Re-Formation of Territory: Privatization and Nationalization in Israel," 9.
[24] Ibid. [25] Allweil, *Homeland: Zionism as Housing Regime, 1860–2011*, 14.
[26] Shadar, *The Foundations of Public Housing*.
[27] Bourdieu, "The Forms of Capital," 241–53.
[28] Kimmerling, *The End of Ashkenazi Hegemony*, 11–20.

hegemony.[29] This would change with the global and local neoliberal turn, which financialized all aspects of individual and social everyday life, and strengthened the importance of one's economic capital.[30] Thus, according to Gutwein, parts of the upwardly mobile old socialist *Mapai* hegemony and the bourgeoisie fully cooperated with the privatization processes that followed the 1977 changeover, transforming their social privileges into economic ones as a means to maintain their hegemonic status.[31] Fittingly, according to Filc, the Israeli neoliberal turn opened the way "to different expressions of exclusionary populism" that privatized the public sphere and commodified the welfare system while highlighting existing ethnic, social, and religious polarizations.[32] This eventually resulted in the accumulation of private wealth by distinguished groups, an emphasis on individualistic values, and a greater focus on living standards, both as social privileges and as a means to promote territorial control; these were all highly visible in the Suburban Settlements.

Settlement and Socioeconomic Classes

The Israeli Suburban Settlement is a spatial phenomenon that emerged in the early 1980s. Interchangeably referred to as *Yeshuv Parvari* or *Toshava*, it was used by the Israeli administrations to attract middle-class and upper-middle-class families to the fringes of the main metropolises,[33] easing the pressure on existing cities while settling areas of national interest. Unlike earlier national decentralization efforts that included peripheral development towns or small-scale rural settlements, the Suburban Settlements were independent localities housing up to 2,000 families, offering spacious and relatively affordable houses in isolated homogeneous communities,[34] all just a car ride away from main Israeli cities. According to the Israeli Central Bureau

---

[29] Bareli and Cohen, *The Academic Middle-Class Rebellion: Socio-Political Conflict over Wage-Gaps in Israel*.

[30] Harvey, *The Condition of Postmodernity*; Harvey, *A Brief History of Neoliberalism*; Graeber, *Debt: The First 5000 Years*, 378.

[31] Gutwein, "The Class Logic of the 'Long revolution', 1973–1977."

[32] Filc, *The Political Right in Israel*, 5.

[33] Benvenisti, *The West Bank Data Project: A Survey of Israel's Policies*, 49; Nahoum Dunsky Planners, "Development of the Hills' Axis: The Seven Stars Plan," 2; Fogel-Hertz-Schwartz Architects and Planners Ltd, "Local Outline Plan: New Mazor GZ/BM/195," 1–8.

[34] Settlement Division, "The 100,000 Plan," 16.

of Statistics, there are currently around twenty localities that fit the description of a Suburban Settlement, all located close to the internal frontiers of the predominantly Arab Galilee, the West Bank, and the Negev,[35] yet in sufficient proximity to the cities of Haifa, Jerusalem, Tel Aviv, and Beer Sheva. They are all characterized by an upper-middle-class Jewish Ashkenazi population[36] and, with the exception of two West Bank settlements, they all belong to the religiously secular and politically central-left sector.[37]

The ability of the settlement enterprise to appeal to a variety of social groups was a well-coordinated project managed by the Settlement Division and the Israeli Government. The Division's plans focused on creating this appeal and thus it classified the different areas in the West Bank according to their potential demands and national importance, categorizing the preferred settlement types in each area according to their size and target group. This included the city (*I'ir*), town (*Kirya*), Suburban Settlement (*Toshava*), Community Settlement (*Yeshuv Kehilati*), and Rural Settlement (*Yeshuv Haklai*).[38] The different types not only differed in their sizes – more than 10,000, 3,000–5,000, 500–2,500, and 500 families respectively – but also in their target population and location. The plans categorized the areas by demand, according to the travel time from the main metropolises – high-demand areas were less than thirty minutes from Tel Aviv and twenty minutes from Jerusalem; medium-demand areas were between thirty-five and fifty minutes from both cities; and those exceeding these travel times were categorized as low-demand zones. The Settlement Division suggested restricting the use of community and rural settlements to medium and low-demand areas while developing several larger *Krayot* (towns) nearby, which would provide the required regional services. *A'rim* (cities) were reserved for the threshold between medium- and high-demand areas, with the latter designated for private development, and offering low-rise houses in

---

[35] Yiftachel, "The Internal Frontier: Territorial Control and Ethnic Relations in Israel," 493.
[36] ICBS, "Population in Jewish Localities, Mixed Localities and Statistical Areas, by Selected Countries of Origin."
[37] ICBS, "Localities in Israel"; Central Elections Committee, "Results of 2015 Elections"; Central Elections Committee, "Results of 2019 Elections."
[38] Benvenisti, *The West Bank Data Project: A Survey of Israel's Policies*, 49; Settlement Division, "The 100,000 Plan," 15–16.

Toshavot (Suburban Settlements) close to the Green Line and the Tel Aviv metropolis.[39]

The Suburban Settlements fulfilled the new demands for better living standards, consisting of spacious private houses, well-developed infrastructure, green areas, and very good educational opportunities. At the same time, the mechanism behind the construction of these settlements enabled some of the privileged middle class to improve their economic situation. The Suburban Settlements were mainly developed by registered associations or private developers. In the case of the associations, they consisted of well-connected middle-class families that were usually affiliated with one of the main political parties, or a powerful organization like the military, the Ministry of Defense, or the aerospace industry. These associations were then able to use their social status and political connections to gain access to state-owned lands, where they were allowed to build their new suburban community. Through their collective strength, they were able to reduce construction costs and to make the dream of a private house even more affordable. Thus, this new mode of production was based on the capability of the associations to transform their social capital into spatial privileges and to improve their members' living standards. Additionally, members eventually became owners of very attractive real estate, gaining concrete capital from their social capital. The same applied to the privately developed settlements. In this mode of production, the developers were initially small-scale contractors with good ties to the government and other important ministries, which eventually supported their entrepreneurial efforts and helped them turn their political capital into an entrepreneurial project as well. Kochav Yair, Alfei Menashe, Oranit, and Reut (Figure 4.2), the focus of this chapter, illustrate how both the association-led and developer-led options were used to attract a specific societal group to the area, gentrifying it and enabling its further development.

Political Capital and Spatial Privileges: The Private Associations

The concept of an association is a development of the former pioneer *Gar'in*; it corresponded with the evolving privatization of the national geopolitical project and the new modes of production it endorsed. Some of the associations began as a *Gar'in*, yet quickly turned into

[39] Settlement Division, "The 100,000 Plan," 16.

Political Capital and Spatial Privileges 119

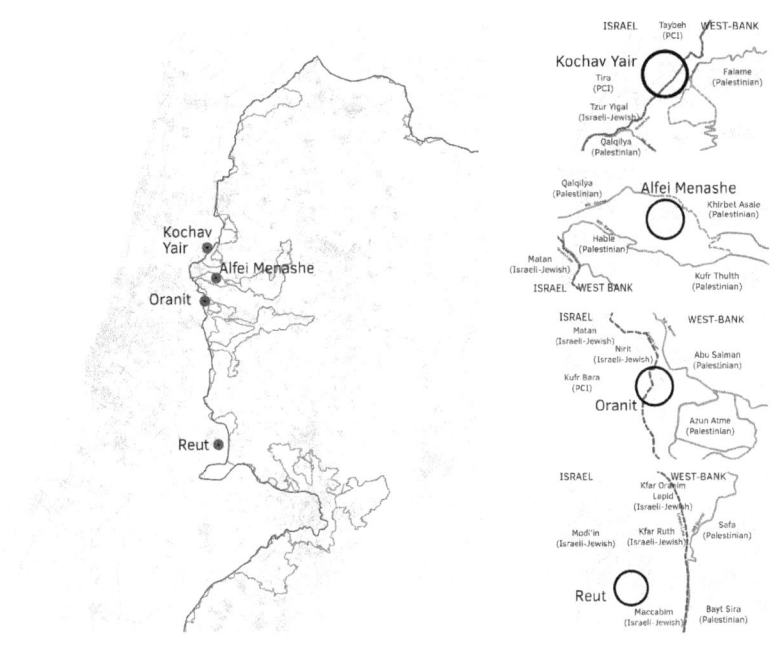

Figure 4.2 Case studies along the Green Line and the West Bank Barrier (illustration by the author) Note: PCI – Palestinian Citizens of Israel.

a well-managed buyers' club, with the objective of securing an appealing suburban environment at affordable prices. As nonprofit civilian organizations, they embody the idea of selective privatization, consisting of members of leading political parties or other powerful institutions – the newly formed bourgeoisie. These associations thus developed simultaneously with the Suburban Settlement phenomenon, establishing isolated and luxurious residential environments for restricted privileged communities.

Kochav Yair constitutes one of the leading examples of the association-led mode of production and the selective spatial privileges it relied on. It was initiated and established by a group of young upper-middle-class families, to whom the state granted the power to develop and settle the site in order to heighten its power in the area. Consequently, while this group of families was initially associated with the right-wing *Herut-Beitar* settlement movement, Kochav Yair quickly lost its political affiliation and turned into an attractive bourgeois Suburban Settlement suitable for the local upper-middle class.[40] It houses a significantly well-established community of 10,000 inhabitants; consisting of several former high-ranking officers and politicians, it is made up almost entirely of single-family houses, with more than 90 percent owner-occupancy.[41]

The site of Kochav Yair was an integral part of state-led frontier domestication efforts and an ideal setting for the suburban desires of the emerging bourgeoisie. The specific location had been chosen by the Jewish Agency (JA) in 1978, as its Settlement Department led an effort to locate potential settlement sites that would enhance the state's control over the Green Line while creating a western counterpart to the West Bank project.[42] Located between the Southern Triangle,[43] the predominantly Arab district of Taybeh and Tira inside Israel, and the West Bank, settling the site prevented a cross-border Palestinian sequence while promoting a stronger Israeli presence. In the early 1980s, the area included some 60,000 Palestinians, on both sides of the former border, and less than 2,000 Israeli Jews.[44] A new Jewish settlement was thus a first step in balancing this Palestinian demographic dominance. The site was initially called Mitzpe Sapir and it was part of three other settlement points in the triangle area that formed the southern version of the Settlement Department's *Mitzpim* Plan; this focused on promoting Jewish presence in northern Galilee, also inside official Israeli territory.[45] Located on the Israeli side of the Green Line and just fifteen kilometers east of Tel Aviv, the site lacked the negative political affiliation of a West Bank settlement and enabled the formation of an exclusive commuter community.

The allocation of the site to the settling families was a clear example of selective privatization. The Settlement Department was in charge of finding potential locations, yet the settlement's type and its future

---

[40] Berger, *Autotopia: Suburban In-between Space in Israel*, 23–49; Eitan, The Construction of Kochav Yair.
[41] ICBS, "Localities in Israel."
[42] Levav, "JNF to Establish 3 More Points in the Triangle Area," 4.
[43] The Triangle is a term that refers to the Arab concentrations to the east of the Green Line, inside the State of Israel. The Northern Triangle refers to the area that includes the towns of Kufr Qara, Ar'ara, Baqa al-Gharbiyye, and Umm al-Fahm, while the Southern Triangle refers to Qalansuwa, Taybeh, Kufr Qasem, Tira, Kufr Bara, and Jaljulia.
[44] ICBS, "Localities in Israel"; PCBS, "Localities in the Palestinian Authority."
[45] Soffer, "Mitzpim in the Galilee – A Decade of Their Establishment."

population were decided by the Ministry of Agriculture, which functioned as a sort of land broker – allocating sites to settlement groups interested in taking part in the greater national mission. Simultaneously, a group of young members of the right-wing *Herut-Beitar* movement, the ideological backbone of the then ruling right-wing Herut party, was organizing to establish a settlement of its own. The group was led by Michael Eitan, head of *Herut-Beitar* Youngsters and later a member of parliament and minister on behalf of the Likud party as well as a key figure in the suburban turn of the Green Line.[46] The group consisted almost entirely of middle-class city dwellers who wanted to improve their living standards and move to a private house, while remaining in proximity to the Tel Aviv metropolitan area. Their demand was thus for a suburban-type settlement, characterized by a relatively high quality of life, which was not more than thirty-minute car ride from Tel Aviv, enabling them to commute to work on a daily basis. The group was first interested in settling in the western edges of the occupied West Bank, just over the Green Line. However, in a meeting in 1981 with the then Minister of Agriculture, Ariel Sharon, Michael Eitan was offered the site of Mitzpe Sapir. The site's proximity to the coastal area and the ideological mission to increase Jewish presence in the predominantly Arab Southern Triangle appealed to the young group, and they accepted Sharon's offer.[47]

Kochav Yair, as it was eventually called, was based on a merger of ideological and individualistic aspirations, constituting an example of a pioneer bourgeois settlement. The group initially functioned along similar lines to the previous ideological *Gar'inim*, and, to emphasize their ideological orientation, they chose to name the settlement after the leader of the pre-state nationalist *Lehi* militia,[48] Avraham Stern, whose nom de guerre was Yair.[49] The *Gar'in* became a registered

---

[46] The successor of Herut.   [47] Eitan, The Construction of Kochav Yair.
[48] *Lehi* (לח״י, לוחמי חירות ישראל; *Lohamei Herut Yisrael*, Israel Freedom Fighters): a Jewish underground paramilitary organization operating against the British Mandate from 1940 until the establishment of the State of Israel. Created by former members of the *Irgun* that opposed the cessation of the struggle against the British Mandate during World War II, it was declared a terrorist organization by the Mandatory government, and for a period also by the State of Israel. In 1980, the State of Israel recognized the *Lehi* as one of the pre-state undergrounds that helped in the national armed struggle.
[49] Kochav, in Hebrew, is literary "star" – *Stern* in German. Therefore, Kochav Yair is a pun that means Yair's Star, but also Yair Stern.

association once the Ministry of Agriculture and the Israel Land Administration decided to enlarge the planned settlement, as appropriate for a more organized and corporate project. As a well-connected agency, the association received unprecedented spatial privileges that included the ability to dictate the profile of new members and the power to control the (sub)urban and architectural characteristics of the future settlement. Thus, the newly admitted members were not reached through the private market, but rather through personal connections and recommendations, managed by the associations; this made sure that new families suited the required pioneer bourgeois profile.[50]

Acting as the developer, contractor, and representative of settling families, the association still wanted to be seen as an ideologically motivated organization. In 1981, fifteen families volunteered to settle the site of Mitzpe Sapir as a temporary outpost – a decision that did not have any practical justification and was mainly a residue of former settlement methods, granting Kochav Yair the aura of a pioneering mission. In an official letter sent to David Levy, the Minister of Construction and Housing, the association voiced their complaints against the ministry's lack of assistance in the settlement's development, stating:

The Jewish Agency, under the orders of the Israeli Government, established a settlement in western Samaria, on the 67 lines, in order to Judaize the area that is populated by tens of thousands of minorities, in a hostile environment ... Herut-Beitar has taken upon itself to establish and develop a settlement in this place, which will be called Kochav Yair.[51]

Claiming that Kochav Yair is located in Western Samaria, and not the Eastern Sharon where it actually resides, the association highlighted the connection to the West Bank project. This is further emphasized by the mention of the Green Line and the "hostile" environment, and by the comment that the association had "taken upon itself" this mission, thus promoting the idea of a pioneering act once more.

The ideological front to the Kochav Yair project ensured wide ministerial support, which further promoted the attractiveness of the project. An interministerial feud concerning overlapping planning responsibilities caused the Ministry of Construction and Housing to

---

[50] Eitan, The Construction of Kochav Yair.
[51] Kochav Yair Association, "Letter to Deputy Prime Minister and Minister of Construction and Housing David Levy," 1.

Political Capital and Spatial Privileges 123

refuse to support the project, yet this did not hinder the support Kochav Yair received from the JA and the Israel Land Administration.[52] Consequently, the latter ensured exclusive use of the site for the settling group and subsidized the sale of the state-owned lots by a "conditional loan of 40% of the land's value, which will turn into a grant for each settler living there for a period of five years after the completion of construction."[53] Eventually, the lack of professional support from the Ministry of Construction and Housing meant that several planning responsibilities were passed to the association, granting it additional spatial privileges and the power to influence the production of the settlement, ensuring that it would turn into the desired suburban environment the settling families wanted. Consequently, the attractive location and affordable prices, as well as the decision to enlarge the project and the practiced spatial privileges, turned Kochav Yair into a highly attractive bourgeois suburb.

As the Kochav Yair project expanded, it retained its selective and exclusive character. While the dominance of the original members declined, admission was still reserved to the well-connected bourgeoisie. The Ministry of Agriculture conducted negotiations with various lobbying groups and allocated 200 lots to *Herut-Beitar*, 100 to the *Lehi* veterans, 100 to members of the Defense Forces, and an additional 100 to members of the South Africa Zionist Federation. This selective privatization, which granted well-connected families such privileges, is perhaps best seen in a letter from the assistant to Michael Dekel, Deputy Minister of Agriculture, to Michael Eitan, asking him to admit "an old member of the *Herut* movement, a son of an old member."[54]

The first zoning plan for Kochav Yair corresponded with the increasing individuality and focus on the private family. Accordingly, the Israel Land Administration issued a scheme that was based on the seclusion and isolation of the family parcel.[55] Unlike a common tract housing development, where a given area is subdivided into smaller parcels, the plan for Kochav Yair started with the single parcel,

[52] Barel, "CEO of MH Warns Apartment Buyers in the West Bank," 1; Maoz, "MA and MH Agree on Cooperation in Construction in JS," 1; Wiener, *Letter to Michael Dekel*, 1–2.
[53] ILA, "Resolution No 262," 1.
[54] Malka, "Letter to Michael Eitan, Jerusalem: Ministry of Agriculture," 1.
[55] ILA, "Kochav Yair."

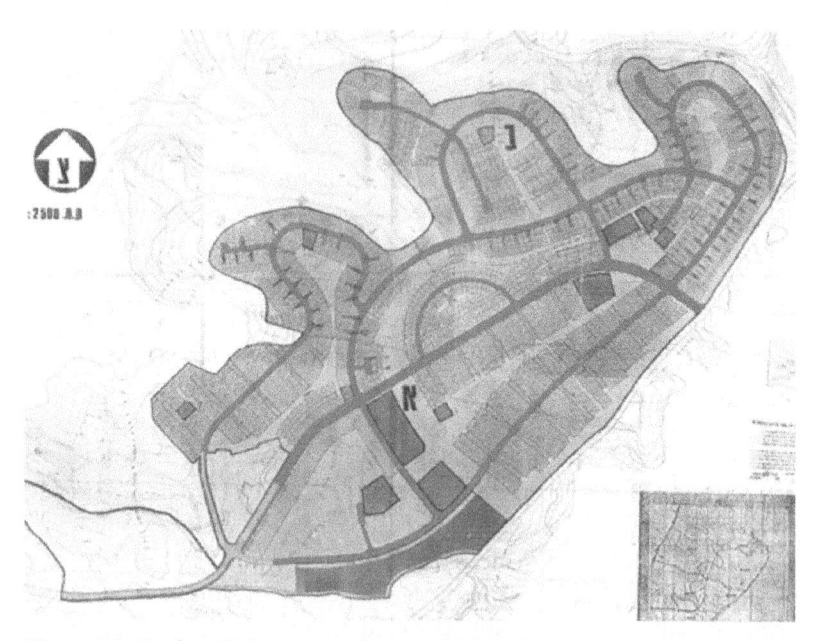

124   4 *Gentrification and the Suburban Settlement*

Figure 4.3 Kochav Yair zoning scheme, 1984 (ILA)

reproducing it across the planned area while creating housing clusters. Together with the almost perfect contour of roads, which followed the site's topography and decreased the requisite groundworks, the proposed arrangement promoted a flowing and continuous car ride through the town, eventually providing the sought-after comfortable car access to each of the parcels. Using separated housing clusters and a system of winding roads, the proposed outline emphasizes the desire to create a commuter town with a focus on detached private households, and less on an integrated and involved community. The repeated use of cul-de-sacs secluded each housing cluster further from the wider context and ensured a higher level of privacy. The use of the private parcel as the basis of the plan, as well as the circular setting, created an abundance of leftover spaces in the intersection of the streets and between the housing clusters, which the planners then used to promote the formation of secluded and isolated housing assemblages (Figure 4.3). Initially, the outline plan included several larger lots, intended for larger housing typologies; however, when the association took over the process it commissioned architect Meir Buchman's office to rearrange the settlement's proposed layout, parceling the larger lots into the same private housing clusters as in the rest of Kochav Yair.[56] This ensured that it would consist only of detached houses suitable for an upper-middle-class suburban community, unlike denser residential buildings that could harm the settlement's morphological and societal homogeneity.

The spatial privileges members of Kochav Yair enjoyed enabled them to produce private houses that suited their profile as upper-middle-class bourgeoisie. Regardless of their former political affiliation, each family became part of the Kochav Yair association based in *Metzudat Zeev*, the headquarters of the Herut movement. Each family was entitled to a private lot in the future settlement, choosing from three options ranging from 500–1,000 m^2, while the exact location was decided through a raffle. In managing the design and construction, the association was interested in promoting individuality on the one hand, while enforcing uniformity, on the other. Therefore, together with Buchman, the association created specific design regulations that were aligned with the ideal Zionist "good house,"[57] and promoted a homogeneous environment made up of two-story detached family units with simplistic white cubic features and a sloping red-tile roof. As Eitan claimed, the association feared the Build Your Own House style "cacophony" where everyone does "whatever he wants," and therefore decided to create a limited number of housing models that each member could choose from.[58] The construction of similar models was also meant to reduce construction costs and ensure a quicker and more efficient procedure. The association approached six different architectural offices, inviting them to propose several housing models according to the different lot sizes, location, and topography. In an event held in *Metzudat Zeev* in 1983, the architects presented their ideas to the first 500 members, who were then supposed to vote for the model of their choice (Figure 4.4).[59]

As bourgeois homes, they followed modest architectural characteristics and focused on the nuclear family and its privacy. Significantly large with an average area of 200 m^2, they consisted of a clear division between the bedroom area and the joint living room and kitchen space, a division heightened by the use of the split-level home, which characterized all

---

[56] Meir Buchman Architects and Planners, "Modification Plan SD/1002/7 A: Kochav Yair."
[57] Allweil, *Homeland: Zionism as Housing Regime, 1860–2011*, 14.
[58] Eitan, The Construction of Kochav Yair. [59] Gil-Ad, Houses in Kochav Yair.

126 4 Gentrification and the Suburban Settlement

Figure 4.4 Promotion drawings of housing models in Kochav Yair, 1984 (Telfed – The South African Zionist Federation)

models.[60] Although the popularity of this typology could be explained by the topography of the site, it should be noted that it was also used in lots that had almost no height differences or any significant topographical features. The family's privacy was further enhanced by orienting the living room area toward the backyard while the bedrooms faced the street. This created a closed façade toward the street, shutting the house off from its neighboring environment, while the more open façade was in the secluded family area (Figure 4.5).

The association's ability to control the entire process enabled it to construct these seemingly luxurious and spacious houses on a tight and limited budget. According to one of the main architects involved in the project, the houses in Kochav Yair were "villas with a budget of social housing."[61] Nonetheless, the well-managed and well-connected association was able to use the recession of the early 1980s, its contacts with leading contractors, and its members' purchasing power to significantly reduce the price of construction materials.[62] With the help of new computer-aided drawing software, the architects were able to replicate plans for the different models and their various implementations.[63] The use of reproduced details and lists of building components were also crucial and, along with the fact that the contractors had to deal with only a small number of architects, construction costs were significantly reduced. To

[60] Riskin, Houses in Kochav Yair and Reut; Gil-Ad, Houses in Kochav Yair.
[61] Gil-Ad, Houses in Kochav Yair.   [62] Eitan, The Construction of Kochav Yair.
[63] Gil-Ad, Houses in Kochav Yair.

Figure 4.5 Houses in Kochav Yair, 1989 (left) and Tzvika Israel, 1986 (right) (Nati Harnik – GPO). Note the small and closed façades toward the street and the open façades toward the backyard.

create some variety and sophistication, the architects tried to design breaks and interruptions in the continuous façades by creating setbacks for balconies and entrances, while using large concrete beams to frame two or more small windows, creating the appearance of a larger one. Maintaining low construction costs met the economic restraints of some of the young families; their access to political power as part of the emerging middle class had not yet translated into economic wealth, and so they were able to build a "villa" at the price of a "social housing" unit.

The managerial rights and support enjoyed by the association enabled a concentrated and efficient construction process. The association enacted a process that included developing the necessary infrastructure before marketing the lots to future buyers. In doing so, it basically invested the development payments made by existing members, which they hoped to get back once the lots in the new neighborhoods were sold. This proved to be highly efficient, as it ensured that all public facilities such as schools, kindergartens, and the country club would be constructed before the settlement reached full capacity. Nevertheless, this speculative management was made possible mainly due to the help of the Israel Land Administration, which gave the association requisite support for the entire settlement before all the lots were marketed, significantly reducing the risk taken. Eventually, despite a short period during the First Intifada when sales were low and some families changing their minds about moving to the settlement, this economic model enabled continuous construction and the admission of new families.[64]

---

[64] Eitan, The Construction of Kochav Yair.

The scope of construction was crucial to Kochav Yair's character as an exclusive settlement. The fact that almost the entire infrastructure and all the houses were developed in several years ensured that the settlement would not turn into a construction site for a long period of time. Building Kochav Yair in three concentrated and consecutive phases also enabled the first 500 families to enjoy the infrastructure and facilities that were intended to serve the entire 1,000 families; these were crucial for the image of an appealing Suburban Settlement. With the completion of the third wave in the early 1990s, Kochav Yair was more or less a done deal, minimizing future extensions or expansion neighborhoods while maintaining the homogeneous societal, architectural, and (sub)urban fabric.[65]

Known as the home of several generals, ministers, and even an acting Prime Minister, Kochav Yair enjoyed the reputation of an ultimate Suburban Settlement with a model high-class community (Figure 4.6). Consequently, it continued to attract the same upper-middle-class sector that had enhanced its elitist nature. To retain this status, Kochav Yair resisted, quite successfully, almost all attempts by the Israel Land Administration and the Ministry of Construction and Housing to expand and change its character. The objections did not only concern plans directly affecting Kochav Yar, but also those regionally, fearing they would damage the area's suburban and bourgeois qualities. In the mid-1990s, for example, residents of Kochav Yair voiced their disapproval of a plan to build a new town in the area of Yarhiv Forest, which is more than 10 km away, opposing the region's possible urbanization.[66] For a period, Kochav Yair was also against the construction of Tzur Yigal on its southern edge, an objection that was eventually moderated with the promise that the new settlement would also be a low-rise, spacious, and significantly small one, designed for upper-middle-class families as well. In 2003, both settlements were merged by the Ministry of Interior into one municipal entity. Still, they maintain their independence as no significant physical connection, such as streets or paths, were created between them and they are still accessible from two different entrances.[67]

---

[65] Mitzpe Afek Council, "Building Permits Archive."
[66] Society for the Protection of Nature in Israel, "Report on the MCH Plans for Kochav Yair and Yarhiv Nirit," 1–3.
[67] Arye Soninio Architects, "Urban Plan ZS/BM/1002/10 (Eyal North) Tzur Yigal."

Political Capital and Spatial Privileges 129

Figure 4.6 Israeli Prime Minister Ehud Barak meeting Yasser Arafat at his private residence in Kochav Yair, 2000 (Amos Ben Gershom – GPO). Note the corner window.

The concept of detachment was an integral part of both the (sub) urban and architectural layouts, and this was also emphasized by the lack of commercial uses. Despite a few stores and public facilities inside Kochav Yair, the main commercial and recreational functions are found on its fringes. This includes the commercial center that is located in the nearby gas station compound, which includes several stores, banks, and cafes, as well as the nearby industrial zone that contains office buildings, shops, and even a supermarket. The gated community aspect is heightened by a physical barrier and a checkpost that separates the residential area from the nearby environment and controls those coming in as well as those going out. To make this procedure more efficient and less troublesome, the access road consists of two lanes, one for Kochav Yair residents and one for guests. A remote identification system automatically opens the barrier for cars owned by residents, while guests are able to enter only after an inspection by the security guards at the entrance. A similar inspection also takes place when exiting Kochav Yair, to prevent car theft and burglary.[68]

[68] Kochav Yair Council, "Security in Kochav Yair."

The inspection of nonresidents is usually visual and based on appearance, meaning that the security guards distinguish by appearance only those who fit the profile of possible guests.[69]

During its construction, Kochav Yair was already considered a success story. Its location attracted young commuters while simultaneously ensuring that the ideological aspect of territorial settlement would be present, ensuring the financial and bureaucratic support of the state and its various administrations as well as that of settling organizations. Yet, as it was on the Israeli side of the line and not on occupied territory, Kochav Yair was attractive to upper-middle-class Israelis from right across the political and religious spectrum. The spacious houses with their intimate character appealed to many seeking such houses in a secluded community in the midst of nature, yet with all the services the cities close by are able to provide. Nevertheless, admittance to the settlement and exposure to the project focused on well-connected families with ties to the association or one of its founding groups. All these aspects were clearly stated in a 1984 promotion film by the South African Zionist Federation, one of the partners in Kochav Yair, that claimed:

> Today, sophisticated technology and a great deal of thought [about] quality of life [has gone into] building Kochav Yair. Located in the vicinity of Ra'anana and Kfar Sava, Kochav Yair is in easy reach of Tel Aviv and is located entirely in the pre-67 borders of Israel. It is easy to work in Tel Aviv and benefit from it culturally, yet to live in a small town. Kochav Yair will have a maximum of 1200 homes, each with a private garden. These homes and the Kochav Yair lifestyle are available at a price no other quality suburb can offer and in travelling distance from the centre.[70]

One of the South Africans moving to Kochav Yair, who was quoted in the promotion film, went further and stated:

> One thing I want to tell you about the houses in Kochav Yair: they are not what one envisions when coming on Aliyah, we are talking about luxury houses, spacious ... so this standard of housing is very high, very similar to what we have in South Africa, very similar.[71]

Kochav Yair is not the only example of an association-led Suburban Settlement that relied on gentrification and place stratification, yet it is

---

[69] The author passed this test a couple of times. [70] Boxer, *Kochav Yair*.
[71] Ibid. Aliyah is Jewish immigration to Israel/Palestine.

perhaps the most famous. Similar initiatives decorated both sides of the Green Line and other internal frontiers, such as the cases of Har-Adar (Ministry of Defense), Na'ale (Israel Aerospace Industries) and Beit Arieh (Israel Aerospace Industries and *Herut-Beitar*) located in the West Bank, or similar initiatives like Lehavim and Meitar in the Negev (Israel Chemicals, Israel Electric Corporation, and Israel Aerospace Industries) and Kfar HaVradim in western Galilee (ISCAR Metalworking). The ability of these associations to lead such a massive construction feasibly and efficiently could not have happened without the support of the various administrations, emphasizing the selective privatization enacted by the state. The focus on the detached family unit and simplistic design features, together with a good perception of the core settling families, offered these select groups the suburban dream of a spacious house and garden in a distinctive community while incorporating them into the national territorial mission. Due to the presence of high-ranking officers and politicians, as well as the proximity to Tel Aviv, Kochav Yair stood out from other cases, making it a synonym for this mode of development. Subsequently, in the early 1990s, when the Israeli Government wanted to construct additional Jewish settlements in the area, it referred to them as "stars" (*Kochavim*) as it sought to create several new reproductions of Kochav Yair – the prototype of the ideal Suburban Settlement – along the Green Line.

Political Capital and Development Monopolies: The Connected Developers

Besides the association mechanism, a similar mode of selective privatization was taking place: private corporations gaining the ability to develop and market a settlement, as seen in the cases of Alfei Menashe and Oranit. The former is a privatized state initiative and the latter a private real-estate venture backed by various state institutions. Although they present two different scenarios, both cases demonstrate the ability of well-connected developers to receive substantial spatial privileges and to incorporate young, secular, middle-class families into the West Bank project.

Both sites are located just a couple of kilometers east of the Green Line, making them ideal locations for a not too ideological territorial Suburban Settlement. Alfei Menashe is three kilometers from the Palestinian city of Qalqilya, and around ten kilometers from the

Israeli city of Kfar Sava. Therefore, it was one of the "five minutes from Kfar Sava" settlements,[72] a term that derived from the marketing technique used by private developers during the 1980s in order to portray the newly built settlements as part of the Israeli central area. Oranit is less than a kilometer inside the Occupied Territories, bordering Horashim forest and the Israeli-Arab localities of Kufr Bara and Kufr Qasem,[73] as well as the Palestinian villages of Azzun Atma and Abu Salem to the east. During the early 1980s, in the vicinity of the site of Oranit, there were more than 10,000 Palestinians and less than 2,000 Israeli Jews, while surrounding the site of Alfei Menashe there were approximately 30,000 Palestinians and some 1,000 Israeli Jews. Therefore, both settlements, with their 10,0000 upper-middle-class inhabitants, formed a crucial step in the demographic turf battle. Belonging to the second highest socioeconomic decile of Israeli localities and affiliated with the secular public and the center of the Israeli political spectrum,[74] both settlements demonstrate how this demographic turf battle was now being conducted by the newly forming Israeli bourgeoisie, and not only by religious right-wing West Bank settlers.[75]

Alfei Menashe initially began as a state-led initiative to house members of the Ministry of Defense. After the site received the authorization of the Israeli Government in August 1979,[76] the Ministry of Defense insisted that the future settlement would house families of military officers and other employees of the Israeli security establishment.[77] Tentatively agreeing to these demands, the Ministry of Construction and Housing and the Ministry of Agriculture first proposed an alternative site for this purpose, highlighting the challenging topography that is more suited to a denser corporate-led construction than a low-rise environment that suited the suburban aspirations of the Ministry of Defense. Rejecting this proposal, the representatives of the Ministry

---

[72] Kislev, "Behind Yeruham, Behind Kfar Sava," 7.
[73] This refers to the Palestinian citizens of Israel.
[74] ICBS, "Localities in Israel"; ICBS, "Population in Jewish Localities, Mixed Localities and Statistical Areas, by Selected Countries of Origin."
[75] ICBS, "Localities in Israel"; ICBS, "Population in Jewish Localities, Mixed Localities and Statistical Areas, by Selected Countries of Origin."
[76] It was simply referred to as the "settlement committee."
[77] Security establishment (*Ma'arach HaBitahon*): an umbrella term that refers to the Israel Defense Forces (IDF), police, the General Security Service (*Shabak*), and the Mossad.

of Defense stated that a site deeper inside the West Bank was out of the question, stressing the importance of proximity to the coastal plain. To ensure the exclusive suburban characteristics, the Ministry of Defense even required a direct road connecting the site to Kfar Sava and insisted that marketing would be restricted to officers and other ministry officials and that only in the case of unsold houses could the project be open to other families, but only after receiving the ministry's prior consent.[78]

The selective privatization continued in the choice of contractors, who received uniquely favorable conditions meant to guarantee the completion of the project. Given the intention of the Ministry of Defense to create a high-end residential environment for its officers, it advocated handing the project over to a single large corporation that would take responsibility for the entire process. Due to the foreseen high development costs, caused by the site's steep and rough topography, the Ministry of Construction and Housing agreed to grant the future corporation easier terms than those usually offered to private developers, including larger governmental loans and higher development grants, as well as a guarantee to purchase 50 percent of all unsold units. Large-scale construction companies were less interested in taking part in this project, and in April 1981 the Ministry of Construction and Housing signed a contract with Tzavta Construction and Housing Ltd, a private corporation made up of eight small-scale construction and development companies with strong ties to the ruling Likud Party and the Ministry of Agriculture. With these connections, Tzavta was able to secure even better conditions than those initially promised, including larger governmental subsidies and even an option to develop 80 percent of the units in the settlement.[79] Subsequently, due to its monopoly over the settlement, the name *Tzavta* became a synonym for Alfei Menashe.[80]

The exclusive status of Alfei Menashe included an inclusive design, covering all aspects of the settlement, prepared according to Ministry of Defense guidelines and carried out by one of Israel's leading architectural firms. The Ministry of Construction and Housing commissioned Avraham Yaski, one of the country's famous and most successful architects, to compose Alfei Menashe's masterplan and to

---

[78] State Comptroller of Israel, "The Establishment of Alfei Menashe," 104–15.
[79] Ibid. [80] Kislev, "Behind Yeruham, Behind Kfar Sava," 7.

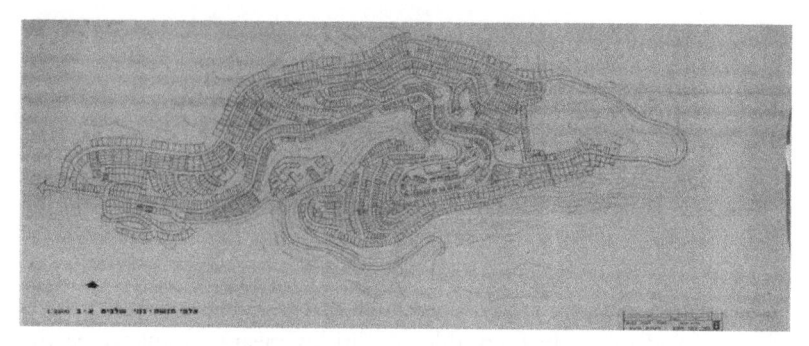

134   4 *Gentrification and the Suburban Settlement*

Figure 4.7 Alfei Menashe, Phases A and B, 1982 (Yaski Architects and Partners – Israel State Archive)

determine its design regulations,[81] emphasizing the desire for a high-class residential environment.[82] Yaski's plan corresponded with these requirements as it consisted of a series of isolated, detached family parcels, placed along the site's topography and system of curving streets, ensuring direct and independent car access for each private household. Retaining the highest point in the settlement as an area for public functions, Yaski repeated the common public center that we have already seen in previous settlements. However, this public area did not form the core of the settlement, but was rather an isolated compound separated from the exclusively residential area. Creating a system of descending terraces, the layout ensured the segregation of each house through height differences while expanding the open panorama. Although it was only commissioned for the first 500 units in Alfei Menashe (Tzavta A), Yaski's plan also included his vision for a larger scheme of almost 1,500 units (Tzavta B) (Figure 4.7). While this larger plan ignored questions of land ownership and municipal boundaries, and for this reason it later had to be adjusted, it offered a unified vision for Alfei Menashe as a residentially oriented Suburban Settlement, consisting of tract houses along curving roads that would become home to a well-established commuter community.[83]

Yaski's plan included very detailed design guidelines that promoted an exclusive yet restrained residential environment based on

[81] Yaski and Partners Architects and Planners, "Tzavta A. Tel Aviv."
[82] Kislev, "Behind Yeruham, Behind Kfar Sava," 7.
[83] Yaski and Partners Architects and Planners, "Detailed Plan 115/4: Alfei Menashe."

singularity and uniformity. Locating the detached houses on the inner rings and the semidetached houses on external roads, Yaski reduced the groundworks and used the site resourcefully. This concern for efficiency was also manifested in the guidelines' emphasis on the quite obvious manner of placing the houses along the topography, assigning each street to a single latitude line. This created the desired uniform sloped terraces and ensured a higher level of perceived density. The design guidelines stressed the need to level up each lot and to construct the houses in two levels – a lower level containing the kitchen and living room, surrounded by a private garden, and an upper level containing the bedrooms. The privacy of the nuclear family was ensured as the kitchen and living room, as well as the backyard, were always removed from the adjacent environment. The guidelines also considered the design of the houses, determining a Mediterranean-like appearance of white cubes with setbacks that blended with the topographical differences, thus not following the common countryside style of a cottage with a sloping roof. Nevertheless, even an apparently avid modernist like Yaski could not avoid the popularity, during the 1980s, of tilted roofs, and permitted their use. He insisted, however, on a unidirectional slope, limiting the diversity of its design and promoting the sought-after clean cubic form (Figure 4.8).

Yaski's proposed design contradicted the regulations of the Ministry of Construction and Housing, and was accepted only because of the demands of the Ministry of Defense. While in sites with similar conditions the Ministry of Construction and Housing determined the construction of denser housing typologies, which reduced development costs, in Alfei Menashe the Ministry of Defense insisted on a multiterraced development of secluded single-family houses (Figure 4.9). With the strong influence of the Ministry of Defense, the Ministry of Construction and Housing and the commissioned architects were not in the position to argue and thus offered no other planning alternatives. A report from the Office of the State Comptroller from 1984 heavily criticized the lack of alternatives and blamed the blind collaboration on the confidence that all the units in Alfei Menashe would be purchased by Israel Defense Forces (IDF) officers. According to the report, the Ministry of Construction and Housing was sure that the high development costs would eventually be paid by the new homeowners from the security forces, who would

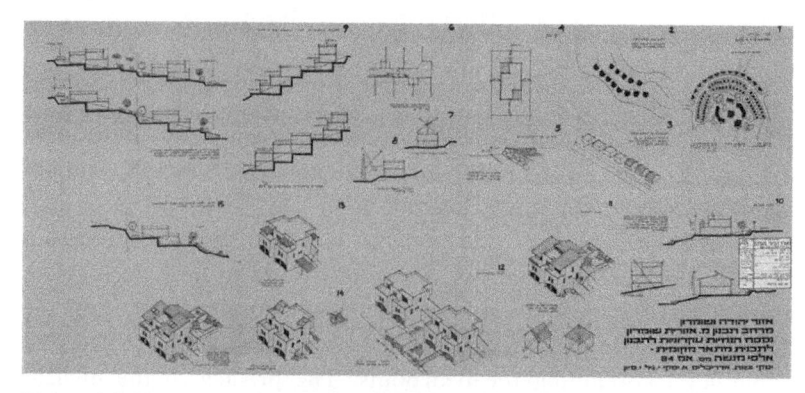

Figure 4.8 Design regulations for Alfei Menashe, 1984 (Yaski Architects and Partners – Israel State Archive)

Figure 4.9 Alfei Menashe, 1984 (Nati Harnik – GPO)

receive financial support from the Ministry of Defense, an assumption that would later prove to be false.[84]

In the design of the houses, Tzavta continued the emphasis on the seclusion of the nuclear family as an essential element of "quality of life." Accordingly, they offered four types of housing, which, though

[84] State Comptroller of Israel, "The Establishment of Alfei Menashe."

they differed in size, number of rooms, and height, all consisted of variations of the same architectural concepts. They were all based on the separation of the different dwelling functions and areas through the use of levels, which helped in merging the units with the site's topography while ensuring the family's segregation from its surroundings. Following Yaski's guidelines, Tzavta proposed different implementation options for each housing type, according to the location of the lot in regard to the adjacent street.

The dependence on military officers proved to be unreliable, causing Tzavta to launch a huge marketing plan that targeted upper-middle-class families as the new desired clientele. While over 400 officers initially expressed their interest in purchasing a house in Alfei Menashe, eventually only 110 did so. In search of new customers, Tzavta initiated an advertising campaign that included several funded promotion articles in leading newspapers and a sales office in downtown Tel Aviv. Choosing newspapers and locating the sales office in the city, Tzavta directed its efforts at established bourgeois families interested in moving to the developing suburbia. Thus, the promotion articles highlighted the size and spaciousness of the houses in Aflei Menashe, as well as the community life and the alleged high level of education it offered.[85] Tzavta also emphasized the financial benefits of purchasing a house in Alfei Menashe, promoting the project not only as a desired residential environment but also as an investment that would reap profits in the near future with ever-increasing property values. Most interesting was the use of the military profile of the settlement for marketing purposes, as Tzavta hoped that the image of a settlement populated by officers would be attractive to potential purchasers looking for an upper-middle-class community.[86] The marketing efforts lasted for more than four years, and included a significant price reduction of almost 20 percent, making Alfei Menashe the only settlement that witnessed a decrease in real-estate prices during the 1980s[87]

With the failure to attract members of the defense forces, the monopoly of Tzavta proved to be challenging and the Ministry of Construction and Housing began applying new selective privatization measures. Besides protests from some of the families that moved to

---

[85] Maariv, "A Fresh Method for New Settlements," 106; Maariv, "God's Little Acre in Alfe Menashe," 41.
[86] Harnish, "Peace Now Wants to Stop Annexation," 1; Kislev, "Behind Yeruham, Behind Kfar Sava"; Pinhas, "Tzavta in Alfei Mensahe: A Success Story," 142.
[87] Kislev, "Behind Yeruham, Behind Kfar Sava."

Alfei Menashe about building defects,[88] the monopoly given to Tzavta was criticized by the Office of the State Comptroller and several members of parliament, almost leading to a criminal investigation due to suspicions of possible corruption and conflict of interests.[89] Consequently, the Ministry of Construction and Housing decided to offer the majority of planned dwelling units in the new neighborhood to other private developers, reclaiming the power to develop space and passing it to smaller contractors.[90] Alfei Menashe continued to develop as suburban patches, fitting the profile of the developers and future settlers and consisting of a variety of housing typologies – multi-family terraced tenements,[91] terraced houses,[92] or the low-rise neighborhood of Kfir Yossef, developed by the *Herut-Beitar* movement according to the Kochav Yair model, planned by the same planners and architects and housing the same bourgeois families.[93] The sporadic development turned Aflei Menashe into an assemblage of selective privatizations (Figure 4.10) that increasingly relied on the corporate sector. Simultaneously, the settlement began to spread over a larger area, strengthening Israeli presence in the West Bank while creating secluded clusters that enabled the development of larger projects over the years without hindering the initial small-scale suburban atmosphere and the upper-middle-class profile of the settlers.[94]

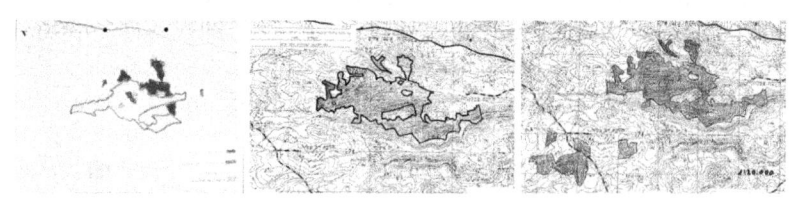

Figure 4.10 Area of Alfei Menashe, 1986 (left), 1988 (middle), and 1992 (right) (IDF)

[88] Naveh, "In Aflei Menahse They Don't Believe Promises," 11.
[89] Bar-Yossef, "Earth on fire," 13; State Comptroller of Israel, "The Establishment of Alfei Menashe."
[90] MCH, "Letter from MCH Legal Department to State Attorney of the Jerusalem District – Tzavta," 2.
[91] Perlstein Architects and Planners, "Detailed Plan 115/2."
[92] Amitai, "Letter from Avraham Amitai CEO of Tzavta to Head of Central District MCH"; Milman, "Letter for CEO of Shikun u Pituah to MCH David Levy."
[93] Eitan, The Construction of Kochav Yair.
[94] DMR Development Planning Ltd, "Alfei Menashe Master Plan Steering Committee," 3.

Oranit constitutes an additional step in the selective privatization of the settlement mechanism and an intriguing case study of the coalition between national and private interests in the efforts to gentrify the Green Line. Developed almost entirely by private initiative, Oranit began as a project of Delta Ltd, a new construction company formed by five quite unrelated individuals, with minimal knowledge and experience in development, real estate, or planning,[95] yet with obvious connections with the ruling Likud party. Purchasing privately owned Palestinian lands, they used their links with Deputy Minister of Agriculture Michael Dekel, who was in charge of new rural settlements in the West Bank and an enthusiastic supporter of private initiative. In 1982, after visiting the site, Dekel promised the project his full support.[96] Accordingly, in 1983 Oranit received the authorization of the Ministerial Settlement Committee, which, in an unprecedented act, confirmed that Delta would be its sole developer.[97] These extraordinary spatial privileges could be explained by the government's interest in optimizing construction by passing its responsibility to a single developer. Yet, considering the company's lack of any evident experience, and Dekel's later conviction for receiving bribes from several West Bank developers, Delta's connections with the Likud Party constitute a much more reasonable explanation for this peculiar decision.

Confident in its political ties, Delta began planning and developing the site even before official governmental authorization had been given.[98] Planned by its developers, the proposed layout of Oranit corresponded with the corporate interest in efficient commodification and thus consisted of a simple tract housing development made up of main streets and diverging cul-de-sacs. Focused on creating an attractive low-rise and low-density residential environment, Delta initially proposed locating the detached houses along the inner and quieter cul-de-sacs while placing denser typologies along the less attractive access roads (these were later concentrated on the settlement's fringes, so as not to interfere with the sought-after distinctive character). Land ownership issues constantly played a major role and despite Delta's intense efforts to purchase all the private parcels, several Palestinian owners

---

[95] Shiloni, Development of Oranit.   [96] Dekel, "A letter to Delta Ltd."
[97] Government of Israel, Decision 1196.   [98] Shiloni, Development of Oranit.

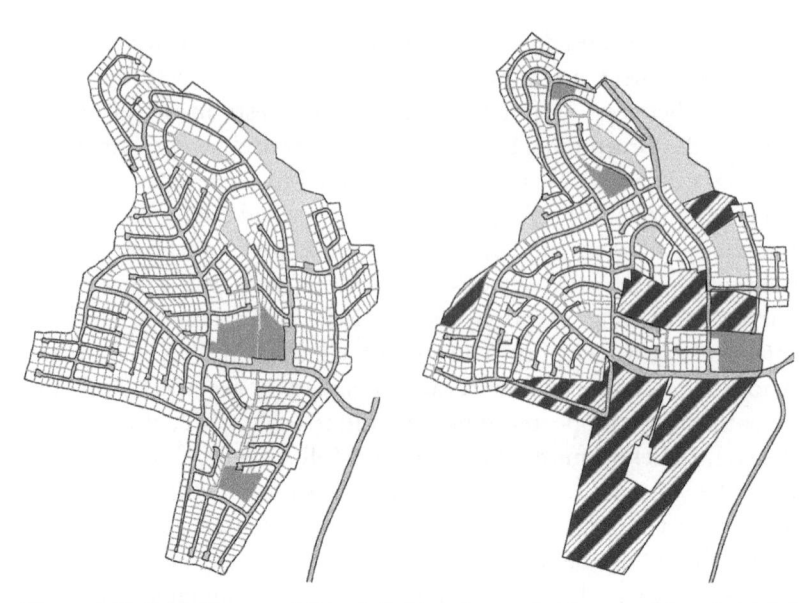

Figure 4.11 Initial layout of Oranit (left) and amended layout of Oranit (right) (illustration by the author)

refused to sell their land to Israelis, leaving undeveloped enclaves inside the settlement (Figure 4.11). Other owners later claimed that their lands were taken from them unwillingly or by fraud, in what became known as the "Lands Affair."[99]

Compatible with the desire to create a bourgeois suburb, the marketing process was highly selective and targeted a specific profile. Labeling Oranit a "city in nature," Delta promoted the image of a tranquil and pleasant small-scale settlement, surrounded by a pristine and pleasant landscape, yet close to the main metropolitan area.[100] The ideal location and the affordable prices of the substantially large houses enabled Delta to engage in a relatively low-key marketing campaign that relied more on word of mouth and targeted specific well-profiled and well-connected families, attracting families with similar profiles and thus ensuring the desired homogeneous character of the future population. These included officials in the Israeli Aerospace

---

[99] Naveh, "Arabs Sold Lands and Then Complained That It Was Stolen in Order Not to Take a Bullet," 13.
[100] Delta Ltd, "Oranit."

Industries, where one of the developers was previously employed, and physicians from Tel-Hashomer Hospital.[101] Consequently, almost all homebuyers were upper-middle-class families from cities in the coastal area and several American Jews interested in moving to Israel.[102]

The bourgeois characteristics extended into the individual family house. Using the term "villa" for the first time, Delta intended to construct 300 of the 500 lots while the remaining 200 were to be developed according to a Build Your Own House method. Following the corporate approach, Delta referred to the settling families as "purchasers" or "clients," and to the act of purchasing a house as an "investment."[103] The clients were able to choose from seven housing prototypes, proposed by Delta, that retained the settlement's homogeneous character and reduced construction costs (Figure 4.12).[104] Despite the involvement of three different offices, which claim to have enjoyed substantial professional freedom, the different models were significantly similar, recreating the popular family-focused and introverted split-level model. Designed along simplistic and quite humble lines, the proposed models fitted the idea of the *good* family house, depicted among nature, with no neighbors, and surrounded by trees and an open landscape (Figure 4.13).[105] The homogeneous character was strengthened further by the construction of almost all the houses by the same contractor and the use of the same designs as in the Build Your Own House lots.[106] Following the construction of the low-rise houses, Delta began to construct denser residential typologies, including tenements and terraced housing units. Nevertheless, these were quite limited and, most importantly, they were detached from the core of the settlement, so as not to compromise its bourgeois character. The denser residential projects were, however, designed to recreate the appearance of a private house, consisting of several units, yet with separated entrances, disguised as white villas with an ornamental tilted roof.

Delta's monopoly in Oranit relied on consecutive state interventions meant to facilitate the success of this seemingly private project. The exclusive status received a strict interpretation by the office of the State Attorney, which claimed that Delta was the only entity with the legal right to commission any new planning schemes or projects in the

---

[101] MCH, "Oranit," 1987. [102] Delta Ltd, "List of Homebuyers in Oranit."
[103] Ibid. [104] Iron, Houses in Oranit. [105] Delta Ltd, "Oranit."
[106] Globes, "High Profits from Sales in Oranit."

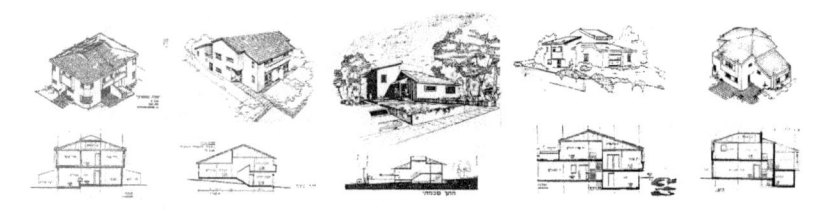

Figure 4.12 House models in Oranit, 1982 (Iron-Kaplan-Shachar Architects)

Figure 4.13 Houses in Oranit, 1985 (Baruch Naeh – Ma'ariv newspaper)

settlement's area.[107] Using Jordanian regulations that are valid in the Occupied Territories, which are much less generous regarding public functions, Delta was able to maximize the number of marketable residential lots.[108] Subsequently, the Israel Land Administration had to assign public lands south of the settlement for the use of a high school and cultural center, contributing public property to a private endeavor. Later, due to the lack of available public lands, the Ministry of Construction and Housing planned to expand Oranit across the

[107] Albeck, "Delta: Oranit." [108] Shiloni, Development of Oranit.

Green Line (on its Israeli side), on state-owned land reserves assigned to the Arab village of Kufr Bara.[109] This plan, which started as a conceptual option in the late 1980s, became very concrete with the official revocation of Delta's exclusive status in 1996;[110] it received the support of leading politicians such as Prime Ministers Rabin and Peres, and even those on the left like Yosi Sarid, a fierce opponent of the settlement enterprise.[111] However, the plan was not implemented, mainly due to the legal restriction on having a single entity on both sides of the Green Line, and the only expansion possibilities were small-scale sites whose ownership was resolved.

The reputation of Oranit as an attractive and legitimate settlement increased during the early 2000s. The prestigious status was already obvious during the early 1990s as families in Oranit were opposed to granting outsiders access to its schools and the newly built sports club.[112] However, with its physical detachment from the Occupied Territories by the Separation Barrier and its de facto absorption into the official area of Israel, Oranit was cleansed from the stigma of a West Bank settlement and from the defense and legal repercussions that came with it. Most of the land issue constrictions were resolved by the Israeli court during the 1990s enabling the settlement's further development. Ashdar Ltd, which had sold its shares in the area during the 1980s[113] due to land ownership issues and the bad publicity that came with it, bought back some 150 dunams[114] that were developed and marketed to individual clients. Concurrently, smaller privately developed projects were also taking place in other parts of the settlement, thus enjoying the spatial privileges granted by the state while adopting denser housing typologies.

The story behind the private-led settlements contains a mixture of economic and national interests. The state, interested in developing Jewish settlement in the area, was willing to hand over its sovereignty to private contractors. Giving them unprecedented spatial privileges that included the power to produce space, the state literally privatized the settlement enterprise. The developers, on the other hand, were able to use the relatively comfortable terms in the West Bank, their ability to

---

[109] MCH, "Oranit," 1991.　[110] Government of Israel, Decision 905.
[111] Elgazi, "A Settlement into the Green-Line," 8.
[112] Oranit Council, "Council Meeting Protocol – 20.3.1993," 1–5.
[113] Priel, "Dozens of Large Development Companies Are Engaged in JS," 2.
[114] Yamin, "Ashdar Purchased 150 Dunams in Oranit."

purchase Palestinian lands in the area, and their ties with the government to gain a monopoly over the process and to conduct a significant money-making and efficient development. At the same time, the families moving into the settlement were attracted by the location, the affordability, and the relatively small and high-class community. These three interests were entangled one with the other, until Delta's and Tzavta's economic interests began to conflict with those of the inhabitants, the local council, and the Ministry of Construction and Housing. Yet, once this issue was resolved, the coalition of interests between the state, private developers, and upper-middle-class families continued, progressing the national settlement mission while generating new housing typologies, and, eventually, creating enclaves of spatial privileges surrounded by Arab-owned lands.

The Omnipotent Spatial Agent: The Military Settlement

The Reut settlement demonstrates the status of military officers as an integral part of the emerging Israeli upper-middle-class and their leading role in the gentrification of national frontiers.[115] Perceived as a stable, ideological, and praiseworthy group, middle-level military personnel became a dominant factor in the development of local suburbia during the mid-1980s.[116] Unlike earlier examples, as in Alfei Menashe where military officers were simply potential customers, by the end of the 1980s they began to organize associations that enabled them to take on the role of entrepreneur. Later, the IDF established an internal unit named the Housing Administration (*Minhelet HaMegorim*), which would become responsible for organizing such housing associations and projects. The young officers' interests in suburban living met those of the government – to enlarge the Jewish population and presence in frontier areas. Moreover, struggling localities that sought to improve their situation saw the potential in attracting military officers and their young families, which would strengthen the local socioeconomic composition and promote the popular image of their town, eventually attracting additional upper-middle-class families as well. The mechanism behind the new military neighborhood

---

[115] Schwake, "An Officer and a Bourgeois: Israeli Military Personnel, Suburbanization and Selective Privatization."
[116] Berger, *Autotopia: Suburban In-between Space in Israel*, 140–48.

was relatively simple. The military, or one of its branches, would organize an association that would manage the construction of a new town or neighborhood. The association would then receive a site from the Israel Land Administration, whether on the edges of an existing town or in frontier areas, and would manage the planning and construction processes while administrating available governmental funding.[117] The Reut project is perhaps the best example of this mechanism, yet it was not the first.

One of the first examples of this new mode of production was the military neighborhood in Yavne. A development town in the larger Tel Aviv metropolis, until the 1980s Yavne was considered a weak and unattractive locality. Its young mayor at that time, Meir Sheetrit, who was keen on bringing a new influx of established young families to his town, together with the Personnel Branch of the Israeli Air Force (IAF), initiated a new residential neighborhood to house IAF officers. The construction of Neot Idan neighborhood was managed by an association organized by the head of the IAF Personnel Branch, Colonel Zvi Gov-Ari, who named it after his eldest son, Idan. This model, which proved very successful both for Yavne and the IAF officers, gained much popularity, and similar initiatives followed. What began as an inner unit of the IAF, later became part of the larger military's Human Resources Directorate, serving officers and noncommissioned officers from all branches of the IDF.

Located in the developing national frontiers and housing one of the state's most privileged groups, Reut is an ideal Suburban Settlement. Today, it constitutes one of the boroughs of the larger city of Modi'in, yet it preceded it and began as a separate residential project for IDF officers. Situated midway between Tel Aviv and Jerusalem, in the then yet undeveloped and relatively pristine regional council of Modi'im,[118] Reut enjoyed a rich natural landscape, open views toward the coastal plain, and a moderate climate. Adjacent to the Green Line, just across the developing new settlement of Maccabim, built in the former no-man's-land between Israel and Jordan, Reut was part of the efforts to settle the previous border area which included some 10,000 Palestinians and hardly any Jewish Israelis. The aura of the military

---

[117] Ibid.
[118] The city of Modi'in should not be confused with the regional council of Modi'im.

officers, together with its location and socioeconomic composition, all turned Reut into an attractive settlement and a suburban success story. Several years after the establishment of the city of Modi'in in 1996, Reut was annexed to it, together with Maccabim. Yet it still retains a relatively distinctive character and is managed by its own borough council.

The Israel Land Administration had already declared the area of Reut as a site for future settlement in the late 1970s, while it was still a military training zone, and by settling it the administration sought to transform its frontier-like nature and to incorporate it into the Tel Aviv metropolis. The army personnel were thus used by the Israel Land Administration to demilitarize the area,[119] confirming the common phrase that "the only one that can move the IDF, is the IDF."[120] Running parallel with the regional planning process, the Israel Land Administration and the IDF had already been surveying possible sites for a military settlement that would form a duplicate of the Yavne project. Nevertheless, unlike Yavne, this project would be much larger with an emphasis on younger officers under thirty-five years of age. This, according to IDF Chief of Staff Lieutenant General Moshe Levi, was the only way to encourage good officers to extend their service considering the existing "budget constraints."[121] Therefore, while the Israel Land Administration proposed other locations for the IDF, the latter insisted on this specific site due to its availability, size, proximity to military bases, and designation for suburban development.[122]

Reut was the outcome of reciprocal interministerial collaboration. Following a mutual understanding between the Israel Land Administration and the IDF, the military housing project needed the approval of the government, and thus also the blessing of the Ministry of Construction and Housing. Therefore, in 1984, Chief of Staff Levi sent an official letter to David Levi, Minister of Construction and Housing,[123] asking for his assistance in the ministerial committee while highlighting the project as "crucial for Israel's security."[124]

[119] Ministry of Defense, "Draft Resolution."
[120] Fogel, Highway 6 Settlements.
[121] Levi, "Letter to Minister of Construction and Housing – Housing Project for Military Personnel," 1.
[122] Eldor, "Letter to CEO of MCH – Modi'in – 2.3.1987."
[123] There were no family ties – Levi is a common family name in Israel.
[124] Levi, "Letter to Minister of Construction and Housing – Housing Project for Military Personnel," 2.

To relieve the minister from budget concerns, Chief of Staff Levi mentioned that the project would be planned, developed, and constructed by the military. In a meeting at the office of the CEO of the Ministry of Construction and Housing that discussed the planning of a future city in the area, which at that time was still preliminary and spoke of possible locations on both sides of the Green Line, it was agreed to allocate the "requested hills" for the Ministry of Defense, as it is "a serious group that had already proven itself in Yavne."[125] Moreover, although ministry officials were less interested in developing another "secluded" and "inefficient" low-rise settlement, they highlighted the importance of attracting a "strong population" to the area, which could "ease directing future ventures."[126] The ministry was therefore willing to support the IDF's demands and to grant it substantial spatial privileges, but for a residential neighborhood that would be a starting point for the planned city.[127] Accordingly, the ministry wanted to refrain from designating the site as a Community Settlement, due to its selective nature, and to coordinate its development with other settlements nearby, east and west of the Green Line, as part of the vision for the entire area.[128]

The far-reaching support for the military housing project concluded in the decision of the Israeli Government to authorize the establishment of Reut in December 1985. The official statement declared the project a "neighbourhood for military personnel" that would eventually "be part of an urban settlement... planned by the Ministry of Construction and Housing."[129] This decision was not well received by all planning agencies, and opinions regarding the national geopolitical need to develop this site rather than others varied. The initial policy of the Ministry of Construction and Housing was to refrain from vast public investment in this region, focusing more on areas of "political preference" while relying on small-scale private investment.[130] Correspondingly, the Authority of Rural and Agriculture Planning and Development (part of the Ministry of Agriculture) and the JA

---

[125] MCH, "Meeting Protocol 1.4.1985," 1.
[126] Eldor, "Letter from the Head of the MCH's Department of Urban Development, Sofia Eldor, to the CEO of MCH, Asher Wiener – 25.10.1984," 1.
[127] Eldor, "Letter to IDF Housing Administration – 20.4.1985."
[128] Eldor, "Letter to Cabinet Secretary, Jerusalem: Ministry of Construction and Housing."
[129] Government of Israel, Decision 1196, 1.   [130] Ravid, *Modi'im Area*, 1.

warned that a development like Reut would eventually harm plans to "populate and strengthen areas of national importance, and especially Jerusalem."[131] Nevertheless, as the decision was already taken, and no one wanted to confront the IDF and its "need to grant 1000 officers housing solutions,"[132] Reut was a done deal. Furthermore, although several towns in the district that were struggling economically, like Ramleh, Lod, and Rosh Ha'ayin, initially protested against the project as they hoped to attract the military families, they ultimately gave in; the Ministry of Construction and Housing promised to promote new plans for low-rise suburban-like neighborhoods in their jurisdiction, with a possibility of attracting military personnel as well.[133]

The spatial privileges the state granted to the IDF were more than the exclusive use of the site; the omnipotent status of the Housing Administration enabled it to control all aspects of the project's development. As both the Israel Land Administration and the government saw the military neighborhood as a preliminary stage in the development of the future city of Modi'in, and due to the IDF's strong political and social capital, the Housing Administration had substantial planning rights. According to retired Colonel Oren, the head of the Housing Administration at that time, although the official decision specified the exact location for the project, the Housing Administration was able to move it by more than a kilometer, bypassing the governmental decree and choosing a site with better topographic conditions.[134] The Administration's authority continued into the planning process, with the Israel Land Administration declaring that the site would be planned and developed by the military. Usually, when issuing a plan for a new residential neighborhood, the entrepreneur requires the consent of the local council. However, as Reut was a new project the IDF was not only the entrepreneur but also the local council, subjected only to the authority of the district level council. Initially, the IDF sought to circumvent this level as well, asking the Ministry of Construction and Housing to create a special independent committee that would speed up the process.[135] The ministry was able to convince the IDF to abandon this audacious demand, but only after assuring it that the district

---

[131] Moran, "Analysis of Population in Modi'in Area," 5.   [132] Ibid., 6.
[133] Eldor, "Letter to CEO of MCH – Modi'in – 2.3.1987."   [134] Oren, Reut.
[135] Morag, "Letter to CEO of MCH: Military Personnel in the Modiin Area."

The Omnipotent Spatial Agent

council would be unable to object to the project as it was backed by both the government and the national planning council.[136]

With the significant spatial privileges exercised by the IDF, it was able to improve its housing production mechanism, controlling planning and construction more efficiently. Initially, the newly established housing association continued to use the same method as Yavne, and was even named *Neot-Idan* B (later Neot-Reut).[137] Although the target group, in this case, was not exclusively the Airforce, but rather the wider military, the Housing Administration remained under the command of the IAF Personnel Branch due to its previous experience. Moreover, while in Yavne the planning process was assigned by the local council,[138] in Reut, it was commissioned by the Housing Administration and the association, enabling them to determine the layout of the future neighborhood according to their needs as a developer and as the representative of future inhabitants. Accordingly, the Housing Administration hired the office of Meir Buchman, which has already been mentioned in the section, Political Capital and Spatial Privileges.[139] The experience of the Housing Administration, the planning expertise of Buchman, the connections and power of the IDF, and the omnipotent status of the association in Reut guaranteed that the project would be planned and accomplished efficiently and resourcefully.

Commissioned by the association, which was simultaneously the developer and the end-user, Reut's layout followed both suburban desires and efficiency aspirations, while lacking any rentability concerns of a private entrepreneur. Buchman's proposed layout was a purely residential housing-oriented setting that resembled other suburban projects of the time. Yet, while the common suburban layout consisted of parcels of different sizes, Buchman focused on a single dimension, creating a nonhierarchical and uniform layout that fitted the egalitarian nature of the military. As the IDF was not a profit-driven developer interested in obtaining the full real-estate potential of the site, Buchman's layout was therefore not the outcome of subdividing a given area into marketable plots, as commonly practiced in a typical tract housing development; it was rather a result of combining parcels

---

[136] Eldor, "Special Planning Committee."
[137] Meir Buchman Architects and Planners, "Detailed Plan GZ/117."
[138] Nahoum Zolotoz Architects, "Outline Plan YV-132-1."
[139] Buchman, Kochav Yair.

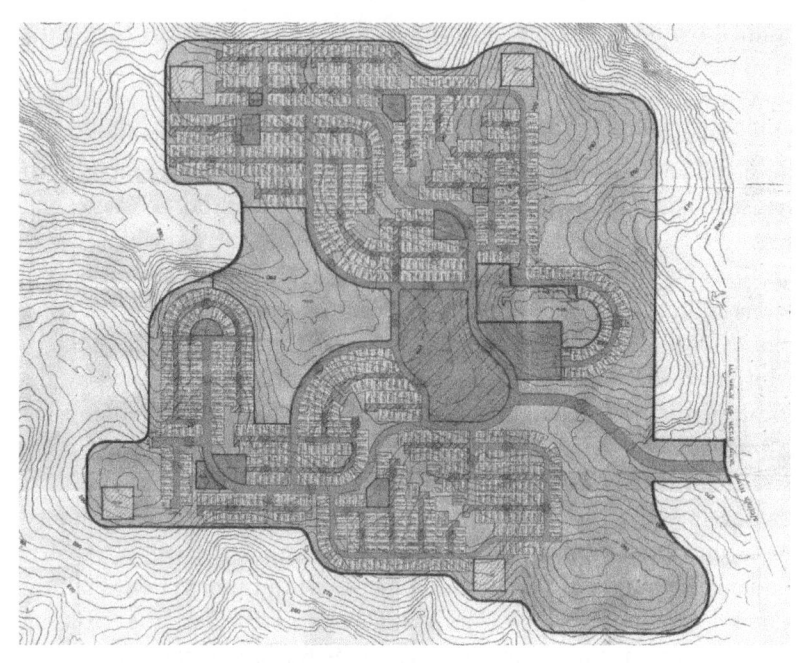

150   4 *Gentrification and the Suburban Settlement*

Figure 4.14 Reut, 1986 (Meir Buchman – MCH)

into housing clusters. Thus, Buchman opted for a system that consisted of a main winding access road and a series of cul-de-sac streets, using the site's topography to form independent compounds of about fifteen houses each (Figure 4.14).

The association's lack of profitability concerns enabled Buchman to plan a secluded settlement surrounded by a well-developed landscape. His plan consisted of 30 percent residential areas, whereas in similar projects these usually make up more than 50 percent.[140] This enabled him to surround the isolated housing clusters with an abundance of open public spaces that addressed the military officers' main wish for a secluded settlement. At the same time, while the common and economically efficient tract housing layout usually located all public functions outside of the settlement, Buchman was free from such considerations and was thus able to propose a public center in Reut, suggestive of its communal character.

[140] Meir Buchman Architects and Planners, "Detailed Plan GZ/117."

The architectural design of the houses in Reut followed the officers' desire for customization and the association's interest in standardization and optimization. As stated in a memo from the Cabinet of the Chief of Staff in 1986, the dwelling units were to be planned with considerations for "quality and costs."[141] With this focus, the association commissioned leading architects such as Chyutin, Riskin, and Bracha and Hakim among others, simultaneously asking for a number of housing models with an option for partial or full construction depending on the needs and economic abilities of each officer. Each family was then able to choose their preferred model with a maximum size of around 250 m². Despite the apparent abundance of choice, the various housing models were significantly similar, following the same spatial characteristics and design regulations determined by Buchman and the association.[142] This included an insistence on single-slope roofs, specific cubic dimensions, and white exterior walls,[143] which gave Reut the appearance of an idyllic suburb, made up of rows of homogeneous white houses (Figure 4.15).[144]

The architectural guidelines imposed by the association went beyond mere design and included specific instructions that ensured the formation of an isolated, introverted, and homogeneous residential environment. Beyond the aesthetic instructions mentioned, the guidelines determined by Buchman and the association included specific parameters for the placement of each house in the lot, creating a buffer zone that disconnects it from the nearby street and emphasizes the centrality of the backyard and the private family area.[145] Accordingly, the different models consisted of a split-level home, which used the site's topography to create an inner division between the family area and the bedrooms while orienting the living room toward the backyard (Figure 4.16). The only case where the association asked to place the family area in the front of the house was in parcels that were higher than the adjacent street. However, this was meant to increase the panoramic view from each living room and not to better connect the family to the community, especially as each plot was then enclosed by retaining walls that secluded it from the street.[146]

---

[141] Chief of Staff Cabinet, "Housing Project – Modi'in Plan," 3.
[142] Buchman, Kochav Yair.   [143] IDF Housing Administration, "Reut B."
[144] Oren, Reut.   [145] Riskin, Houses in Kochav Yair and Reut.
[146] Oren, Reut.

Figure 4.15 Houses in Reut, with the West Bank in the background, 1994. Tzvika Israel (GPO)

Figure 4.16 Model for a house in Reut B, 1991 (Architect Arik Riskin – IDF)

In full control of the entire construction process, the association was able to enforce broad standardization that significantly increased the homogeneity of Reut while optimizing its development. Although each family was able to select the model of its choice, its location was decided by the association, as the latter wanted to create single-model compounds that would consist of the same housing type. This would enhance the uniformity of the residential environment, fitting for a military-led project, while rationalizing the construction process.[147]

[147] Mentzel, Reut and Rosh Ha'ayin.

Optimizing the process further, the association established a parallel development company, Megorei Modi'in Ltd, run by the same officers, yet as a private corporation, and was thus able to manage the procedure economically, ensuring quality of construction at relatively low prices.[148] Consequently, the first phase of Reut, which included around 1,000 housing units, was a concentrated construction effort that the association was able to conclude in around three years. This was an unprecedented case of nongovernmental suburban development that enabled the construction of 500 additional houses directly afterward.[149]

Three decades after its completion, Reut continues to be a privileged housing project, even after the construction of Modi'in, which it was supposed to merge with. With a single gated entrance and no physical connections to other localities nearby, Reut was run by the same local council as Maccabim and functioned as a separated upper-middle-class gated settlement. By the early 2000s, when the Ministry of Interior wanted to merge the two with Modi'in, the citizens of Reut tried to resist, fearing they would lose their unique small-scale suburban character. Eventually, even though Reut officially became a part of the city of Modi'in-Maccabim-Reut, it still retains its unique quality, tone, and independence. The borough of Reut is still managed by the Neot Reut Association, which is in charge of running the daily municipal services and developing the area, while Reut and Modi'in still maintain their segregation through a series of open green spaces and lack of connecting streets. Therefore, Reut is still an idyllic bourgeois Suburban Settlement, home to the country's social elite.

With the omnipotent status of the IDF personnel involved in its development, Reut presents a unique case in the selective privatization of the Israeli settlement mechanism. The unprecedented spatial privileges exercised by the IDF enabled it to control almost all aspects of Reut's production. This eventually led to a unique settlement that was an outcome of the developers' desires for quality suburban lifestyle, as well as their interests in an optimized, efficient, and resourceful construction process. The suburban features that characterize Reut are therefore not simply a tool used by the state in order to attract officers

---

[148] Maccabim Reut Local Council Construction Committee, "Permit 910127/4560."
[149] Fogel, Highway 6 Settlements; Eitan, The Construction of Kochav Yair.

and their families to its frontier, but rather an outcome of the unique development method that turned the military into both the producer and consumer of the new settlement. Thus, it was not the built environment in itself that functioned as a territorial tool, but rather the ability to develop it.

The success of Reut in offering military officers an exclusive residential environment while gentrifying the Green Line turned it into a prototype for further IDF and Israel Land Administration cooperation. Consequently, following Reut, the Housing Administration continued to develop additional housing projects on the Israeli periphery. First to be developed were the military neighborhoods of Rosh Ha'ayin, which the Ministry of Construction and Housing and IDF had suggested developing in 1987 as a way to appease the town's discontent over choosing the site of Reut for the military housing project.[150] Consequently, the underprivileged and neglected Rosh Ha'ayin of the 1980s attracted young and well-established families and was thus able to continue developing, becoming one of Israel's emerging cities. Later, smaller compounds were developed in the new city of Modi'in or in new neighborhoods in other underdeveloped peripheral towns like Nazareth-Illit, Karkur, Akko, Gadera, and Beer Sheva.[151] Nevertheless, in all the ensuing projects the Housing Administration had to work with an existing local council and a prevailing local masterplan, which decreased its exclusive status and ability to dictate every aspect of the project. At the same time, as a representative of the IDF, the Housing Administration was still able to negotiate over key planning issues for the benefit of the military families. The logic behind these projects was maintained, as it included promising officers large houses at cheap prices while extending their service and gentrifying underdeveloped areas.[152] These military neighborhoods were secluded and segregated residential areas, as implied by their names, which almost always consisted of the words *Naveh* or *Neot* (Hebrew for oasis). These oases, with their unique method of gentrification, transformed the public image of the areas they were built in, turning them from frontier regions or impoverished towns to fertile

[150] Eldor, "Letter to CEO of MCH – Modi'in – 2.3.1987."
[151] IDF Housing Administration, "Nofei Ramot. Marketing Brochure, Petah Tikva."
[152] Bar-Eli, "IDF Housing Administration Offers Officers Offers They Can't Refuse."

grounds for larger investments, and the Israel Land Administration was thus willing to continue privatizing both property and planning rights.

For years the slogan of the IDF's education corps was "The nation builds the army that builds the nation" [*A'm Bone Tzava Boneh A'm*].[153] Regardless of whether this is valid in Israeli society in the individualistic twenty-first century, it still implies IDF's role as an integral part of local culture and identity. However, in the case of Reut, the claim that *the nation builds an army that creates real estate* may be more apt, as it was through this unique case of selective privatization that the state sought to develop its frontier, leading to one of the largest development projects in its history – Modi'in.

Localized American Suburbs and State-Oriented Gentrification

As we have seen in this chapter, the Suburban Settlements were an outcome of new privatized modes of production that relied on varying powers to produce space. Thus, more than the appeal of the suburban dream house, it was the spatial privilege of being able to produce it that facilitated settling both sides of the Green Line during the 1980s, whether in the mode of the private association, the connected developer, or the omnipotent spatial agent. The Suburban Settlement therefore correlates with Logan and Alba's analysis of place stratification, as it is based on the ability of favored groups to use their privileges to secure their desired residential preferences.[154]

The varying modes of production presented in this chapter demonstrate the various privileged groups and how they were incorporated in the settlement enterprise. Kochav Yair's mode of production was based on the state giving a small group of privileged families permission to build an exclusive and secluded Suburban Settlement by granting them the power to plan, develop, and inhabit state-owned lands. Consequently, these families significantly improved their living standards, as they were able to affordably obtain a spacious private house in a homogeneous secluded community while transforming their social and political capital into real estate. In Aflei Menashe, the mode of production first relied on privileged military personnel and specific

---

[153] Sasson-Levy, "Where Will the Women Be? Gendered Implications of the Decline of Israel's Citizen Army," 183.
[154] Logan and Alba, "Minority Proximity to Whites in Suburbs: An Individual-Level Analysis of Segregation," 244.

well-connected contractors, yet as these were either uninterested in the site or unable to develop it properly, the state then approached other privileged contractors and civic groups, passing to them the power to develop and inhabit the settlement. In Oranit, it was the private developers' political capital that was put to use, as government support granted them a monopoly over the construction process, and an almost unlimited power to plan, construct, commodify, and market space. Reut, on the other hand, demonstrates a unique mode of production, in which the military was simultaneously the client, developer, planner, and local council; consequently, it enjoyed unprecedented spatial privileges and is illustrative of a genuine case of selective privatization.

Nevertheless, in all the cases, it was the bourgeoisie that formed the main clientele, whether this was due to them being the privileged group that gained the power to produce space, or due to selective marketing strategies, enacted by private developers to create the image of an attractive high-class residential project. Therefore, while all the cases were supported by right-wing politicians whose main electoral power came from the blue-collar and middle-class *Mizrahi* sector, it was eventually the upper-middle class, center-left Ashkenazi sector that inhabited these settlements.

The ability of the bourgeoisie to both produce and consume space concluded in the similar architectural and (sub)urban characteristics of all the case studies presented in this chapter. The appeal to upper-middle-class families was the settling tool applied by the state, and architecture and planning were thus the product of this specific tool. Applying this new settlement tool, the state promoted the development of a new typology – the Suburban Settlement – which differed significantly from former Israeli urban and rural precedents. While in the communal rural settlements and in the quasi-socialist development towns the focus was on creating a unified community, in the Suburban Settlements the focus was on the individual family. This was echoed in the use of the single unit as the focal point of the entire planning process. At the same time, differences in the modes of production created distinctive variations of the Suburban Settlement model. In Kochav Yair, the process was carried out by a nonprofit-oriented association and the layout was based on duplicating the basic parcel and paving the site with it. In Reut, where the association enjoyed more significant privileges, this reproduction of a basic parcel was even more enhanced, leading to a layout based on secluded clusters surrounded by an abundance of open green areas. In Oranit, as well as in Alfei Menashe, as the development was handled by a private corporation, the site was resourcefully subdivided into smaller plots, efficiently utilizing the land's real-estate potential. Therefore, the layout of this new settlement typology derived from its settlers' interest in social seclusion and from its developers' economic incentives.

Characterized by homogeneous lines, the architectural qualities of all the settlements fitted the distinctive profile of the new pioneer bourgeoisie. The repetitively used split-level houses, whether in single, double, or terraced formation, continued the sequence of separations and enhanced the focus on private family life. The tract housing development and the focus on the private parcel as the basis of planning were clearly inspired by the American suburban model. In that sense, the chase of the bourgeoisifying Israeli middle-class for better living standards in the developing suburbia corresponded with the American Dream of a detached private house, a garden, and a car. Nevertheless, American suburbia was not implemented as a blueprint, but rather received an Israeli interpretation. The main difference was in the positioning of the houses and their relation to the surrounding environment. In the American example, houses are usually built parallel to the access street, while orienting an entrance porch and the living room to it. Here, the private front yard forms a symbolic buffer zone between the public and the private spheres, while enhancing the homogeneous character of the neighborhood. In the Israeli version, the houses were constructed mainly perpendicular to the street, minimizing the relation to it, while orienting the living room toward the backyard, as far as possible from the neighboring environment. Augmenting the seclusion further, the front yard, which functions mostly as a parking area, is cut off from the street by a wall. Therefore, in the Israeli suburban dream the private households function as independent entities or *monades*, an extreme case of its American inspiration.

In his writing on the Americanization of Israel, Uri Ram claims that globalization is a dual process, using the example of "McFalafel" to illustrate the Americanization of the local, but also the localization of the American.[155] In a way, the Israeli version of the American suburb,

---

[155] Ram, "Glocommodification: How the Global Consumes the Local – McDonald's in Israel"; Ram, *The Globalization of Israel*, 179–206.

realized in Suburban Settlements, constitutes the spatial version of the McFalafel phenomenon. This McFalafel was precisely what the bourgeois families were looking for, as its anti-communal features formed a contra to all former socially oriented Israeli residential models, transferring the Tower and Stockade approach from the level of the community to that of the family. As Chapters 5 and 6 show, the secluded family unit would continue to form the main focus of planning in all future residential developments.

Using the upper-middle class to domesticate the Green Line was a coordinated gentrification process that turned the former frontier area into suburbia. Through this state-supported endeavor, this hegemonic group was *seduced* by the privileged spatial rights, as Kim Dovey would claim, to settle along the Green Line and enable its domestication. Turning the area from a region inhabited by pioneer-like settlers into a dormitory of doctors, academics, high-ranking officers, and senior officials concluded in its legitimization; it eventually became an integral part of the national consensus. As we have seen, the development of all the case studies promoted the economic feasibility of larger housing projects, whether inside the settlements or surrounding them. Consequently, the projects that we will encounter in Chapters 5 and 6 were no longer the same low-rise, detached residential environments, but rather high-rise, denser housing typologies. The Suburban Settlement thus functioned as a real-estate avant-garde, gentrifying the area and preparing it for mass suburbanization.

5 | Mass Suburbanization and the Stars Settlements

Supply-Side Territoriality

From Gentrification to Suburbanization

Following its gentrification during the 1980s, the Green Line became an attractive and appealing area. This enabled a growing reliance on private capital as the state enacted a supply-side territorial approach, securing developers' interests as a means to ensure the area's continuous development. Subsequently, unlike earlier modes of production that relied on spatial privileges granted to organized settlers or small-scale developers, there was now a shift to granting private entrepreneurs the power to develop and market space.[1] Accordingly, in this new mode of production, profitability became a crucial feature in all development phases and the new outline schemes had to take into account the private developers' investment and financial interests; these eventually reshaped the built environment. The development of the Green Line during the 1990s was incorporated into the Israeli Government's attempts to solve the upcoming housing crisis caused by the mass Jewish immigration from the post-Soviet bloc, and turned into a corporate-led mass-suburbanization project intended to enlarge the national supply of dwelling units while enhancing the state's power over its frontiers.

This chapter focuses on the *Stars* settlements, which present a new mode of privatized territoriality based on new modes of production and a new set of spatial privileges (Figure 5.1). These seven new sites were initiated by the state in the early 1990s as part of national efforts to expand existing housing reserves. Focusing on the Stars, the chapter explains how the settlement mechanism relied on supply-side territoriality and new modes of spatial production. Analyzing the spatial features of the Stars, it demonstrates how this newly applied supply-side

---

[1] Schwake, "Supply-Side Territoriality: Re-Shaping a Geopolitical Project According to Economic Means."

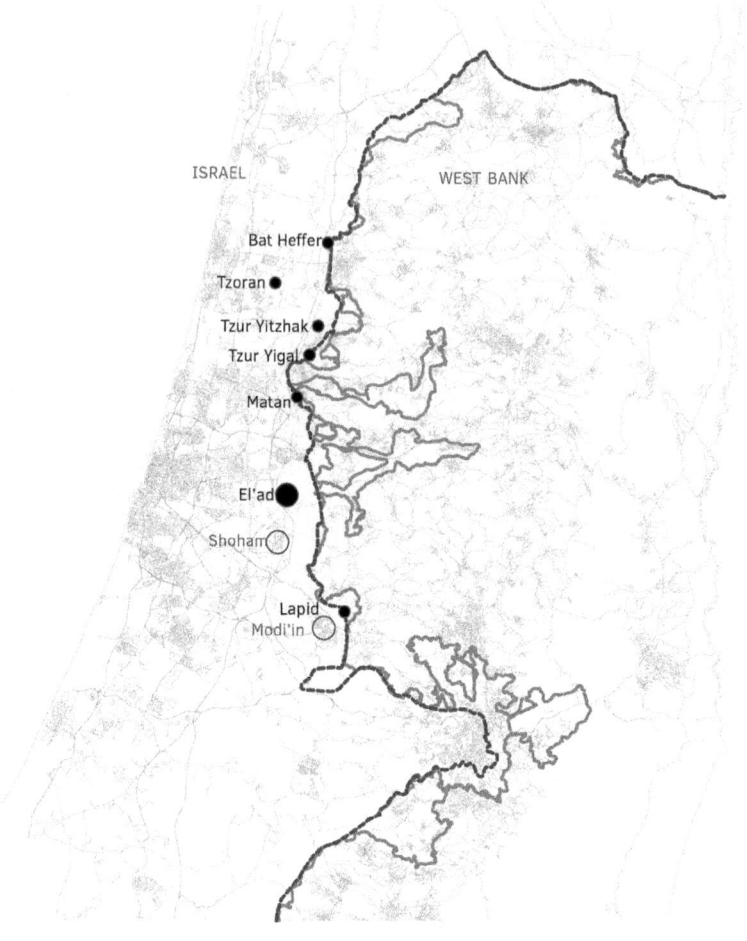

Figure 5.1 Case studies along the Trans-Israel Highway and the West Bank Barrier (illustration by the author)

approach affected the production of the built environment, starting with low-rise residential environments and then evolving into new urban–suburban hybrids that transformed the area along the Green Line into real estate – eventually finalizing its domestication.

Peace Talks, Immigration, and a National Housing Crisis

The early 1990s was a period of significant political changes. The declining violent uprising of the First Intifada and the Arab-American coalition during the first Gulf War, as well as improving relations between the USA and Russia, created an opportunity to revive the Israeli–Arab/Palestinian peace process. This led to the Madrid Conference, during the right-wing government of Yitzhak Shamir.[2] Although the immediate consequences were eventually limited, a crucial rapprochement between both sides enabled future talks. Moreover, as part of the negotiations, the US administration promised the Israeli Government substantial financial aid for the absorption of Jewish immigrants coming from the collapsing USSR. With the election of Yitzhak Rabin as Prime Minister in 1992, the peace talks between Israel and Palestinian representatives were restarted, eventually leading to the Oslo Accords, a series of agreements signed by the State of Israel and the Palestinian Liberation Organization (PLO)[3] as part of the Israeli–Palestinian peace process, and intended to lead to a permanent solution. As an interim agreement, the autonomous Palestinian Authority was created, as a momentary self-governing body, in charge of the newly created areas, A+B, in the West Bank and the Gaza Strip. These consisted of the major Palestinian cities and towns, while Israel retained control over all other areas (Area C). The agreements included mutual recognition between the PLO and the State of Israel, while leaving the issues of the nature of a future Palestinian State and its borders, the status of Jerusalem, and the question of Palestinian refugees to be dealt with in later agreements.

The political and diplomatic efforts, together with new waves of immigration, affected the development and suburbanization of the Green Line. In 1989, Mikhail Gorbachev lifted all immigration restrictions on the Jewish population in the USSR, enabling the State of Israel to absorb hundreds of thousands of Jewish families, carrying its role as

[2] Shamir, Yitzhak (יצחק שמיר; 1915–2012): an Israeli politician and head of state. Former leader of the Zionist right-wing Paramilitary organization Lehi. After the establishment of the State of Israel, he joined the Mossad until 1965. Later, he served as a member of parliament (1973–94), Speaker of the Knesset (1977–80), Foreign Minister (1980–6), and Prime Minister (1986–1992), all on behalf of the Likud Party.

[3] Palestinian Liberation Organization (PLO; منظمة التحرير الفلسطينية, *Munadhamat A'Tahrir Al Falastiniah*): an umbrella organization consisting of several Palestinian national movements and established in 1964. In 1974 it gained observer status at the United Nations and was later recognized by the majority of the international community as a legitimate (and, by some, *the sole*) representative of the Palestinian people (including Israel, in 1993, though it had considered it as a terrorist organization until 1991).

home of the entire world Jewry while aiding in the local demographic competition with the Arab Palestinian population. Estimations spoke of more than one million immigrant in only a few years, enlarging the local population by 20 percent, which at that time included less than five million inhabitants, and, in 1990–91 alone, more than 300,000 USSR Jews came to Israel.[4] This ignited, once again, national plans of absorption and redistribution of the country's population,[5] while consequently causing an increase in the overall demand for dwelling units. Assurances to the US administration that its financial support of this immigration would not be invested in new West Bank settlements, and later the construction freeze the Rabin government placed over the Occupied Territories as part of the peace talks with the PLO, caused the state to focus its new development efforts outside of the West Bank. At the same time, strengthening Israeli presence along the Green Line would help create an Israeli sequence with (some of) the inner settlement blocs, limiting the creation of Jewish enclaves in a future Palestinian State and thus ensuring the attachment of these settlement blocs to the State of Israel, in case of a territorial compromise. Moreover, a stronger Israeli presence all along the Green Line would prevent any Palestinian claims to lands outside the West Bank as compensation for the Jewish Settlement blocs that remained annexed to Israel, thus preventing any potential land swaps and minimizing the size of a future sovereign Palestinian entity.[6]

The involvement of private capital in the developments along the Green Line grew substantially during the 1990s. In the first plans for the area, during the tenure of Ariel Sharon as Minister of Construction and Housing, the government's strategy was to enlarge the supply of dwelling units by encouraging private developers. The new Rabin government, though led by the seemingly socialist Labor Party, did not rescind the privatization process, and even expanded it significantly.[7] Among the leading measures the government took were the privatization of several state-owned companies and, eventually, the construction of the planned transnational highway. By the 1990s, privatization was thus a given fact, supported by almost the

[4] Tolz, "Jewish Emigration from the Former USSR since 1970," 1–27.
[5] Efrat, "Geographical Distribution of the Soviet-Jewish New Immigrants in Israel," 355–63.
[6] Adiv and Schwartz, *Sharon's Star Wars: Israel's Seven Star Settlement Plan.*
[7] Hason, *Three Decades of Privatisation.*

entire political spectrum.[8] At the same time, the areas on the Israeli side of the Green Line, as we have seen, were ideological enough to be seen as areas of national priority, yet not too ideological so as to be left outside the national consensus. Thus, their development was supported by almost the entire political spectrum as well, turning into an ideal platform for the suburban turn of the 1990s. This mass suburbanization eventually completed the domestication of the former frontier and incorporated it into the greater Tel Aviv metropolis.

Supply-Side Territoriality

In the process of suburbanization, there are usually two main forces that generate urban immigration. First, there are the *pull factors* of suburbia, which usually consist of a better quality of life, manifested in a large private house, a well-established community, and proximity to nature. Second, there are the *push factors* of the city, such as crime, taxes, and ethnic/economic tensions.[9] While this is usually true for the upper-middle class, or *white suburbanization*,[10] for the lower classes there is more of an urban *spill over*, caused by high rents that push the poor to the fringes of cities, creating an extension of the low-income ghettos.[11] The pull factors of the suburbanization along the Green Line during the 1980s were created by the state. Allocating lands to homogeneous communities or subsidizing construction costs and mortgages, the state stimulated demand for housing units in the area while supporting the decentralization efforts, just as we saw in the previous chapter.

With the ongoing privatization of the Israeli economy, the development method used for its built environment transformed significantly. The state's role as both planner and developer began to change with the growing dependence on private construction companies; this first involved private contractors and later developers and entrepreneurs. The state withheld its status as planner, but relied on marketing the

[8] Rabinowitz and Vardi, *Driving Forces: Trans-Israel Highway and the privatization of Civil Infrastructures in Israel*.
[9] Marshall, "White Movement to the Suburbs: A Comparison of Explanations," 975.
[10] Ibid.
[11] Lake and Cutter, "A Typology of Black Suburbanization in New Jersey since 1970," 172.

planned parcels to private contractors, who were later supposed to develop the lots and to sell the constructed units to private families.[12] Like other neoliberal economies, Israel began to apply a *supply-side* housing policy, which included a variety of economic measures, policies, and deregulations,[13] all intended to "enable[e] the markets to work."[14] In this housing approach, dwelling units are supplied by safeguarding the interests of the developers in the hope that this would eventually benefit the end-users.[15]

In the Israeli territorial version of supply-side housing policy, the Ministry of Construction and Housing sought to develop the frontier by turning it into real estate. Thus, it had to make sure that the new settlements were *marketable*, meaning that the building rights and regulations also had to ensure the profitability of construction. In 1990, the Israeli Government took an additional crucial step toward a supply-side housing market as it exempted income from rented properties from overall taxed income. Enacting a maximal 10 percent tax rate, the state sought to encourage homeowners to put their properties on the market so as to enlarge the national housing stock.[16] The financial support to settling families could, on the one hand, be seen as *demand-side* housing policy, while, on the other, it could be seen as an extension of the supply-side strategy, as it was intended to create a demand for housing in a specific area,[17] ensuring that the supplied apartments would eventually be bought. Therefore, once the government began to safeguard the interests of the private housing market in order to bound additional space and to enforce its sovereignty, we can define the new settlement phase as one based on *supply-side territoriality*.

During the 1980s, the involvement of private developers west of the Green Line was minimal. As we saw in the previous chapter, private developers were drawn to the West Bank by the state through the financing of construction costs and the promise to purchase unsold

[12] Carmon, "Housing Policy in Israel: Review, Evaluation and Lessons," 200–08.
[13] Brenner and Theodore, "Cities and the Geographies of 'actually Existing Neoliberalism'," 349–52.
[14] Rolnik, *Urban Warfare: Housing under the Empire of Finance*, 20; World Bank, "Housing: Enabling Markets to Work."
[15] Galster, "Comparing Demand-side and Supply-side Housing Policies: Submarket and Spatial Perspectives," 561–77; Graeber, *Debt: The First 5000 Years*, 377.
[16] Israeli Tax Authority, "Israeli Tax Authority."
[17] Gutwein, "The Class Logic of the 'Long Revolution', 1973–1977."

units; on the Israeli side of the frontier there were mainly contractors, commissioned by one of the housing associations.[18] Demand for suburban housing did exist, yet not to the extent of large-scale private investment, and the 1980s' recession prevented private developers from engaging in large-scale projects with marginal governmental support. Nevertheless, the area's state-led gentrification turned it into an exclusive environment and eventually made future investments much more plausible, as suggested by the Ministry of Construction and Housing regarding so called strong families, like Israel Defense Forces (IDF) officers, who function as "a factor that attracts additional populations to the area, 'creates' hundreds of housing units per year and is able to assist the ministry from an organisational point of view."[19] Thus, with the state anticipating a national shortage in dwelling units it now had the necessary infrastructural, financial, and speculative circumstances to enable private developers and entrepreneurs to take over the development of the area. This led to an accelerated process of mass suburbanization – starting with mass-produced, low-rise residential environments and ending with high-rise suburbia.

With the transition to a supply-side approach, the residential parcel became the focus of planning. Enacting an optimized marketable system, the Ministry of Construction and Housing began implementing specific dimensions for each housing type, which planners were then in charge of implementing in their proposed outlines. The art of urban planning was thus the ability to create a harmonious system of fixed parcels, while the essence of the architectural task was to optimize the building rights of each parcel, generating optimal sizes and numbers of dwelling units.

The Modi'in project of the mid-1990s is perhaps the best example of this transition. The idea of establishing the city (or even a city) of Modi'in first arose in the late-1960s and the initial thoughts included a new suburban town on the fringes of Gush Dan (in a different location from today). The concept was of a satellite town that would redistribute the population inside the Tel Aviv metropolitan area more equally.[20] In the late 1970s, the current site of the city as a potential settlement area was mentioned in the Hills Axis plan,

---

[18] Maggor, "State, Market and the Israeli Settlements: The Ministry of Housing and the Shift from Messianic Outposts to Urban Settlements in the Early 1980s," 140.
[19] MCH, *Meeting regarding Construction for Military Personnel 2.9.1990*, 1.
[20] IPD, "Modi'in."

which would become part of the overall national effort to develop an eastern counterpart to the coastal plain along the hilly area of the Green Line.[21] The idea reemerged in the 1980s, when the emphasis was on enlarging the supply of residential units east of Tel Aviv.[22] Intended to control the suburbanization of the metropolitan area by directing it eastwards along the connection between Tel Aviv and Jerusalem, the Ministry of Construction and Housing wanted to develop the city "by private developers [and] by means of various governmental incentives."[23] Modi'in, according to the director of the ministry's urban department at the time, was "based on economic efficiency, private initiative and indirect government involvement;"[24] it thus focused on encouraging private investment instead of relying on public funds.

While the planning and execution of the first phases in Modi'in was a decade-long coordinated process managed by the Ministry of Construction and Housing, the smaller settlements nearby, the Stars, were developed in a significantly shorter period of time. Built in order to rapidly answer present needs, they were thus more an outcome of an improvised process controlled by private developers than a long and complex procedure. The story of their development therefore provides a more genuine narrative on the selective privatization of the local settlement mechanism and the enacted modes of production, and explains the architectural typologies and (sub)urban models it generated.

From Private Associations to Private Corporations: The Low-Rise *Stars*

The *Stars (HaKochavim)*, is a term that refers to a series of localities that were developed along the Green Line in the 1990s; they form a new step in the privatization of the Israeli settlement mechanism. The term usually includes the new sites of Harish, Bat Hefer, Tzoran, Matan, Tzur Yigal, El'ad, Tzur Yitzhak, Shoham, and sometimes even the city of Modi'in. Although the *Stars* today refers to a variety of settlements of different sizes and socioeconomic backgrounds, the original idea

[21] Kipnis, "Potential of Developing Urban Housings along the Hills Axis."
[22] Eldor, "Letter from the Head of the MCH's Department of Urban Development, Sofia Eldor, to the CEO of MCH, Asher Wiener – 25.10.1984."
[23] Eldor, "A New Town in Modi'in," 2.   [24] Eldor, 3.

was to develop small-scale suburban localities along the Green Line, that would attract young families seeking better living conditions. Despite the intensified settlement efforts, as discussed in the previous chapter, in the early 1990s there were barely 100,000 Jewish Israelis living in the immediate vicinity of the Green Line, on both its sides, while there were almost 250,000 Palestinians.[25] Continuing the demographic turf battle, the Israel Land Administration and the Ministry of Housing and Construction began to search for additional state-owned lands in the area which could house additional settlements. Eventually, these new sites were integrated with the state's larger plans to stimulate the development of the area by promoting the enlargement of existing localities, the acceleration of ongoing planning efforts, and the transformation of several sites from suburban to more urban settlements.

As a geopolitical and economically liberal project, the Stars were promoted by the right-wing, pro-laissez faire Likud government. One of the main driving forces behind the Stars was parliament member Michael Eitan, whose leading role in the development of Kochav Yair we discussed in the previous chapter. Eitan, along with several other politicians and planning officials, was interested in repeating the success of Kochav Yair and thus began to promote plans for multiple Suburban Settlements. The method was very simple as it included the cooperation of the Israel Land Administration to find and assign vacant parcels along the Green Line and the government's financial support for young families interested in relocating to the area. At first, Eitan's plan included seven new settlements, which he called the *Seven Stars*. Stars (*Kochavim*), referred to the Kochav Yair model, and also to the Seven Stars Flag that nineteenth-century Zionist leader and thinker Theodor Herzl had suggested for the future Jewish state.[26]

Territorially focused, the Stars were initially intended to settle both sides of the Green Line. Nevertheless, with the generous financial aid from the US government, which opposed its money being invested in the West Bank, all the new Stars were supposed to be built on official Israeli territory. Their objective was thus to enlarge the main metropolitan area eastwards and to fortify Israeli presence along the Green Line. This stronger presence would later limit any potential cross-border connections between Palestinian localities in the West Bank and those

---

[25] ICBS, "Localities in Israel"; PCBS, "Localities in the Palestinian Authority."
[26] Eitan, The Construction of Kochav Yair.

inside Israel and minimize the option of land swaps between Israel and any future Palestinian entity.[27]

As a territorial project, efforts to detect potential sites were directed by the geopolitical importance of every possible location; each spot was analyzed according to concepts of scarcity (of settlements), interconnections (between Jewish settlements), and separations (between Arab areas). As a parliament member and head of the subcommittee for Construction and Housing, Eitan was in charge of coordinating the work of the Israel Land Administration, the Ministry of Construction and Housing, and parliament, while working closely with the Jewish Agency and heads of the regional councils. At the same time, as a supply-side-oriented project, discussions were attended by representatives of the Association of Israeli Contractors and each site was examined according to the practicality of its fragmentation into marketable parcels. For example, the report stated that as Kibbutz Yad Hannah Meuhad, where a suggested site had previously been assigned, was going through a process of liquidation, the Israel Land Administration would be economically able to retake the "parcels" in question. Still, it was the territorial importance that the report highlighted, emphasizing the "high importance of the site of this settlement on the Green Line, as in this area there are only a few small Jewish settlements."[28] The same applied to Sha'ar Ephraim, where the report claimed that "[we] must state that beside Nitzane Oz, the settlement is surrounded by large Arab towns ... [it] is on the Green-Line in the narrowest part of the State of Israel, only 15 km from the seashore." The geopolitical agenda is made even more obvious in the recommendation for a "lookout or a military base" near the Arab villages of Ibtin, Marja, and Beit a Siqa.[29]

For the "Stars Plan" to become an integral part of the state's mode of production it needed the support of the Ministry of Construction and Housing, ensuring the involvement of the state's various capacities and turning the new plan into a large-scale national project. The prosettlement Minister of Construction and Housing, Ariel Sharon, endorsed the project in a personal meeting with Eitan in October 1990, asking "why only seven?," thus advocating for a larger scale of

---

[27] Soffer, The Stars; Gazit and Soffer, *Between the Sharon and Samaria*, 77–87.
[28] ILA, "Planning and Establishing New Settlements along the Green-Line," 2.
[29] Ibid.

The Low-Rise Stars 169

Figure 5.2 Detailed lots of proposed sites: *upper row* (from left) Yad Hannah (Bat Heffer), Tzur Yigal, Matan, and Kfar Ruth (Lapid); *lower row* (from left) Holot Geulim (Tzoran), Khirbet Mazor (El'ad), and Budrus (not built) (ILA)

development.[30] With the ministry on board, its rural division took the lead, as its vision called for small-scale suburban localities as well. With the first report's geopolitical analysis, the Directory of Rural Settlement and the Israel Land Administration collaborated in analyzing further the feasibility of each site, and recommending alternative sites for those that were less practical (Figure 5.2).[31]

As part of the state's new mode of production, the Stars were integrated into the new supply-side approach that advocated for corporate efficiency and profitability as a means to reignite the stagnating construction industry and to mitigate the upcoming housing crisis. Therefore, besides the financial aid and guarantees to developers, in 1990 the government implemented special measures in the Planning and Building Law, designed to swiftly authorize and execute large-scale residential projects.[32] In the existing planning routine, a new urban

[30] Eitan, The Construction of Kochav Yair.
[31] MCH Directorate of Rural Construction, "Land Allocation for New Settlements."
[32] Alterman, *Planning in the Face of Crisis.*

outline plan was required to go through several planning administrations, in a process that could take several years; the new measures were therefore made to reduce this process to a few months. The Ministry of Interior, in charge of the national planning process, formed a special housing committee in each planning district, which assembled all the necessary authorities into a single team, dealing with and authorizing only feasible large-scale residential compounds. This enabled the mass production of housing units that would increase the overall national supply, wherever possible. Initially valid for six months, the government repeatedly extended the special measures, and all the Star sites were authorized by one of the special Housing Committees.

The Stars Plan was officially authorized by the Israeli Government in December 1990 as a demographic and geopolitical project. Being part of the early 1990s immigration policy, it was discussed and approved by the Ministerial Committee for Aliyah and Integration.[33] Decision A/82 thus stated that:

[As] part of the governmental policy regarding Aliyah and integration [we have decided] to authorize the "Seven Stars" plan for the development of communal-suburban settlements along road number 6, which constitutes part of the larger plan for nation-wide housing solutions for new O'lim and those entitled to [support] by the Ministry of Construction and Housing.[34]

The authorized plan had three main objectives: "1. Preparing housing solutions ... by enlargement of housing supply. 2. Establishing a mixed communal fabric of new O'lim and Israelis ... 3. Creating a settlement sequence in the Hills Axis, [with] the aim to thicken the [Jewish] settlement in the area, and to execute the population dispersal policy."[35]

Highly suburban, with a significant emphasis on commuting and a growing dependence on private initiative, the Stars Plan suited the metropolitan-based national planning approach that relied on enhancing existing economic centers. The government's decision declared that the plan would consist of twelve new settlement points, offering

---

[33] Aliyah (עליה): literally meaning "ascent," a term used to describe Jewish immigration to Palestine, and later the State of Israel. It is common to refer to the first waves of Zionist immigration in 1882 as the first Aliyah (*Haliyah Harishona*). Jewish immigrants to Israel are referred to as *O'lim* (ascenders), while emigrants are referred to as *Yordim* (descenders).
[34] Ministerial Committee Aliyah, "Decision A/82," 3.   [35] Ibid., 4.

28,000 dwelling units to 100,000 inhabitants, which would be developed by the Ministry of Construction and Housing, housing associations, and housing companies. While larger than the preliminary plan, the decision continued the initial suburban focus, stating that the new settlements "would be of communal suburban character, while especially focusing on maintaining the principles of quality of life and environment," and that these would rely on "existing employment, education and cultural centres in Gush Dan and the central cities." Creating a series of dormitory suburbs, the plan thus relied on developing the "needed roads and connections to the Tel Aviv metropolis" that were crucial to its success.[36]

Alongside the government's approval, the Ministry of Construction and Housing began the planning and development process by defining the preferred clientele and a suitable residential environment that would enable each of the sites to become marketable real estate. In 1990, the ministry had already commissioned different planning offices for each of the locations and provided them with detailed programs regarding the character of each settlement, the nature of the future environment, the density and type of dwelling units, as well as the desired socioeconomic composition of the future population. Attuned to the initial suburban focus, the guidance consisted of low-rise, low-density Suburban Settlements with an emphasis on private units, with detached, semidetached and terraced options. Correspondingly, the target population was predominantly what the ministry referred to as "housing improvers" – young upper-middle-class families that were interested in better living standards in a suburban community.[37]

The comparable target groups and planning guidelines eased the fragmentation and homogenization of space expected from the increasing involvement of the private sector, resulting in similar property-oriented layouts. With the focus on creating a tract development scheme that parceled each site into individual private plots and a system of primary and secondary roads, the various layouts were very alike and relied on the same planning principles. Lacking an apparent hierarchy, the proposed outlines were concentrated on the private lot, the privacy of the private family, and car accessibility. The implementation of these principles varied, as the planners had to adjust to each site's restrictions and topographical characteristics. The outline

[36] Ibid., 5.   [37] Fogel, Highway 6 Settlements.

172 5 *Mass Suburbanization and the* Stars *Settlements*

of Tzoran, a site with minimal height differences and size limitations, consisted of an open grid of primary roads and cul-de-sac streets that could have continued endlessly having not been bound, thus, forming an abstraction of the contemporary suburban ideal. In all other sites, which were located on hillier terrain and closer to the Green Line, highways and other localities, the planners had to project the abstract suburban grid on the given topography while squeezing it between the fixed boundaries. Nevertheless, despite the small nuances, the suburban characteristics of all the plans were quite evident, promoting the cost-efficient formation of homogenous communities housing car-dependent commuters (Figure 5.3).

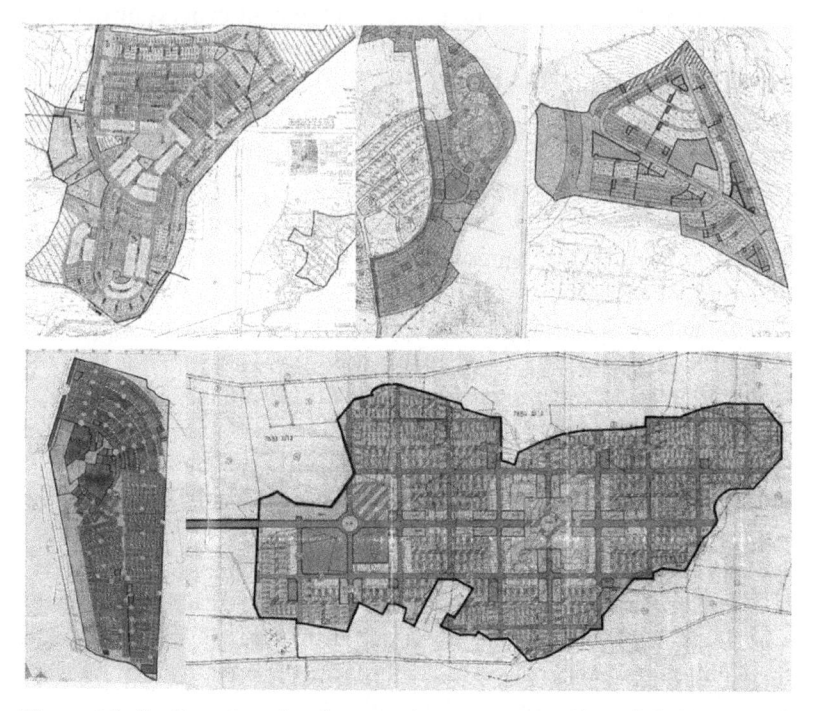

Figure 5.3 Outline plans for the new sites: *upper row* (from left) Tzur Yigal, 1991 (note Kochav Yair to the north, Kibbutz Eyal to the west and the Green Line determining its eastern border), Matan, 1991 (note Yarhiv to the west and the Green Line to the east), and Lapid, 1991 (note the Green Line to the west, Kfar Ruth to the south and a road to the east); *lower row* Bat Heffer, 1991 (note the Green Line on the right and an existing road and the future transnational highway on the left) and Tzoran, 1991 (ILA)

As an early example of the supply-side territorial approach, the initial mode of production regarded the future settlers as part of the supplying side, and the state sought to motivate their interests as a means to stimulate the development process. Therefore, it initially planned to develop the Stars using the method of organized housing associations – nonprofit organizations in charge of constructing houses for its registered members. First, the Ministry of Construction and Housing planned and authorized the new settlements. Then, commissioning one of the governmental construction companies, *Shikun U'Pituah* or *A'rim*, to conduct the groundworks and develop the necessary infrastructure, the ministry converted each site into parcelled compounds that would then be tendered out to different associations. These were basically exclusive marketing agencies that ensured the suited profile of upper-middle-class (Jewish) families, and they conducted selective and elaborate marketing campaigns that targeted their preferred clientele while emphasizing the promise of better living standards (Figure 5.4).[38] Despite having seemingly restricted spatial privileges, the new associations therefore retained the power to shape the character of the future community, enacting different selection criteria and ensuring a homogenous composition. Accordingly, being Jewish was cited as one of the main criteria for new members joining one of the associations that would inhabit parts of Matan and Lapid.[39] Later, this criterion was eased into one that was more politically correct, listing military service as a necessity, which, as the Arab population in Israel is not mandatorily drafted, practically also means being Jewish.[40]

Figure 5.4 A single-family house (left), a double-family house (middle), and a terraced house (right) in Tzur Yigal, 1991 (Gil-Ad Architects)

---

[38] Tzur Yigal Association, "Tzur Yigal."
[39] Yahad Shiveti Yisrael, "Association Rules," 5.
[40] ZP Association, "Association Rules," 5.

Eventually, due to the amateur nature of the nonprofit associations and the state's interests in mass development, the Ministry of Construction and Housing was quite reluctant to continue with this model and began to rely more on private corporations, thus enhancing its supply-side approach.[41] While a few associations were able to manage the process efficiently, in the long run, both the ministry and the Israel Land Administration saw them as inefficient and unreliable partners. In respect of the first tenders, the majority of associations that were granted compounds were unable to keep to the demanding schedule and witnessed a significant loss of members. Consequently, the ministry began tendering entire compounds to private contractors instead, and while housing associations had earlier been in charge of almost half of each settlement, in later projects like Bat Heffer all of the various compounds were exclusively tendered to private developers (Figure 5.5), thus enacting an enhanced supply-side mode of production.

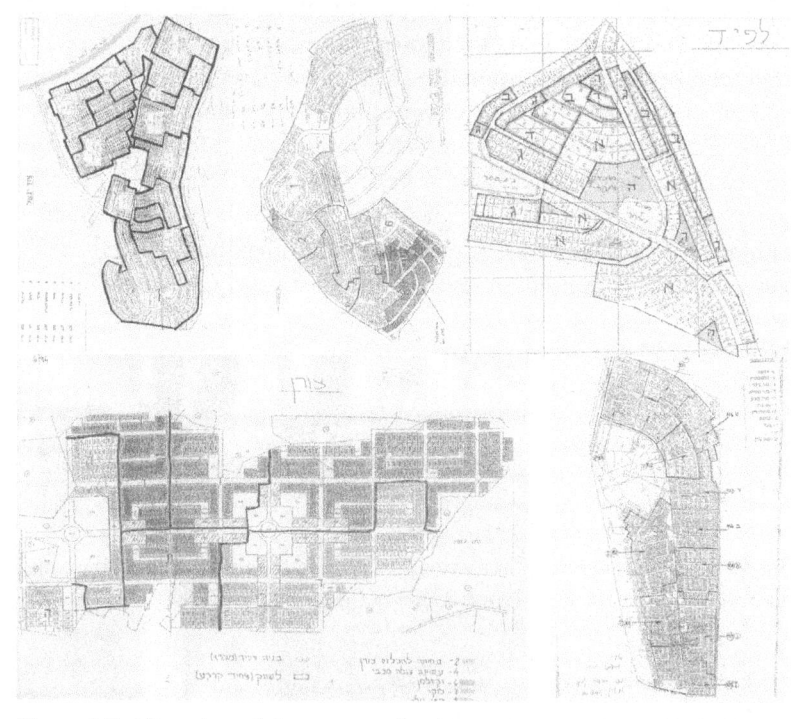

Figure 5.5 Allocation of the areas to developers, 1996: *upper row* (from left) Tzur Yigal, Matan (Yarhiv), and Lapid (Kfar Ruth); *lower row* (from left) Tzoran and Bat Heffer (ISA)

---

[41] MCH, "Construction through Associations," 137–51.

The corporate mode of production carried out by the Ministry of Construction and Housing significantly homogenized the new settlements, putting in place limited suburban models and housing types. Whether developed by an association or by a private contractor, all the new projects consisted of a single housing model, implemented in the different lots, with differing size options. Consequently, due to the uniform architecture of its houses, each part of the settlement received an obvious and undeviating character. Focusing on the privacy of the nuclear family, the houses repeated the popular seclusion method that separated the inner parts from the surrounding environment. Yet the 1980s' popular split-level model disappeared, and almost all the houses in the Stars were unilevel, whether one-story or two-stories high. At the same time, the emphasis on seclusion was enhanced through the central role separating fences and walls began to play; these formed an integral part of the planning principles and design regulations while creating a continuous uniform barrier to each row of houses. Suiting a suburban environment, the single-slope, red-tiled roof remained a must, adorning all the new houses. Eventually, the recreated compounds of reproduced white cubes covered with red roofs, surrounded by stripes of greenery, roads, and parking places became the hallmark of Green Line suburbia (Figure 5.6).

The strategy behind the Stars was a supply-side housing policy integrated with the national geopolitical project. To provide housing solutions for the new ex-Soviet Jewish immigrants, the overall supply of dwelling units had to be increased. Enlarging this supply did not only mean constructing new apartments for the use of the new *O'lim*, but also releasing those in the coastal plain that were already occupied by offering the inhabiting families better living standards in the new developing suburbia. This, as explained in the plan, also met other national objectives, which included strengthening Israeli presence in the area and expanding the Tel Aviv metropolis eastward. In light of the national privatization measures, the state granted specific private developers and housing associations the power to construct and inhabit space, as long as they enhanced the state's power over it. Ultimately, although the plan mentioned the integration of *O'lim* in the new settlements, this rarely happened. In the sites presented here more

Figure 5.6 Houses in Bat Heffer, 2002 (Avi Ohayon – GPO). In the background is the settlement's surrounding wall placed on the Green Line.

than 95 percent of the population had been born in Israel,[42] and they were mostly well-paid, upper-class,[43] secular Ashkenazi Jewish families, owning more than 90 percent of the houses.[44]

The Stars Plan was based on a descending order of supply-side mechanisms that eventually led to a new settlement typology. To stimulate the housing market, the government regarded upper-middle-class families as part of the supplying side, giving them the option to affordably purchase a new suburban house as a means to *supply* vacant apartments in the coastal plain. Looking for more efficient development, the government eventually chose to involve more private developers by tendering entire compounds, thus enabling the developers to optimize the construction process and *supply* the needed private houses in a faster and more reliable manner. The supply-side approach had a great effect on the seemingly monotonous new suburban environments that consisted of repetitive rows of private houses and

---

[42] Ministry of Aliyah Integration, "O'lim 1989–2015 According to Settlements."
[43] ICBS, "Wages and Income from Work by Locality and Various Economic Variables – 2013."
[44] ICBS, "Population in Jewish Localities, Mixed Localities and Statistical Areas, by Selected Countries of Origin."

reproduced residential compounds. In the sites that were developed later, the supply-side factor would continue to evolve, leading to an even more evident monotony.

Slumurbia: El'ad

El'ad, with its unique societal composition and a relatively high-rise environment, presents an exceptional case study of the privatizing settlement mechanism and is a unique mode of production. Housing some 50,000 inhabitants, it is the second largest Jewish locality between the cross-country highway and the Green Line. Officially urban and populated mainly by large, low-income, Ultra-Orthodox (*Haredi*) religious Jewish families with an average of seven children per household, El'ad is nowhere near the standard of the low-rise bourgeois Star suburbs it was initially part of. It is characterized by a much higher, denser, and more affordable built environment than all the other settlements in the region.

The part the Ultra-Orthodox sector took in the territorial project of political Zionism was not a natural one. In fact, relations between the sector, which forms more than 10 percent of the local population, and the State of Israel are quite complex. The Ultra-Orthodox's disapproval of any changes in the Jewish way of life creates a situation where being more religious does not automatically mean more nationalistic, with the sector's main leaders initially opposed to the idea of an independent Jewish state due to is reliance on secular ideals; some segments still do not acknowledge the State of Israel today. Conversely, large parts of the sector eventually took a very active part in the local political system, while maintaining a secluded and clearly introverted community life; this includes living in distinct residential areas, a segregated educational system, and low participation in the workforce, while focusing on religious studies at a *Yeshiva*,[45] all meant to ensure an isolated everyday life. The two main Ultra-Orthodox concentrations are in Jerusalem and Bnei Brak, a city in the Tel Aviv metropolis, which form the sector's cultural and spiritual centres. The sector's accelerated natural growth, which derives from its emphasis on childbearing, has led to an ever-growing shortage of dwelling units in both cities, ultimately leading to an increase in the need for more Ultra-Orthodox neighborhoods. At the same time,

---

[45] A Jewish religious educational institution.

as a significantly poor group, the Ultra-Orthodox sector is unable to compete in the "free market" and therefore needed to develop its own internal one, with government assistance.[46]

The state's concern to address the housing shortage of one of its poorest communities might seem like a continuation of the welfare approach, yet it is in fact an additional case of selective privatization. In the privatizing Israeli economy, the commodified social services became political goods, provided to privileged groups and sectors in exchange for their support for the ruling regime. The participation of the Ultra-Orthodox parties of *Agudat Yisrael*, and later, *Yahdut HaTorah*, *Degel HaTorah*,[47] and *Shas*[48] in almost all coalitions and governments since 1977, no matter whether right or left, highlights their realpolitik approach. They have supported key governmental decisions, such as peace agreements and territorial withdraws, on the one hand, or wars and military campaigns, on the other, in return for economic support for the sector's institutions and its special needs and demands.[49] This creates what Gutwein refers to as an alternative welfare system that runs parallel to the prevailing neoliberal agenda and reinforces it, directing state funding through alternative channels – religious institutions in this case – while increasing the power of the Ultra-Orthodox leadership in return for their support for the ruling government.[50] This enabled the further seclusion of the Ultra-Orthodox sector, which is highly visible in state-endorsed Ultra-Orthodox housing projects and settlements that simultaneously meet both the sector's desires for social seclusion and national territorial interests to distribute the local Jewish population.

Eventually, the Ultra-Orthodox sector became part of the state's strategy of decentralization and an active agent in the domestication of the Green Line, a role that it refrained from playing until the late 1980s. As proximity to the main centres in Jerusalem and Bnei Brak was crucial, the new sites for Ultra-Orthodox settlements had to be on

---

[46] Cahaner, "Between Ghetto Politics and Geopolitics: Ultraorthodox Settlements in the West Bank," 126.
[47] These are political parties that are the main representatives of the Ultra-Orthodox Ashkenazi sector.
[48] A party which represents the Ultra-Orthodox Mizrahi sector, as well as parts of the traditional and orthodox Mizrahi communities.
[49] Cahaner, "Between Ghetto Politics and Geopolitics: Ultraorthodox Settlements in the West Bank."
[50] Gutwein, "The Settlements and the Relationship between Privatization and the Occupation."

the new periphery along the Green Line. Not surprisingly, the largest West Bank settlements are actually the Ultra-Orthodox cities of Beitar-Illit and Modi'in Illit, which house almost 30 percent of the entire Jewish population in the Occupied Territories. While both these cities form a suburban extension to Jerusalem, the city of El'ad on the Israeli side of the Green Line, is an extension of Bnei Brak.

El'ad was originally an integral part of the low-rise Stars Plan. In the plan it was named *Ancient Mazor*, a reference to the historic Roman remains near moshav Mazor and the ruins of the depopulated Arab villages of Al-Muzayri'a and Qula.[51] The site had already been reserved for a future military compound and the new plan was to turn it into a new Suburban Settlement. Nevertheless, in a meeting between Minister of Housing Ariel Sharon, who took full control of the Stars Plan, his deputy, Rabbi Avraham Ravitz from the Degel HaTorah party, and several Ultra-Orthodox leaders, it was decided to assign the site to the Ultra-Orthodox public, granting it the spatial privilege to exclusively inhabit the future settlement. Compatible with the initial development method of the Stars, the development process was put under the management of an Ultra-Orthodox housing association, *Beit U'Menuha*,[52] despite the project's exceptional scope.

Still, the El'ad's initial plans resembled those for the other Stars settlements.[53] In the ministry's program the *Star* of *New Mazor* was described as a settlement of 3,000 low-rise dwelling units, consisting of private detached and semidetached houses, serving secular families looking for better living standards.[54] Later, as the Ministry of Construction and Housing adjusted the project to the needs of the Ultra-Orthodox sector, it abandoned the small-scale, low-rise suburban vision, improving its affordability and cost efficiency while simultaneously expanding the overall number of dwelling units. Accordingly, the upper-middle-class Suburban Settlement of white houses covered with red roofs gave way to a denser, mass-produced residential environment and the ministry's new requirements began to speak of more than 6,000 dwelling units and a population of almost 35,000 inhabitants.

[51] Khalidi, *All That Remains: The Palestinian Villages Occupied and Depopulated by Israel in 1948*.
[52] MCH, "Meeting at the Office of the Minister of MCH in Tel Aviv – 6.9.1990."
[53] Fogel, Highway 6 Settlements.
[54] MCH, "Program for a Detailed Urban Plan: Ancient Mazor."

Enacting a more corporate-led mode of production, the Ministry of Construction and Housing appointed the government company *A'rim* Ltd to manage the planning, development, and marketing processes. In doing so, the ministry moved to a more commercial method and gave up the initial intention to develop El'ad through the *Beit U'Menuha* housing association.[55] The latter tried to object to this change of policy and even sued the State of Israel for reneging on their agreement. Yet their claims were rejected by the Tel Aviv District Court, which ruled that the promises made earlier by Minister Ariel Sharon were illegal.[56]

The more corporate approach made the intention to assign the entire project to a specific sector of the population a complicated task. Consequently, El'ad could not be assigned exclusively to Ultra-Orthodox families and the emphasis was therefore on a "religious public." The Ministry of Construction and Housing could not officially enforce a selective marketing process and instead had to do this through planning, promoting an urban layout with civil and cultural infrastructure that would appeal to the Ultra-Orthodox sector rather than the general secular population. The official focus was thus "the need of religious families ... with all that implies," and this included an emphasis on economically constructed large dwelling units.[57] In enforcing these planning measures, the ministry believed that secular families would eventually stay away from El'ad, as they would not want to live within a population with strong religious characteristics and modes of everyday life. The ministry therefore doubted the intentions of organized secular groups that claimed they wanted to purchase apartments in the new project and regarded them as mere provocations, meant to protest against the luring conditions given to religious families.[58] The ministry's assumptions proved correct as eventually these organizations did not make any real attempts to purchase apartments in the town.[59]

The promoted plan for El'ad focused on generating an efficient and resourceful urban layout that would optimize the development process. The Ministry of Construction and Housing commissioned the office of

[55] Beit U'Menuha, "Decisions regarding Mazor (El Ad)."
[56] Tel Aviv District Court, Beit U'Menuha against the State of Israel.
[57] A'rim, "El'ad – Mazor," 2.
[58] Petersburg, "Ultra-Orthodox Trying to Prevent National Religious to Settle in El'ad"; Wasserman, "MCH: Contractors That Purchased Lands in El'ad Are Prohibited from Selling Units to Seculars," 5.
[59] Krispel, El'ad.

Hertz, Fogel & Schwartz to conduct the planning process, which would dictate the urban layout and main design regulations. The company, which had also been in charge of the district outline plan ten years earlier, was an experienced team of planners that worked closely with the various government ministries and planning administrations. With the new vision, the planners had to set aside their initial suburban concepts, drafting a large-scale masterplan, which could later be processed into smaller, more detailed outline schemes. Using a system of wide access roads, the masterplan proposed an arrangement of 50 m deep mono-use blocks, divided into two rows of 1,000 m^2 residential parcels. With a single façade facing the street, this layout enabled a highly efficient partition that reduced construction and development costs while increasing profitability and the marketability of each lot.[60] The same logic, just on a smaller scale, was applied to the low-rise residential compounds; here, the planners did not use the common cul-de-sac typology and preferred to create residential areas that could be divided into two rows of plots, each accessible from a different road.

The strict division between the different functions and residential areas suited the Ultra-Orthodox demands for social segregation. Despite the superficial homogeneity of the Ultra-Orthodox sector, it in fact consists of numerous groups and congregations. Therefore, in separating the residential functions from the areas for large public buildings, while designating a small-scale public function in each housing compound, the masterplan allowed for the formation of isolated communities, concentrated around their own religious institutions (Figure 5.7). Correspondingly, the lack of public open spaces in the center of town is very noticeable; the planners thought these would be less needed by this unique population, and located them in the northern and southern fringes of the residential areas. Moreover, with the majority of males being full-time *Yeshiva* students, the need for a large number of occupational opportunities was quite redundant; as a suburb of Bnei Brak, the planners predicted that those that did work would retain their existing jobs outside of El'ad.[61] Despite an anticipated population of more than 40,000 inhabitants, the plan therefore lacked almost any commercial or industrial zones.

---

[60] Fogel, Highway 6 Settlements.
[61] Fogel-Hertz-Schwartz Architects and Planners Ltd, "Local Outline Plan: New Mazor GZ/BM/195."

Figure 5.7 El'ad masterplan, 1992 (MCH)

The detailed instructions that followed the masterplan included further guidelines that corresponded with the vision of a resourceful and cost-efficient development. Processing the overall vision into smaller zoning schemes, the planners drafted the building and design regulations and parcelled areas into marketable lots, whether for low-rise or high-rise construction. The division into smaller parcels meant that the buildings could be constructed adjacent to one another, making a sequence of buildings, thus enabling a single contractor to efficiently develop a given compound and ensuring the profitability of the process. Characterized as a low-income Ultra-Orthodox community, the planners predicted that the likelihood of maintaining a plastered white façade would be very low, and therefore sought to require cladding each building with limestone. This, they thought, would also contribute to a more "Jerusalem-like appearance," which corresponded with the population's religious profile,[62] and the initial instructions even included tilted red roofs. However, to reduce construction costs and to increase future revenues, the Ministry of Construction and Housing and the developers objected to all additional expenses, reducing the limestone cladding to 30 percent of the front façade while limiting the tilted roofs to areas with significant topography.[63]

[62] Fogel, El'ad, 12. [63] Fogel, Highway 6 Settlements.

Slumurbia: *El'ad* 183

With tight profit margins and the emphasis on cost efficiency, the developers of El'ad were all large-scale construction corporations that could afford to take the risk. After some setbacks, the marketing process began in mid-1996; it took the Ministry of Construction and Housing two years from the approval of the first detailed plan to start tendering the site.[64] The ministry eventually chose to give the various contractors the rights over several joint compounds, which they were able to plan, develop, construct, and sell to private individuals. This limited the number of possible contractors, as they needed to have the necessary expertise and guaranties for a project of such scope. Moreover, as a low-cost project, the construction had to be very efficient, and so only highly experienced firms were able to compete. Tenders were made using a fixed price method, in which contractors vouched for a maximum value per dwelling unit as part of their bid. Consequently, the already limited profit margins were further reduced, limiting the competition even more. Eventually, the chosen contractors were leading companies including *Solel Boneh*, *Ashdar*, *Minrav*, and *Heftziba*.[65]

To ensure the development of El'ad, the state made several supply-side interventions that guaranteed the interests of the private sector. First, in order to facilitate the targeted low-income Ultra-Orthodox population, the state offered an additional subsidy of 25 percent for development costs, on top of the earlier ministerial and governmental grants.[66] Second, the ministry, together with A'rim, decided to develop El'ad as a *closed market*, meaning that all unused funds would be invested back in the town's infrastructure, thus improving the town's appearance and functioning and attracting more developers and contractors.[67]

To secure the purchasing power of the Ultra-Orthodox sector and to optimize sales, the chosen private developers were hardly involved in the marketing process. As a low-cost project, the contractors did not invest too much in advertising and commercials and preferred to promote their projects through the various religious associations and congregations. The contractors would contact, or be contacted by, a certain Hasidic or Ultra-Orthodox group that would become responsible for spreading the word and organizing families interested in moving to El'ad. The religious associations thus functioned as

---

[64] Petersburg, "Tender for Apartments in El'ad Begins," 13.
[65] MCH, "El'ad."   [66] Government of Israel, Decision 778.
[67] MCH, "El'ad: Adjusting Land Costs and Analysing Apartment Prices."

advertising and sales agencies for the contractors, and individuals who contacted the private developers were usually referred to one of these associations.[68] In doing so, the contractors were able to ensure sales and to minimize promotion costs, while the religious associations were able to reserve entire compounds for the use of their members, or for families affiliated with their religious approach. Furthermore, the contractors could not lawfully prevent nonreligious families from purchasing apartments, and by passing the marketing process to the religious associations, the contractors and the Ministry of Construction and Housing were able to restrict sales to the orthodox and the Ultra-Orthodox sector without encountering any legal repercussions.[69]

The prodevelopment approach promoted further selective privatization measures and adjusted the development process to the considerations of private contractors. Accordingly, the Ministry of Construction and Housing endorsed continual construction and, in what was clearly a corporate-oriented move, it started the works on the second stage before completing the first one, thinking that increased construction would promote the image of a successful and attractive project that would attract additional developers and potential buyers.[70] The slow development of the first phase was also an outcome of the relatively low sales to the Ultra-Orthodox sector, causing contractors to market units to families from the orthodox sector, while also reducing the speed of construction. Consequently, in the first phase almost half of the dwelling units were sold to national-religious families, leading to a minor conflict in which the Ultra-Orthodox sector sought to minimize the presence of all other religious streams in El'ad.[71]

With the support of the state, Ultra-Orthodox leaders thus tightened their relationships with the private developers, ensuring their exclusive status in larger segments of the town while also increasing the Ultra-Orthodox character of El'ad, limiting TV services and issuing a special subsidized and gender-separated bus service to Bnei Brak.[72] The intensified exclusive Ultra-Orthodox approach enabled the Ministry of

[68] Kessler, "Savione HaShem," 12–16.
[69] HaModiya, "Arrangement for the Construction of the Hasidic Qirya," 5; Cohen, "A New Ultra-Orthodox Qirya in El'ad."
[70] El'ad Council, "Marketing Quarter B in El'ad."
[71] Maor, "Half of 200 Homebuyers in Ultra-Orthodox El'ad – National Religious."
[72] Petersburg, "Ultra-Orthodox Trying to Prevent National Religious to Settle in El'ad."

Construction and Housing to avoid its biggest concern – setbacks caused by developers postponing construction due to predicted low sales. The new connections and deals between the developers and various Ultra-Orthodox congregations ensured that all apartments were sold before construction began, guaranteeing the necessary capital before the project started. Subsequently, all the apartments were bought almost entirely by Ultra-Orthodox families.[73] Nevertheless, not all contractors were successful in affordably managing such low-budget projects and one of the companies, *Heftziba*, an expert in ventures of this sort, went bankrupt in 2007.

The enacted mode of production concluded in the use of minimal building types and apartment typologies. Although more than 20 private developers were involved in the city, hiring more than 20 different architects and completing more than 700 buildings, the architectural product was highly repetitive. Almost all the residential buildings, except for the semidetached houses,[74] followed two main housing models that were reproduced all around El'ad. The first is the elongated complex, usually referred to as a *train building* (*Shikun Rakevet*). This typology consists of four-story buildings with two apartments on each floor, consisting of a living room and kitchen area at the entrance, taking up the back to the front façade, with the bedrooms parallel to it.[75] The second main housing type is the H building, which consists of four apartments on each floor, resembling the first typology, yet differing in the number and orientations of the exterior façades. Lacking a rear façade, the kitchen, located near the living room and at the entrance of each unit, is ventilated through a cavity in the side façade, creating a more enclosed and efficiently used space.

These housing typologies were not unique to El'ad, yet their implementation was. The units' inner arrangement had minimal requirements of areas and spaces, which is highly visible in the buildings' outline. Therefore, unlike similar projects at that time, the buildings in El'ad were strictly cubic, characterized by a marginal envelope surface. The windows and openings reflected the affordability of the project as well,

---

[73] Taskir, "Survey of Homebuyers in El'ad."
[74] El'ad Local Construction Committee, "Permit 960087 (El'ad)."
[75] El'ad Local Construction Committee, "Permit 960033 (El'ad)"; El'ad Local Construction Committee, "Permit 960034 (El'ad)"; El'ad Local Construction Committee, "Permit 960046 (El'ad)"; El'ad Local Construction Committee, "Permit 990025 (El'ad)."

as they were significantly minimal, unlike the desire of that time to create open façades. Moreover, the chosen low-cost building materials and inexpensive details consisted of plastered walls and affordable cladding stones where they were required. All of this led to a significantly uniform environment, made out of repetitive sealed cubes with small holes as windows. An additional distinguishing architectural feature is the *Sukkah* terrace that is noticeable in all the buildings in El'ad. According to the Jewish Torah, during the feast of *Sukkot*, it is mandatory to dine and sleep in a *Sukkah* (hut), made of temporary materials and located under the open sky. The ability to fulfill this custom in an apartment building is quite problematic, due to the usually small common balcony that is generally not located directly under the sky. Consequently, tenements housing highly religious families would usually include *Sukkah* balconies, a series of large terraces that do not overlap, facilitating the placement of a kosher *Sukkah*. Accordingly, the regulations for this type of balcony were mentioned in the masterplan for El'ad, excluding them from the overall built area that was allowed, so giving developers greater building rights and ensuring that the *Sukkah* terraces would not be built instead of livable areas.[76] As a result, the buildings in El'ad are covered by an exterior layer of retreating or *jumping* large balconies, which simultaneously breaks the town's cubic appearance and enhances its uniformity (Figure 5.8).[77]

El'ad is the outcome of a unique mode of production that relied on the collaboration between the state, religious sectors, and private capital, eventually creating a new local urban–suburban hybrid. Unlike previous settlements in the area, which were designed according to the *pull factors* of the suburban environment, El'ad was developed to answer the *push factors* of the urban. In a survey conducted by the Ministry of Construction and Housing in 2000, the families in El'ad stated "the ability of purchasing an apartment" and the proximity to Bnei Brak as the main reasons for moving to the new settlement. "Quality of life," on the contrary, was the least stated motive.[78] The affordability of the dwelling units, as well as the high subsidies, might seem like a Keynesian residue from welfare state housing policies. On the other hand, the applied selective welfare approach highlights that in

[76] Fogel-Hertz-Schwartz Architects and Planners Ltd, "Local Outline Plan: New Mazor GZ/BM/195."
[77] El'ad Local Construction Committee, "Permit 20020179 (El'ad)."
[78] Taskir, "Survey of Homebuyers in El'ad."

Figure 5.8 Dwelling types in El'ad, 2007 (left–right) single-family houses, "Rakevet" buildings, and H-buildings (Moshe Milner – GPO). Note the "jumping" balconies.

privatizing Israel affordable housing became a political commodity, traded for the sake of electoral allegiance. As a city assigned to one the weakest socioeconomic groups, with minimal taxable commercial and industrial uses, El'ad is among the poorest 20 percent of all Israeli localities. It constitutes an example of state-designed *slumurbia*, and its spatial morphology thus derives from the attempt to profit from this low-budget project.

High-Rise Suburbia: Tzur Yitzhak

The last developed Star, Tzur Yitzhak, included a greater involvement of private capital and concluded in a unique hybrid of a high-rise suburb, representing an advanced stage of the privatization of the Israeli geopolitical project. It began as an integral part of the Stars Plan and turned into a new, denser, and urban-like variation of it. Initially referred to as Tzur Nathan B, or simply the Tzur Nathan project, as it was planned as an expansion of a nearby rural settlement bearing the same name. Like the other Stars, it was originally the responsibility of the Ministry of

Construction and Housing's rural division, and supposed to resemble the other low-rise suburban settlements built in the area. Nevertheless, with the change in the ministry's policy, the project moved to a new mode of production, involving a larger number of dwelling units using higher and denser housing typologies.[79]

With the increasingly metropolitan-based approach, the state began to endorse a more "urban" image to the area while enhancing the supply-side approach, thus influencing Tzur Yitzhak's mode of development. The ministry moved the project, together with all the other Stars settlements, from its rural division to its urban one.[80] As all the other settlements were already under construction or in advanced planning stages, this decision did not really affect their nature. The Tzur Nathan project, however, was in the initial stages, which meant that the "urban" characteristics of its future environment would be much more evident. While the Ministry of Construction and Housing endeavored to promote a more urbanized character for the area,[81] the new outline plan for the central district categorized the project as an extension of the rural Tzur Nathan, but referred to it as a Community Settlement,[82] thus turning it into a rural, suburban, and urban hybrid[83] – a combination that would continue to mark the settlement over the years.

The new vision for an urban complex resulted in several objections from the nearby rural settlement of Tzur Nathan, which were appeased only after the latter was enabled to take part in the new mode of production. As the commissioned planners began composing an outline scheme for the new project that would turn the site into marketable parcels, the nature of these parcels was not yet clear. The Ministry of Construction and Housing and the Israel Land Administration were considering a residential project of 5,000 units, while Tzur Nathan and the regional council wanted to maintain the area's small-scale rural characteristics. Eventually, the parties agreed that the project would include around 3,000 units, with Tzur Nathan, the site's lessee, having the right to develop a third of all planned units.[84] In the meantime,

---

[79] MCH Directorate of Rural Construction, "Program for Tzur Nathan."
[80] MCH Directorate of Rural Construction, "The Stars Settlements."
[81] Halufa – Dov Kehat Ltd, "Kochav Yair – Options for Municipal formation."
[82] Fogel-Hertz-Schwartz Architects and Planners Ltd, "District Outline Plan TMM/3/21."
[83] MCH Urban Planning Unit, "List of the Stars Settlements."
[84] Tal, "Development Momentum"; Tal, "Tzur Nathan: Forgot the VLKH."

concerned that the new urban compound would change its rural nature, Tzur Nathan was interested only in the potential real-estate revenues from the new project and opposed the option of being part of the same locality. Thus, the Israeli Government, after receiving recommendations from the Ministry of Construction and Housing, the Israel Land Administration, and the regional council, decided to turn the new project into an independent settlement called Tzur Yitzhak, named after the former Prime Minister Yitzhak Rabin, who was murdered in 1995 while in office.[85]

The proposed outline proceeded with the fragmentation and homogenization of space while creating a new residential environment somewhere between urban and suburban models. The layout consisted of a system of wide car-oriented roads, rather than streets, that created three main residential areas, each defined by a circular setting surrounding a core with an open green space or a public institution. Seemingly urban, the project's vision was based on strong references to the surrounding suburban environment, lacking any apparent hierarchy, commercial uses, and other functions that went beyond the settlement's role as a dormitory town. Semiurban, the proposed environment included buildings of relatively moderate height, mainly two to five stories, with the exception of a ten-story tenement in the middle of the project. Additionally, tilted roofs adorned all the buildings and the vast system of open green spaces and connecting paths promoted a suburban-like appearance, offering a new interpretation of the term "urban" (Figure 5.9).[86] The project was thus planned as an enlarged and expanded version of the previous Stars settlements, and while the former layouts fragmentized and homogenized space two-dimensionally, the new plan did so three-dimensionally.

The urban turn and the increasing dependence on private developers delayed the completion of the project for an additional five years, causing the Ministry of Construction and Housing to find alternative supplying sides. One of the main reasons for the delays was the ministry's inability to market the project. By the end of the 1990s, after an extensive period of state-initiated or sponsored construction, the local market witnessed a state of recession that decreased both demand for new dwelling units and the willingness of developers and entrepreneurs to invest in large-scale projects. This affected the development of Tzur

---

[85] National Committee for Planning and Construction, "Meeting Number 534."
[86] Nir, Tzur Yitzhak.

Figure 5.9 Illustration of the Tzur Nathan project, 1997 (Meir Nir – Courtesy of Meir Nir)

Yitzhak, which the ministry initially thought would receive the same interest as other residential projects in the area; it thus authorized a similar mode of production that relied on private entrepreneurship.

The ministry rejected the attempts of housing associations to take part in the process, and when the *Pioneers of Tzur Nathan* association and its 1,800 registered families expressed their interest in participating in "settling thousands of Jews in ... the outskirts of Taybeh" as part of the mission to "stop the Arab expansion," the ministry was initially not impressed, counting on a private initiative of a much larger scale.[87] Yet, with the recession, the state had to return to earlier modes of production and the selective marketing techniques they relied on. The Ministry of Construction and Housing first thought of granting the IDF personnel branch the spatial privilege to develop the site, hoping to attract military families to the project as a means to accelerate development. However, as the latter was not interested, the ministry eventually marketed the lots to housing associations,[88] hoping that the relatively homogenous and select character would attract a critical mass of upper-middle-class families and ignite investment interest in the project.[89]

To promote the stagnated marketing process, the Ministry of Construction and Housing and the government construction corporation

[87] Rabin, "Building in Tzur Nathan," 2.
[88] Maor, "Marketing to Associations, the Improved Version."
[89] Lori, "The Strike of Real Estate Monsters Continues, This Time in the Tzur Yitzhak Version."

A'rim Ltd acted to ensure the profitability of future developers by granting them the power to reparcel the site. A'rim was well aware of and attentive to the demands of private developers. For instance, as each urban outline plan usually includes an architectural appendix, A'rim argued that such an appendix would be redundant as the private contractors developing each lot would eventually compose one of their own, which would better suit their economic interests.[90] With this statement, A'rim essentially gave away its responsibility for the nature of the future environment, granting prospective developers the spatial privilege of developing space according to their economic interests. Later, the Ministry of Construction and Housing, the Israel Land Administration, and the regional committee initiated and supported a series of new spot planning schemes that would make Tzur Yitzhak more attractive for investment. These included increasing the number of overall dwelling units, raising the height of buildings, merging parcels, and raising the number of permitted buildings per lot – all in order to "optimally use the building rights"[91] and adjust the existing outline to "the demands of the market."[92]

With private developers receiving additional powers to form space, they were able to secure the profitability of their investment. The changes they proposed were seemingly minor and were thus only subject to the local planning committee, ensuring an easier and quicker bureaucratic procedure. Such minor modifications cannot enlarge the overall permitted area for residential use, yet they can redistribute the inner functions inside the settlement, exchange lots, and alter the total number of units, buildings, and floors, thus ensuring the feasibility of construction. For instance, the original plan designated a strip of housing along the northern edges of the project that created marketing problems due to the proximity to the Arab city of Taybeh – not a feature that upper-middle-class Jewish families were seeking. Two local outline plans from 2008 and 2010 authorized exchanging residential lots with inner ones designated for public institutions.[93] Consequently, the schools and kindergartens, which were not subjected to marketing and real-estate interests, were to be located in the strip close to Taybeh, an area with substantially less economic potential. These amendment plans also allowed the construction of the same

---

[90] Bar, "Tzur Nathan."
[91] Golan Architects, "Town Outline Plan SD/MK/101/15/3," 2.
[92] Cohen Lifshitz Architects, "Urban Outline Plan SD/MK/101/15/8," 2.
[93] Mintz-Melamed Architects and Planners, "Local Outline Plan SD/MD/101/15/1."

Figure 5.10 Tzur Yitzhak, 2010 (Ori~)

residential square meterage in a smaller number of buildings, with a larger number of floors and apartments, thus increasing the ratio of units per stairwell. Construction costs therefore decreased, while higher quality apartments marketed as luxurious "villas in the air" were created[94] (Figure 5.10).

All of these aspects are clearly indicated in the marketing brochures for one of the projects built in Tzur Yitzhak, described as "an apartment in nature." The brochure includes a general map of the new settlement, an exemplary plan of an apartment, a view from a living room, and the usual explanatory text. The map, which points to the location of the project in Tzur Yitzhak, also states that the strip of schools on the northern edges is turned toward Taybeh, clarifying that it is not the housing units that do so. Moreover, the apartments are depicted as autonomous dwelling units, disconnected from all adjacent ones, a virtue that is highlighted by their outline, which mimics that of private houses. The

[94] Y. H. Dimri, "The Most Prestigious Villas in the Sharon Area Are in the Sky."

High-Rise Suburbia: Tzur Yitzhak

living room oriented toward a nonexisting open view and the promotion text enhance this idea further:

Along the Samarian slopes, opposite to HaMarzeva Valley, right near Alexander stream and the blossoming Tzur Yitzhak forest. There, amid nature, with no barrier to the view and the open air, stands a residential project. The project overlooks the entire settlement of Tzur Nathan in the Sharon, and is close to Highway 6 and 531, so it is easy to get to employment and recreation places in Gush Dan and the Sharon cities in general.[95]

This quote illustrates the logic of the new Tzur Yitzhak, a notion of living in an open landscape, away from city life, but accessible to all the major highways. One is supposed to seek employment, recreation, and cultural life outside the settlement. Inside the settlement, one should only desire to be at home with one's family.

The refragmentation and rehomogenization of Tzur Yitzhak transformed the initially planned suburban residential environment into a high-rise housing semiurban development. While the changes that were made to increase the profitability of the project could perhaps also be explained as beneficial to future inhabitants, it is quite hard to make such a claim in this case. For example, although the original plans included underground parking and positioning the buildings so that the entrance was at street level, the new plans raised the entrance level above the street, thus raising the ground floor over the entrance level, and allowed for above ground parking places. This eventually resulted in sharp height differences between the residential buildings and the surrounding environment; and it is difficult to understand the social or aesthetic benefits that derive from the long continuous and closed supporting walls that were included in the amended plans, which function as the buildings' main façades.[96]

The changes in the plan for Tzur Yitzhak also affected its architectural design. Except for modifications in the height, scale, and number of units, the new regulations enabled the redistribution of the overall permitted area along different floors. This supported the construction of larger apartments on the upper floors, where real estate is of a higher value. Consequently, this resulted in giving the buildings in Tzur Yitzhak a mushroom-like appearance, dictated according to the value of a square

---

[95] Hanan Mor Ltd, "Apartment in Nature – the Green Spot in Tzur Yitzhak."
[96] Drom HaSharon Local Council Construction Committee, "Permit 20090085 (Tzur Yitzhak)."

meter that corresponded with the floor on which it was located. The intensified prodevelopment approach eventually determined almost every aspect of the built environment of Tzur Yitzhak, from the zoning plan to the apartment, leading to a settlement made up of isolated buildings, surrounded by parking places and supporting walls.

The prodevelopment approach assisted in overcoming the rough start Tzur Yitzhak initially experienced. Besides the marketing problems and the recession in the construction industry, the violent events of the Second Intifada, which began the same year as approval of the outline plan, resulted in a further decrease in interest in dwelling units in this particular area.[97] Eventually, the construction of Highway 6 and the West Bank Separation Barrier, together with the end of the Second Intifada and the post-2008 national housing crisis, turned Tzur Yitzhak into an attractive real-estate project, with substantial rises in property values that doubled in less than ten years,[98] reigniting the circle of supply and demand.

The eastern part of the settlement would undergo a large number of changes, brought about by the developers' interests in further optimization. This area was mostly handled by the Tzur Nathan council, which received building rights according to the aforementioned agreement with the Israel Land Administration. Here, the involvement of the Ministry of Construction and Housing was minimal, and it even stated that it had no interest in developing this area.[99] To properly develop it, Tzur Nathan teamed up with a private entrepreneur, creating a unique public–private partnership, in which the public agency lacked almost all concerns other than financial interests. After the approval of the first outline plan in 2000, the partnership, together with the Israel Land Administration, submitted three different amendment plans to the local committee, which the latter approved. Despite the official objective of rearranging the public parcels in the site, the amendment plans were used to redistribute building rights inside the new neighborhood,[100] eventually creating a series of mid-rise "boutique buildings"[101]

[97] MCH, "Tzur Nathan – SD/101/15/D."
[98] Buso, "Once an Apartment Was Worth Half a Million Shekels."
[99] Bar, "Tzur Nathan," 1; Steinmentz, "Tzur Nathan," 1.
[100] Dov Koren Architects, "Local Outline Plan SD/101/15/5"; Dov Koren Architects, "Local Outline Plan SD/101/15/12"; Dov Koren Architects, "Local Outline Plan SD/101/15/18."
[101] Drom HaSharon Local Council Construction Committee, "Permit 20090215 (Tzur Yitzhak)."

surrounded by sixteen-story residential towers. This was a huge extension of the initially approved five-story layout.[102]

The transformations in the supply-side mode of production turned Tzur Yitzhak into an undefinable settlement type. Completely suburban, yet with sixteen-story residential towers, it is entirely different from previously constructed settlements nearby. This new type of high-rise suburbia was not implemented exclusively in Tzur Yitzhak, however, and since the late 1990s it has begun to mark the entire area along the Green Line, be it in new settlements like El'ad, Modi'in, Modi'in Illit, Shoham, and Harish, or in the expansion of previous low-rise ones like Rosh Ha'ayin or Alfei Menashe. Nevertheless, in Tzur Yitzhak there was not only a question of appearance and design but also an issue of managerial and municipal governance. With its low-rise suburban neighbors refusing to merge with it,[103] Tzur Yitzhak is officially a Community Settlement, a definition that is usually reserved for small-scale, semirural settlements. In practical terms, it is more of a hybrid of suburban ideas and seemingly urban ones, functioning as a gated compound of high-rise residential buildings placed on a hilltop.

The State Creates a Market That Shapes the State

Following their previous gentrification, both sides of the Green Line were ready for mass suburbanization during the 1990s. Fueled by geopolitical considerations and a desire for a vast production of dwelling units, the development of the area turned into a national project executed by private capital. Consequently, as shown in this chapter, the former association-led mechanism was weakened and eventually abandoned, as the state preferred to rely on the experience and profit incentives of private developers. Endorsing this new mode of production, the state commodified its frontier, hoping that this would generate a circular process of supply and demand. To create the needed real-estate market, it made major administrative and planning interventions that were meant to promote an efficient and swift development process that would secure the investments of private entrepreneurs. Enacting such a top-down process meant that the state took back the power to plan and form space, which it had previously granted to the early

[102] Mevnim Ltd, "Marom HaSharon."
[103] Levi, "A Committee of the Interior Ministry Recommended."

housing associations and developers active in the area. The spatial privileges were thus mainly property rights and the ability to develop a specific site.

As mass-produced projects, the architectural and (sub)urban models introduced in the Stars settlements were the product of the new supply-side perspective and the growing involvement of the private sector. The earlier focus on the detached house and the seclusion of private family life from the wider communal context was not forsaken, but rather enhanced by market incentives to produce an ever-growing number of units. In this sense, the commodification of space, manifested in the tract housing developments, suited the detached suburban lifestyle urban families were looking for when moving away from the cities. Lacking almost any employment and recreational opportunities and made up of free-standing residential buildings, the newly evolving high-rise suburbia could be understood as a vertical tract housing development, subdividing a particular area in all three dimensions. Disconnected through retaining walls and parking places, with an outline imitating the layout of a detached private house, the recently designed buildings form a collection of isolated dwelling units, thus constituting a scaled version of the earlier Suburban Settlements.

With growing reliance on the market, the profitability of a particular urban plan became a leading concern. Consequently, the (sub)urban and architectural form of the new environment was heavily dictated by speculative interests. With an increase in demand for housing units, the state focused on creating more urban-like settlements, which are a more economically efficient use of a given site, concentrating efforts and enlarging profits. At the same time, as demand decreased, the state acted to create one, solving the "market failure" by promising the economic feasibility of the project and, with it, the continuation of the development of the entire area. Later, as the state was entirely dependent on private capital, it endorsed a new mode of production, granting private developers additional spatial privileges by giving them the power to form space through the promotion of new schemes or by amending existing ones. In doing so, it hoped to meet the developers' speculative interests and to ensure the realization of the project – completing the domestication of the frontier and securing the state's power over space. Thus, this state-created market eventually began to physically shape the same state that created it.

During the 1990s, the settlement development mechanism turned into a supply-side territorial policy, focused on creating a market as a means to promote spatial control. Whereas classic supply-side housing strategies are usually used to meet the public need for dwelling units, in this case the state intervened in order to regenerate it. Harish, the focus of the next chapter, illustrates how the supply-side territorial approach continued to develop, leading to the financialization of the national settlement mechanism.

6 | *Financialization and Harish City*
Merging Financial and Geopolitical Frontiers

Forming a Crisis

The increasing privatization of the Israeli settlement mechanism – and its growing reliance on the private sector – eventually resulted in a gradual process of *financialization*. In this new mode of production, the focus is on economic feasibility and its use as a means to involve the private sector in the construction of new territorial settlements.[1] Accordingly, following the post-2008 national housing crisis, the Israeli Government sought to appease growing public pressure by stimulating the real-estate market, increasing the focus on property, and regenerating the financial aspect of development once again. The government's main strategy relied on tendering state-owned lands, deregulation of the planning process, and offering economic incentives to private developers, with an emphasis on large-scale developments that would increase the overall supply of residential units. Consequently, undeveloped planned cities, new urban quarters, and various settlements, the execution of which had been continuously halted, swiftly became sites of rapid construction. With a strong focus on the geographical periphery and areas of so-called national priority, the state hoped to use the increasing need for dwelling units to develop previously underdeveloped peripheral and frontier areas, thus opening new financial frontiers in order to domesticate national ones.

This chapter focuses on the city of Harish, a unique case study whose various attempts at development demonstrate the gradual privatization of the Israeli settlement mechanism, the various modes of production it relied on, and the different architectural and urban models these produced. The first attempts included a kibbutz, a Community Settlement, and, later, a Suburban Settlement. While for more than three decades

---

[1] Schwake, "Financialising the Frontier: Harish City."

these attempts recurrently failed, it was the post-2008 crisis that enabled the current development of Harish, turning it into the fastest growing city in the history of the State of Israel.

Focusing on Harish, the chapter illustrates the financialization of the national settlement project, explaining how the state apparatus was used to create a real-estate market in a particular area, supplying the dwelling units that were needed while expanding the national territorial project. Analyzing the different modes of production that the development of Harish utilized, the chapter demonstrates how the ability to produce space turned into the main settlement tool. First, a turf battle between different groups seeking spatial privileges that was eventually won by large-scale corporations is investigated; this led to a new phase in the privatization of the settlement mechanism. The Green Line was thus domesticated by the completion of its transition into a real-estate market, while, at the same time, new architectural and urban typologies were promoted – planned and designed to absorb and generate private investment while enhancing the state's control over space.

Financializing the Frontier

The worldwide financialization of the built environment forms a new phase in the capitalist mode of production. As an advanced step in the global neoliberal turn, it continues the worldwide liquidation of the welfare state approach concluding in the "financialisation of everyday life."[2] Real-estate-oriented urban development is not a neoliberal invention, and one can trace speculative approaches to planning back to the nineteenth century, and even earlier.[3] Lefebvre's critique of the modern state's mode of production focused on pre-neoliberal apparatuses and its efforts to create "manageable, calculable and abstract grids," simultaneously homogenizing and fragmenting space as a means to turn it into interchangeable commodities.[4]

Financialization is thus not the simple speculative production and consumption of space, but rather a "multidimensional, contested and conflictual process," controlled by financial actors and funded by

[2] Graeber, *Debt: The First 5000 Years*, 347.
[3] Moreno, "The Urban Process under Financialised Capitalism," 260.
[4] Brenner and Elden, "Henri Lefebvre on State, Space, Territory," 367; Lefebvre, "Space and the State," 233.

asset-backed securities, hedge funds, holding companies, and securitization.[5] The postwar capitalist mode of spatial production analyzed by Lefebvre seems innocuous in comparison to the current neoliberal one, and, while homeownership was already an integral part of capitalist society, in neoliberalism real estate as investment became the only way to participate in the new economic order.[6] Consequently, market-led instruments became the main factors in urban policies, and planning turned into a finance-oriented strategy focused on constantly promoting additional speculation and investment as a means to persistently reignite the economic system.[7] Thus, the spatial fixity of real estate is mediated by the financialization of new investment frontiers, intended to expand the boundaries of urban development.

Financialized urban development relies on a "complex meshwork" of "multiple opportunities for value-creation," eventually turning cities "into real estate controlled and managed within financial markets."[8] Urban planning thus becomes a framework focused on promising the "yield," the return on investment, that the financiers of urban development anticipate,[9] and, as Samuel Delaney has noted, "more important than whether the buildings can be rented out ... is whether investors *think* the buildings can be rented out."[10] Consequently, built space turns into an assemblage of assets, "packed together with mortgages and traded on the market as a financial instrument."[11] Not surprisingly, once use-value entirely gives way to exchange-value, this transformation into assets leads to a greater level of standardization and homogenization of the built environment.[12]

Financializing the Israeli geopolitical project meant tying it to the rationale of real-estate investment. Therefore, what began by depending on the economic interests of developers and entrepreneurs and on the

---

[5] Gotham, "Creating Liquidity Out of Spatial Fixity: The Secondary Circuit of Capital and the Subprime Mortgage Crisis," 360.
[6] Harvey, *The Limits to Capital*.
[7] Tasan-Kok, "Changing Interpretations of 'Flexibility' in the Planning Literature: From Opportunism to Creativity?," 187; Rolnik, *Urban Warfare: Housing under the Empire of Finance*.
[8] Moreno, "The Urban Process under Financialised Capitalism," 260–64.
[9] Moreno, "Always Crashing in the Same City: Real Estate, Psychic Capital and Planetary Desire," 157.
[10] Delaney, quoted in ibid., 163 (emphasis added).
[11] Haila, *Urban Land Rent: Singapore as a Property State*, 72.
[12] Rolnik, *Urban Warfare: Housing under the Empire of Finance*, 233.

quest of Israeli families for better living standards or more affordable housing solutions, eventually turned into a series of market-oriented measures that included mass marketing of state-owned lands, tax exemptions for entrepreneurs, and accelerated bureaucracy. Advancing to a new mode of production, the state focused on merging financial frontiers with geopolitical ones, facilitating the survival of its territorial agenda in a time of increasing neoliberalism. This financialized territorial approach received a boost following the 2008 world economic crisis, which initially derived from overfinancialized real estate and was, ironically, followed by further financialization as a means to reignite investment and regenerate the economy.[13] In the case of Harish, the financialized mode of production was intended to help solve the national housing crisis while simultaneously enhancing the state's control over the Green Line.

The Crisis and Emergency Measures

The 2008 world financial crisis significantly affected the Israeli housing market. Initially, it seemed that this small and relatively isolated economy would be left untouched by the global confusion, with the local banking system and stock exchange witnessing modest fluctuations. Eventually, however, the post-2008 years became a period of rapidly increasing real-estate prices. The usual explanation is the lack of sufficient development during the late 1990s, following the early 1990s construction boom. Other explanations point the finger at the low interest rate set by the Israeli Central Bank, parallel to similar decisions worldwide. This, together with stock market uncertainty, turned real estate into the most common investment method.[14] As Boruchov shows, although official state claims spoke of a "real" deficit of tens of thousands of dwelling units annually, a proper analysis of the statistics indicates a significantly lower number. Demand for housing was thus not only due to the annual production of dwelling units lagging behind the yearly increase in households; it was also due to the increasing profitability of real-estate investment.[15]

[13] Peck, Theodore, and Brenner, "Neoliberal Urbanism Redux?," 1093.
[14] Boruchov, "On Target: The Housing Crisis and Damage to the Planning System," 63–70.
[15] Boruchov, "On Target: The Housing Crisis and Damage to the Planning System," 80–85.

Or, in other words, the increasing demand was not only for the *use-value* of housing but also (or even mainly) for its *exchange-value*.[16] But regardless of whether it was a question of lack of supply or high demand, increasing housing prices led to huge demonstrations in summer 2011, which became known as the Israeli Social Justice Protests.[17] They focused on the rising living costs of the local middle class, and especially emphasized ever-increasing rental prices and property values.[18]

In the post-2008 housing crisis, the Israeli Government continued with its decades-long supply-side housing approach, which sought to promote the construction of dwelling units by stimulating the private market.[19] As in similar neoliberal economies, bureaucracy and regulations turned into the new public enemy that prevented the public from receiving the services it believed it was entitled to.[20] Accordingly, prime minister Netanyahu promised a "Supertanker" against bureaucracy, which would enable the immediate construction of hundreds of thousands of dwelling units in a short period of time.[21] Using the supertanker metaphor, the large firefighting aeroplane Israel had borrowed from the USA in the efforts to extinguish the Carmel fires a year earlier, Netanyahu expressed his desire to promote massive government interventions that would bypass existing planning and construction procedures.[22] Netanyahu's supertankers included a new National

---

[16] Harvey, *Seventeen Contradictions and the End of Capitalism*, 15–25.
[17] Alfasi and Fenster, "Between Socio-Spatial and Urban Justice: Rawls' Principles of Justice in the 2011 Israeli Protest Movement"; Marom, "Activising Space: The Spatial Politics of the 2011 Protest Movement in Israel."
[18] Allweil, *Homeland: Zionism as Housing Regime, 1860–2011*, 1–26.
[19] Carmon, "Housing Policy in Israel: Review, Evaluation and Lessons"; Barzilai, "Fantasies of Liberalism and Liberal Jurisprudence State Law: Politics and the Israeli Arab-Palestinian Community."
[20] Harvey, *A Brief History of Neoliberalism*, 61; Graeber, *The Utopia of Rules*, 6–29.
[21] Charney, "A 'Supertanker' against Bureaucracy in the Wake of a Housing Crisis: Neoliberalizing Planning in Netanyahu's Israel," 1224; Somfalvi and Lahav, "Natanyahu on Housing: Supertanker for Bureaucracy."
[22] Charney, "A 'Supertanker' against Bureaucracy in the Wake of a Housing Crisis: Neoliberalizing Planning in Netanyahu's Israel," 1224; Mualem, "Playing with Supertankers: Centralization in Land Use Planning in Israel: A National Experiment Underway," 270; Eshel and Hananel, "Centralization, Neoliberalism, and Housing Policy Central–Local Government Relations and Residential Development in Israel," 238.

Housing Committee, deregulation and acceleration of planning processes, and easing the private development of state-owned lands.[23]

The main challenge facing the Israeli Government, to enlarge supply in areas of high demand, caused it to try to expand the main metropolises into the peripheries and internal frontiers. With the local neoliberal turn and its metropolitan-based planning strategy, the government did not abandon its territorial agenda and continued to invest in the development of settlements in areas of national interest.[24] With limited state-owned lands in areas of high demand and the national desire to continuously expand its power over space, the state sought to extend the areas of high demand while incorporating parts of the geographical peripheries and internal frontiers.[25] This eventually created a neoliberal frontier domestication mechanism by developing a real-estate market in areas of national interest, merging social, territorial, and entrepreneurial interests. To stimulate the interest of the private market, the state promoted special measures, like tendering state-owned lands at very low prices and creating new planning committees that bypassed the existing hierarchy.

The story behind the development of Harish, the focus of this chapter, illustrates the gradual privatization of the Israeli settlement mechanism, which led to its eventual financialization. This new city was an integral part of the government's recurrent efforts to enhance the state's control over the Green Line and the Wadi A'ara area, which, despite the development of the Reihan Bloc, was still predominantly Palestinian (Figure 6.1). From the late 1970s, the government led several unsuccessful attempts to develop the site, corresponding with the methods we have seen in previous chapters. However, it was the post-2008 housing crisis that eventually facilitated the mass development of the site, demonstrating a new mode of privatized production. Financializing the development of Harish, the state turned housing development into an ever-growing market, harnessing the interests of the private sector. Focusing on Harish's development stages and the modes of production they relied on, this chapter illustrates the gradual privatization of its development. Furthermore, by analyzing the architectural and urban products of each stage, the chapter clarifies the changing

---

[23] Rubin and Felsenstein, "Supply Side Constraints in the Israeli Housing Market: The Impact of State Owned Land," 267.
[24] Shachar, "Reshaping the Map of Israel: A New National Planning Doctrine."
[25] Charney, "A 'Supertanker' against Bureaucracy in the Wake of a Housing Crisis: Neoliberalizing Planning in Netanyahu's Israel," 1240–43.

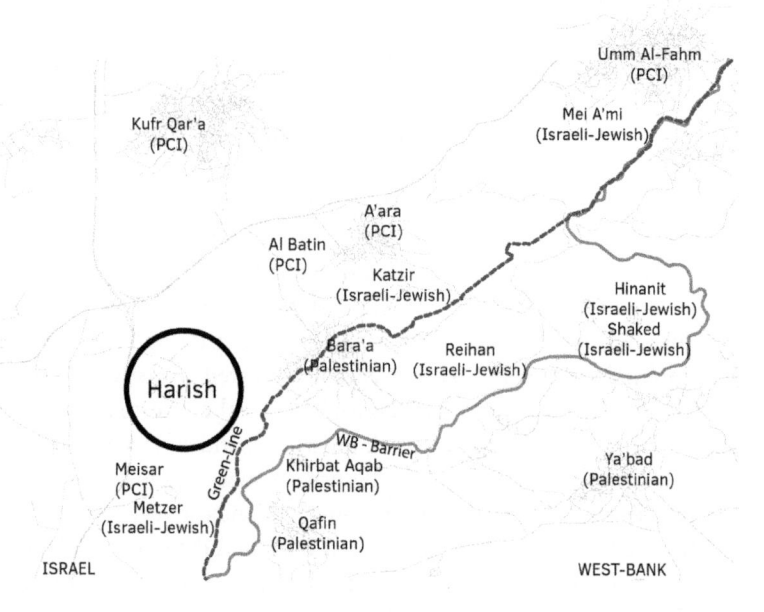

Figure 6.1 Harish in 2015, located on the Green Line between the West Bank Separation Barrier and the Arab area of Wadi A'ara (illustration by the author). Note: PCI – Palestinian Citizens of Israel.

public–private alliance and its influence on the production of space. Concluding with the current phase in the development of Harish, the chapter presents the spatial characteristics of the financialized settlement mechanism.

Kibbutz Harish and Moshav Katzir: Early Rural and Neo-Rural Attempts

During the past four decades, Harish has undergone various endeavors and transformations corresponding with changes in the local spatial development mechanism and the modes of production it has utilized. These include a frontier *Nahal* outpost that was supposed to be developed into a kibbutz, a Community Settlement, a large Suburban Settlement, a city for the Ultra-Orthodox sector, and, eventually, the current corporate-led mode. These variations ran parallel to local economic and political transformations and demonstrate the changing relation between the national agenda and the private market, as well as the growing reliance of the former on the latter. Overall, the case of Harish expresses the state's efforts to create new real-estate markets in order to promote national territorial considerations and to harness the interests of the private market to those of the state.

Today, Harish is still a city in the making, anticipating a future large-scale development. As of early 2019, it consists of around a 2,000 inhabited apartments with a population of just over 10,000. Currently, across the new town, there are some 4,000–6,000 dwelling units in various construction and approval phases; tens of thousands additional units are planned.[26] While the original target for 2020 was a city with a total population of 60,000, new objectives aim toward 100,000 inhabitants by 2030, balancing the approximately 150,000 Palestinians living in the adjacent area on both sides of the Green Line.[27] These ambitious intentions, if fulfilled, will turn Harish into the fastest developing city in the history of the State of Israel, surpassing all former precedents.

The site of Harish has long been part of the national geopolitical agenda. The first attempts to settle the site were made in the late 1970s as part of the Israeli Government and the Jewish Agency's (JA) Judaization campaign in northern Galilee. The state-led endeavors focused on establishing an array of small-scale Jewish settlements on state-owned lands, across the predominantly Arab area. These efforts turned into an official scheme named the Lookouts Plan, as they consisted of an initial temporary settlement phase, which usually included a provisional site on a vacant hilltop that later would become permanent. While the main focus was the upper Galilee, in what would later become the Misgav regional council, the JA located a few southern sites, west of the Green Line and in the mainly Arab populated areas of Wadi A'ara and the Triangle. The site of Harish was one of these sites, which also included the future settlements of Kochav Yair and Katzir, thus forming a counterpart to the settlement efforts inside the West Bank.[28]

The new site of Harish was also part of the state's strategic Nahal Eron Plan. Nahal Eron, or using its Arab name, Wadi A'ara, is an area

[26] ICBS, "Localities in Israel."
[27] ICBS, "Localities in Israel"; PCBS, "Localities in the Palestinian Authority."
[28] Soffer, "Mitzpim in the Galilee – A Decade of Their Establishment," 24–29; Falah, "Israeli 'Judaization' Policy in Galilee," 69–85.

in northern Israel with a significant Arab majority, who live mainly in the cities and towns of Umm al-Fahm, Kufr Qara, and Ar'ara, as well as in several smaller villages. The site's location near another group of Palestinian localities inside Israel, which includes Baqa al-Gharbiyye, Jat, Meiser, and Zemer,[29] and its proximity to the Green Line, meant that the Israeli Government was concerned about the formation of a significant Arab territorial sequence across both sides of the former border. It has constantly promoted the establishment of new Jewish settlements, which would prevent this potential sequence from forming and thus secure its control over this area. These settlements included the kibbutzim of Metzer, Magal, and Barkai in the early 1950s, the moshav of Mei Ami as part of the 1960s' Frontier Fortresses Plan,[30] and the Reihan Bloc of the 1980s that extended these efforts into the West Bank.

Besides the usual emphasis on rural and small-scale settlements, the various planning administrations were interested in promoting a new city in the area. Already, in the late 1970s, Baruch Kipnis' Hills Axis plan for the development of urban settlements along the Green Line mentioned three possible sites for a city in Wadi A'ara. These, according to Kipnis, "would enable introducing a big urban Jewish settlement in the Nahal Eron region, which constitutes a consecutive Arab area."[31] Discussing the potential sites, the Israel Land Administration preferred an option close to the Green Line, which would "break" the Arab sequence on both sides of the border, rather than those better connected to the coastal plain, thus favoring the territorial perspective over feasibility.[32]

Despite the growing urban focus, the JA decided to proceed with the rural mode of production, indicating the lack of economic feasibility for a larger-scale project. The masterplan for Settlement Development in the West Bank, which prevailed over the more urban idea, designated the area of Nahal Eron as a hybrid of agricultural and industrial villages with a population of around fifty families.[33] The early plan did not mention

---

[29] A merger of the villages of Bir al-Sika, Ibtan, Marja, and Yama.
[30] Tal, *The Frontier Fortresses Plan*.
[31] Kipnis, *Potential of Developing Urban Housings along the Hills Axis*, 18.
[32] Israel Planning Administration, "An Analysis for a New Jewish Settlement in Wadi A'ara," 2.
[33] Drobles, "Master plan for Settlement Development in Judea and Samaria, 1979–1983," 4.

the site of Harish directly, but, by the early 1980s, it was included in two different plans for the development of the area. Produced by the Settlement Division, the first plan declared both Harish and the nearby site of Katzir as Community Settlements, and therefore not agricultural ones.[34] Similar to other settlements developed at that time, they enjoyed a reputation of being rural-like or neo-rural, bearing names with strong farming connotations like Plough (Harish) and Harvest (Katzir). The plan of the Settlement Division a year later declared Harish as a kibbutz of the National Kibbutzim Movement, to be settled on a temporary basis in 1982, initially consisting of 15 interim units and later growing to 200 families engaged in intensive agriculture, cotton, and dairy farming.[35] It would thus become a rural settlement per se.

The first step resembled former rural examples and depended on the fusion of communal life, agriculture, and territory. In 1982, a settling group from the Nahal corps arrived at the site of Harish and established a temporary outpost. The Settlement Department had already conducted the necessary planning for the provisional site a year earlier, deeming it suitable for preprivatization development. Consequently, this supposedly temporary station resembled other frontier Nahal settlements and was made up of rows of prefabricated dwelling units and a communal clubhouse (Figure 6.2). Concurrently, the JA and the National Kibbutzim Movement promoted a plan to turn the temporary site into a permanent kibbutz, drafted by the technical department of *HaShomer HaTzair* movement, the intended settling body.[36] Following the classic kibbutz outline, the plan consisted of a communal public core, surrounded by the members' dwelling units, which were divided between regular, children's, and youth compounds, all sharing a common, open, green car-free space.

In keeping with the decline in rural settlement, Kibbutz Harish was short-lived. Despite its official "civilianization," the temporary site of Harish continued housing mainly Nahal settling groups, which lived and worked in it yet never turned it into an official permanent settlement; the plans for a full-scale kibbutz were therefore never fulfilled. The kibbutzim crisis of the 1980s, which left the movement almost

---

[34] Settlement Division, "A Proposal for Settlement Development in the Eron-Reihan Hills."
[35] Settlement Division, "Development Plan for Jewish Settlement in the Eron Hills-Reihan Region."
[36] HaShomer HaTzair Technical Department, *Outline Plan M/146*.

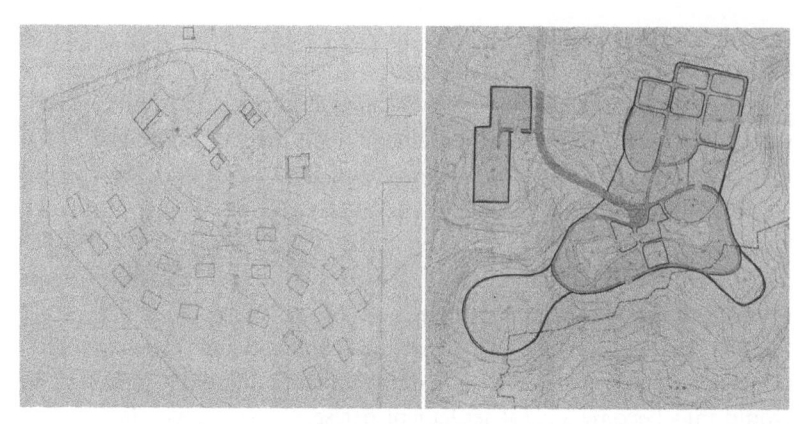

Figure 6.2 Temporary site of Harish, 1981 (Harish outline plan for Kibbutz Harish, 1984 – WZO)

bankrupt, as well as the inability to find a proper civilian settling group, eventually led to the failure of Harish as a communal rural settlement and by the early 1990s the site was evacuated.

While Harish was considered a failure, neighboring Katzir was more successful. Established in the same wave as Harish, Katzir was planned neither as a kibbutz nor as a *moshav*, but rather as a Community Settlement. Therefore, it was an outcome of a different, and more privatized, mode of production. It started as a temporary site as well, yet it was housed by a civilian settling group, organized by the JA, and not by the Nahal corps. The Agency was thus in charge of assembling the settling families and it prepared a small group of ten members who were granted the spatial privilege of settling the site. A year later, a group of ten additional families joined the original members, all of whom would live in temporary trailer-type, light-weight units supplied by the JA, while efforts to plan and expand the settlement were underway.[37]

As a Community Settlement, Katzir started out with a communal core that later formed the center of a future development, suiting its neo-rural profile. Similar to other Community Settlements, the layout of the initial phase consisted of temporary dwelling units, and it was made up of two parallel rows of houses, placed along the topographic lines. The JA planners located the public area of the settlement, including the secretariat and the members club, at the site's highest point,

[37] Lanir, "You Plowed and Harvested," 26.

which also formed the official entrance and the main parking lot. A series of pedestrian paths connected the settlement's center to each of the dwelling units, creating a well-integrated and communal compound based on private households, yet sharing a collective open space.

The plans for the expansion of Katzir were slightly more suburban and less communal compared with Kibbutz Haris. While the vision of the first phase focused on creating the communal basic core, the logic of the later phase was to form a series of detached lots that could be developed separately by newly admitted families. Thus, the new layout was a tract housing development made up of four dead-end streets that formed two rows of private parcels that could then be marketed to future members.[38] Despite its ability to attract several upper-middle-class families, the expansion plan was not completely fulfilled, and Katzir remained relatively empty. This was mainly due to the site's remote location and poor accessibility, which enhanced its pioneer-like image on the one hand, yet, on the other, prevented it from becoming an appealing settlement and limited its ability to attract additional families to the area.[39] In the 1980s Katzir was thus still an ex-urban settlement, built on the geographic periphery of the seam-zone, and not yet an ideal Suburban Settlement. Still, the border of the total area of Katzir, which was more than five times larger than the developed area, indicated future intentions to turn it into a much larger settlement. Forming a small-scale settlement with vast land reserves was a common territorial tactic, repeatedly used by Israeli planning administrations in order to limit the expansion of Arab localities, as constantly stated in a variety of settlement plans, both for the West Bank and pre-1967 borders.[40] However, while in previous cases land reserves had usually been farming plots, in this case they were merely a statement of intent regarding future actions.

Katzir-Harish: The Suburban Turn

By the early 1990s, the Israeli Government had already developed a new comprehensive vision for the area, with Harish and Katzir playing a major role in it. Both sites were incorporated into the wider

---

[38] Arye Sonino Architects, "M/139."
[39] Lanir, "You Plowed and Harvested," 26.
[40] Soffer, "Mitzpim in the Galilee – A Decade of Their Establishment," 24–29; Falah, "Israeli 'Judaization' Policy in Galilee."

Stars Plan, the development of Suburban Settlements along the Green Line. With the new vision, the Ministry of Construction and Housing shifted from state-led rural frontier settlement to a privatized mode that relied on the production and consumption of real estate as a means to encourage development. Corresponding to the new mode of production, both settlements lost their former frontier-like and ex-urban characteristics, turning into suburban residential environments. To encourage development further, the Ministry of Interior united both settlements into one council, and, though they maintained relative independence, they now formed a new locality named Tel Eron.

The new plans for Katzir transformed the initial small-scale layout into a large Suburban Settlement, adding two additional sites while expanding the original one (Figure 6.3). Adapting to topographic conditions and land ownership issues, the new plan, "Katzir: Emergency Site," consisted of separate "bubbles" of residential areas and a broken outline rather than a well-integrated plan.[41] As a new suburban environment, the proposed layout of Katzir was a tract housing development, which subdivided the site into uniform residential parcels. Based on a nonhierarchical system of access roads and cul-de-sac streets, the new plan focused on the private family lot, its autonomy and detachment, as well as commuting ability. In this sense, the proposed plan corresponded with other Suburban Settlements at that time. Yet, while other Stars utilized corporate-led or organized construction, Katzir was planned as a Build Your Own House project, and, unlike other upper-middle-class suburbs, Katzir also included several prefabricated units, issued for the use of Jewish immigrants from the former Soviet Union.

Figure 6.3 Outline plan of Katzir, 1981 (left), 1985 (middle), 1994 (right) (MCH)

[41] Lavi-Bar Architects and Planners, "Outline Plan M/196a Katzir: Emergency Site," 1–3.

With its relative distance from the Tel Aviv metropolis, Katzir was a decade behind in the mechanism of frontier settlement and was thus not able to rely on a completely privatized mode of production. Its remote location and lack of accessibility prevented the formation of the necessary conditions that would attract private developers. Its designation as a Community Settlement, with an active admissions committee that secured its members' spatial privilege of controlling its societal composition, hindered the potential of an intensive private-led construction project. Thus, Katizr became famous for refusing to admit the Arab Ka'adan family from the neighboring town of Baqa al-Gharbiyye. The settlement's admissions committee, backed by the JA and the Jewish National Fund, claimed that the lands of the settlement were designated as National Lands (*Admot Leom*), and thus intended for the exclusive use of the Jewish (not Israeli) nation.[42] The Israeli High Court of Justice eventually overturned this decision and enabled the Ka'adans to move to Katzir;[43] however, the case demonstrates the relative backwardness in promoting privatized geopolitical development in Wadi A'ara, and the need to apply nonmarket-oriented selection criteria as the site was not developed enough to use market-oriented criteria. In sites closer to the Tel Aviv metropolis, selection committees were not needed, mainly because housing associations, targeted promotion, and relative high prices guaranteed the desired upper-middle-class Jewish composition. In remote locations, ethnic homogeneity was maintained only through stricter benchmarks,[44] indicating the difficulty of creating a simple real-estate-oriented development that would prevent Katzir from becoming another reproduced suburb.

With the new vision for the area, Harish anticipated a future on a much larger scale and the Ministry of Construction and Housing began promoting its development as a Suburban Settlement. Enacting a new mode of production, the ministry commissioned a private architectural firm to produce a new outline plan for the site. In 1994, the new plan for a settlement of around 4,000 units received the official approval of the district planning committee, under the emergency regulations of 1990.[45] Typically suburban, the plan proposed a low-rise, low-density

[42] Barzilai, "Fantasies of Liberalism and Liberal Jurisprudence State Law: Politics and the Israeli Arab-Palestinian Community," 426–30.
[43] Israel High Court of Justice, Ruling 6698/95.
[44] Yacobi and Tzfadia, *Rethinking Israeli Periphery*, 35–52.
[45] Moshe Zur Architects and Planners, "Harish."

residential environment, with great emphasis on integrating with the natural landscape – going so far as to require the planting of a tree in each of the front yards.[46] The core of the plan was a *HaParsa* (the horseshoe) neighborhood, which was intended to become the first project of Harish, followed by the northern part and then the eastern neighborhood named *HaMagaf* (the boot). With four different housing types, the plan allocated each to a specific compound, creating homogenous residential quarters that would be gradually developed: starting with single- and double-family houses initially, and moving to denser three-story and terraced tenements in later phases (Figure 6.4).

Matching the new mode of corporate suburban production, the outline of Harish was a tract housing development that resourcefully subdivided the site into smaller lots. Using an excessive system of roads, the plan was highly car oriented, and while the main arteries created the residential areas, the secondary streets subdivided them into smaller marketable compounds and parcels. With the focus on production and consumption, the plan created housing complexes consisting of a single housing model, to be tendered to private contractors. Accordingly, the basis of this plan was the residential parcel and the ability to reach it with a private car. Each housing typology, low- or high-rise, dictated the specific dimensions of residential lots, which would facilitate an optimized future construction process. Forming two rows of the same housing type, the plan ensured an optimal ratio between roads and residential areas, dictating the distance between two parallel streets according to the dimensions of the housing parcels it served. The site's topography granted the proposed road system an almost perfect form, decreasing the necessary groundworks while creating a continuous, flowing car ride through the town, and providing the sought-after ease of access to each of the plots. While highly efficient for the residential lots, this circular setting created an abundance of leftover spaces in intersection areas. Due to their irregular proportions these spaces were of low economic feasibility for corporate residential development, thus becoming ideal spots for open areas and public buildings that are not subject to the rentability constraints of the real-estate market.

The proposed order of development also corresponded with the new mode of production. The first neighborhood to be developed included

[46] Ibid., 9.

Figure 6.4 Compounds of Harish, 1992 (Moshe Zur Architects – MCH)

mainly double-family homes and terraced houses, with several tenements in its center. The next area, the northern section, included a higher percentage of tenements, yet it was still mainly of lower density. The last phase of development was made up almost entirely of higher-density tenements. This resembled former examples, where the Ministry of Construction and Housing used low-rise and seemingly more prestigious units to attract well-established upper-middle-class families. They would then help in promoting a positive and esteemed image that would lead to an increase in the area's economic potential, creating the financial feasibility needed for the construction of higher-density dwelling units.

As a corporate-oriented plan, it was based on a clear marketing strategy that relied on a covert system of spatial privileges, intended to attract suitable middle-class families that would encourage demand and ensure the project's success. A market analysis, conducted by Tznovar Consultants Ltd for the Ministry of Construction and Housing, showed that in the surrounding area of Harish there was an expected surplus in both low- and high-rise housing. Yet, the report stated, these predictions could be overlooked if the ministry was able to promote Harish as an attractive settlement with high living standards, a strong proximity to nature, and a comfortable commute to the main metropolitan region. The report therefore suggested directing the first marketing efforts to attract "strong" young families, which, in return, would give Harish the required image of a settlement with an appealing community.[47] To promote this image further, the report also recommended marketing Harish as a "Green Urban Settlement" that blends with the natural landscape and has an environmentally aware community.[48] It also stated that the first units in Harish would need to be significantly cheaper than similar ones in the area. At the same time, the report warned against lowering prices too much, due to the potential of attracting families with a weaker socioeconomic profile as this would harm the desired image of the settlement. Thus, the suggested strategy was to target marketing at the desired type of family, which would gentrify Harish and enable development to continue according to an economic rationale. The internal report essentially concluded that there was not a market-based logic to build a new town, and it thus suggested tools that would promote the formation of such a market.

With the ministry's intentions of promoting concentrated construction, it tendered the first compounds to a single developer, a decision that would hinder the desired marketing strategy. Ashdar Ltd, the chosen corporation with a speciality in prefabricated units, had already played a leading role in the construction of a variety of settlements and several key national projects.[49] Due to its status and experience, it gained the privilege of being the single developer of the first compounds. This was a highly cost-efficient project that consisted of a series of ten three-story apartment complexes surrounding an inner courtyard, with a total of 250 dwelling units. The entire compound was made up of a single

[47] Tznovar Consultants Ltd, "Populating Harish Katzir," 1–10.   [48] Ibid., 5.
[49] Ashtrom, "Milestones."

Katzir-Harish: The Suburban Turn

Figure 6.5 First houses in Harish, 2000 (Moshe Milner – GPO). Note the high-rise buildings in the middle and the low-rise buildings at the back, surrounded by the street layout and parcels for future projects.

residential model that included eight similar double-bedroom apartments. Ashdar planned and constructed the buildings using prefabricated concrete slabs, coated with limestone and assembled on site, thus utilizing an industrialized and affordable construction process. The second and seemingly more luxurious compound included some fifty double-family houses, which were semidetached units, spread over two floors and covered by a pitched red roof. Yet, just like the denser apartment buildings, they were also made of prefabricated concrete walls covered with limestone (Figure 6.5).

Marketing and populating the apartments in Harish did not go as the Ministry of Construction and Housing expected, causing it to implement various selective promotion campaigns. According to an internal report, the ministry was unable to balance "geopolitical considerations" with "marketing concerns," causing it to rely on an inadequate private mode of development. Consequently, marketing the first 300 units was difficult and the fact that they were made of prefabricated concrete slabs did not help.[50] Due to the oversupply of apartments, the

[50] MCH Urban Planning Department, "Meeting Regarding Tel-Eron – 15.9.1993," 2.

ministry housed several families of former Soviet Union immigrants, mainly from the Caucasus area, while still trying to market the rest of the units. After two unsuccessful years, the ministry contacted Hever, the consumer club of Israel Defense Forces (IDF) personnel, in order to interest its members – military officers – in purchasing the remaining vacant units. Offering this group the chance of a house in Harish at an affordable price, the ministry hoped the respected public profile of the military would promote the image of the settlement, and thus help future development and marketing efforts.[51] Eventually, several IDF personnel purchased some 230 units in Harish, yet almost none of them actually lived in the settlement, preferring to rent out their properties. The failure to successfully market the first phase caused the Ministry of Construction and Housing to halt the tenders for the remaining compounds, and even to cancel the infrastructure development for the northern neighborhood.[52] At the same time, the idea of Harish as a settlement affiliated with the IDF interested the ministry, and, after receiving Hever's promise to assist in the marketing efforts, it began working on a new tender for some 200 Build Your Own House plots for military personnel.[53]

Although the ministry ceased construction of the remaining compounds, it continued efforts to reignite the development process by facilitating a more productive process of production and consumption.[54] The ministry's perspective was that an intense effort would eventually lead to the development of Harish and it thus hired an entire team of planners to produce a new masterplan, in an attempt to merge the isolated neighborhoods into one urban system. The changes and adjustments varied, one from the other, ranging from a low-rise military settlement to an Ultra-Orthodox town.[55] The focus was constantly on reigniting the development process, and, by 1997, the Ministry of Construction and Housing had invested tens of millions of US dollars in an unexecuted project.[56] As the ministry's urban planning unit took the lead, the new plans for Harish included exploring the option of creating a city of almost 200,000 inhabitants,

[51] Tel Iron Council, "Council Meeting 01/95," 1.
[52] Davidovic, "Haifa District – Harish – Tender #," 1.
[53] Dvir, "Meeting Protocol Regarding Tendering Lots in Harish 17.3.1996," 1.
[54] Eiges, "Development Works in Harish," 1.
[55] Dvir, "Meeting Protocol Regarding Tendering Lots in Harish 17.3.1996," 1.
[56] Karp, "Harish," 1; Meridor, "Harish," 1.

stretching over an area of around 1,000 km², including lands east of the Green Line.[57] The ministry persistently resisted readjusting its large-scale vision, and insisted on enlarging it further, assuming that as the project grew the interests of developers would grow as well.

By the late 1990s, the inconsistency between the plans of the Ministry of Construction and Housing and the demands of the market turned Harish into an ill-developed town. The repeated attempts to reignite the construction process failed, and, consisting only of a few buildings, Harish was not a small-scale Community Settlement, but rather an uncompleted urban project. The population of Harish was composed of Jewish Caucasian families from the former Soviet Union, and, mostly, tenants who rented apartments from property owners who were not keen on living in the undeveloped settlement. The Israeli Police and the Ministry of Interior relocated members of the Arab family of Karaja from the town of Lod to Harish in the late 1990s, in an attempt to resolve a long turf battle and vendettas – a step that, to say the least, did not improve the image of the town.[58] To make a comparison with Katzir, which shared a local council with Harish, on a scale measuring the socioeconomic deciles of localities in Israel, the population of the former was eight (with ten being the richest, and one the poorest), while the latter was two. The violent events of the Second Intifada, which started in 2000, and the mass demonstrations held by Palestinian citizens of Israel, especially in the Wadi A'ara area, did not improve the attractivity of Harish. Thus, while the ministry attempted to tender some 300 units to 5 different developers in 1999, these were conclusively revoked three years later, mainly due to a unanimous lack of interest.[59]

Promoting the image of Harish to assist its development involved both its residents and contractors. In a letter to the Ministry of Construction and Housing, the Katzir-Harish council highlighted the need for an "aggressive" marketing strategy,[60] demanding an elaborate public relations campaign focused on well-established groups, with an emphasis on employees in the high-tech industry, the military, and upper-middle-class families from the greater Tel Aviv area. The

---

[57] Freund, "Survey for the Extension of Harish," 1–5.
[58] Sandrov, "Local Council Katzir-Harish," 1.
[59] Zimmerman, "Tender 10025/99 HaParsa Neighbourhood – Harish," 1.
[60] Katzir-Harish Council, "Strategic Outline for the Development of Harish-Katzir," 2.

requested campaign included promotional pieces, in color, in "elitist" newspapers that would improve the popular image of Harish and address the sought clientele.[61] Other promotion techniques included a greater emphasis on Harish as a "green" town, such as naming the streets after the names of the area's fauna and flora. Disappointed by the ministry's lack of collaboration with attempts to improve the image of Harish, a group of organized residents sent an angry petition to the CEO of the prime minister's office. Emphasizing their despair – as well as their national leverage – they stated that should the current situation continue they would sell their apartments to the "highest bidder, meaning Arabs in the area";[62] similar statements were made by contractors active in Harish. Nevertheless, the expectations of the Ministry of Construction and Housing became quite pessimistic, and the head of the Haifa District, went as far as describing Harish as a site of "prostitution and drugs, which no sane person would like to live in."[63]

Harish: The Next City of Israel

By the early 2000s, it became clear that creating a market-led development in Harish in the current conditions was impossible, causing the state to implement a different mode of production and a new set of spatial privileges. An official report by the Ministry of Construction and Housing even stated that successful marketing Harish could be a double-edged sword, as it would also appeal to the Arab population in the area who would then also be interested in moving into Harish.[64] The report mentioned the Ka'adan case in Katzir and the fact that, unlike Katzir, Harish did not have an admissions committee that could prevent additional Arab families from joining. Therefore, as the appeal to the private market was not successful, and as a successful development might in any case lead to the Arabization of the planned settlement, the report suggested renewing the plans for an Ultra-Orthodox town.[65] The ministry had already considered this idea twice in the past, under two different administrations, but in the end it decided to drop the idea following negative feasibility assessments that indicated the likely failure of such a project.[66] However, as it was only the Ultra-Orthodox sector that had

[61] Ibid., 5. [62] Harish Representatives, "Harish Settlement," 1.
[63] Marom, "Tender 10025/99 – HaParsa Neighbourhood – Harish," 2.
[64] Rubenstein, "Harish Survey," 1–2. [65] Ibid.
[66] Rubenstein, "Proposal for the Planning of Harish."

Harish: The Next City of Israel

the ability to bring tens of thousands of (Jewish) families to the area, this scenario seemed to be the only way out.[67]

For the Ministry of Construction and Housing, an Ultra-Orthodox Harish was essentially the last opportunity to apply a privatized mode of spatial production. Approaching this sector did not mean that the ministry had given up on a market-oriented development, but rather that it wanted to implement a mode of production that matched the rationale of the Ultra-Orthodox real-estate market. The Israeli Ultra-Orthodox sector has, to some extent, its own internal economic system, which operates in parallel with the wider Israeli economy. As we discussed in the previous chapter, with a significantly low socioeconomic profile, considerably high fertility rates, and a fundamental need to live in secluded neighborhoods, the Ultra-Orthodox sector is constantly facing a housing crisis.[68] As the existing centers of Bnei Brak and Jerusalem were unable to continue supplying the needed dwelling units, the leaders of the Ultra-Orthodox sector, the Ministry of Construction and Housing, and some affiliated entrepreneurs and housing associations initiated and promoted several Ultra-Orthodox-oriented neighborhoods and settlements such as El'ad, Beitar Illit, Modi'in Illit, and others. The main components in an Ultra-Orthodox market-oriented development are its mass community and loyalty. Private developers would focus on cheap construction, while making deals with rabbis and leaders of the Ultra-Orthodox streams, who would guarantee the purchase of all units in a specific project. Relying on internal loans and mortgage systems, like the *Gemach* funds[69] – interest-free loans organized by each community – the Ultra-Orthodox sector is able to grant families the economic tools needed to purchase an apartment. This, of course, would only be done if the family belonged to the same Ultra-Orthodox community and was intending to use the loan to purchase an apartment in one of the community's residential projects, facilitating alliances with private developers and the creation of restricted compounds.[70]

The new vision for Harish followed negotiations with representatives and contractors from the Ultra-Orthodox sector that ensured their participation in the development process. As they all agreed to cooperate in this project, representatives from the Ministry of Construction and

---

[67] Rubenstein, "The Minister's Decisions regarding Harish."
[68] Cahaner, "Between Ghetto Politics and Geopolitics: Ultraorthodox Settlements in the West Bank,"; Fogel, Highway 6 Settlements; Kehat, Harish.
[69] *Gemilut chasadim* – "acts of kindness." [70] Fogel, Highway 6 Settlements.

Housing promised to adjust development and marketing to the needs and abilities of the Ultra-Orthodox sector. Moreover, they also guaranteed the status of Harish as a site of national priority, which includes zero pricing for state-owned lands and substantial government grants and funding.[71] In return, the Ultra-Orthodox leaders guaranteed that the different streams would eventually purchase the future dwelling units, bringing tens of thousands of Jewish families to the predominantly Arab area of Wadi A'ara[72] and ensuring a new privatized territorial-focused mode of spatial production.

The original suburban layout was not economically feasible for the new target group and the promoted mode of production. The lack of suitability was not only due to cultural differences, but, above all, because of the need for a substantially affordable construction process. Consequently, the ministry recommended transforming the approved fabric of private households into a series of larger parcels, containing four-story apartment buildings, with some twenty dwelling units each. Restricting the height of the buildings to four floors derives from the Ultra-Orthodox sector's avoidance of using electricity on Saturdays, as part of the religious practice of not working on the Sabbath. This limited the use of elevators that would be required in high-rise tenements – which would already suffer from extensive pressures due to the substantially large size of a usual Ultra-Orthodox family that often consists of 8–10 members.[73] The extreme homogenization of Harish, which included turning it into an environment of four-story buildings, was compatible with the lifestyle of large Ultra-Orthodox families and facilitated a reasonably affordable development; the Ministry of Construction and Housing hoped that a concentrated and uniform process would significantly reduce construction costs to less than half of the costs of a similar project.[74] This corresponded with the demands of Ultra-Orthodox leaders who, besides their focus on affordability, called for large-scale concentrated construction, which would prevent Harish from following former Ultra-Orthodox precedents like the ill-developed settlement of Emmanuel inside the West Bank.[75]

---

[71] Assaf, "Meeting of the Minister with Representatives of the Ultra-Orthodox Sector – 15/01/2001," 1.
[72] Rubenstein, "Harish Survey," 1–3.   [73] Kehat, Harish.
[74] Rubenstein, "Proposal for the Planning of Harish."
[75] Rubenstein, "Discussion Regarding the Decision for Harish."

The replanning of Harish was based on a new overall vision, rather than simple adjustments, which affected all planning levels. The Ministry of Construction and Housing commissioned Mansfeld-Kehat architects for the task, and the locally renowned firm first began to analyze the overall potential of the site, composing a skeleton plan for the city that outlined in general the future vision for Harish. This was followed by a new masterplan and then by detailed outline schemes. Focusing on the Ultra-Orthodox sector, the planners encountered several issues that would not usually exist in other urban contexts. Besides the previously mentioned issue of height limitations and desired building sizes, Mansfeld-Kehat needed to adjust the areas needed for public buildings and the proposed system of roads.

In a usual planning process in Israel, the planners would base all their calculations on the overall number of dwelling units. However, while a dwelling unit usually consists of 3–4 individuals, in the case of an Ultra-Orthodox community the number is closer to 7–8. This means that the same number of units would need a much larger quota of public areas, facilities, and infrastructure. Moreover, as Ultra-Orthodox families typically do not own a private vehicle and rely mainly on public transport and internally organized shuttle services, the planned road system had to be adjusted for larger means of transportation; it thus consisted of wider access streets and almost no cul-de-sac paths.[76] As the planner Haim Kehat stated, becoming an Ultra-Orthodox city basically meant that Harish needed to be a significantly affordable residential environment for large families that rely on communal transportation.[77] Accordingly, the masterplan, which deliberately stated the objectives of an Ultra-Orthodox city, included an overall number of 8,800 dwelling units, divided into the same three main residential quarters, but with a significantly higher density in order to meet the sought-after population combination and size. Typical for an Ultra-Orthodox environment, the masterplan contained several design and planning guidelines, such as the instruction to coat 70 percent of the façades in stone and the permission to construct special *Sukkah* balconies.

While the masterplan was naturally of a more general nature, the detailed scheme for *HaParsa* neighborhood was much more detailed, and completely changed the previously approved urban fabric.[78]

[76] Kehat, Harish. [77] Ibid.
[78] Mansfeld-Kehat Architects and Planners, "Local Outline Plan Harish/1/A."

Except for the already constructed complexes, the new layout consisted of a system of wide continuous access roads, and larger oblong residential parcels. Accordingly, this engendered buildings with a single main façade and three incidental ones so that the contractors needed to invest less in their development. This scaled version of tract development was based on an optimal ratio between roads and lots, grounding the subdivision of the site on the same economic considerations as in a typical Suburban Settlement, yet in a larger context. The plan also divided the entire neighborhood into some seventy different residential compounds, with an intention to tender each of them to a single developer (Figure 6.6). Most important, however, was the relative flexibility facilitated by the plan, which was manifested in gradual construction and relatively adjustable instructions for the overall building rights, which stated the minimum size of an average apartment and a minimum number of units per dunam.[79]

To promote the planning process, the Ministry of Interior created a special planning committee for Harish, bypassing the existing planning hierarchy. This committee was autonomous from the district of Haifa, which Harish originally belonged to, and thus directly accountable to the national planning committee. As Harish was now an independent entity, the former merger with Katzir was revoked, and the latter returned to being under the control of the regional council of Menashe.[80] This helped to accelerate the entire procedure, while also limiting the public's ability to object to the plan. However, the special committee's decision to designate Harish solely for the Ultra-Orthodox sector did lead to several objections from the general secular public. All of these were declined by the National Appeals Committee, which stated that there was no legal impediment to the decision to designate the new town as an Ultra-Orthodox locality.[81] Nevertheless, the Appeals Committee directed the planners to add some functions and flexibility to the plan, in the event that Harish was populated by non-Ultra-Orthodox families.[82] Simultaneously with the approval of the detailed plan for HaParsa neighborhood, the planning of the town's remaining quarters continued.

In 2001 the Ultra-Orthodox sector was the only optional target group; by 2010, however, the situation was entirely different.

---

[79] Ibid., 12.
[80] State Comptroller of Israel, "Local Government Audit Reports," 613.
[81] Ibid. [82] Ibid.

Harish: The Next City of Israel 223

Figure 6.6 Compounds plan of HaParsa neighborhood, Harish, 2012 (Mansfeld-Kehat Architects – MCH)

Post-2008 Israel was facing a major housing crisis, which may have been due to insufficient construction or the low interest rates that made real estate a solid investment.[83] Following the huge public discontent, the Israeli Government continued and even enhanced its supply-side housing policy,[84] igniting a vicious circle of increasing property values and the increasing profitability of real-estate investment.[85] Owning an apartment, even for mere investment, became a crucial component in

---

[83] Boruchov, "On Target: The Housing Crisis and Damage to the Planning System," 63–65; Eshel and Hananel, "Centralization, Neoliberalism, and Housing Policy Central–Local Government Relations and Residential Development in Israel," 237–39; Mualem, "Playing with Supertankers: Centralization in Land Use Planning in Israel: A National Experiment Underway," 269–83; Charney, "A 'Supertanker' against Bureaucracy in the Wake of a Housing Crisis: Neoliberalizing Planning in Netanyahu's Israel."
[84] Rubin and Felsenstein, "Supply Side Constraints in the Israeli Housing Market: The Impact of State Owned Land," 266–75.
[85] Boruchov, "On Target: The Housing Crisis and Damage to the Planning System," 85.

the economic stability of the average Israeli family. Suddenly, remote housing projects like Harish turned into attractive pieces of real estate. In addition, by 2010 the new Trans-Israel Highway had reached the area, and the newly constructed West Bank Separation Barrier had cut Harish off from the neighboring Palestinian environment causing it to lose its peripheral and frontier-like appearance. Consequently, the intention to exclusively designate Harish for the Ultra-Orthodox sector led to widespread national objections from the secular and National-Orthodox (*dati leumi*) public. In 2012, the Haifa district court ruled in favor of the appeal submitted against the state's intentions, forcing it to open up the marketing process to the general Israeli public, religious and nonreligious alike, and thus to revoke the discriminating spatial privileges.[86]

The tendering and marketing process for Harish turned into a turf battle between the Ultra-Orthodox and non-Ultra-Orthodox sector. While the various Ultra-Orthodox streams and communities were already represented by their own housing associations, several secular and National-Orthodox groups began to organize their own associations with the intention of competing in the open public housing tenders. Although he state had begun to prefer private developers during the 1990s due to the housing associations' lack of experience,[87] in areas like Harish, which were still not attractive to private developers, the housing associations were a useful tool to ignite the first construction stages. Moreover, as these associations consisted of registered members, they provided potential property owners with certainty regarding the profile of their future neighbors. This facilitated the creation of associations with specific ethnic or religious profiles, while limiting the inclusion of less desirable families, such as Arabs. In this way, the housing associations functioned as a sort of admissions committee, guaranteeing socioeconomic and ethnic profiles that could secure the appeal of the following construction stages.

The first tender in 2012 proved to be a crucial turning point for Harish. In the first phase, the Israel Land Administration and the Ministry of Construction and Housing tendered some 4,500 dwelling units in 29 compounds. Participants included several Ultra-Orthodox housing associations, secular and National-Orthodox organizations,

[86] State Comptroller of Israel, "Local Government Audit Reports," 619.
[87] MCH, "Construction through Associations," 137–51.

and a few private contractors. A group of twelve Ultra-Orthodox associations were very well-organized and were thus able to submit a much higher bid than the other participants. However, their coordination led the Israel Land Administration to conclude that they were acting as a cartel, which contradicted the rules of the tender and led to their disqualification. Eventually, a single Ultra-Orthodox association acquired a compound in Harish, as well as two private contractors that were affiliated with the Ultra-Orthodox sector, making up less than 10 percent of the overall tendered units.[88] The majority of the compounds were eventually won by secular and National-Orthodox associations, as well as three private developers, who submitted significantly low bids and eventually sold most of their lots to associations.[89]

With the secular "success" the development of Harish shifted from relying on the simple production and consumption of real estate, to a new financialized mode. While, just ten years earlier, Harish had been a place that "no sane person would like to live in,"[90] by 2015 construction tenders were won mainly by private entrepreneurs and Harish became entirely corporate-led. To stimulate the proinvestment climate, the Ministry of Construction and Housing authorized additional detailed plans for three new neighborhoods, while the Israeli Government declared the city a site of national priority, promising a total of one billion Israeli shekels to stimulate the development process.[91] This was followed by the development of an additional neighborhood, where the Ministry of Construction and Housing chose to tender all of the compounds to a single developer. Symbolically, this new corporately developed neighborhood was built on the ruins of the former Kibbutz Harish. To provide a solution for the Ultra-Orthodox sector, which became a NIMBY in Harish's booming real-estate market, the Israeli Government designated the future town of Kasif on the southern Negev for their exclusive use[92] – reasonably far from the expanding demand areas of the Israeli middle class.

Adapting the existing plan to the new financialized mode of production meant that the proposed urban and architectural setting had to

---

[88] State Comptroller of Israel, "Local Government Audit Reports," 619; Levi, "Harish for Everyone."
[89] Levi, "Harish for Everyone."
[90] Marom, "Tender 10025/99 – HaParsa Neighbourhood – Harish," 2.
[91] State Comptroller of Israel, "Local Government Audit Reports," 629.
[92] Abovich, "After Harish Comes Kasif."

secure the anticipated yield of private entrepreneurs and investors. This was not a complicated task as the Israeli planning law has several specific regulations that enable some flexibility in the implementation of local outline plans. These support developers in increasing the overall permitted number of dwelling units by 30 percent, as well as the permitted number of floors.[93] As the planners had initially considered substantially larger apartments and allowed quite generous building rights, the developers were able to significantly increase the number of apartments and to add additional floors,[94] maintaining the original ratio between residential and public areas while optimally fulfilling the city's real-estate potential.

The layout of Harish enabled the continuous recreation of the same housing typology, promoting a homogenous, standardized and economically feasible development that fitted the new mode of production. Like the plans of the early 1990s, the residential parcel formed the basis of the plans in the 2000s. Nevertheless, while earlier plans included some variations, the new vison was based mainly on recreating the same dimensions for each single parcel: the typical residential building with four apartments on each floor, as prescribed by the Ministry of Construction and Housing and mentioned earlier.[95] This would become the basis of the new plans, with a single size residential property determining the dimensions of each parcel, which, in turn, dictated the distance between streets, and the allocation of public functions. The dimensions of the basic, uniform apartment therefore ordained the layout of Harish, its urban hierarchy, and even the everyday life of those living there, creating the necessary framework for the commodification of the future city.

The planned density of Harish also fitted the new mode of production. The initial suburban plan included some 4,000 units in a usable area of 1,863 dunams of which 655 were for residential use. The gross density was thus 2.2 units per dunam with a net density of around 6 units.[96] The new two plans of 2014 and 2015, with a usable area of 3,155 dunams, offered some 8,500 units in around 880 dunams of residential plots.[97] The new gross density was 2.6 per dunam while the

---

[93] Ministry of Interior, "Planning and Building Regulations (Considerable Deviation from Plan)."
[94] Kehat, Harish.   [95] Rubenstein, "Proposal for the Planning of Harish."
[96] Moshe Zur Architects and Planners, "Harish," 4.
[97] Mansfeld-Kehat Architects and Planners, "Local Outline Plan Harish/1/A," 3; Yaar Architects, "Local Outline Plan Harish/1/b," 3–4.

Harish: The Next City of Israel 227

net density was almost 10, and as the former increased by a mere 20 percent the latter increased by 60 percent, compared with the original plans. Therefore, while the overall supply of units was not significantly larger, the potential of each parcel became much more attractive to private developers, improving the site's cost efficiency while only slightly increasing the number of planned dwelling units.

For a city of its size, Harish has a very limited number of housing types. Essentially, it consists of a single residential model, which the different contractors, developers, and entrepreneurs repeatedly implemented. Corresponding to the proposed layouts, the vast majority of buildings in Harish are made up of the same simple five-room dwelling unit, based on a joint family area that forms the core of the apartment, with the bedrooms attached to it. This basic model is easily adapted by offering a closed kitchen or semiclosed option to more conservative families, or it can be tailored to a site's conditions by applying a terraced option (Figure 6.7). This housing type, which makes up more than 90 percent of the buildings in Harish, constitutes the ultimate optimization of corporate construction, completing the transformation of the house into an asset to be sold, rented, or leveraged for further investment. The transformation of the house into a commodity was thus completed, while presenting an example of neoliberal vernacular.

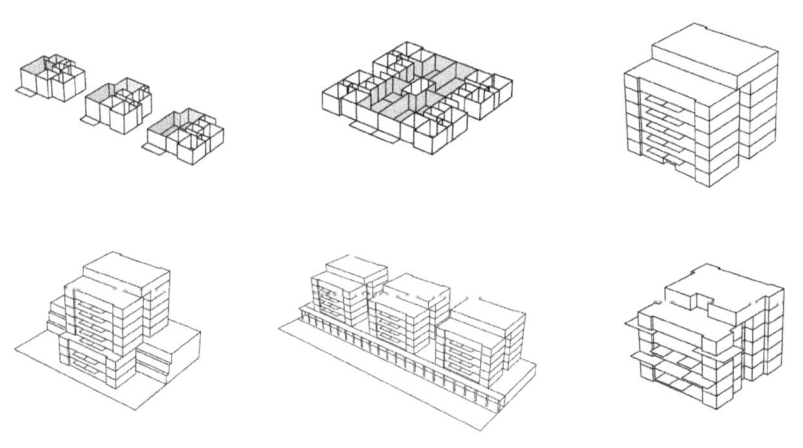

Figure 6.7 *Upper row* – types of apartments (left), typical floorplan (middle), and a typical building (right); *lower row* – implementations of a typical building (illustration by the author)

Like almost all the new settlements built along the Green Line over the past forty years, Harish is a housing-only development. With the intention to attract as many (Jewish) families to the area as possible, in a relatively short period of time, the Ministry of Construction and Housing and the various planning administrations focused on creating an abundance of dwelling units. These developments, however, almost always relied on the existing social infrastructure as well as the employment and service centers in Gush Dan. Creating purely residential environments was also a tool to promote an image of high living standards, as industry, commerce, and business did not usually fit with the sought-after tranquil suburban setting. Correspondingly, a study by the Office of the State Comptroller of Israel showed that in 2016 more than 70 percent of property owners in Harish were employed in the greater Tel Aviv area.[98]

Besides the usual critique that single-use zoning schemes generate badly planned environments, they also create local councils that lack feasibility. A lack of sufficient business-related uses, which are the most important element of city property taxes, can lead to a significant deficit, leaving local councils bankrupt or heavily depending on government aid.[99] In 2013, Harish was in need of an additional 930,000 m^2 of land for commercial use, just so the council could avoid a budgetary deficit.[100] To protect the council from an economic crash, the Israel Land Administration, as of 2021, is currently seeking to involve Harish in some of the newly developed industrial areas close by, making sure that it receives a portion of the property taxes paid there. Additional state interventions therefore continues, in order to keep stimulating the market.

With the intention of stimulating investment, the development of Harish was accompanied by a substantial and aggressive marketing strategy. While the suggestions for such a campaign during the 1990s remained on paper, by 2015 Harish became more of a public relations campaign than a housing project. The first advertising and promotion was carried out by the housing associations that competed for the first tenders, which sought to admit as many members as possible. Besides the emphases on affordable housing, reasonable commuting distances,

[98] State Comptroller of Israel, "Local Government Audit Reports," 627.
[99] Local Government Administration, "Economic Resilience of Local Authorities."
[100] State Comptroller of Israel, "Local Government Audit Reports," 623.

and the usual proximity to nature, the associations also focused on the sense of community, and on the right of the non-Ultra-Orthodox sector to live in Harish. In that sense, intending to purchase an apartment in the new city became an act of civil protest, and the housing associations commonly used slogans like "our Harish" and "Harish for everyone." Another was "Harish is Green, not Black," emphasizing the struggle between the Ultra-Orthodox sector (black) and the aspirations of secular families for a suburban community (green).[101] When private developers took over, they continued with a similar approach, although they used varied and broad promotion techniques.

This is perhaps best represented in *Harish City*, a private internet platform, consisting of a website, as well as Instagram and Facebook pages, that brings together all the development updates and marketing of all the entrepreneurs active in the city. It focuses on promoting an image of a young community, living in affordable houses with high living standards, surrounded, of course, by nature, yet close to urban centers. The "greenwashing" campaign continued in the rebranding efforts by the Harish local council, which included changing the names of previous neighborhoods – *HaParsa* (horseshoe) and *HaMagaf* (boot) – to more appealing ones like *HaPrahim* (flowers), *HaHoresh* (Grove), *Maof* (bird flight), *Avne Hen* (Gems), and *Tzavta* (together). The fierce public relations campaign included endless color pieces, intended to promote the same young image. Notably, almost all the promotion articles included an interview with a lesbian couple who own a local diner, thus adding some "pinkwashing" to the "greenwashing" efforts while cynically using the LGTB community as a means to market real estate.[102]

In order to continually attract private investors in the new financialized mode of production, the state enacted a strategy of "too big to fail." It enlarged the municipal borders of Harish and its intended target population, hoping that the intensified development and state-guided funding would attract additional private investment. Harish was thus Netanyahu's promised "Supertanker," flooding the market with tens of thousands of new dwelling units. However, this approach

---

[101] Eitiel, "Harish Is Green, not Black."
[102] Shaked, "Eyal Berkowitz: 'I Recommend Young Couples to Think of Harish'"; Patilon, "Derech Eretz Avenue Continues to Populate: Get to Know the New Businesses"; Arad, "You Will Be Recorded in History as the First Reporter to Write Anything Good about Harish"; Ynet, "Harish: Not What You Thought."

eventually overstimulated the national real-estate market, leading to increases in housing prices, instead of lowering them.[103] Not surprisingly, according to estimations by the Ministry of Construction and Housing, half of the apartments in Harish were bought by investors relying on derivative rents.[104] No wonder that the constant rise in property values in Harish is constantly used as a marketing tool for new housing projects in the town,[105] creating a paradox whereby the success of the city that was built in order to tackle increasing real-estate prices is proven by an increase in real-estate prices.

The Architecture of Exchange-Value

Harish is representative of the gradual financialization of the national project of settlement development. Along its different phases, from the kibbutz to the future city of Israel, one can clearly identify the manner in which the settlement mechanism transformed and how the conception of space changed accordingly. Along the different phases, the state granted a variety of select groups diverse spatial privileges in order to promote the national geopolitical agenda. In the rural and neo-rural phases, the state sought to attract pioneer settlers by granting them the power to cultivate and exclusively inhabit space. As these attempts were unsuccessful, the government sought to turn Harish into a Suburban Settlement, attracting developers by giving them the power to construct and commodify space, and appealing to young privileged families by offering them the power to consume it. The objective was to create a desirable suburban environment and to persuade upper-middle-class families to move to the area; they would then help to generate the image of an attractive suburb and facilitate the settlement's further development.

However, as the area was still a geographical periphery, both developers and upper-middle-class families were uninterested in the spatial rights the state wanted to provide. To solve this market failure, while preventing the formation of an Arab town, the state focused on the power to exclusively use space as a means to appeal to the

---

[103] Boruchov, "On Target: The Housing Crisis and Damage to the Planning System," 63–64.
[104] Levi and Bahor-Nir, "Harish: A City for Rent."
[105] Cohen and Horesh, "How to Market 86 Buildings in Harish When the Market Slows."

Ultra-Orthodox sector. With the housing crisis and the intention to expand the existing areas of demand into its internal frontiers, the Israeli Government focused on making Harish attractive to private developers through affordable tenders and a speedy planning procedure. The financialization of frontier settlement therefore occurred when the power to speculate in spatial development became the leading method to attract entrepreneurs, contractors, and investors to develop the frontier and to complete its domestication.

With the financialization of the settlement mechanism, its architectural and urban characteristics transformed and turned into by-products of the new mode of production. Consequently, while earlier plans focused on the private household, they later focused on the residential parcel as a means to optimally subdivide a given area into a typical number of private lots. As spatial speculation became the leading force behind frontier settlement, the emphasis on the *use-value* of the private parcel gave way to a growing focus on its *exchange-value*, and how to efficiently and feasibly extract the economic potential of a given site. Thus, when replanning Harish, the emphasis was on subdividing the site into a system of residential parcels, which would enable private entrepreneurs to generate an optimal layout and number of apartments. As Harish turned into a high-rise residential environment, the number of units did not significantly increase. The net density of a residential parcel, on the other hand, rose substantially, increasing the profitability of the residential area so that the planned units could actually be constructed.

As exchange-value took the lead, architecture turned into the art of optimally using the building rights of a given residential parcel to generate profit. Subsequently, almost all the buildings in Harish followed very similar spatial features, with a few minimal variations between the different apartments, thus functioning as three-dimensional grids that generated cubic commodities. With some design nuances in façades, meant to create a seemingly unique envelope to the same reproduced volume, the new financialized environment completed the transition from the state-led, reproduced urban environment of the 1950s and 1960s to the corporate-led, reproduced quasi-urban landscape of the 2010s.

Neoliberalist market-oriented approaches allegedly lead to the decentralization of society and the economy, in opposition to state intervention and decreasing national and political interests. However, as Harish shows, this is, de facto, rarely the case. To create a market in

Harish that private developers would invest in, the Israeli Government took an *if you build it, they will come* approach – continually investing public funds to enlarge the project and create a probusiness environment. At the same time, as the role of the state increased, compatible with a neoliberal development approach, state involvement was used to enforce the logic of the market on all aspects of the urban system.[106] The measures enacted in Harish thus turned the planning process and planning system into the "new ally of market forces,"[107] and market forces into the ally of the greater national territorial project – promoting real-estate speculation in order to domesticate geopolitical frontiers.

[106] Brenner and Theodore, "Cities and the Geographies of 'Actually Existing Neoliberalism'."

[107] Lovering, "Will Recession Prove to Be a Turning Point in Planning and Urban Development Thinking?," 238; Charney, "A 'Supertanker' against Bureaucracy in the Wake of a Housing Crisis: Neoliberalizing Planning in Netanyahu's Israel," 1238.

7 | Conclusions

Ends and Means, Tools, and Products

The first time I visited a settlement was in November 2008, when I spent a weekend in Yitzhar. Located in the heart of the West Bank and populated by one the most extreme, right-wing, fanatic groups of settlers, Yitzhar was the last place one might expect to find a gentile like myself. In order not to arouse any suspicions or to fall out with my weekend neighbors, I could not refuse an invitation from one of the families to the traditional Shabbat dinner. To avoid the awkward silence around the supper table, and in an attempt to be courteous to my hosts, I thought I should compliment them, and I said they had a lovely panoramic view. The husband, Niryah, who would later be arrested by the Israeli police for alleged terrorism, was highly offended by my attempt at a compliment and replied angrily, "we are not here for the view."

Niryah's comment was constantly in the back of my mind during my fieldwork for this project, especially while conducting interviews. Dealing with case studies that most Israelis would consider lite settlements, or even nonsettlements due to their location west of the Green Line, I was not surprised that most of my interviewees spoke from a mixture of national and personal perspectives. Mentioning "quality of life" on the one hand, and the defense and security of their settlement on the other, I understood that the image they tried to portray was of an ideological group of people, who also knew when and how to seize the opportunity to upgrade their living standards by moving to a private house in a new settlement. Thus, they were ideological but not extremists, and perhaps also opportunists, yet not "parasites" who abuse the state to further their interests. These conversations reminded me of a satirical sketch from the Israeli *HaHamishia HaKamerit* television program during the 1990s, where one of the actors, Rami Heuberger, plays the role of a settler who is trying to explain the quality of life in a West Bank settlement:

> Look at this view. Vegetation, boulders, rocks, animals ... you have everything here. Look at the horizon, how bright it is. Look at the houses, how nice they are ... the kids are playing in the yard. Look at how everything was built here with faith, love, honesty ... Do you feel the breeze? Do you see the skies? Aren't they bluer here? Breathe! Breathe! It's not Tel Aviv here, you can breathe with all the lungs ... You know, I open my eyes here in the morning, birds on the windows, sunsets over the mountains ... This house, for example, built to stand for years, three floors. With room for many children, and grandchildren "Inshallah"[1] ... The basketball that I installed in the yard ... The pool is almost finished, just left to pave around it ... And I'm not a religious person, but add to all of this the sense of mission, and the power of the concept of ancestral land, which all have real meaning here, a tangible one ... isn't this worth 1,200,000 [shekels]?[2]

In a settler-chic look with a military Doobon coat, a checkered flannel shirt and a mustache, yet lacking the religious yarmulke headcover, Heuberger exhibits the typical image of a secular Israeli settler (Figure 7.1). Surrounded by white cubic houses with red-roofs and a Caterpillar truck, the scene depicts a stereotypical quality of life settlement. Starting with the natural landscape and vibrant community life, then mentioning the quality of the houses, national pretensions, and ending with real-estate value, Heuberger's monologue illustrates the fusion of ends and means, objects and tools of the Israeli settlement project. This is precisely what the settlement mechanism is: It perhaps

Figure 7.1 Screen shots of Rami Heuberger in *HaHamishia HaKamerit* (Mater Productions)

---

[1] "Inshallah" is Arabic – when a settler uses an Arab phrase it indicates a sort of appropriation.
[2] Tzur, *HaHamishia HaKamerit*.

has a main territorial objective, yet it always included additional intentions and purposes – beginning with the Jewish national renaissance, through agricultural work, and ending with the current market-led development. Nevertheless, the privatization of this mechanism meant that its additional purposes were of an individualistic nature, unlike former spiritual national endeavors or state-led socialization plans. Thus, using personal interests in self-fulfillment, seclusion, and investment as settlement tools, these were intended to promote the national geopolitical agenda while producing a variety of new architectural and urban models.

The Privatized Settlement Mechanism

The settlements described in this book illustrate the gradual privatization of the national settlement project. As we have seen, the larger objective remained the state's power over space, achieved through the construction of new settlements in the former frontier area of the Green Line. Yet, to ensure their unceasing development, the state constantly sought to involve a variety of private families (as part of organized groups), developers, and entrepreneurs, various settlement tools, which were the spatial privileges that gave these new agents the power to produce, consume, and market space. These changes ensured the ceaseless continuation of the Israeli territorial project. We began our journey in 1977 with a few thousand Jewish Israelis living in small rural settlements west of the Green Line, and around 150,000 Palestinians on both sides; by 2020 there were some 400,000 Jewish Israelis living in over 30 new neo-rural, suburban, and urban settlements, both inside the West Bank and on official Israeli territory.[3] Consequently, a demographic balance with the Palestinian population was created and the former border was successfully obscured.

With the increasing privatization, the national settlement project went through different phases, each with its own mode of production, which progressively included more organized and economically efficient private allies. Starting with the first case studies of Community Settlements during the early 1980s, through the suburbanization of the mid- to late 1980s and 1990s, and up until the recent corporate-led development, a continuous process can be noted where the settlement

---

[3] ICBS, "Localities in Israel"; PCBS, "Localities in the Palestinian Authority."

agents became private entrepreneurial corporations, and the spatial rights they were granted became real-estate oriented. In this sense, the privatization of the settlement mechanism was intended to increase the profitability of the planned residential environments, turning them into what Raquel Rolnik refers to as "bankable" projects,[4] in order to enhance the national territorial agenda. Thus, the state's noninterventionist laissez-faire approach was intended to eventually increase its control, turning the settlements of the Trans-Israel Highway into a privately developed national project, just like the road that passes between them.

Each of the different modes of production generated its own architectural and urban typologies. As we have seen in the previous chapters, the location of the new settlements was dictated by territorial aspirations and while the strategic geopolitical agenda created new ink spots on the map, the various settling agents that the state relied on dictated how these spots would materialize.

In the early privatization phases, the Community Settlement was still a settlement tool, and not yet a mere outcome of economic calculations. The state initially retained its role as planner and developer of the new sites, attracting organized groups by granting them the power to exclusively populate a small-scale, ex-urban settlement. Here, the appeal was to meet the desire of the settling groups for a pioneer-like experience away from the cities its members originated from. The planning administrations imitated former rural models, which, though lacking all means of production, were supposed to replicate some of the communal values of previous pioneer settlements. On the one hand, the Community Settlements symbolize the primary transformations in the settlement efforts, disconnecting them from the former link with practical farming and labor, while starting a new mode of life based on individualistic interests in self-fulfillment. On the other hand, as the state still reserved its power to produce space, the architectural and urban characteristics of the new settlements were an outcome of pre-privatization mechanisms.

As a neo-rural territorial tool, the new Community Settlements were, at first, far from being luxurious suburban communities. Influenced by earlier settlement patterns and featuring several pioneer-like residues, they consisted of spartan houses in peripheral locations. At the same

---

[4] Rolnik, *Urban Warfare: Housing under the Empire of Finance*, 95.

time, unlike the former pioneer rural settlements that were both a physical and a spiritual avant-garde, the Community Settlements were mainly intended to function as segregated homogeneous localities. The individual interests of the settling groups changed as well, and while the Community Settlements began as an attempt to create a contrast to city life by establishing ex-urban communities, they eventually turned into an integral part of the expanding national suburbanization process. Consequently, "quality of life" was not measured by the remoteness from urban centers, but rather by luxurious living standards and short commuting distances.

The transformations in the Community Settlement model corresponded with the growing ability of private actors to produce space; this shifted the focus from communal features to individual and corporate interests. Subsequently, the first phases, consisting of an array of small private households sharing a communal open space and a public core, gave way to more house-oriented typologies, with a focus on detaching the family from the wider collective context. The emphasis was on car accessibility and on detached private parcels that could be developed by future residents. Later on, with the growing involvement of private developers, these urban and architectural typologies of self-fulfillment gave way to uniform and economically efficient housing models, thus completing the shift from the individual's power to customize space, to the developer's power to commodify it.

The suburban turn of the 1980s led to a new mode of production where the power to produce space became the focus of the settlement mechanism. While in the late 1970s the spatial rights granted by the state were manifested in the ability to settle secluded ex-urban communities, the suburban efforts of the 1980s relied on the power to affordably construct spacious houses at a reasonable distance from the Tel Aviv metropolis. Being a substantial spatial privilege, it was granted by the state either to favored groups, like members of a ruling political party, large unions, or the military, or to well-connected developers that obtained the permission to develop a certain site. These "private initiative settlements,"[5] as the different administrations referred to them, witnessed minimal professional involvement by the Ministry of Construction and Housing, and thus followed the desires and aspirations of their settlers and developers. As the power to develop new

[5] Settlement Division, "The 100,000 Plan," 8.

settlements became the main territorial tool, the architecture and layout of the new sites was therefore a product of the new settlement mechanism. Advertising campaigns were limited, and used only as a backup to word-of-mouth marketing efforts. The suburban lifestyle was thus not a means, but rather an artifact of the newly enacted settlement tool.

The suburban turn of the mid-1980s illustrates the changes in both modes of production and patterns of consumption. In the state's attempts to involve the upper-middle class in its territorial project, it granted them the ability to develop new settlements. Consequently, the new residential environments followed bourgeois, individualistic forms of consumption. With respect to the design of the houses, this was echoed in the recurring attempt to create a private and secluded family area, cut off from the surrounding environment, and the frequent use of the split-level unit. The external use of vegetation, fences, walls, and closed façades, and the inner orientation of the various uses, generated an urban system subdivided into smaller entities that had no relationship with each other. In this sense, the suburban private parcel is similar to Leibniz's *monads* – self-sufficient substances that form the universe. They are coordinated one with the other, yet there is no causal relationship between them as they "have no windows through which something can enter or leave."[6]

The mass suburbanization and the supply-side approach of the 1990s created a new mode of privatized territoriality. The earlier gentrification efforts generated the appeal of living along the Green Line, depicting it as a natural and pristine environment, populated by well-established communities. Subsequently, the state-led planning, tendering, and promotion efforts of a decade later turned the area into a flourishing real-estate market that attracted additional families, contractors, and investors. Initially, the intention was to rely on organized housing associations; however, the increasing public appeal and the growing economic potential enabled the state to use larger developers, thus going a step further in the privatization process and turning the power to commodify and market space into the main settlement tool. With the commodification of the built environment, the state hoped to generate a process of supply and demand that would lead to the continuous development of the area and complete the

[6] Leibniz, *Monadology*, 219.

A Privatizing Settlement Mechanism

239

domestication of the frontier. Profitability and marketability became leading values in the settlement mechanism, while urban planning and architectural design turned into a framework intended to promote market-oriented environments and profitable dwelling units. The shift toward the self-sufficient monads suited the new modes of production, which used the new parcel-oriented approach to subdivide a given site into a series of marketable residential lots. Thus, while Allweil depicts the development of Israeli settlements as a housing regime,[7] by the 1990s it would be more accurate to refer to it as a commodity regime, as the use-value of housing gave way to its exchange-value.

The commodification of the built environment was a one-way street that eventually turned architecture and planning into by-products of the privatized settlement mechanism. Once the state had endorsed the market-oriented approach, there was no way back. Therefore, in the event of market failure, the state and its planning agencies supported new outline plans and adjustments in order to meet the speculative interests of private developers, and to ensure that the planned dwelling units would eventually materialize. The rights granted to private entrepreneurs thus included a substantial power to plan space and turn it into a feasible residential project. Subsequently, the state financialized the settlement mechanism, creating a market that would become the main ally of the territorial agenda, and later dictate the formation of the built environment. This reached a pinnacle in the case of Harish, which has been vastly transformed over the past forty years, concluding in the current corporate-led urban project. While the state made many attempts to stimulate the process, it was eventually the market- and financial-oriented approach, relying on ever-increasing investment, that became the main driving force behind the development of the future city of Israel.

A Privatizing Settlement Mechanism

Over the forty years of privatization surveyed in this project, the role of the individual in the national settlement mechanism changed drastically with the evolving modes of production. While, in the Community Settlement, the individual retained some of the pioneer characteristics and features, these seemingly self-sacrificing attributes gave way to the

---

[7] Allweil, *Homeland: Zionism as Housing Regime, 1860–2011*, 5.

individualistic interests of better living standards in the Suburban Settlement. Consequently, farmers or pioneers, who enhanced the territorial efforts through their plows, were replaced by upper-middle-class commuters. These *neo-settlers*, as Yacobi and Tzfadia refer to them,[8] promoted the national territorial agenda through their private houses and the distance covered by their cars during their daily commute. Finally, the market-oriented financial development replaced the commuters with shareholders willing to take part in the national project by literally owning a piece of it. Real estate, therefore, became the last virtue of the patriot.

The changes in the role of the individual in domesticating the Green Line corresponded with the way the state chose to enforce its power. According to Kim Dovey's analysis of the spatial mediation of power, discussed in Chapter 1, there are five different modes the state uses to ensure the individual's compliance: force, coercion, manipulation, seduction, and authority.[9] *Force* is a situation in which the individual basically has no choice other than compliance, like the Palestinians who lived in the area in 1948 and were forced to leave. *Coercion* is compliance due to fear of the consequences – the dilemma of many Mizrahi immigrants that the government settled in the area during the 1950s, who feared that lack of obedience would cut them off from the welfare system. *Manipulation* is when the individual is tricked into thinking that they are acting from free choice, like the pioneer-like settlers of the late 1970s. *Seduction* is when the individual is lured by their desires, as in the ability to produce space in the 1980s and 1990s.[10] Therefore, the spatial privileges granted in the Community and Suburban Settlements turned the favored groups that were given these privileges into settlement agents, thus enhancing the state's spatial dominance while freely incorporating more individuals into its territorial agenda. While extremely successful, however, this was not yet a mode of *authority*.

Tying individuals to the state by turning them into homeowners was a common practice during the twentieth century.[11] The famous quote

---

[8] Yacobi and Tzfadia, "Neo-Settler Colonialism and the Re-formation of Territory: Privatization and Nationalization in Israel," 1–19.
[9] Dovey, *Framing Place. Mediating Power in Built Form*, 3.   [10] Ibid., 10–12.
[11] Wright, *Building the Dream: A Social History of Housing in America*; Jackson, *Crabgrass Frontier: The Suburbanization of the United States*, 45–72; Hayden, *Redesigning the American Dream: Gender, Housing, and Family Life*, 3–38;

from US President Roosevelt highlights this assumption further: that as "a nation of homeowners, of people who own a real share in their own land," America is an invincible power.[12] Therefore, as *shareholders* in suburbia, citizens are *seduced* by the ability to form their own exclusive communities. Segal and Weitzman, as well as Gutwein, claim that as Israelis become homeowners and shareholders in the settlement enterprise they will more likely affiliate themselves with the right-wing territorial agenda and its representatives in parliament, ensuring the continuity of right-wing political parties.[13] Nevertheless, while the seduction mechanism speaks of metaphoric shareholders, in the financialized mode of production, the speculating individuals and investors became real shareholders, tied not only to the continuation of the settlement enterprise but also to its constant growth. Thus, while the modes of compliance cited above imply overt attempts to enforce the state's power over space, the financialization of the settlement mechanism is closer to the mode of *authority*, where power relations become an integral part of the social structure, making them less obvious and undisputable.[14]

As Rabinowitz and Vardi argue, the Israeli neoliberal turn was accompanied by an undisputed consensus in favor of privatization, so that laissez-faire became the only means to improve and optimize the state apparatus.[15] This widespread support, the authors claim, was not an outcome of a great conspiracy, but rather in opposition to the decades-long state-controlled economy; it was also due to the perception of Israel as a state facing the constant threat of war, whose government needed to focus on security and defence while leaving "marginal" issues, like the economy, aside. Consequently, the market economy became the natural way of operating.[16] Harnessing the development of the Green Line to the seemingly natural process of the

---

Vale, *From the Puritans to the Projects: Public Housing and Public Neighbors*, 92–104; Allweil, *Homeland: Zionism as Housing Regime, 1860–2011*, 17–19.
[12] Allweil, *Homeland: Zionism as Housing Regime, 1860–2011*, 17.
[13] Segal and Eyal, *A Civilian Occupation: The Politics of Israeli Architecture*; Gutwein, "The Settlements and the Relationship between Privatization and the Occupation."
[14] Delso, "Concrete Punishment: Time, Architecture and Art as Weapons in the Israeli–Palestinian Conflict," 60.
[15] Rabinowitz and Vardi, *Driving Forces: Trans-Israel Highway and the privatization of Civil Infrastructures in Israel*, 11–27.
[16] Ibid., 15–18.

"free market," the state thereby turned its territorial project into an integral part of the social structure. Yet, rather than seeing this as a well-designed conspirative strategic plan, it would be much more accurate to think of it as series of ad hoc privatization measures, enacted on a rolling basis in order to bind the national territorial vision to the prevailing economic conditions.

As an ethno-territorial project, the privatization of the settlement mechanism was a means to improve the state's geopolitical apparatus and eventually nationalize space. As seen in the case studies analyzed in this book, the selective privatization measures were enforced by the state in order to relocate a specific sector of the population to a given area, granting them privileges that enabled them to consume and/or produce space. Privatization was not, therefore, simply a tool to fulfill the national settlement agenda, but actually an integral part of it. The state-directed gentrification process, as well as the state's support for exclusive measures like admissions committees and housing administrations, ensured that the "free market" would serve certain geopolitical aspirations while preventing the Arabization of space. This ethnocentric process of *privatize and rule* was a thus clear attempt to adapt the "free market" to the state's territorial interests. In return, the "free market" augmented the state's involvement and its control over space, turning the trans-Israel settlements not only into the products of a privatized national project but also of a national project of privatization.

Post-Socialist Neoliberalism?

The privatization of the Israeli settlement mechanism constitutes a local implementation of a global phenomenon. Besides the unique geopolitical agenda that is omnipresent, this process is exceptional in the manner that it was executed. While the main texts on neoliberalism discuss it as a return to power of the prewar financial elites and their economic and societal values, the case of Israel is significantly different. Being a relatively young state with an ethnocentric quasi-socialist background, Israel lacked an old financial hegemony, and the privatization of its economy therefore did not conclude in the revival of old economic elites, but rather in the formation of a new one. This consisted of well-connected individuals that either benefited from their former role as governmental contractors, becoming leading entrepreneurs, or those who used their connections to purchase state-owned corporations.

In the settlement mechanism it is possible to identify two main groups: previous small contractors that turned into large-scale concerns, and formerly public or state-owned companies that were sold to well-connected businessmen and entrepreneurs. Ashtrom and Ashdar, for example, which supplied prefabricated concrete units for the frontier Community Settlements in the late 1970s, had turned into a billion-dollar concern by the early 2000s, involved in real estate, infrastructure, and holdings, with a portfolio that includes the construction works of the Trans-Israel Highway as well as numerous residential neighborhoods and high-rise buildings in the area. Another example is Shikun U'Binui and Solel Boneh, originally owned by the socialist central workers' union, the Histadrut. Purchased by the Arison Group, they became involved in large-scale, high-rise residential projects such as El'ad or Tzur Yitzhak, while also becoming one of the main forces behind the Trans-Israel Highway.

The liquidation of the state-controlled monopoly over the development of the built environment did not conclude in a more competitive market that benefited the end-users, but rather in a private cartel that continuously protects its own interests. As noted by Rabinowitz and Vardi, the termination of the Israeli state-monopoly resolved into acute market concentration, in which a small number of post-governmental firms controls all aspects of the industry.[17] As shown in this book, these unique circumstances, which one could refer to as post-socialist neoliberalism, are very apparent in the settlement mechanism; the development of all the case studies discussed here was eventually controlled by a restricted number of developers and contractors who directed the process, and it concluded with larger, concentrated construction segments.

In their analysis of neoliberalization, Peck, Theodore, and Brenner, describe it as a "less-than-happy marriage" between economic interests and local mechanisms.[18] Nevertheless, as we have seen in this book, the settlements along the Trans-Israel Highway, on both sides of the Green Line, were an outcome of a happy, stable, and fruitful marriage between geopolitics and geoeconomics. Accordingly, the offspring this marriage produced continue to serve territorial and economic

[17] Ibid., 18–20.
[18] Peck, Theodore, and Brenner, "Neoliberal Urbanism Redux?," 1093.

agendas, whereas social, individual, environmental, and communal issues have increasingly been set aside. As private entrepreneurs became the main executors of the state's territorial agenda, their leverage steadily increased. Subsequently, their ability to dictate, directly or indirectly, the formation of the built environment increased as well. This eventually led to the reproduction of similar housing typologies all across the settlements of the Trans-Israel Highway, recreating and duplicating the same residential environments. In the long run, the old quasi-socialist monotonous horizontal development towns, which were the focus of 1950s' national decentralization efforts and are the closest example of alienated housing projects, gave way to the reproduced, high-rise suburbs of the 2000s – allegedly an outcome of a more liberal economic approach. As state concentration was replaced by market concentration, the former monotonous housing estates were replaced by uniform market-led residential towers.

Architecture without Architects: The Neoliberal Vernacular

Every first-year architecture student can quote Louis Sullivan: that "form follows function." As the Israeli settlement mechanism consisted of a coalition of private and national interests, its form had to follow a variety of functions. At the strategic level, the form of the different territorial enclaves and exclaves was dictated by the geopolitical considerations of creating a consecutive Israeli sequence, while the lower levels were subjected to the relevant mode of production in the privatizing settlement mechanism. Thus, while pro-laissez-faire approaches usually highlight the self-fulfillment potential in the process of privatization – Karl Polanyi suggests "[private]property in land" is an essential part of the concept of "individual liberty"[19] – this was quite the contrary in the case of the trans-Israel settlements. Despite a restricted period during the early 1980s, when a small and very privileged group was able to plan and construct houses according to the desires and needs of its members, the process indicates a gradual diminishing of individual ability to influence the production of space. Even then, these unprecedented privileges were part of a state-directed gentrification process, intended to enable the corporate development of a given area, as seen in the early Suburban

[19] Polanyi, quoted in Rolnik, *Urban Warfare: Housing under the Empire of Finance*, 151.

Settlements that were later surrounded by high-rise residential projects. Self-fulfillment was therefore briefly facilitated – so as to eventually replace it with market-oriented development.

Eventually, the form of the built environment had to adapt to new functions with the financialized mode of production. As private entrepreneurs and investors took the lead, the emphasis was on the profitability of planning and construction. Consequently, as seen in the case studies Tzur Yitzhak (Chapter 5) and of Harish (Chapter 6), this concluded in a limited number of housing models that were an outcome of speculative calculations and intended to optimize the distribution of the overall building rights in a given site. As private investment became the main force behind the development of new residential environments, the role of architects and planners turned into the capacity to create three-dimensional grids of real estate. The planner was in charge of dividing space into marketable tracts, while the architect was in charge of extracting the maximal economic potential from a given plot. Fittingly, design turned into an attempt to create a unique and singular façade, camouflaging the commodification of built space while promoting a seemingly user-friendly environment and hiding the financial considerations that produced it.

As entrepreneurial and speculative interests have fueled all recent developments, this created the same reproduced housing models right across the Trans-Israel Highway. Raquel Rolnik, writing on the financialization of housing production, points to increasing standardization which includes the "uniformization of measurements, materials, components and even forms of execution and management."[20] Thus, the current financialized mode of production, whether in São Paulo or in Harish, produces a new mode of architecture without architects and a compatible neoliberal vernacular. As seen in this book, the Israeli neoliberal vernacular was the final and perhaps the most efficient tactic ensuring the continuation of the national geopolitical project – encouraging perpetual private investment while completing the homogenization of the built environment. In his ground-breaking book, *The Decline of the West*, the German historian Oswald Spengler wrote, "Gothic cathedrals and Doric temples are mathematics in stone."[21] Building on Spengler, we could easily claim that housing in the neoliberal age is speculation in concrete.

---

[20] Rolnik, *Urban Warfare: Housing under the Empire of Finance*, 223.
[21] Spengler, *The Decline of the West*, 44.

Bibliography

A'rim. "El'ad – Mazor." Ministry of Construction and Housing. ISA-moch-Programs-000ujzc: A'rim. Israel State Archive, 1993.

Abovich, Yaacov. "After Harish Comes Kasif." *JDN*, October 11, 2013. www.jdn.co.il/news/israel/278938/.

Abreek-Zubeidat, Fatina, and Ronen Ben-Arie. "To Be at Home: Spaces of Citizenship in the Community Settlements of the Galilee." In *The Politics of Nihilism: From the Nineteenth Century to Contemporary Israel*, edited by Nitzan Lebovic and Roy Ben-Shai, 205–26. New York: Bloomsbury Academic, 2014.

Abu Kishk, Bakir. "Arab Land and Israeli Policy." *Journal of Palestine Studies* 11, no. 1 (1981): 124–35.

Adiv, Michal, and Assaf Schwartz. *Sharon's Star Wars: Israel's Seven Star Settlement Plan*. Jerusalem: Hanitzotz A-Sharara, 1992.

Adorno, Theodor. *The Culture Industry: Selected Essays on Mass Culture*. London: Routledge, 2007.

Adorno, Theodor, and Max Horkheimer. *Dialectic of Enlightenment*. Palo Alto, CA: Stanford University Press, 2007.

Agnew, John. "The Territorial Trap: The Geographical Assumptions of International Relations Theory." *Review of International Political Economy* 1, no. 1 (1994): 53–80.

Aigen. *35 Years for Sal'it* [Documentary], 2014. www.youtube.com/watch?v=9vQXrvHyPmY&t=246s.

Alba, Richard D., and John R. Logan. "Variations on Two Themes: Racial and Ethnic Patterns in the Attainment of Suburban Residence." *Demography* 28 (1991): 431–53.

Albeck, Plea. "Delta: Oranit." The State Attorney's Office. ISA-moch-CentralRegion-00097hy. Israel State Archive, 1990.

———. "The Site of Ya'arit." ISA-moch-UrbanPlanning-000z12o. Israel State Archive, 1984.

Alfasi, Nurit, and Tovi Fenster. "Between Socio-Spatial and Urban Justice: Rawls' Principles of Justice in the 2011 Israeli Protest Movement." *Planning Theory* 13, no. 4 (2014): 407–27.

Allegra, Marco. "'Outside Jerusalem – Yet So Near': Ma'ale Adumim, Jerusalem, and the Suburbanization of Israel's Settlement Policy." In *Normalizing Occupation. The Politics of Everyday Life in the West Bank Settlements*, edited by Ariel Handel, Marco Allegra, and Erez Maggor, 48–63. Bloomington, IN: Indiana University Press, 2017.

"The Politics of Suburbia: Israel's Settlement Policy and the Production of Space in the Metropolitan Area of Jerusalem." *Environment and Planning A* 45 (2013): 497–516.

Allweil, Yael. *Homeland: Zionism as Housing Regime, 1860–2011*. London: Taylor & Francis, 2016.

Almog, Oz. *The Sabre – A Profile*. Tel Aviv: Am Oved, 1997.

Alterman, Rachelle. *Planning in the Face of Crisis*. New York and London: Routledge, 2002.

Amitai, Avraham. "Letter from Avraham Amitai CEO of Tzavta to Head of Central District MCH." ISA-moch-DirectorGeneral-000qpp6. Israel State Archive, 1987.

Ampa Israel. "Ampa Israel Website." http://ampa-israel.co.il.

Appelbaum, Levia, and David Newman. *Between Village and Suburb: New Forms of Settlement in Israel*. Rehovot: National Institute of Agriculture, 1989.

Arad, Roei. "You Will Be Recorded in History as the First Reporter to Write Anything Good about Harish." *Haaretz*, May 22, 2019. www.haaretz.co.il/magazine/.premium-MAGAZINE-1.7272134.

Archer, John. *Architecture and Suburbia: From English Villa to American Dream House, 1690–2000*. Minneapolis, MN: University of Minnesota Press, 2005.

Arendt, Hannah. *The Origins of Totalitarianism*. Milton Keynes, UK: Random House, 1951.

Ariel Yazamut. "Project Information" [Promotion]. Ariel Yazamut official website, 2017. www.ayz.co.il.

Arye Soninio Architects. "M/139." Israel Land Administration. Haifa, 1984.

"Urban Plan ZS/BM/1002/10 (Eyal North) Tzur Yigal." Israel Land Administration. Tel Aviv, 1991.

Ashtrom. "Milestones." Ashtrom group official website, 2015. www.ashtrom.co.il/%D7%A6%D7%99%D7%A8-%D7%96%D7%9E%D7%9F.

Assaf, Yigal. "Meeting of the Minister with Representatives of the Ultra-Orthodox Sector – 15/ 01/2001." Ministry of Construction and Housing. ISA-moch-HaifaRegion-000t76e. Israel State Archive, 2001.

Azrayahu, Maoz. "Rabin's Road: The Politics of Toponymic Commemoration of Yitzhak Rabin in Israel." *Political Geography* 31, no. 2 (2012): 73–82.

Bar, Arieh. "Zur Nathan." Tel Aviv: A'rim, 1999. ISA-moch-CentralRegion-000v5zh. Israel State Archive.

Bar-Eli, Avi. "IDF Housing Administration Offers Officers Offers They Can't Refuse." *The Marker*, March 30, 2007. www.themarker.com/realestate/1.506918.

Bar-Yossef, Avinoam. "Earth on Fire." *Maariv*, December 13, 1986.

Barel, Zvi. "CEO of MH Warns Apartment Buyers in the West Bank." *Haaretz*, September 1, 1983.

Bareli, Avi, and Uri Cohen. *The Academic Middle-Class Rebellion: Socio-Political Conflict over Wage-Gaps in Israel*. Vol. 30. Leiden and Boston: Brill, 2018.

Barnstone, Deborah Ascher. *The Transparent State: Architecture and Politics in Postwar Germany*. London and New York: Routledge, 2005.

Barzilai, Gad. "Fantasies of Liberalism and Liberal Jurisprudence: State Law, Politics and the Israeli Arab-Palestinian Community." *Israel Law Review* 34, no. 3 (2000): 426–51.

Bauman, Zygmunt. *Community Seeking Safety in an Insecure World*. Cambridge: Cambridge University Press, 2001.

Beit U'Menuha. "Decisions regarding Mazor (El Ad)." ISA-moch-moch-000ejyx: Beit U'Menuha. Israel State Archive, 1993.

Ben-Porat, Amir. *Where Are Those Bourgeois?* Tel Aviv: Magnes, 1999.

Bennet, Naftali. Facebook Profile. www.facebook.com/NaftaliBennett/about/. Speech at the INSS. Tel Aviv, 2014.

Benvenisti, Meron. *Report: Demographic, Economic, Legal, Social, and Political Developments in the West Bank*. Jerusalem and Boulder, CO: Jerusalem Post and Westview Press, 1987.

Sacred Landscape. Berkeley, CA: University of California Press, 2002.

The West Bank Data Project: A Survey of Israel's Policies. Washington, DC: AEI Press, 1984.

Berger, Tamar. *Autotopia: Suburban In-Between Space in Israel*. Tel Aviv: Hakibbutz Hameuchad, 2015.

Betts, Paul. "The Bauhaus as Cold War Legend: West German Modernism Revisited." *German Politics and Society* 14, no. 12 (2010): 75–100.

Billig, Miriam. "The Jewish Settlements in Judea and Samaria (1967–2008): Historical Overview." *Israel Affairs* 21, no. 3 (2015): 331–47.

Boruchov, Eliahu. "On Target: The Housing Crisis and Damage to the Planning System." *Planning* 15, no. 2 (2018): 63–85.

Bourdieu, Pierre. *Distinctions*. New York: Routledge, 1984.

"The Berber House." In *Rules and Meanings*, edited by Mary Douglas, 98–110. Harmondsworth, UK: Penguin, 1973.

"The Forms of Capital." In *Handbook of the Theory and Research for the Sociology of Education*, edited by John G. Richardson, 241–58. New York: Greenwood Press, 1986.

Boxer, Bonnie. *Kochav Yair* [Promotion video]. South African Zionist Federation, 1984. www.youtube.com/watch?v=pUFGazWYXwk&t=1s.

Brenner, Niel, and Stuart Elden. "Henri Lefebvre on State, Space, Territory." *International Political Sociology* 3 (2009): 353–77. https://doi.org/10.1111/j.1749-5687.2009.00081.x.

Brenner, Niel, and Nik Theodore. "Cities and the Geographies of 'Actually Existing Neoliberalism'." *Antipode* 34, no. 4 (2002): 349–79.

Brenner, Niel, Bob Jessop, Martin Jones, and Gordon MacLeod. "State Space in Question." In *State/Space: A Reader*, edited by Niel Brenner, Bob Jessop, Martin Jones, and Gordon MacLeod, 1–26. Hoboken, NJ: Wiley-Blackwell, 2003.

Brown, Adrienne. *The Black Skyscraper: Architecture and the Perception of Race*. Baltimore, MD: John Hopkins Press, 2017.

Buchman, Meir. Kochav Yair. Interview by Gabriel Schwake, March 4, 2019.

Buso, Nimrod. "Once an Apartment Was Worth Half a Million Shekels." *The Marker*, June 10, 2016. www.themarker.com/realestate/1.3078545.

Cahaner, Lee. "Between Ghetto Politics and Geopolitics: Ultraorthodox Settlements in the West Bank." In *Normalizing Occupation: The Politics of Everyday Life in the West Bank Settlements*, edited by Marco Allegra, Ariel Handel, and Erez Maggor, 112–27. Bloomington, IN: Indiana University Press, 2017.

Carmon, Naomi. "Housing Policy in Israel: Review, Evaluation and Lessons." *Israel Affairs* 7, no. 4 (2001): 181–208.

Central Elections Committee. "Results of 2015 Elections." Jerusalem: Central Elections Committee, 2015. www.votes20.gov.il.

——. "Results of 2019 Elections." Jerusalem: Central Elections Committee, April 9, 2019. https://votes21.bechirot.gov.il/.

Charney, Igal. "A 'Supertanker' against Bureaucracy in the Wake of a Housing Crisis: Neoliberalizing Planning in Netanyahu's Israel." *Antipode* 49, no. 5 (2017): 1223–43.

Chevalier, Michel. "Neo-Rural Phenomena." *Espace géographique* (Special Issue in English) (1993): 175–91.

Chief of Staff Cabinet. "Housing Project – Modi'in Plan." Tel Aviv: IDF, 1986. ISA-moch-UrbanPlanning-000ze5p. Israel State Archive.

Chyutin, Michael, and Bracha Chyutin. *Architecture and Utopia: Kibbutz and Moshav*. Jerusalem: Magnes, 2010.

Cohen, A. "A New Ultra-Orthodox Qirya in El'ad." *Yated Ne'eman* 21 (1997): 4.

Cohen, Avi. Interview in Reihan. Interview by Gabriel Schwake, October 29, 2018.
Cohen, Adi, and Hadar Horesh. "How to Market 86 Buildings in Harish When the Market Slows". *The Marker*, January 30, 2019. www.themarker.com/realestate/.premium-1.6892363.
Cohen, E. "Problems of Development Towns and Urban Housing Quarters." *The Economic Quarterly* 49, no. 50 (1966): 117–31.
Cohen Lifshitz Architects. "Urban Outline Plan SD/MK/101/15/8." Israel Land Administration, Tel Aviv, 2008.
Cohen, Shaul. "Israel's West Bank Barrier: An Impediment to Peace?" *Geographical Review* 96, no. 4 (2006): 682–95.
Cohen, Uri, and Nissim Leon. "The New Mizrahi Middle Class: Ethnic Mobility and Class Integration in Israel." *Journal of Israeli History Politics, Society, Culture* 27, no. 1 (2008): 51–64.
Davar. "Attempts to Sabotage Water Carrier Foiled'. *Davar*, November 15, 1965.
"First Experiment in Eastern Sharoin." *Davar*, January 26, 1983, 7.
"Rozolio: Setbacks in Settlement in Undisputed Areas." *Davar*, August 23, 1978.
"The Three Settlements." *Davar*, August 19,1977, 2.
Davidovic, L. "Haifa District – Harish – Tender #." Haifa: Ministry of Construction and Housing, 1995. ISA-moch-Programs-000ud58. Israel State Archive.
Dekel, Michael. "A Letter to Delta Ltd," 1982. ISA-moag-DeputyMinister-0013xu9. Israel State Archive.
Delso, Rodrigo. "Concrete Punishment: Time, Architecture and Art as Weapons in the Israeli–Palestinian Conflict." *Political Geography* 66 (2018): 57–66.
Delta Ltd. "List of Homebuyers in Oranit." Petah Tikva: Delta, 1982. ISA-moag-DeputyMinister-0013xu9. Israel State Archive.
"Oranit." Karnei Shomron: Delta, 1982. ISA-moag-DeputyMinister-0013xu9. Israel State Archive.
Dirsuweit, Teresa, and Alex Wafer. "Suburban Road-Closures and the Ruinous Landscapes of Privilege in Johannesburg." *Journal of African Studies* 42, no. 3 (2016): 395–410.
DMR Development Planning Ltd. "Alfei Menashe Master Plan Steering Committee." DMR Development Planning Ltd, 2000. ISA-moch-Programs-000tfd3. Israel State Archive.
Dor, Gabi. Development of Nirit. Interviews by Gabriel Schwake, November 2018.
Douer, Yair. *Our Sickle Is Our Sword*. Tel Aviv: Yad Tevenkin, 1992.

Bibliography

Dov Koren Architects. "Local Outline Plan SD/101/15/5." Tel Aviv: Israel Land Administration, 2008.
"Local Outline Plan SD/101/15/12." Tel Aviv: Israel Land Administration, 2011.
"Local Outline Plan SD/101/15/18." Tel Aviv: Israel Land Administration, 2015.
Dovey, Kim. *Framing Place. Mediating Power in Built Form*. London: Routledge, 1999.
Drobles, Matityahu. "Master Plan for Settlement Development in Judea and Samaria, 1979–1983." Jerusalem: World Zionist Organization, 1978. ISA-moag-DeputyMinister-0013y6y. Israel State Archive.
Drom HaSharon Local Council Construction Committee. "Permit 416/87 [Nirit]," 1987. Drom HaSharon Regional Council Engineering Archives.
"Permit 98288 [Nirit]," 1998. Drom HaSharon Regional Council Engineering Archives.
"Permit 20090085 (Tzur Yitzhak)," 2009. Drom HaSharon Regional Council Construction Committee Archives.
"Permit 20090215 (Tzur Yitzhak)," 2009. Drom HaSharon Regional Council Construction Committee Archives.
Dvir, Ran. "Meeting Protocol Regarding Tendering Lots in Harish 17.3.1996." Ministry of Construction and Housing, 1996. ISA-moch-Programs-000ud58. Israel State Archive.
Efrat, Elisha. "Geographical Distribution of the Soviet-Jewish New Immigrants in Israel." *GeoJournal* 24, no. 4 (1991): 355–63.
"Israel's Planned New 'Crossing Highway'." *Journal of Transport Geography* 2, no. 4 (1994): 274–77.
"New Development Towns of Israel (1948–93)." *Cities* 11, no. 4 (1994): 247–52.
Efrat, Elisha, and Jacob Dash. *The Israel Physical Master Plan*. Jerusalem: Planning Department, Ministry of Interior, 1964.
Efrat, Zvi. *The Israeli Project: Building and Architecture 1948–1973*. Tel Aviv: Tel Aviv Museum of Art, 2005.
The Object of Zionism: The Architecture of Israel. Leipzig: Spector Books, 2019.
Eiges, Itay. "Development Works in Harish." Ministry of Finance, 1994. ISA-moch-Programs-000ud59. Israel State Archive.
Eitan, Michael. The Construction of Kochav Yair. Interview by Gabriel Schwake, February 23, 2019.
Eitiel, Yoav. "Harish Is Green, Not Black." *Geffen*, June 21, 2013. www.gfn.co.il/inner.asp?page=213192&item=&search=.

El'ad Council. "Marketing Quarter B in El'ad," 1997. ISA-moch-DirectorGeneral-000q0hs. Israel State Archive.
El'ad Local Construction Committee. "Permit 960033 (El'ad)," 1997. El'ad Local Construction Committee Archives.
"Permit 960034 (El'ad)," 1997. El'ad Local Construction Committee Archives.
"Permit 960046 (El'ad)," 1997. El'ad Local Construction Committee Archives.
"Permit 960087 (El'ad)," 1997. El'ad Local Construction Committee Archives.
"Permit 990025 (El'ad)," 1999. El'ad Local Construction Committee Archives.
"Permit 20020179 (El'ad)," 1999. El'ad Local Construction Committee Archives.
El-hanani, Edith. "Feelings of Ethnic Discrimination in Two Development Towns." *Megamot* 1 (1983): 97–99.
Elden, Stuart. "Thinking Territory Historically." *Geopolitics* 15, no. 4 (2010): 757–61.
Eldor, Sofia. "A New Town in Modi'in." Jerusalem: Ministry of Construction and Housing, 1992. ISA-moch-CentralRegion-000pca4. Israel State Archive.
"Letter from the Head of the MCH's Department of Urban Development, Sofia Eldor, to the CEO of MCH, Asher Wiener – 25.10.1984," 1985. ISA-moch-UrbanPlanning-000ze5p. Israel State Archive.
"Letter to Cabinet Secretary." Jerusalem: Ministry of Construction and Housing, 1985. Israel State Archive.
"Letter to CEO of MCH – Modi'in – 2. 3.1987," 1987. ISA-moch-UrbanPlanning-000ze5p. Israel State Archive.
"Letter to IDF Housing Administration – 20. 4.1985', 1985. ISA-moch-UrbanPlanning-000ze5p. Israel State Archive.
"Special Planning Committee," 1986. ISA-moch-DirectorGeneral-000qpom. Israel State Archive.
Elgazi, Yossef. "A Settlement into the Green-Line." *Ha'aretz*, April 9, 1996.
Engle, Randi, Jennifer Langer-Osuna, and Maxine McKinney de Royston. "Toward a Model of Influence in Persuasive Discussions: Negotiating Quality, Authority, Privilege, and Access within a Student-Led Argument." *Journal of the Learning Sciences* 23, no. 3 (2014): 245–68.
Eshel, Sharon, and Ravit Hananel. "Centralization, Neoliberalism, and Housing Policy Central–Local Government Relations and Residential Development in Israel." *Politics and Space* 37, no. 2 (2018): 237–55.
Falah, Ghazi. "Israeli 'Judaization' Policy in Galilee." *Journal of Palestine Studies* 20, no. 4 (1991): 69–85.

Filc, Dani. *Hegemony and Populism in Israel*. Tel Aviv: Resling, 2006.
— *The Political Right in Israel*. London and New York: Routledge, 2010.
Findley, Lisa. *Building Change: Architecture, Politics and Cultural Agency*. New York: Routledge, 2005.
Fogel, Uri. El'ad, September 1996. ISA-moch-DirectorGeneral-000q0hs. Israel State Archive.
— Highway 6 Settlements. Interview by Gabriel Schwake, March 26, 2019.
Fogel-Hertz-Schwartz Architects and Planners Ltd. "District Outline Plan TMM/3/21." Tel Aviv: Israel Land Administration, 2002.
— "Local Outline Plan: New Mazor GZ/BM/195." Tel Aviv: Israel Land Administration, 1992.
Foucault, Michel. *Discipline and Punish*. 2nd ed. New York: Vintage Books, 1995.
— *Society Must Be Defended*. Translated by Jamey Macey. New York, NY: Picador, 2003.
Freund, Yitzhak. "Survey for the Extension of Harish." Tel Aviv: Israel Land Administration, 1997. ISA-moch-HaifaRegion-000t76e. Israel State Archive.
Galster, George. "Comparing Demand-Side and Supply-Side Housing Policies: Sub-market and Spatial Perspectives." *Housing Studies* 12, no. 4 (1997): 561–77.
Garb, Yaacov. "Constructing the Trans-Israel Highway's Inevitability." *Israel Studies* 9, no. 2 (2004): 180–217.
Gazit, Pnina, and Arnon Soffer. *Between the Sharon and Samaria*. Haifa: University of Haifa, 2005.
Giddens, Anthony. *Central Problems in Social Theory*. London: Macmillan, 1979.
Gil-Ad, Yaacov. Houses in Kochav Yair. Interview by Gabriel Schwake, February 25, 2019.
Gilboa, Arik. Interview in Salit. Interview by Gabriel Schwake, November 26, 2018.
Glick, Moshe. "Nadlan – Nof HaSharon," 2010. https://bit.ly/3oWR6q8.
Glick, Yafa. "Nirit: Labour Pain." *Tzomet Hasharon*, April 9, 1987, 21.
Globes. "High Profits from Sales in Oranit," June 24, 1985.
Golan Architects. "Town Outline Plan SD/MK/101/15/3." Tel Aviv: Israel Land Administration, 2006.
Gonen, Amiram, and Gad Cohen. "Multi-Faceted Screw-up of Neighborhoods in Jerusalem." *City and Region (Ir Veezor)* 19, no. 20 (1989): 9–27.
Gonen Architects and Planners. "Shaked: Urban Outline Plan 102/3." Tel Aviv: Israel Land Authority, 1998.

Gordis, Avishay Ben-Sasson, and Yonatan Levi. *Israel's National Security and West Bank Settlements*. Jerusalem: Molad – Center for the Renewal of Democracy Ltd, 2017.

Gotham, Kevin Fox. "Creating Liquidity Out of Spatial Fixity: The Secondary Circuit of Capital and the Subprime Mortgage Crisis." *International Journal of Urban and Regional Research* 33, no. 2 (2009): 355–71.

Government of Israel. Decision 778 (1996).

Decision 905 (1996).

Decision 1196 (1985).

Treaty between the Government of Israel and the JNF. Jerusalem: Government of Israel, 1960.

Graeber, David. *Debt: The First 5000 Years*. New York: Melville House, 2011.

The Utopia of Rules. New York: Melville House, 2015.

Gramsci, Antonio. *Selections from Cultural Writings*, edited by Quintin Hoare and Geoffrey Nowell-Smith. Cambridge, MA: Harvard University Press, 1985.

Guimond, Laurie, and Myriam Simard. "Gentrification and Neo-Rural Populations in the Québec Countryside: Representations of Various Actors." *Journal of Rural Studies* 26 (2010): 449–64.

Gush Emunim. "Proposal for Settlement in Judea and Samaria." Jerusalem, 1977. ISA-moag-DeputyMinister-0013y71. Israel State Archive.

Gutwein, Daniel. "Pioneer Bourgeoisie." In *Culture, Memory and History*, edited by Meir Chazan, 685–746. Tel Aviv: Tel Aviv University, 2012.

"The Class Logic of the 'Long Revolution', 1973–1977." *Iyunim Bitkumat Israel (Studies in Israeli and Modern Jewish Society)* 11 (2017): 21–57.

"The Settlements and the Relationship between Privatization and the Occupation." In *Normalizing Occupation: The Politics of Everyday Life in the West Bank Settlements*, edited by Ariel Handel, Marco Allegra, and Erez Maggor, 21–33. Bloomington, IN: Indiana University Press, 2017.

Haila, Anne. *Urban Land Rent: Singapore as a Property State*. Chichester, UK: John Wiley and Sons, 2016.

Halliday, Joyce, and Mike Coombes. "In Search of Counterurbanisation: Some Evidence from Devon on the Relationship between Patterns of Migration and Motivation." *Journal of Rural Studies* 11, no. 4 (1995): 433–46.

Halufa – Dov Kehat Ltd. "Kochav Yair – Options for Municipal formation." Tel Aviv: Ministry of Construction and Housing, 1996. ISA-moch-UrbanPlanning-000bsoc. Israel State Archive.

HaModiya. "Arrangement for the Construction of the Hasidic Qirya." *HaModiya*, September 5, 1997.
Hanan Mor Ltd. "Apartment in Nature – The Green Spot in Tzur Yitzhak." Hanan Mor Ltd official website, 2017. https://hmg.co.il.
Handel, Ariel, Galit Rand, and Marco Allegra. "Wine-Washing: Colonization, Normalization, and the Geopolitics of Terroir in the West Bank's Settlements." *Environment and Planning* 47 (2015): 1351–67.
Harif, Yossef. "Prof Zamir: Haven't Yet Finished My Examination Regarding Reihan and Dotan." *Maariv*, November 9, 1979.
Harish Representatives. "Harish Settlement," 2001. ISA-moch-DirectorGeneral-0004zak. Israel State Archive.
Harnish, Dane. "Peace Now Wants to Stop Annexation." *Davar* 14, no. 1 (1983): 1.
Harvey, David. *A Brief History of Neoliberalism*. Oxford: Oxford University Press, 2005.
　Seventeen Contradictions and the End of Capitalism. Oxford: Oxford University Press, 2014.
　The Condition of Postmodernity. Oxford: Blackwell Publishers, 1990.
　The Limits to Capital. London: Verso, 2006.
HaShomer HaTzair Technical Department. "Outline Plan M/146." Haifa: Israel Land Administration, 1985.
Hason, Yael. *Three Decades of Privatisation*. Tel Aviv: Adva Center, 2006.
Hatuka, Tali, Roni Bar, Michael Jacobson, Hila Lothan, Merav Battat, and Jessica Fain. *Neighborhood-State*. Tel Aviv: Resling, 2012.
Hayden, Dolores. *Redesigning the American Dream: Gender, Housing, and Family Life*. 2nd ed. New York, NY: W. W. Norton & Company, 2002.
Heilbronner, Oded. "The Israeli Victorians." *Iyonim Betkumat Israel* 28 (2017): 128–68.
Hein, Carola. "The What, Why, and How of Planning History." In *The Routledge Handbook of Planning History*, edited by Carola Hein, 1–11. London: Routledge, 2018.
Hines, J. Dwight. "In Pursuit of Experience: The Postindustrial Gentrification of the Rural American West." *Ethnography* 11, no. 2 (2010): 285–308.
Hirst, Paul. *Space and Power: Politics, War and Architecture*. Cambridge, UK: Polity Press, 2005.
Hobsbawm, Eric. *Globalisation, Democracy and Terrorism*. London: Little, 2008.
　"Identity Politics and the Left." Institute of Education, London, 1996. http://banmarchive.org.uk/articles/1996%20annual%20lecture.htm.

Nations and Nationalism since 1780. Cambridge, UK: Cambridge University Press, 1992.

Holston, James. *The Modernist City: An Anthropological Critique of Brasilia*. Chicago, IL: University of Chicago Press, 1989.

Homee. *Website for Rural Living*, 2019. www.homee.co.il/.

ICBS. "Localities in Israel." Tel Aviv: Israel Central Bureau of Statistics, 2016.

"Population in Jewish Localities, Mixed Localities and Statistical Areas, by Selected Countries of Origin." Jerusalem: Israeli Central Bureau of Statistics, 2016.

"Socio-Economic Index Value 2013, Cluster of Locality." Jerusalem: Israeli Central Bureau of Statistics, 2013.

"Wages and Income from Work by Locality and Various Economic Variables – 2013." Jerusalem: Israeli Central Bureau of Statistics, 2017.

IDF Housing Administration. "Nofei Ramot Marketing Brochure." Petah Tikva: IDF Housing Administration, 2019.

"Reut B." Petah Tikva: IDF Housing Administration, 1991. Private collection.

ILA. "Kochav Yair." Tel Aviv: Israel Land Administration, 1984.

"Planning and Establishing New Settlements along the Green-Line." Israel Land Administration, 1990. Michael Eitan's private archive.

"Resolution No 262." Israel Land Administration, 1982.

Ilan, Giora. "Letter to the Jewish Agency regarding Payment for House Redemption," 1984. ISA-moag-DeputyMinister-0013xx9. Israel State Archive.

IPD. "Modi'in." Tel Aviv: Institute of Planning and Development, 1968. Central Zionist Archive.

Iron, Gadi. Houses in Oranit. Interview by Gabriel Schwake, November 3, 2019.

Isaac, Jeffrey. "Beyond the Three Faces of Power." In *Rethinking Power*, edited by Thomas Wartenberg, 32–55. Albany, NY: SUNY Press, 1992.

Israel High Court of Justice. Ruling 6698/95, 2000.

Ruling 8573/08 – Uzi Arnon against the Ministry of Interior, 2013.

Israel Planning Administration. "An Analysis for a New Jewish Settlement in Wadi A'ara." Jerusalem: Ministry of Interior, 1978. ISA-MOIN-InteriorPlans-0003yiu. Israel State Archive.

"Meeting regarding Nirit Outline Plan." Ministry of Interior, 1986. ISA-MOIN-InteriorPlans-0002ohr. Israel State Archive.

Israeli Tax Authority. "Israeli Tax Authority." Israeli Tax Authority official website, 2019. www.gov.il/en/departments/israel_tax_authority/govil-landing-page.

JA and WZO. "A Plan for the Development of Jewish Settlements in the Ara Hills – Reihan." Haifa: Jewish Agency and the World Zionist Organization, 1980. Central Zionist Archive.
"Nahal Eron Project." Haifa: Jewish Agency and the World Zionist Organization, 1989. Central Zionist Archive.
Jabareen, Yosef, and Hakam Dbiat. *Architecture and Orientalism in the Country*. Haifa: The Technical Institute of Israel, 2014.
Jackson, Kenneth T. *Crabgrass Frontier: The Suburbanization of the United States*. Oxford: Oxford University Press, 1985.
Jencks, Charles. *The Language of Post-Modern Architecture*. New York, NY: Rizzoli International, 1977.
Jerusalem District Court. Arnon et al. against the District Judea–Samaria Residential Neighbourhoods Ltd (2017).
Judea–Samaria Residential Neighbourhoods Company. "Residential Neighbourhoods in Judea and Samaria." Tel Aviv: Judea–Samaria Residential Neighbourhoods, 1981.
"Ya'arit." Tel Aviv: Judea–Samaria Residential Neighbourhoods, 1984. ISA-moch-UrbanPlanning-000z12o. Israel State Archive.
Karp, Willi. "Harish." Haifa: Ministry of Construction and Housing, 1997. ISA-moch-Programs-000ud59. Israel State Archive.
Katzir-Harish Council. "Strategic Outline for the Development of Harish-Katzir." Katzir-Harish Council, 2001. ISA-moch-DirectorGeneral-0004zak. Israel State Archive.
Kehat, Haim. Harish. Interview by Gabriel Schwake, August 27, 2019.
Kemp, Adriana. "The Frontier Idiom on Borders and Territorial Politics in Post-1967 Israel." *Geography Research Forum* 19 (1999): 78–97.
Kessler, Adi. "Savione HaShem." *Tel Aviv*, June 6, 1997.
Khalidi, Walid. *All That Remains: The Palestinian Villages Occupied and Depopulated by Israel in 1948*. Washington, DC: Institute for Palestine Studies, 1992.
Kimmerling, Baruch. *The End of Ashkenazi Hegemony*. Tel Aviv: Keter Publishing House, 2001.
Zionism and Territory: The Socio-Territorial Dimensions of Zionist Politics. Berkeley, CA: Institute of International Studies, University of California, 1983.
Kipnis, B. "Potential of Developing Urban Housings along the Hills Axis." Haifa: Ministry of Construction and Housing, 1979.
Kislev, Ran. "Behind Yeruham, behind Kfar Sava." *Haaretz*, February 17, 1989.
Knesset of Israel. Israel as the Nation State of the Jewish People, 2018.
Kochav Yair Association. "Letter to Deputy Prime Minister and Minister of Construction and Housing David Levy," 1981. ISA-moag-DeputyMinister-0013y15. Israel State Archive.

Kochav Yair Council. "Security in Kichav Yair." Kochav Yair-Tzur Yigal Council official website, 2015. www.kyair.org.il/Lists/List2/DispForm.aspx?ID=12.
Kotler, Yair. "The Construction Frenzy in Judea and Samaria – at Skyrocketing Prices." *Maariv*, January 10, 1982.
Krispel, Zuriel. El'ad. Radio interview by Eithan Danziger. *Artuz 7*, December 26, 1997. ISA-moch-DirectorGeneral-000q0hs. Israel State Archive.
Lake, Robert W., and Susan Caris Cutter. "A Typology of Black Suburbanization in New Jersey since 1970." *Geographical Review* 70, no. 2 (1980): 167–81.
Lane, Barbara M. *Architecture and Politics in Germany, 1918–1945*. Cambridge, MA: Harvard University Press, 1985.
Lanir, Niva. "You Plowed and Harvested." *Davar*, September 23, 1983.
Laniv Engineering. "Villa in Nature." Hadera, 2016.
Lavi-Bar Architects and Planners. "Outline Plan M/196a Katzir: Emergency Site." Haifa: Israel Land Administration, 1994.
Lefebvre, Henri. "Space and the State." In *State, Space, World*, edited by Niel Brenner and Stuart Elden, 223–53. Minneapolis, MN: University of Minnesota Press, 2009.
   The Production of Space. New York, NY: John Wiley and Sons, 1991.
   Writings on Cities. Translated by Elenoere Kofman and Elizabeth Lebas. Oxford: Blackwell Publishers, 1996.
Leibniz, Gottfried. *Monadology*. Translated by Robert, UK Latta. Dumfries & Galloway, UK: Anodocs Books, 2017.
Leonard, Pauline. "Landscaping Privilege: Being British in South Africa." In *Geographies of Privilege*, edited by France Winddance Twine and Bradley Gardener, 97–120. London and New York: Routledge, 2013.
Levav, Amos. "First Members of the Caucasian Gari'n Arrive in Reihan B." *Maariv*, December 1, 1981.
   "In Reihan Are Worried from Controversy over Other Settlement with the Same Name." *Maariv*, December 9, 1979.
   "JNF to Establish 3 More Points in the Triangle Area." *Maariv*, October 28, 1980.
Levi, Dotan. "A Committee of the Interior Ministry Recommended'. *Calcalist*, October 10, 2016. www.calcalist.co.il/local/articles/0,7340,L-3699656,00.html.
   "Harish for Everyone." *Calcalist*, January 17, 2013. www.calcalist.co.il/real_estate/articles/0,7340,L-3593333,00.html.
Levi, Dotan, and Dianna Bahor-Nir. "Harish: A City for Rent." *Calcalist*, February 2, 2018. www.calcalist.co.il/local/articles/0,7340,L-3730631,00.html.

Levi, Moshe. "Letter to Minister of Construction and Housing – Housing Project for Military Personnnel," 1984. ISA-moch-UrbanPlanning-000ze5p. Israel State Archive.
Levi-Barzilai, Vered. "A House with an Attached Tank." *Haaretz*, October 16, 2001.
Liechty, Mark. *Suitably Modern Making Middle-Class Culture in a New Consumer Society*. Princeton, NJ: Princeton University Press, 2002.
Local Government Administration. "Economic Resilience of Local Authorities." Jerusalem: Ministry of the Interior, 2013.
Logan, John R., and Richard D. Alba. "Minority Proximity to Whites in Suburbs: An Individual-Level Analysis of Segregation." *American Journal of Sociology* 98 (1993): 1388–1427.
Logan, John, and Harvey Molotch. *Urban Fortunes: A Political Economy of Place*. Los Angeles, CA: University of California Press, 1987.
Logan, John R., Weiwei Zhang, and Miao David Chunyu. "Emergent Ghettos: Black Neighborhoods in New York and Chicago, 1880–1940." *American Journal of Sociology* 120, no. 4 (2015): 1055–94. https://doi.org/10.1086/680680.
Lori, Aviva. "The Strike of Real Estate Monsters Continues, This Time in the Tzur Yitzhak Version." *Ha'aretz*, March 2, 2011.
Lovering, John. "Will Recession Prove to Be a Turning Point in Planning and Urban Development Thinking?" *International Planning Studies* 15, no. 3 (2001): 15.
Maariv. "A Fresh Method for New Settlements." *Maariv*, March 20, 1983.
"God's Little Acre in Alfe Menashe." *Maariv*, October 29, 1985.
"Ideology and Money." *Maariv*, December 14, 1982.
"Samaria: Uri Bar on Road." *Maariv*, October 30, 1985.
Maccabim Reut Local Council Construction Committee. "Permit 910127/4560," 1991. Modi'in-Maccabim-Reut Local Construction Committee Archives.
MacCannell, Dean. *The Tourist: A New Theory of the Leisure Class*. Berkeley, CA: University of California Press, 1976.
MacIver, Robert Morrison. *The Modern State*. London: Oxford University Press, 1926.
Maggor, Erez. "State, Market and the Israeli Settlements: The Ministry of Housing and the Shift from Messianic Outposts to Urban Settlements in the Early 1980s." *Israeli Sociology* 16 (2015): 140–67.
Malka, C. "Letter to Michael Eitan, Jerusalem: Ministry of Agriculture,"1982. ISA-Moag-DeputyMinister-0013y15. Israel State Archive.
Mansfeld-Kehat Architects and Planners. "Local Outline Plan Harish/1/A." Haifa: Israel Land Administration, 2012.

Maor, Ziv. "Half of 200 Homebuyers in Ultra-Orthodox El'ad – National Religious." *Haaretz*, August 17, 1997.
"Marketing to Associations, the Improved Version," August 23, 2002. www.haaretz.co.il/misc/1.819455.
Maoz, Shlomo. "MA and MH Agree on Cooperation in Construction in JS." *Haaretz*, January 18, 1983.
Marcuse, Herbert. *One-Dimensional Man*. Boston, MA: Beacon Press, 2012.
Marcuse, Peter. "Housing Policy and the Myth of the Benevolent State." *Social Policy* 9, no. 4 (1978): 21–26.
Marom, Avi. "Tender 10025/99 – HaParsa Neighbourhood – Harish," 2001. ISA-moch-DirectorGeneral-0004zak. Israel State Archive.
Marom, Nathan. "Activising Space: The Spatial Politics of the 2011 Protest Movement in Israel." *Urban Studies* 50, no. 13 (2013): 2826–41.
City of Concept: Planning Tel Aviv. Tel Aviv: Babel Press, 2009.
Marshall, Harvey. "White Movement to the Suburbs: A Comparison of Explanations." *American Sociological Review* 44, no. 6 (1979): 975–94.
Marx, Karl. *Capital: A Critique of Political Economy*. Vol. 1. London: Penguin, 1992.
Mbembe, Achille. "Necropolitics." *Public Culture* 15, no. 1 (2003): 11–40.
MCH. "Construction through Associations." Ministry of Construction and Housing, 1993. Michael Eitan's private archive.
"El'ad." Ministry of Construction and Housing, 1996. ISA-mof-Budget-0010kuo. Israel State Archive.
"El'ad: Adjusting Land Costs and Analysing Apartment Prices." Ministry of Construction and Housing, 1997. ISA-moch-moch-000elrw. Israel State Archive.
"Letter from MCH Legal Department to State Attorney of the Jerusalem District – Tzavta." Jerusalem: Ministry of Construction and Housing, 1999. Israel State Archive.
"Meeting at the Office of the Minister of MCH in Tel Aviv – 6.9.1990." Tel Aviv: Ministry of Construction and Housing, 1990. ISA-moch-moch-000ejyx. Israel State Archive.
"Meeting Protocol 1.4.1985." Jerusalem: Ministry of Construction and Housing, 1985. ISA-moch-UrbanPlanning-000ze5p. Israel State Archive.
"Meeting Regarding Construction for Military Personnel 2.9.1990." Jerusalem: Ministry of Construction and Housing, 1990.
"Oranit." Jerusalem: Ministry of Construction and Housing, 1987. ISA-moch-CentralRegion-00097hx. Israel State Archive.
"Oranit." Jerusalem: Ministry of Construction and Housing, 1991. ISA-moch-CentralRegion-000qpze. Israel State Archive.

"Program for a Detailed Urban Plan: Ancient Mazor." Ministry of Construction and Housing, 1990. Courtesy of Uri Fogel.

"Tzur Nathan – SD/101/15/D." Ministry of Construction and Housing, 1999. ISA-moch-CentralRegion-000ykrt. Israel State Archive.

MCH Directorate of Rural Construction. "Land Allocation for New Settlements." Tel Aviv: Ministry of Construction and Housing, 1990. Michael Eitan's private archive.

"Program for Tzur Nathan," 1995. ISA-moch-Programs-000upmn. Israel State Archive.

"The Stars Settlements." Ministry of Construction and Housing, 1995. ISA-moch-Programs-000upmn. Israel State Archive.

MCH Directorate of Rural Construction and New Settlements. "Plan for the Development of New Suburban Settlements along Highway 6." Ministry of Construction and Housing, 1990. Michael Eitan's private archive.

MCH Urban Planning Department. "Meeting Regarding Tel-Eron – 15.9.1993." Jerusalem: Ministry of Construction and Housing, 1993. Israel State Archive.

MCH Urban Planning Unit. "List of the Stars Settlements." Ministry of Construction and Housing, 1998. ISA-moch-moch-000uls4. Israel State Archive.

Meir Buchman Architects and Planners. "Detailed Plan GZ/117." Tel Aviv: Israel Land Administration, 1988.

"Modification Plan SD/1002/7 A: Kochav Yair." Tel Aviv: Israel Land Administration, 1987.

Mentzel, Dan. Reut and Rosh Ha'ayin. Interview by Gabriel Schwake, July 5, 2019.

Meridor, Dan. "Harish," 1997. ISA-moch-Programs-000ud59. Israel State Archive.

Mevnim Ltd. "Marom HaSharon," 2016. www.mhasharon.co.il.

Milman, D. "Letter from CEO of Shikun u Pituah to MCH David Levy," 1987. ISA-moch-DirectorGeneral-000qpp6. Israel State Archive.

Ministerial Committee Aliyah. "Decision A/82." Jerusalem: Israeli Government Secretariat, 1990. ISA-moch-CentralRegion-000ynfn. Israel State Archive.

Ministry of Agriculture. "Renewal of Settlement Momentum in Judea and Samaria." Jerusalem: Ministry of Agriculture, 1984. ISA-moag-DeputyMinister-0013y2 g. Israel State Archive.

Ministry of Aliyah Integration. "O'lim 1989–2015 According to Settlements." Jerusalem: Israeli Central Bureau of Statistics, 2016.

Ministry of Defense. "Draft Resolution." Tel Aviv: Ministry of Defense, 1985. ISA-moch-UrbanPlanning-000ze5p. Israel State Archive.

Ministry of Environmental Protection, *Residential Building Patterns in Israel*. Jerusalem: Ministry of Environmental Protection, 2015.

Ministry of Interior. "Planning and Building Regulations (Considerable Deviation from Plan)." Ministry of Interior, 2002.

Mintz-Melamed Architects and Planners. "Local Outline Plan SD/MD/101/15/1." Tel Aviv: Israel Land Administration, 2010.

Mitzpe Afek Council. "Building Permits Archive." Official website of Mitzpe Afek Regional Council. Mitzpe Afek Regional Council Engineering Department, 2019. www.vmm.co.il/.

Molnar, Virag. *Building the State Architecture, Politics, and State Formation in Post-War Central Europe*. London and New York: Routledge, 2013.

Morag, Moshe. "Letter to CEO of MCH: Military Personnel in the Modiin Area," 1986. ISA-moch-DirectorGeneral-000qpom. Israel State Archive.

Moran, Hannah. "Analysis of Population in Modi'in Area." Tel Aviv: Ministry of Agriculture and Jewish Agency, 1986. ISA-moch-UrbanPlanning-000ze5p. Israel State Archive.

Moreno, Louis. "Always Crashing in the Same City: Real Estate, Psychic Capital and Planetary Desire." *City* 22, no. 1 (2018): 152–68.

——— "The Urban Process under Financialised Capitalism." *City* 18, no. 3 (2014): 244–68.

Morris, Benny. *The Birth of The Palestinian Refugee Problem Revisited*. Cambridge, UK: Cambridge University Press, 2004.

Moshe Ravid Architects and Planners. "Harish." Haifa: Ministry of Construction and Housing, 1992. Israel Land Administration.

——— "Sal'it: Urban Outline Plan 112/1/2," 1999. Israel Land Administration.

Movement for New Urban Settlements. "The Community Settlement." Jerusalem, 1975. ISA-moag-DeputyMinister-0013y71. Israel State Archive.

Mualem, Nir. "Playing with Supertankers: Centralization in Land Use Planning in Israel: A National Experiment Underway." *Land Use Policy* 75 (2018): 269–83.

Nahoum Dunsky Planners. "Development of the Hills' Axis: The Seven Stars Plan." Tel Aviv: University of Haifa, 1991. Israeli Institute of Technology.

Nahoum Zolotoz Architects. "Outline Plan YV-132-1." Tel Aviv: Israel Land Administration, 1983.

Naim, Yossi. "Lot Sizes in Toshavot and Community Settlements with Mountainous Topography." Jerusalem: Settlement Division, 1982. ISA-moag-DeputyMinister-0013xxu. Israel State Archive.

National Committee for Planning and Construction. "Meeting Number 534." Ministry of Interior, 2012.

Naveh, Baruch. "Arabs Sold Lands and Then Complained That It Was Stolen in Order Not to Take a Bullet." *Maariv*, December 18, 1985.

"In Aflei Menahse They Don't Believe Promises." *Maariv*, August 7, 1984.

Neuman, Boaz. *Land and Desire in Early Zionism*. Waltham, MA: Brandeis University Press, 2011.

Neupane, Gita, and Meda Chesney. "Violence against Women on Public Transport in Nepal: Sexual Harassment and the Spatial Expression of Male Privilege." *International Journal of Comparative and Applied Criminal Justice* 38, no. 1 (2014): 23–38.

Newman, David. "Gush Emunim and Settlement-type in the West Bank." *British Society for Middle Eastern Studies* 8, no. 1 (1981): 33–37.

"Settlement as Suburbanization: The Banality of Colonization." In *Normalizing Occupation: The Politics of Everyday Life in the West Bank Settlements*, edited by Ariel Handel, Marco Allegra, and Erez Maggor, 24–47. Bloomington, IN: Indiana University Press, 2017.

Nir, Meir. Tzur Yitzhak. Interview by Gabriel Schwake, March 26, 2019.

Nirit Council. "Guard Duty in Nirit." Nirit Council, 1985. Nirit Council website. www.nirit.org.il/.

Nitzan-Shiftan, Alona. *Seizing Jerusalem: The Architectures of Unilateral Unification*. Minneapolis, MN: University of Minnesota Press, 2017.

"Whitened Houses." *Theory and Criticism (Teoria vebekoret)* 16 (2000): 227–32.

Niu, Ben, and Tan Gang. "Enforcing User-Space Privilege Separation with Declarative Architectures." In Proceedings of the Seventh ACM Workshop on Scalable Trusted Computing. Raleigh, NC: Association for Computing Machinery, 2012. https://doi.org/10.1145/2382536.2382541.

Oranit Council. "Council Meeting Protocol – 20. 3.1993." Oranit Council, 1993. ISA-MOIN-MOIN-000z2 ft. Israel State Archive.

Oren, Amikam. Reut. Interview by Gabriel Schwake, March 25, 2019.

Pais, Jeremy, Scott South, and Kyle Crowder. "Metropolitan Heterogeneity and Minority Neighborhood Attainment: Spatial Assimilation or Place Stratification?" *Social Problems* 59, no. 2 (2012): 258–81.

Patilon, Rina. "Derech Eretz Avenue Continues to Populate: Get to Know the New Businesses." *Harish City*, November 2, 2019. https://bit.ly/3FJCX5K.

PCBS. "Localities in the Palestinian Authority." Ramallah: Palestinian Central Bureau of Statistics, 2008.

Peck, Jamie, Nik Theodore, and Niel Brenner. "Neoliberal Urbanism Redux?" *International Journal of Urban and Regional Research* 37, no. 3 (2013): 1091–99.

Perlstein Architects and Planners. "Detailed Plan 115/2." Tel Aviv, 1985. Israel Land Administration.
Petersburg, Ofer. "Tender for Apartments in El'ad Begins." *Yediot Ahronot*, March 21, 1996.
"Ultra-Orthodox Trying to Prevent National Religious to Settle in El'ad." *Yediot Ahronot*, August 22, 1997.
Pinhas, Ruthie. "Tzavta in Alfei Mensahe: A Success Story." *Maariv*, December 27, 1985.
Portugali, Juval. "Jewish Settlement in the Occupied Territories: Israel's Settlement Structure and the Palestinians." *Political Geography Quarterly* 10 (1991): 26–53.
Prescott, John Robert Victor. *Political Frontiers and Boundaries*. New York: Routledge, 1987.
Priel, Aharon. "Dozens of Large Development Companies Are Engaged in JS." *Maariv*, March 20, 1983.
Pripaz, E. "Nahal Reihan: Moshav Shitufi." *Davar*, June 28, 1979.
Pullan, Wendy. "Frontier Urbanism: The Periphery at the Centre of Contested Cities." *The Journal of Architecture* 16, no. 1 (2011): 15–35. https://doi.org/10.1080/13602365.2011.546999.
Rabin, Dan. "Building in Tzur Nathan," 1999. ISA-moch-CentralRegion -000v5zh. Israel State Archive.
Rabinowitz, Dan, and Itai Vardi. *Driving Forces: Trans-Israel Highway and the Privatization of Civil Infrastructures in Israel*. Tel Aviv: Van Leer Institute Jerusalem/Hakibbutz Hameuchad, 2010.
Ram, Uri. "Glocommodification: How the Global Consumes the Local – McDonald's in Israel." *Current Sociology* 52, no. 1 (2004): 11–31.
The Globalization of Israel. New York: Routledge, 2008.
Ravid, M. "Modi'im Area." Tel Aviv: Ministry of Construction and Housing, Administration of Rural Construction, 1983.
Razin, Elad. "Urban Economic Development in a Period of Local Initiative: Competition among Towns in Israel's Southern Coastal Plain." *Urban Studies* 27 (1990): 685–703.
Reihan Council. 'Reihan'. Reihan Council official website, 2018 [no longer available].
Riskin, Arieh. Houses in Kochav Yair and Reut. Interview by Gabriel Schwake, March 14, 2019.
Rolnik, Raquel. *Urban Warfare: Housing under the Empire of Finance*. New York: Verso, 2019.
Ron, James. *Frontiers and Ghettos: State Violence in Serbia and Israel*. Berkeley, CA: University of California Press, 2003.

Rose, Damaris. "Rethinking Gentrification: Beyond the Uneven Development of Marxist Urban Theory." *Environment and Planning D: Society and Space* 2 (1984): 47–74.
Rosen, Gilad, and Eran Razin. "Enclosed Residential Neighborhoods in Israel: From Landscapes of Heritage and Frontier Enclaves to New Gated Communities." *Environment and Planning A* 40 (2008): 2895–913.
Rotbard, Sharon. "Wall and Tower." In *A Civilian Occupation*, edited by Rafi Segal and Eyal Weizman, 39–58. London: Verso, 2003.
——. *White City, Black City: Architecture and War in Tel Aviv and Jaffa*. Cambridge, MA: MIT Press, 2015.
Rotem, Tzahar. "Nirit Regrets: They Do Not Want a Neighborhood of Alfei Menashe." *Haaretz*, August 25, 2011. www.haaretz.co.il/misc/1.992036.
Rozin, Orit. *A Home for All Jews: Citizenship, Rights, and National Identity in the New Israeli*. Waltham, MA: Brandeis University Press, 2016.
Rubenstein, Moshe. "Discussion Regarding the Decision for Harish." Ministry of Construction and Housing, 2001. ISA-moch-HaifaRegion-000t76e. Israel State Archive.
——. "Harish Survey." Ministry of Construction and Housing, 2000. ISA-moch-DirectorGeneral-0004zaj. Israel State Archive.
——. "Proposal for the Planning of Harish." Ministry of Construction and Housing, 2001. ISA-moch-HaifaRegion-000t76e. Israel State Archive.
——. "The Minister's Decisions Regarding Harish." Ministry of Construction and Housing, 2001. ISA-moch-HaifaRegion-000t76e. Israel State Archive.
Rubin, Ziv, and Daniel Felsenstein. "Supply Side Constraints in the Israeli Housing Market: The Impact of State Owned Land." *Land Use Policy* 65 (2017): 266–76.
Said, Edward. *The Question of Palestine*. New York: Times Books, 1979.
Sal'it Council. *40 Years for Sal'it* [Documentary], 2019.
Samaria Local Construction Committee. "Permit 8/1 [Sal'it]," 1987. Samaria Regional Council Engineering Archives.
——. "Permit 8–7/1/1 [Sal'it]," 2013. Samaria Regional Council Engineering Archives.
——. "Permit 8/77 [Sal'it]," 1987. Samaria Regional Council Engineering Archives.
——. "Permit 8/84 [Sal'it]," 2018. Samaria Regional Council Engineering Archives.
——. "Permit 8/908/0 [Sal'it]," 1981. Samaria Regional Council Engineering Archives.

"Permit 12-38/99-01 [Reihan]," 2001. Samaria Regional Council Engineering Archives.
"Permit 15-231/99 [Shaked]," 2000. Samaria Regional Council Engineering Archives.
"Permit 852/84 [Sal'it]," 1984. Samaria Regional Council Engineering Archives.
"Permit 1008 [Shaked]," 2007. Samaria Regional Council Engineering Archives.
"Permit 1503/85 [Hinanit]," 1985. Samaria Regional Council Engineering Archives.
Sand, Shlomo. *The Invention of the Jewish People*. New York: Verso, 2009.
Sandrov, Dovi. "Local Council Katzir-Harish." Local Council Katzir-Harish, 2000. ISA-moch-DirectorGeneral-0004zaj. Israel State Archive.
Sassen, Saskia. *Territory, Authority, Rights*. Princeton, NJ: Princeton University Press, 2006.
Sasson-Levy, Orna. "Where Will the Women Be? Gendered Implications of the Decline of Israel's Citizen Army." In *The New Citizen Armies: Israel's Armed Forces in Comparative Perspective*, edited by Stuart Cohen, 173–95. New York: Routledge, 2010.
Schattner, David, and Gideon Biger. "The Real 'Fathers' of the 'National Water Carrier' of Israel." *Cathedra* 159 (2017): 89–124.
Schnabel, Ariel. "In the Twisted World of the Extreme Left, Every Settler Is a Spy." *Makor Rishon*, September 15, 2017. www.makorrishon.co.il/nrg/online/1/ART2/895/016.html.
Schwake, Gabriel. "An Officer and a Bourgeois: Israeli Military Personnel, Suburbanization and Selective Privatization." *Planning Perspectives* 36, no. 1 (2020): 183–94. https://doi.org/10.1080/02665433.2020.1781683.
    "Financialising the Frontier: Harish City'. *Cities* 107 (2020). https://doi.org/10.1016/j.cities.2020.102945.
    "Normalizing War: Protective Spaces and National Resilience." In *War Diaries: Design after the Destruction of Art and Architecture*, edited by Elisa Dainese and Aleksandar Staničić. Charlottesville, VA: University of Virginia Press, 2021.
    "Post-Traumatic Urbanism: Repressing Manshiya and Wadi Salib." *Cities* 75 (May 2018): 50–58.
    "Settle and Rule: The Evolution of the Israeli National Project." *Architecture and Culture* 8, no. 2 (2020): 350–71. https://doi.org/10.1080/20507828.2020.1730624.
    "Supply-Side Territoriality: Re-shaping a Geopolitical Project According to Economic Means." *Space and Polity* 25 (2020): 75–96.
    "The Americanisation of Israeli Housing Practices." *The Journal of Architecture* 25, no. 3 (2020): 295–316.

"The Bourgeoisification of the Green-Line: The New Israeli Middle-Class and the Suburban Settlement." *Political Geography*, 2020. https://doi.org/10.1016/j.polgeo.2020.102223.

"The Community Settlement: A Neo-Rural Territorial Tool." *Planning Perspectives* 36, no. 2 (2021): 237–57. https://doi.org/10.1080/02665433.2020.1728569.

Scott, James. *Seeing Like a State: How Certain Schemes to Improve the Human Condition Have Failed*. New Haven, CT: Yale University Press, 1999.

Segal, Rafi, and Weizman Eyal. *A Civilian Occupation: The Politics of Israeli Architecture*. London: Verso, 2003.

"The Mountain." In *A Civilian Occupation: The Politics of Israeli Architecture*, 79–99. London: Verso, 2003.

Segev, Tom. *Elvis in Jerusalem: Post-Zionism and the Americanization of Israel*. New York: Metropolitan Books, 2002.

Settlement Department. "Hinanit Local Outline Plan'. Jerusalem: World Zionist Organization, 1980. Central Zionist Archive.

"Mitzpe Yarhiv." Tel Aviv: Jewish Agency, 1980.

"Outline Plan for Reihan." Jerusalem: World Zionist Organization, 1979. Central Zionist Archive.

"Outline Plan for Sal'it." Haifa: World Zionist Organization, 1977.

Settlement Division. "A Proposal for Settlement Development in the Eron-Reihan Hills." Haifa: World Zionist Organization, 1980. Central Zionist Archive.

"Community Settlements." Jerusalem: World Zionist Organization, 1978. ISA-moag-DeputyMinister-0013xta. Israel State Archive.

"Development Plan for Jewish Settlement in the Eron Hills – Reihan Region." Haifa: World Zionist Organization, 1981. Central Zionist Archive.

"Population Dispersal Policy and Development of Judea and Samaria." World Zionist Organization, 1982. ISA-moag-DeputyMinister-0013xtb. Israel State Archive.

"The 100,000 Plan." Jerusalem: World Zionist Organization, 1981. ISA-moag-DeputyMinister-0013y6y. Israel State Archive.

Shachar, Arieh. "Reshaping the Map of Israel: A New National Planning Doctrine." *Annals of the American Academy of Political and Social Science* 555, no. 1 (1998): 209–18.

Shadar, Hadas. *The Foundations of Public Housing*. Tel Aviv: Ministry of Construction and Housing, 2014.

Shafir, Gershon. "From Overt to Veiled Segregation: Israel's Palestinian Arab Citizens in the Galilee." *Middle East Studies* 50 (2018): 1–22.

Shaked, Lidor. "Eyal Berkowitz: 'I Recommend Young Couples to Think of Harish'." *Harish24*, January 8, 2018. https://bit.ly/3DBYtYd.
Shapira, Anita. *Land and Power: The Zionist Resort to Force, 1881–1948*. 2nd ed. Stanford, CA: Stanford University Press, 1999.
Sharet, Moshe. *Political Diary B*. Tel Aviv: Am Oved, 1968.
Sharon, Arieh. *Physical Planning in Israel*. Jerusalem: Israeli Government, 1951.
Sheikh, Faheem. "Pan-Arabism: A Tool of Ruling Elites or a Politically-Relevant Ideology?" *Policy Perspectives* 13, no. 2 (2016): 93–107.
Shenhav, Yehouda. *The Arab Jews: A Postcolonial Reading of Nationalism, Religion, and Ethnicity*. Redwood, CA: Stanford University Press, 2006.
Shiloni, Giora. Development of Oranit. Interview by Gabriel Schwake, July 3, 2019.
Shomron Regional Council. "Building Permits Archive." Shomron Council Engineering Department, 2018. Shomron Regional Council official website [no longer available].
Sklair, Leslie. "Iconic Architecture and Urban, National, and Global Identities." In *Cities and Sovereignty: Identity Politics in Urban Spaces*, edited by Diane E. Davis and Nora Libertun Duren, 179–95. Bloomington, IN: Indiana University Press, 2011.
Smith, Darren P., and Deborah A. Phillips. "Socio-Cultural Representations of Greentrified Pennine Rurality." *Journal of Rural Studies* 7, no. 4 (2001): 457–69.
Society for the Protection of Nature in Israel. "Report on the MCH Plans for Kochav Yair and Yarhiv Nirit." Tel Aviv: Society for the Protection of Nature in Israel, 1995. ISA-moch-UrbanPlanning-000bsoz. Israel State Archive.
Sofer, Dror. Nirit: Sofer Architects. Interview by Gabriel Schwake, February 21, 2019.
Soffer, Arnon. "Mitzpim in the Galilee – A Decade of Their Establishment." *Karaa* 34 (1992): 24–29.
The Stars. Interview by Gabriel Schwake, January 11, 2018.
Sofian, Sandra. *Healing the Land and the Nation: Malaria and the Zionist Project in Palestine, 1920–1947*. Chicago, IL: University of Chicago Press, 2007.
Somfalvi, Atila, and Avital Lahav. "Natanyahu on Housing: Supertanker for Bureaucracy." *Ynet*, July 3, 2011. www.ynet.co.il/articles/0,7340,L-4038871,00.html.

Sontag, Susan. "Fascinating Fascism." In *Under the Sign of Saturn*, 73–105. New York: Picador, 1980.
Spengler, Oswald. *The Decline of the West*. New York: Vintage Books, 2006.
Stanek, Łukasz. "French Post-War Architecture and Its Critics." In *Architecture and the Welfare State*, edited by Mark Swenarton, Tom Avermaete, and Dirk Heuvel, 113–32. New York: Routledge, 2015.
State Comptroller of Israel. "Local Government Audit Reports." Jerusalem: Office of the State Comptroller of Israel, 2016.
——— "The Establishment of Alfei Menashe." Jerusalem: Office of the State Comptroller of Israel, 1984.
Steinmentz, Leah. "Tzur Nathan." Israel Land Administration, 1993. ISA-moch-CentralRegion-000v5zh. Israel State Archive.
Tal, Dalia. "Development Momentum." *Globes*, October 14, 1999.
——— "Tzur Nathan: Forgot the VLKH." *Globes*, November 22, 1999.
Tal, Einat. *The Frontier Fortresses Plan*. Haifa: University of Haifa, 2016.
Tasan-Kok, Tuna. "Changing Interpretations of 'Flexibility' in the Planning Literature: From Opportunism to Creativity?" *International Planning Studies* 13, no. 3 (2008): 183–95.
Taskir. "Survey of Homebuyers in El'ad." Jerusalem: Ministry of Construction and Housing, 2000. ISA-moch-moch-000eoi6. Israel State Archive.
Tel Aviv District Court. Beit U'Menuha against the State of Israel, 1995.
Tel Iron Council. "Council Meeting 01/95." Tel Iron: Tel Iron Council, 1995. ISA-MOIN-InteriorLocalgov-000hhvo. Israel State Archive.
Tessler, Mark. *A History of the Israeli–Palestinian Conflict*. Bloomington, IN: Indiana University Press, 1994.
Thatcher, Margaret. Margaret Thatcher's Interview in *Women's Own*, September 23, 1987. (THCR 5/2/262): COI transcript. Thatcher Archive.
The Subcommittee on Immigration and Naturalization of the Committee on The Judiciary: United States Senate Ninety-Fifth Congress. "The Colonization of the West Bank Territories by Israel." Hearings protocol. Washington DC: Printed for the use of the Committee on the Judiciary, 1978.
Tolz, Mark. "Jewish Emigration from the Former USSR since 1970." *Demoscope* 497, no. 6 (2012): 1–27.
Tönnies, Ferdinand. *Community and Civil Society*, edited by Jose Harris. Cambridge, UK: Cambridge University Press, 2001.
Trans-Israel Ltd. "TransIsrael." Trans-Israel road company official website, 2014. www.transisrael.co.il/.

Trezib, Joachim. *Die Theorie der zentralen Orte in Israel und Deutschland: Zur Rezeption Walter Christallers im Kontext von Sharonplan und 'Generalplan Ost'*. Berlin: De Gruyter Oldenbourg, 2014.

Troen, Illan. "Frontier Myths and Their Applications in America and Israel: A Transnational Perspective." *The Journal of American History* 86, no. 3 (1999): 1209–30.

Turner, Frederick Jackson. *The Frontier in American History*. New York: Holt, Rinehart & Winston, 1962.

Tzabari, Guy. "Nirit: From a Community Settlement in the Sharon Region to a Semi-Settlement." *Channel 10*, August 11, 2008.

Tzfadia, Erez. "Abusing Multiculturalism: The Politics of Recognition and Land Allocation in Israel." *Environment and Planning D: Society and Space* 26 (2008): 1115–30.

——— "Public Housing as Control: Spatial Policy of Settling Immigrants in Israeli Development Towns." *Housing Studies* 21, no. 4 (2006): 523–37.

Tznovar Consultants Ltd. "Populating Harish Katzir." Giva'ataim, 1993. ISA-MOIN-InteriorLocalgov-000hhvo. Israel State Archive.

Tzur, Eitan. *HaHamishia HaKamerit* [Comedy], 1995. www.youtube.com/watch?v=65sUsV3gBYY.

Tzur Yigal Association. "Tzur Yigal." Tzur Yigal Association, 1992.

Tzuriel, Yossef. "Samaria Is Open for Settlement." *Maariv*, May 3, 1979.

Vale, Lawrence. *Architecture, Power and National Identity*. 2nd ed. New York and London: Routledge, 2008.

——— *From the Puritans to the Projects: Public Housing and Public Neighbors*. Cambridge, MA: Harvard University Press, 2009.

——— "The Temptations of Nationalism in Modern Capital Cities." In *Cities and Sovereignty: Identity Politics in Urban Spaces*, edited by Diane E. Davis and Nora Libertun Duren, 196–205. Bloomington, IN: Indiana University Press, 2011.

Van Slyck, Abigail. "The Spatial Practices of Privilege." *Journal of the Society of Architectural Historians* 70, no. 2 (2011): 210–39.

Wachman, Avraham. "The Double Column Plan." Haifa: University of Haifa, 1975.

Walter, Yossef. "Nahal Reihan Outpost Goes on Site." *Maariv*, December 9, 1977.

Wasserman, Noa. "MCH: Contractors That Purchased Lands in El'ad Are Prohibited from Selling Units to Seculars." *Globes*, May 17, 1997.

Waxman, Yaacov. "Green Light for Three Settlements over the Green-Line." *Maariv*, August 18, 1977.

Weismann, Shaul. "Private Settlements in Samaria." Ministry of Agriculture, 1983. ISA-moag-DeputyMinister-0013xu4. Israel State Archive.

Weizman, Eyal. *Hollow Land*. London: Verso, 2007.

"Principles of Frontier Geography." In *City of Collision*, edited by Philip Misselwitz and Tim Rieniets, 84–92. Basel: Birkhäuser, 2006.

Wiener, Asher. Letter to Michael Dekel. Jerusalem: Ministry of Construction and Housing, 1983.

Wilton, Robert. "Colouring Special Needs: Locating Whiteness in NIMBY Conflicts." *Social & Cultural Geography* 3, no. 3 (2002): 303–21.

World Bank. *Housing: Enabling Markets to Work*. Washington, DC: World Bank, 1993.

Wright, Gwendolyn. *Building the Dream: A Social History of Housing in America*. Cambridge, MA: MIT Press, 1983.

Yaar Architects. "Local Outline Plan Harish/1/b." Tel Aviv, 2014. Israel Land Administration.

Yacobi, Haim. "Architecture, Orientalism and Identity: The Politics of the Israeli-Built Environment." *Israel Studies* 13, no. 1 (2008): 94–118.

Constructing a Sense of Place: Architecture and the Zionist Discourse. London: Routledge, 2017.

Yacobi, Haim, and Erez Tzfadia. "Neo-Settler Colonialism and the Re-formation of Territory: Privatization and Nationalization in Israel." *Mediterranean Politics* 24, no. 1 (2018): 1–19.

Rethinking Israeli Periphery. London and New York: Routledge, 2011.

Yahad Shiveti Yisrael. "Association Rules." Yahad Shiveti Yisrael Association, 1991.

Yamin, Guy. "Ashdar Purchased 150 Dunams in Oranit." *Globes*, January 8, 2006. www.globes.co.il/news/article.aspx?did=1000047710.

Yaski and Partners Architects and Planners. "Detailed Plan 115/4: Alfei Menashe," 1986. ISA-moch-CentralRegion-000qpzf. Israel State Archive.

"Tzavta A. Tel Aviv." Tel Aviv: Ministry of Construction and Housing, 1982. ISA-moch-CentralRegion-000gw6 n. Israel State Archive.

Y. H. Dimri. "The Most Prestigious Villas in the Sharon Area Are in the Sky" [Promotion article], 2017. www.themarker.com/labels/rooftop/1.4606802.

Yiftachel, Oren. "Bedouin-Arabs and the Israeli Settler State." In *Indigenous People between Autonomy and Globalization*, edited by Duanc Champagne and Ismael Abu-Saad, 21–47. Los Angeles, CA: University of California Press, 2003.

Ethnocracy. Philadelphia, PA: University of Pennsylvania Press, 2006.

"From Sharon to Sharon: Spatial Planning and Separation Regime in Israel/Palestine." *HAGAR Studies in Culture, Polity and Identities* 20, no. 1 (2010): 73–106.

"Nation-Building or Ethnic Fragmentation? Frontier Settlement and Collective Identities in Israel." *Space and Polity* 1, no. 2 (1997): 149–69.

"The Internal Frontier: Territorial Control and Ethnic Relations in Israel." *Regional Studies* 30, no. 5 (1996): 493–508.

Yiftachel, Oren, and Nufar Avni. "'Privati-nation' – Privatization, Nationalization, Housing and Gaps." *Planning (Tichnun)* 16, no. 1 (2019): 225–47.

Yiftachel, Oren, and Alexander Kader. "Landed Power: The Making of the Israeli Land Regime." *Teoria VeBikoret* 16 (Spring 2000): 67–103.

Ynet. "Harish: Not What You Thought." *Ynet*, June 30, 2019. www.ynet.co.il/articles/0,7340,L-5537800,00.html.

Zakim, Eric. *To Build and Be Built*. Philadelphia, PA: University of Pennsylvania Press, 2006.

Zimmerman, Sarah. "Tender 10025/99 HaParsa Neighbourhood – Harish." Ministry of Construction and Housing, 2002. ISA-moch-DirectorGeneral-0004zak. Israel State Archive.

ZP Association. "Association Rules." ZP Association, 1990.

Index

100,000 Plan, 68
1948 Arab–Israeli war, 32
1949 Armistice Agreements, 50
1950s, 4, 37–39, 43, 206, 231, 240
1960s, 7, 11, 37, 39, 43–44, 47, 64, 111–12, 165
1970s, 2, 4–5, 7, 11, 14, 17, 25, 43, 61, 64–65, 68–69, 80, 88, 112, 146, 165, 203, 205–6, 237, 240, 243
1977, ix, 4, 14, 17, 39, 44, 52, 56, 61, 112, 116, 178
1980s, 5, 11, 14, 17–18, 45, 47–48, 53, 68–69, 81, 83–84, 88, 94, 96, 100, 109–10, 126, 132, 135, 143–45, 154, 159, 163–64, 166, 175, 178, 195, 207, 235, 237–38, 240, 244
1982, x, 12, 50, 96, 113–14, 134, 142, 207
1985 Economic Stabilization Plan, 45
1990s, 5, 14, 18, 47, 54–55, 85, 92, 100–1, 128, 131, 159–60, 162–63, 165–66, 170, 179, 189, 195, 201, 208–9, 217, 226, 228, 233, 235, 238, 240
2000s, 5, 42, 57, 86, 100, 153, 218, 226, 243–44
2008 world economic crisis, 201
2010s, 231
2011 Israeli Social Justice Protests, 202

A'rim, 180, 183
Abu Salem, 132
admissions committee, 69, 83, 211
Admot Leom, 25, 33, 211
Africa–Israel, 48
Agency House, 63
Agricultural Centre, 87
Agudat Yisrael, x, 129, 178
Albeck, Plia, 99

Alfei Menashe, x, 14, 18, 104, 111, 118, 133–37, 138, 144, 157
Aliyah, 130, 170
Alon Plan, 72
Alon, Yigal, 51
architecture, 134, 136, 213, 244
Area A, 17, 88
Area C, 161
area of high demand, 53, 203
area of national priority, 163, 198, 220
Arison Group, 243
Asbestonim, 89
*Ashda*r, 77, 143, 183, 243
Asher Wiener, 54
Ashkenazi, 44–45, 112–13, 117, 156, 178
Ashkubit, 77, 89
Ashtrom, 243
Azzun Atma, 132

B'nai Brith, 75
Bank Hapoalim, 49
Bank Leumi, 48
Baqa al-Gharbiyye, 120, 206, 211
Barkai (kibbutz), 206
Bat Heffer, xi, 14, 169, 172, 174
Begin, Menachem, 44, 54
Beit U'Menuha, 179–80
Beitar Illit, 179, 219
Ben Gurion, David, 39, 45
Bennet, Naftali, 58
Bnei Brak, 177–78, 181, 184, 186, 219
bourgeois, 18, 110–11, 125, 156–57
bourgeoisie, 111–15, 120–21, 123
British Mandate, 23, 32
Buchman, Meir, 124–25, 149–51
built environment, 1, 3, 5, 8–9, 11–12, 18–20, 24, 43, 60, 64, 111, 159–60, 163, 186, 191, 194, 238–39, 243–45

273

built space, xi, 3–4, 6–8, 13, 17, 20, 169
Build Your Own Home, 92, 101, 103, 115, 125, 141

Central Bureau of Statistics, 117
Central Places Theory, 35
Christaller, Walter, 35
Chyutin, Michael and Bracha, 151
coastal plain, 35, 50–51, 54–55, 57, 68, 76, 85, 93, 116, 133, 145, 166, 175
Community Settlement(s), 5, 14, 17, 52, 58, 62, 66–70, 80, 85–86, 88, 93, 96–97, 99, 103–5, 107–8, 117, 147, 188, 198, 204, 207–8, 211, 217, 235–37, 239–40, 243
compound model, 89, 107
counterurban, 52, 70, 99, 107
cul-de-sac, 90, 96–97, 101–2, 108, 124, 139, 181, 210, 221

decentralization, 35, 41, 51, 55, 110, 116, 163, 178, 231, 244
Degel HaTorah, 178–79
Dekel, Michael, 53, 94, 123, 139
Delta, 139–42, 144
demand side, 164
density, 16, 135, 139, 211, 231
Derech Eretz, 48
development town(s), 34, 37–39, 51, 62, 116, 156, 244
Double Column Plan, ix, 51, 56
Drobles Plan, 68
Drobles, Matityahu, 75
Drom HaSharon, 92
dwelling units, 16, 19, 28, 31, 38, 57, 61, 78, 89, 103, 107–8, 113, 138, 151, 159, 162, 164–65, 175, 177, 179–80, 184, 186, 189, 192, 195–98, 201, 205, 207–8, 214, 219–21, 224–26, 227–29, 239

Eitan, Michael, 121, 123, 167, 173
exchange-value, 202, 231
ex-urban, 17, 40, 62, 64, 68–69, 82–83, 107, 209–10, 236–37
Eyal (kibbutz), 71, 172

Falame, 72
Fordist–Keynesian, 34, 43
former Soviet Union, 179, 217

free market, 58, 178, 242
frontier, 1, 8, 17–18, 21, 26, 28, 30, 39, 46, 50–51, 55, 57–58, 61, 62–63, 66, 72, 81, 83–84, 88, 93, 107, 110, 113, 120, 144, 146, 154–55, 158, 163–65, 195–96, 203–4, 207, 210–11, 224, 231, 235, 239, 243
Frontier Fortresses Plan, 206

Galilee, 51, 70, 113, 117, 120, 205, 209
Gar'in, 81, 89, 107
Gaza Strip, 161
Gemeinschaft, 66
gentrification, 5, 18, 54, 65, 109, 111, 130, 144, 154–55, 158–59, 195, 238, 242, 244
geopolitical, xiv, 2–5, 10, 12, 16, 20–21, 60–61, 77, 169–70, 175, 195, 205, 230, 235–36, 242, 244–45
Gesellschaft, 66
Geulat Adama, 29
Gorbachev, Mikhail, 161
Green Line, 2, 5, 16–18, 21, 42, 48, 50–51, 55, 57–58, 60–61, 68, 76, 87, 95, 100, 104, 109–11, 116, 118, 120–22, 131, 139, 143, 145, 147, 154, 158–59, 161–64, 166–67, 172, 177–78, 195, 203, 205–6, 210, 217, 228, 233, 235, 238, 240–41
Gulf War, 161
Gush Dan, 24, 53, 57, 165, 171, 228, *See* Tel Aviv Metropolis
Gush Emunim, ix, 51–52, 54, 56, 68, 105

Hagshama, 30, 41, 70
Hagshama Atzmit, 41, 70
Hagshama Leomit, 70
Haifa, 105, 113, 117, 218, 222, 224
Halutz, 30
HaOved HaTzioni, 76
Harish, xi, 16, 19, 105, 166, 197–98, 204–5, 207–9, 212–14, 217–21, 222–24, 227–28, 230–31, 239, 245
HaShomer HaTzair, 207
Heftziba, 183, 185
Herut party, 112, 121
Herut-Beitar, 75, 119, 121–23
Hever, 216

Index

Hills' Axis(plan), ix, 55–56, 165, 170, 206
Hinanit, ix, 70, 79, 81–82, 104–5, 109
Histadrut, 49, 243
home, 25, 94, 99, 105, 125, 128, 134, 151, 193
house, x, xi, 5, 31, 41, 79, 84–85, 92, 95, 104–5, 108–109, 110, 118, 121, 125–26, 131–32, 137, 141, 145, 151–52, 155, 157, 163, 173, 176, 179, 196, 215–16, 227, 233–34, 237–38, 240
housing, ix, 3, 8, 11, 18–19, 24, 28, 34, 37–38, 42, 55, 57–58, 86, 88, 90, 92, 99, 102, 104, 107, 109, 113, 115–16, 123–26, 130, 135, 137, 144–47, 149, 151–52, 154, 157–60, 163–65, 170–71, 175, 178–80, 185–86, 190, 194, 196–97, 201, 203, 210–12, 214, 219, 223, 224, 227–31, 237–38, 242, 244–45
Housing Administration (HA), 144, 148–49, 152, 154
housing associations, 144, 165, 175, 190, 196, 211, 219, 224, 228, 238

Israeli Air Force (IAF), 145, 149
Israel Defense Forces (IDF), 50, 135, 138, 144–46, 148–49, 152, 154–55, 190, 216
industrial towns, 24, 34–35, 37, 39
internal frontiers, 33, 57, 61, 69, 117, 203, 231
Intifada, 55, 57, 101–3, 127, 160, 194, 217
Israel Land Administration (ILA), 33, 89, 91, 99, 122–24, 127, 145, 167–69, 172, 174, 182, 188–89, 191, 194, 206, 208, 223–24, 228
Israeli Government, 10, 17, 19, 33, 38, 47, 55, 57, 117, 122, 131–32, 147, 161, 164, 170, 202–3, 205, 209, 223, 232
Israeli High Court of Justice, 25, 104
Israeli Project, 11
Israeli-Arab, 132, *See* Palestinian Citizens of Israel

Jaljulia, 120
Jerusalem, 51, 72, 113, 117, 145, 148, 161, 166, 177–78, 182, 219
Jewish Agency (JA), 12, 23, 72, 79, 120, 122, 147, 205, 211
Jewish National Fund (JNF), ix, 29–30, 39, 67
Judea–Samaria Residential Neighbourhoods Company, 95

Katzir, xi, 105, 204–5, 207–11, 217–18, 222
Keynesian, 34, 186
Kfar Sava, 130, 132–33
Kibbutzim crisis, 207
Kibbutzim Movement, 45, 207
Kibush Haavoda, 29
Kibush HaShmama, 28
Kochav Yair, x, 14, 18, 111, 118, 120–31, 172, 205
Kufr Bara, x, 120, 129, 132, 143
Kufr Jamal, 72
Kufr Qara, 120, 206
Kufr Qasem, 132
Kufr Sur, 72

Labor Settlement, 29
laissez-faire, 4, 236, 241, 244
Lehi, 121, 123
Levi, David, 146
Levi, Moshe, 50, 146
liberalization, 2, 39
Likud, 44, 52, 121, 133
living standards, 21, 38, 41, 53–54, 65, 68–70, 84, 95, 97, 109–11, 116, 118, 121, 155, 157, 171, 173, 175, 179, 214, 228–29, 237, 240

Maccabim, 145, 153
Madrid Conference, 161
Magal (kibbutz), 206
Mansfeld-Kehat, 221, 223
Mapai, 28, 34, 44–45, 109, 112, 115
market economy, 17, 21, 41, 241
marketable, xiii, 97, 103, 142, 164–65, 182, 239, 245
Matan, xi, 14, 166, 169, 172, 174
Mazor, xi, 169, 179
McFalafel, 157
Metzer (kibbutz), 206

middle class, 18, 53, 55, 64, 67, 69, 98, 110–13, 115–16, 118, 120–21, 127–28, 131, 144, 153, 156–57, 202, 214, 230
military, 27, 50, 72–74, 112, 118, 132, 137, 144–49, 152, 154–55, 168, 178–79, 190, 216–17, 234, 237
military personnel, 144, 147, 155, 216
Ministry of Agriculture (MA), 39, 53, 121, 147
Ministry of Construction and Housing (MCH), xiii, 12, 40, 53, 84, 91, 94, 113, 123, 132, 135, 144, 146–47, 170, 184, 189, 211, 213–17, 219–21, 224, 228, 230, 237
Ministry of Defense, 57, 73, 118, 147
Mitzpe; Mitzpim, 12, 88, 120–22
Mizrahi, 38, 44, 50, 112–13, 115, 156, 178, 240
mode of production, 4–5, 16–19, 52, 54, 58, 61, 63, 66, 70, 74, 80, 83–84, 99–100, 104, 106–7, 118–19, 145, 155–56, 159, 168–69, 173, 174, 177, 180, 185–86, 188, 195–96, 198–201, 206, 208, 210–11, 220, 225–26, 229
Modi'im, 145
Modi'in, 145, 148, 153–55, 165–66, 179, 219
Moshav, ix, 31–32, 64, 66, 74, 85, 88, 109, 179, 204, 206, 208
Moshavim Movement, 87–88
Movement for New Urban Settlement, 66

Nahal, 39, 77, 81, 105, 204–8
Nahal Eron. *See* Wadi A'ara
nation-building, 14, 27, 32–33, 42, 63
National Outline Plan 35, 55
National-Orthodox, 224
nation-state, 16, 25, 27–28, 42
Nation-State Bill (2018), 25
Negev, 25, 51, 113, 117
neoliberal, 2, 9, 21, 42–43, 65, 116, 164, 178, 202–3, 241, 244
neoliberalism, 17, 19, 43, 49, 66, 242–43
neo-rural, 5, 17, 54, 62, 64–65, 67, 70, 77, 80, 82, 86, 103, 106–7, 110, 113, 204, 207–8, 230, 236
neo-rurality, 64–65

Neot-Idan, 149
Neot-Reut, 149
Netanyahu, Benjamin, 202, 229
Netivei Israel, 47, 49
Nir, Meir, 190
Nirit, x, 14, 62, 70, 90–92, 103, 109
Nitzane Oz, 168

O'lim, 170, 175
Occupied Territories, 1, 4, 13, 51, 67, 72, 88, 104, 132, 143, 162, 179
officers, 112, 120, 132–33, 135, 137, 144–46, 148, 153–54, 158, 216
Oranit, x, 14, 18, 111, 118, 139, 142–43, 156–57
Oren, Amikam, 148
Oslo Accords, 161
outline plan, xi, 55, 208, 210
outpost, 72–73, 76, 81, 89, 122, 204, 207

Palestinian Authority, 161
Palestinian Citizens of Israel, 72, 132
Peres, Shimon, 45, 143
periphery, 35, 37, 41, 76, 110, 154, 179, 198, 209, 230
Place Stratification Model, 10, 114
planning, xiii, 1, 5–6, 8, 12, 17, 26, 35, 37, 47–48, 55, 63, 68, 70, 77, 89, 94, 96, 99, 110, 122, 135, 139, 141, 147–48, 154, 156–58, 165–67, 180–81, 195, 198, 202–3, 206–7, 209, 211, 221–22, 226, 228, 231–32, 236, 238–39, 245
PLO, 161–62
Population dispersal, 170
power over, 3, 8, 10–11, 16–18, 20, 23, 27, 61–62, 79, 107, 110, 115, 119, 159, 175, 196, 203, 235, 241
power to, 3, 8, 10–11, 16–19, 61–62, 74, 81, 92, 94, 103, 107, 110–11, 115, 119, 122–23, 138, 143, 155, 175, 195–96, 230, 235–39
Practical Zionism, 23, 30
prefabricated, 73, 77, 79, 81, 85–86, 207, 210, 214–15, 243
privacy, 7, 113, 124–25, 135, 175
privatization, 2–5, 8, 10–11, 13–14, 17, 19–21, 39, 43–46, 48–49, 61, 62, 107, 116, 120, 123, 131, 133, 139,

155, 162–63, 166, 175, 178, 198, 207, 235–36, 238–39, 241–42
production, 1, 3, 5, 8–13, 16, 20, 31, 52, 55, 62, 65–66, 79, 81, 83, 111, 113, 123, 149, 160, 195, 201, 231, 236, 239, 241, 244–45
profitability, 5, 45, 102–3, 107, 164, 181, 201, 223, 236, 239, 245
property values, 101–2, 107, 137, 194, 202, 223, 230
Public Works Department, 47
pull factors, 163, 186
push factors, 163

Qalansuwa, 120
Qaliqilya, 131
quality of life, x, 12, 40, 67, 69–70, 96, 104–6, 108, 113–15, 121, 130, 136, 163, 171, 209, 233–34, 237
quasi-socialist, 34, 43, 109, 156, 242, 244

Rabin, Yitzhak, 48, 161
red roof, 102, 179, 215
Reihan, 70
Reihan Bloc, 14, 100, 107
rentability, 159, 212
Reut, x, 14, 18, 111, 118, 144–45, 147–48, 150–52, 154–55
Riskin, Aryeh, 151–52
Rosh Ha'ayin, 148, 154, 244
rural areas, 64
Rural Settlement, 19, 31, 67, 71, 74, 80, 107, 206–7
rurbanization, 64

Sal'it, 14, 62, 70, 73–74, 78, 84–85, 100–1, 106–7
Samaria, 53, 68, 76, 86–87, 94, 96, 98, 103, 106, 122
Sarid, Yosi, 143
Seam-Zone, 51–52
selective privatization, 11, 46, 166, 242
Separation Barrier, 1, 19, 57–58, 194, 224
Settlement Department, 67, 69–70, 72, 88–89, 120, 207
Settlement Division, 12, 52–53, 67, 70, 76, 81–82, 86, 88, 96, 101, 114, 117, 207

settlement mechanism, 1–2, 12, 14, 16, 18, 20–21, 24–25, 34, 41, 43, 61–62, 75, 107, 159, 166, 177, 198, 230–32, 234–35, 237–39, 241–44
Shaked, 70
Shamir, Yitzhak, 161
Sharon, 35
Sharon, Arieh, 32, 35
Sharon, Ariel, 52, 77, 80, 121, 162, 179–80
Sharon (area), 105, 193
Shas, 178
Shertok, Moshe, 21
Shikun Rakevet, 185
Shikun U'Binui, 49, 243
Shoham, 166
Slumurbia, 177, 187
Socialist Zionism, 40
Solel Boneh, 183
spatial agents, 13, 16
spatial privilege(s), 3–4, 9–11, 13, 16–17, 21, 38, 41, 46, 52–53, 62, 69, 84, 94, 102, 107, 122–23, 125, 143, 147–48, 153, 159, 179, 190–91, 196, 208, 211, 214, 218, 224, 230, 235, 237, 240, 242
speculations, 2, 4, 13, 19, 232, 245
split-level model, 175
split-level unit, 238
star model, 84, 97, 108
Stars Plan, ix, 55–56, 170, 179, 210
Stars (settlements), 18, 131, 159, 166, 170, 179, 196, 210
state-owned lands, 32, 37, 57, 88–89, 118, 155, 167, 198, 203, 205, 220
Suburban Settlement(s), 5, 18, 54, 58, 109–11, 115–18, 128, 131, 134, 145–46, 155–56, 158, 167, 179, 196, 204, 209–10, 212, 222, 230, 240, 245
suburbanization, 5, 14, 18, 54, 65, 107–10, 113, 158–59, 161, 163, 165–66, 195, 237–38
suburbia, 106, 110, 137, 144, 157–58, 163, 165, 175, 196, 241
Supertanker, 202, 229
supply side, 159, 164–65, 175, 183, 196–97, 202, 223, 238

Taybeh, 72, 96, 120, 190, 192
Tel Aviv metropolis/Tel Aviv metropolitan area, 1, 4, 53, 109, 116, 118, 163, 175, 177, 211, 237
tenements, 212
territorial, 3–5, 8–10, 12, 14, 17, 20, 23–24, 28, 32, 34, 37, 41, 54–55, 58, 61, 63, 66, 70, 72, 116, 130–31, 162, 164, 177–78, 197, 199, 203, 205–6, 209, 232, 235–36, 238–42, 244
territoriality, 17
Tira, 120
Toshava, 116–17, *See* Suburban Settlement
tract development, 97, 222
tract housing, 18
Trans-Israel Highway, ix, 1, 3, 5, 15, 17, 19, 43, 46, 48, 57–58, 60, 224, 236, 243–45
Trans-Israel Road Ltd, 47–48
Triangle (area), 120–21, 205
Trumpeldor, Joseph, 29
Tzavta, 133–34, 136–37, 229
Tzoran, xi, 14, 166, 169, 172, 174
Tzur Nathan, xi, 71, 190, 193–94
Tzur Yigal, xi, 14, 128, 166, 169, 172–74
Tzur Yitzhak, 14, 166, 191–93, 239, 243, 245

Ultra-Orthodox, 177–78, 180, 182–84, 216, 218–19, 221–22, 224, 229
Umm al-Fahm, 120, 206
upper-middle class, 4–5, 18, 53–54, 64, 95, 102, 110–11, 113, 115–16, 119, 125, 128, 130, 137, 141, 144, 153, 156, 158, 163, 171, 179, 190, 209, 217, 230, 238, 240
use-value, 202, 231
USSR, 7, 161

Wadi A'ara, 203, 205–6, 217, 220
Weitz, Ra'anan, 72
welfare state, 14, 34, 186
West Bank, x, 1, 4, 12–13, 19, 25, 50–54, 57, 66, 69, 75, 82–83, 88, 93, 95–96, 99, 101, 104, 113, 117, 119–22, 131, 139, 143, 161–62, 179, 194, 205, 224, 233–34
World Zionist Organization (WZO), ix, 39, 52, 56, 67

Ya'arit, 14, 62, 70, 93–99, 109
Yahdut HaTorah, 178
Yarhiv, xi, 128, 172, 174
Yaski, Avraham, 134–35, 137
Yeshuv Parvari, 116, *See* Suburban Settlement

Zionism, 20, 28, 44, 109, 177
Zionist Federation, 23, 123, 130
Zionist-Socialist, 28

Lightning Source UK Ltd.
Milton Keynes UK
UKHW050103210422
401764UK00004BB/57

9 781316 512890